PhoneGap 3.x
Mobile Application
Development HOTSHOT

Create useful and exciting real-world apps for iOS and
Android devices with 12 fantastic projects

Kerri Shotts

BIRMINGHAM - MUMBAI

PhoneGap 3.x Mobile Application Development HOTSHOT

First published: February 2013

Second Edition: May 2014

Production Reference: 1200514

Published by Packt Publishing Ltd.
Livery Place
35 Livery Street
Birmingham B3 2PB, UK.

ISBN 978-1-78328-792-5

www.packtpub.com

Cover Image by Suresh Mogre (suresh.mogre.99@gmail.com)

Credits

Author
Kerri Shotts

Reviewers
Gerard Braad
Steve Husting
Dhaval Nagar
Julio César Sánchez
Rajpal A. Vishal

Acquisition Editors
Aarthi Kumaraswamy
Kevin Colaco

Content Development Editor
Susmita Panda Sabat

Technical Editors
Monica John
Neha Mankare
Edwin Moses
Shiny Poojary

Copy Editors
Alisha Aranha
Roshni Banerjee
Sarang Chari
Brandt D'Mello

Project Coordinator
Swati Kumari

Proofreaders
Simran Bhogal
Maria Gould
Ameesha Green
Paul Hindle

Indexers
Hemangini Bari
Mariammal Chettiyar
Tejal Soni

Graphics
Abhinash Sahu

Production Coordinator
Aditi Gajjar Patel

Cover Work
Aditi Gajjar Patel

About the Author

Kerri Shotts has worked with computers for nearly 24 years. Her love for technology and programming started when she was introduced to her first computer: a Commodore 64. She obtained a degree in Computer Science and went on to become a software test engineer. After that, she was an Oracle database administrator for several years. Now, she works as a Technology Consultant creating, implementing, and maintaining custom applications (both desktop and mobile), websites, graphics and logos, and much more for her clients. You can find her blog posts at her website (www.photokandy.com), and she is active on the Google Group for PhoneGap. When she isn't working, she enjoys photography, music, and fish keeping. She is the author of two other books, *Instant PhoneGap Social App Development* and *PhoneGap 2.x Mobile Application Development Hotshot*, both published by Packt Publishing.

Firstly, I will thank my family for their incredible support, even with the late night clacking of the keyboard. Thanks also to those who have made PhoneGap and Cordova such an awesome tool, and I am also thankful to those who support it on the forums. A special thanks to the technical reviewers of this book—you're all amazing! Finally, thanks to Packt Publishing and their editorial staff for making sure that everything came out just right.

About the Reviewers

Gerard Braad is an all-rounder when it comes to IT. He has used many programming languages on both the frontend and backend as well as mobile solutions. He is currently working in the Beijing office of ThoughtWorks.

> I would like to thank the contributors and community for improving PhoneGap/Cordova by suggesting new features, bugfixes, and writing great how-tos. However, I would also like to thank all the application authors who have used PhoneGap, since it shows what HTML and JavaScript are capable of doing.

Steve Husting wears various hats by day, including that of a website worker, in a company that designs and manufactures radio-controlled hobby cars. By night, he writes, does calligraphy, and creates iPhone and Android apps. He posts his findings about PhoneGap app development on his blog, `http://iphonedevlog.wordpress.com`, which is geared towards beginners.

Dhaval Nagar is an experienced Java and mobile developer who started developing JEE applications in 2006. He has been developing mobile/tablet applications since 2011 and has experience working on all major mobile platforms. His first experience with mobile devices began in 2008 on a Psion handheld computer.

At present, he is running his own software development and consulting business. Prior to that, he was working as a software architect, developing large-scale industrial software using Java, EJB, JMS, Spring, and so on. Now, he is focused on developing Cordova-based mobile applications for Android, iOS, Windows Phone, and BlackBerry platforms. Besides mobile applications, he is also working on JavaScript-based frameworks such as NodeJS, Meteor, Famo.us, and AngularJS.

He lives in Surat, Gujarat, India, and can be reached at `dhaval@jumpbyte.com`

Julio César Sánchez has been a professional software developer since 2007. Over the years, he has worked with different technologies, most of them related to the Web. In 2010, he discovered PhoneGap and has been following the PhoneGap Google Group since then— learning, helping other developers, and even contributing by creating PhoneGap plugins. He spends a part of his spare time developing mobile apps and writing tutorials about PhoneGap development for the website `http://www.phonegap.es`. You can visit his personal website to know more about him and his work at `http://www.jcesarmobile.com` or follow him on Twitter `@jcesarmobile`.

Rajpal A. Vishal is a mobile application developer with extensive experience in developing multi-platform mobile applications using Appcelerator Titanium and PhoneGap. He has contributed plugins to both the communities and is currently pursuing his Master's in Computer Science from Northeastern University, Seattle.

First and foremost, I would like to thank the author of this book for producing a great book for the readers, and I would also like to thank everyone related to this book.

www.PacktPub.com

Support files, eBooks, discount offers and more

You might want to visit www.PacktPub.com for support files and downloads related to your book.

Did you know that Packt offers eBook versions of every book published, with PDF and ePub files available? You can upgrade to the eBook version at www.PacktPub.com and as a print book customer, you are entitled to a discount on the eBook copy. Get in touch with us at service@packtpub.com for more details.

At www.PacktPub.com, you can also read a collection of free technical articles, sign up for a range of free newsletters and receive exclusive discounts and offers on Packt books and eBooks.

http://PacktLib.PacktPub.com

Do you need instant solutions to your IT questions? PacktLib is Packt's online digital book library. Here, you can access, read and search across Packt's entire library of books.

Why Subscribe?

- ▸ Fully searchable across every book published by Packt
- ▸ Copy and paste, print and bookmark content
- ▸ On demand and accessible via web browser

Free Access for Packt account holders

If you have an account with Packt at www.PacktPub.com, you can use this to access PacktLib today and view nine entirely free books. Simply use your login credentials for immediate access.

Table of Contents

Preface   **1**

Project 1: Your First Project   **11**

What do we build?   13

Installing Node.js and configuring SDKs   16

Installing Cordova/PhoneGap   25

Creating your first project   28

Managing your project's platforms   30

Managing your project's plugins   32

Building your project   38

Deploying your project to a simulator/device   41

Game Over..... Wrapping it up   44

Can you take the HEAT? The Hotshot Challenge   44

Project 2: Localization and Globalization   **45**

What do we build?   46

Creating the template   47

Creating a new project based on an existing template   49

Introducing the YASMF v0.4 framework   52

Determining the user's locale   53

Formatting numbers and dates   57

Translating text   65

Game Over..... Wrapping it up   71

Can you take the HEAT? The Hotshot Challenge   71

Project 3: Mobile Application Design   **73**

What do we build?   73

Designing the user interface   75

Designing the data model   82

Implementing the Base Note data model	87
Implementing the Note Storage model	95
Implementing the note list view	101
Implementing the text note edit view	110
Implementing the CSS	115
Putting it all together	123
Game Over..... Wrapping it up	128
Can you take the HEAT? The Hotshot Challenge	128

Project 4: The File API — **129**

What do we build?	129
Covering the File API	131
Covering Promises and Q.js	142
Covering YASMF's FileManager file	145
Changing the Note Storage model	148
Game Over..... Wrapping it up	157
Can you take the HEAT? The Hotshot Challenge	157

Project 5: Working with Audio — **159**

What do we build?	159
Covering the Media API	161
Designing the user interface	174
Designing the data model	175
Implementing the data model	176
Covering Hammer.js	179
Covering the view stack	182
Implementing the user interface	187
Putting it all together	198
Game Over..... Wrapping it up	200
Can you take the HEAT? The Hotshot Challenge	201

Project 6: Working with Still Images — **203**

What do we build?	203
Designing the user interface	204
Defining the data model	205
Covering the Camera API	207
Implementing the data model	218
Implementing the user interface	221
Putting it all together	225
Game Over..... Wrapping it up	229
Can you take the HEAT? The Hotshot Challenge	230

Project 7: Capturing Video   **231**

What do we build?   231
Designing the user interface   232
Covering the Capture API   234
Covering native, native-like, and non-native alerts   240
Implementing the data model   250
Implementing the user interface   252
Putting it all together   257
Game Over..... Wrapping it up   260
Can you take the HEAT? The Hotshot Challenge   261

Project 8: Sharing Content   **263**

What do we build?   263
Handling device events   264
Working with the sharing plugin   271
Modifying the text note edit view   273
Modifying the image note edit view   277
Game Over..... Wrapping it up   279
Can you take the HEAT? The Hotshot Challenge   280

Project 9: Devices of Different Sizes   **281**

What do we build?   282
What is responsive design?   283
Response 1 – scaling up   293
Response 2 – changing the layout   294
Response 3 – split view   298
Game Over..... Wrapping it up   309
Can you take the HEAT? The Hotshot Challenge   309

Project 10: Maps and GPS   **311**

What do we build?   311
Designing our app's UI and its look and feel   313
Exploring geolocation   315
Designing our data models   319
Loading the Google Maps API   320
Implementing our data models   322
Implementing our path edit view   328
Putting it all together   335
Game Over..... Wrapping it up   337
Can you take the HEAT? The Hotshot Challenge   337

Project 11: Canvas Games and the Accelerometer   **339**

What do we build?   339
Designing the game   341
Implementing the Start view   344
Implementing the Options view   349
Implementing the Game view   352
Generating levels   358
Drawing on the canvas   364
Performing updates   369
Touched-based input   375
Accelerometer-based input   378
Game Over..... Wrapping it up   380
Can you take the HEAT? The Hotshot Challenge   381

Project 12: Building a Backend – Working with Parse   **383**

What do we build?   384
Configuring Parse   385
Modifying the Options view   391
Submitting scores   396
Displaying scores   399
Modifying the Start view   404
Game Over..... Wrapping it up   405
Can you take the HEAT? The Hotshot Challenge   406

Appendix A: User Interface Resources   **407**

Flat versus skeuomorphic   407
Human Interface/Design Guidelines   408
Mobile pattern references   409
User interface frameworks/libraries   410
User interface tips   410

Appendix B: Tips, Tricks, and Quirks   **413**

Tips   413
Android quirks   419
The Android Emulator is slow   421
iOS quirks   422

Index   **425**

Preface

Mobile applications can be developed using various approaches, programming languages and frameworks. Most apps are developed using native tools, that is, they are written in programming languages such as Java or Objective-C and use native software development kits (SDKs). This usually offers the greatest flexibility and performance, but at a cost. What happens when your app needs to work across many different platforms? Often, this involves rewriting a larger portion of the app from scratch. Once another platform is added to the mix, the entire process is repeated. Given that most apps are written by small teams, or even a single individual, this quickly becomes unsustainable. There's got to be a better way!

All current mobile platforms support web apps. These applications are coded entirely in HTML, Cascading Style Sheets (CSS), and JavaScript. There may also be a server-side component, depending on the app's purpose. As long as the app doesn't need to interact with the device's capabilities at a deeper level than that provided by the browser, this is fine. But the moment the app needs to access these capabilities (such as the physical file system), the browser environment quickly becomes too restrictive.

Cordova aims to bridge the gap between web apps and native device functionality. You can write HTML, CSS, and JavaScript, and Cordova will provide a native shell in which that code executes. This native shell is different for each platform, but it provides core device functionality in a consistent way that simplifies cross-platform development.

PhoneGap is Adobe's extension to Cordova. PhoneGap provides a slightly different interface, and it provides a remote building service that reduces the need to have a complete software development stack installed on your development machine. You are free to use either PhoneGap or Cordova in this book; we will focus on the latter and try, where possible, to point out the differences if there are any.

Because Cordova and PhoneGap wrap your HTML, CSS, and JavaScript code into a native shell, you can also submit your app to various app stores (most app stores don't accept web app submissions). If you do submit your app, you need to keep in mind that app stores often have human interface guidelines and are often very strict about how your app should behave. When you submit an app to an app store, it should reflect and respect the conventions of that platform. Furthermore, many app stores will refuse an app that is only a wrapper for a remote website. Instead, your app should consist of client-side HTML, CSS, and JavaScript code. Should your app need to communicate with a server, it can do so via XMLHttpRequest (XHR).

While many books that cover Cordova and PhoneGap will cover the framework and its documentation, this book is different. We'll introduce you to full applications. Each one is designed to take advantage of one or more native device features but is also fully functional, interesting, and useful.

This book focuses on the iOS and Android platforms and shows you how to write cross-platform code that works on both platforms in a single code base. Even so, it should be relatively easy to get these apps up and working on any other platform supported by Cordova and PhoneGap, such as BlackBerry OS, Windows Phones, and so on, with minor modifications.

What this book covers

Project 1, Your First Project, introduces you to project creation and management via the Cordova/PhoneGap command-line interfaces. We'll create a simple project and execute it on a simulator or device.

Project 2, Localization and Globalization, deals with creating a template that can be used for this and future projects using Cordova's command-line interface. We'll cover localization and globalization across four locales: English (UK and US) and Spanish (Spain and US). We'll be introduced to jQuery/Globalize and the mechanisms behind number and currency formatting as well as a translation matrix implementation.

Project 3, Mobile Application Design, the first version of a note-taking app called Filer. We'll be introduced to RequireJS (dependency management) and Yet Another Simple Mobile Framework (YASMF). We'll be designing the user interface and user interactions and will implement the required data models and views. We'll cover using LocalStorage and why it isn't a great idea for persistent data storage.

Project 4, The File API, explores persistent data storage, which is required by most apps, and Filer is no exception. We'll create Version 2 of our Filer app by modifying Filer to use the device's physical filesystem. We'll be introduced to the HTML5 File API and the core plugin Cordova uses to provide this functionality.

Project 5, Working with Audio, explains that notes don't need to be text-only; in this project, we'll create the third version of Filer by adding support for audio notes. We'll be introduced to the Media API and the corresponding plugin. We'll add a swipe-to-delete gesture using Hammer.js, and we'll cover the view stack, the view lifecycle, and view-to-view animations.

Project 6, Working with Still Images, deals with extending Filer to allow the user to take a picture using the device's camera and attach it to a note. We'll be introduced to the camera API and associated plugin, and we'll also discuss how to display many image thumbnails at once in a memory-efficient manner.

Project 7, Capturing Video, discusses rounding out the media capabilities of the app by adding video support in version four of Filer. We'll be introduced to the HTML5 Video tag, and we'll work with the Media Capture API and plugin.

Project 8, Sharing Content, covers adding shared capabilities to Filer. We'll be introduced to a third-party plugin that provides access to e-mail and various social networks. We'll also cover how to share text and images.

Project 9, Devices of Different Sizes, pursues two different mechanisms for filling the screens of larger, tablet-sized devices since we have only focused on phone-sized devices so far. We'll be introduced to split view controllers as well as various mechanisms for building apps that respond to screen size.

Project 10, Maps and GPS, deals with building a totally new app that records the location of a user over a given period of time. We'll use the Geolocation API and plugin to access the user's location, and we'll use Google Maps to display the recorded route to the user.

Project 11, Canvas Games and the Accelerometer, focuses on creating a simple game called Cave Runner that uses the HTML5 canvas and uses the device's accelerometer as one of the input mechanisms.

Project 12, Building a Backend – Working with Parse, extends Cave Runner by adding a simple backend to keep track of high scores. We'll be introduced to Parse and their JavaScript API used to store and retrieve data.

The online project, *Using Native Controls*, will take the app from *Project 10, Maps and GPS*, and add various native controls to make it look and feel even more native.There are times when we need our app to blend into the native environment in a better way than what we can provide via HTML, CSS, and JavaScript. While this project is tailored for iOS, the concepts can be extended to other platforms. This project is only available online at `https://www.packtpub.com/sites/default/files/downloads/79250S_Chapter_13_Native_Controls.pdf`.

Appendix A, User Interface Resources, covers various user interface and design patterns that are used in mobile applications.

Appendix B, Tips, Tricks, and Quirks, expands on the idea that each platform has its quirks, and even though we're writing cross-platform code, we will sometimes encounter glitches. In this appendix, we'll cover some of the quirks we encountered while writing the apps in this book as well as cover some tips and tricks learned from experience.

What you need for this book

To build/run the code supplied for the book, the following software is required (divided by platform, where appropriate):

	Windows	Linux	OS X
For iOS Apps			
IDE			XCode 5+
OS			OS X 10.8.4+
SDK			iOS 6+
For Android Apps			
IDE	Eclipse 3.6.2+ or Android Studio Preview		
OS	XP or newer	Any modern distribution supporting: GNU C library 2.7+ (if 64-bit, must be able to run 32-bit apps); Ubuntu must be 8.04+	OS X 10.5.8+
Java*	JDK 6 or higher	JDK 6 or higher	JDK 6 or higher
SDK	Version 15+	Version 15+	Version 15+
For all platforms			
Apache Cordova / PhoneGap	3.x**	3.x**	3.x**
ANT	1.8+	1.8+	1.8+

* A JRE is not sufficient.

** The code accompanying this book has been tested with Cordova 3.4. It should work with any 3.x version. The code also relies on core and third-party plugins; check the README file in the code package for this book for specific plugin versions, if applicable.

While not required, it is considered good practice to work using source control. Git is an easy-to-use source control management solution, and the one I use.

Websites and download locations that can be useful are as follows:

- Xcode: `https://developer.apple.com/xcode/`
- iOS SDK: `https://developer.apple.com/devcenter/ios/index.action`
- Eclipse: `http://www.eclipse.org/downloads/packages/eclipse-classic-421/junosr1`
- Android SDK: `http://developer.android.com/sdk/index.html`
- Apache Cordova: `http://cordova.apache.org`
- PhoneGap: `http://phonegap.com`
- Git: `http://git-scm.com/downloads`

Who this book is for

If you are a developer who has experience with HTML, CSS, and JavaScript and desires to use your experience to build mobile applications, this book is for you. You should understand HTML, be able to understand CSS, and have a reasonable working knowledge of JavaScript. You should also be able to set up a development environment and should be comfortable with a text editor or integrated development environment.

This book is also for any native developer who wants to create apps that can target multiple platforms with limited modifications. Cordova and PhoneGap provide mechanisms that make it easy to build a single HTML/CSS/JavaScript codebase that works across many platforms.

Conventions

In this book, you will find several headings appearing frequently. To give clear instructions of how to complete a procedure or task, we use:

What do we build?

This section explains what you will build.

What does it do?

This section explains what the project will achieve.

Why is it great?

This section explains why the project is cool, unique, exciting, and interesting. It describes what advantage the project will give you.

How are we going to do it?

This section explains the major tasks required to complete your project.

- ▶ Task 1
- ▶ Task 2
- ▶ Task 3
- ▶ Task 4

What do I need to get started?

This section explains any prerequisites for the project, such as resources or libraries that need to be downloaded, and so on.

Task 1

This section explains the task that you will perform.

Getting ready

This section explains any preliminary work that you may need to do before beginning work on the task.

Getting on with it

This section lists the steps required in order to complete the task.

What did we do?

This section explains how the steps performed in the previous section allow us to complete the task.

What else do I need to know?

The extra information in this section is relevant to the task.

In this book, you also will find a number of styles of text that distinguish between different kinds of information. Here are some examples of these styles, and an explanation of their meaning.

Code words in text, database table names, folder names, filenames, file extensions, and pathnames are shown as follows: "We can include other contexts through the use of the `include` directive."

A block of code is set as follows:

```
var userLocale = navigator.language || navigator.browserLanguage ||
navigator.systemLanguage || navigator.userLanguage;
```

When we wish to draw your attention to a particular part of a code block, the relevant lines or items are set in bold:

```
var theUID = this.getAttribute("data-uid");
var aNote = noteStorageSingleton.getNote(theUID);
```

Any command-line input or output is written as follows:

```
cordova create ./HelloWorld helloworld.phonegaphotshot.com HelloWorld
```

New terms and **important words** are shown in bold. Words that you see on the screen, in menus or dialog boxes for example, appear in the text like this: "Click on the **Downloads** tab, and find the **Command Line Tools** option."

Warnings or important notes appear in a box like this.

Tips and tricks appear like this.

Reader feedback

Feedback from our readers is always welcome. Let us know what you think about this book—what you liked or may have disliked. Reader feedback is important for us to develop titles that you really get the most out of.

To send us general feedback, simply send an e-mail to feedback@packtpub.com, and mention the book title via the subject of your message.

If there is a topic that you have expertise in and you are interested in either writing or contributing to a book, see our author guide on www.packtpub.com/authors.

Customer support

Now that you are the proud owner of a Packt book, we have a number of things to help you to get the most from your purchase.

Downloading the example code

You can download the example code files for all Packt books you have purchased from your account at http://www.packtpub.com. If you purchased this book elsewhere, you can visit http://www.packtpub.com/support and register to have the files e-mailed directly to you.

If GitHub is more your style, you can also download the code for this book from https://github.com/kerrishotts/PhoneGap-HotShot-3-x-Code-Bundle.

Errata

Although we have taken every care to ensure the accuracy of our content, mistakes do happen. If you find a mistake in one of our books—maybe a mistake in the text or the code—we would be grateful if you would report this to us. By doing so, you can save other readers from frustration and help us improve subsequent versions of this book. If you find any errata, please report them by visiting http://www.packtpub.com/submit-errata, selecting your book, clicking on the **errata submission form** link, and entering the details of your errata. Once your errata are verified, your submission will be accepted and the errata will be uploaded on our website, or added to any list of existing errata, under the Errata section of that title. Any existing errata can be viewed by selecting your title from http://www.packtpub.com/support.

Piracy

Piracy of copyright material on the Internet is an ongoing problem across all media. At Packt, we take the protection of our copyright and licenses very seriously. If you come across any illegal copies of our works, in any form, on the Internet, please provide us with the location address or website name immediately so that we can pursue a remedy.

Please contact us at copyright@packtpub.com with a link to the suspected pirated material.

We appreciate your help in protecting our authors, and our ability to bring you valuable content.

Questions

You can contact us at questions@packtpub.com if you are having a problem with any aspect of the book, and we will do our best to address it.

Project 1
Your First Project

When designing a mobile app, the first thing you need to decide is if this app will be a native app, a web app, or a hybrid app. Each uses different technologies to build, and it is important to consider the pros and cons of each before deciding on what your project will use.

Native apps work by leveraging the built-in system frameworks present on the device. The apps are written in languages that are compiled for quick execution, such as Objective C for iOS development or Java for Android development. Since these apps run native code (that is, code compiled directly for the platform, often down to assembly language or some other bytecode), they are very fast. As they use the built-in frameworks, they get a lot of features (including look and feel) nearly for free. The problem with native frameworks, however, is that they aren't cross-platform. For example, the code you write for iOS will not work on Android. If your app needs a wide variety of platform support, this can mean considerable development time as the app needs to be rewritten for each platform it supports. If you're the only developer, this means you need to learn each native framework and language in order to write your apps—often a lengthy endeavor.

Web apps, on the other hand, solve some of these difficulties by being inherently cross-platform (as long as web standards are adhered to). Furthermore, any HTML, CSS, and JavaScript knowledge you might have can be leveraged, so there may be less to learn at the outset. However, web apps have serious problems as well: they have very limited access to the capabilities of the device, and they are slower than native apps (given that they run inside a browser using an interpreted language, JavaScript). Furthermore, web apps don't inherit the native look and feel of the app. Although distribution and updates are easy (all you need is a web server), no app store will list your app, and so discovery by your users is difficult.

Hybrid apps try to be the best of both worlds. Since hybrid apps use some native code, the app has access to the native features of the device. It also means that app stores will allow the app in their stores, allowing easy discovery. Because hybrid apps use web technology, your code is largely cross-platform (assuming you follow the Web standards), and easy to port to other platforms. Of course, there are still downsides: the web portion of a hybrid app will likely still run slower than a native app. However, there is an upside: if you need that extra performance, hybrid apps allow you to write native code when needed.

Apache Cordova is a framework that allows you to write hybrid apps. These apps can be published to the app store of your choice, and they permit cross-platform development. Should you need access to the native features of the device, there are core native plugins that can be added, which permit access to the camera, accelerometer, microphone, and so on. There is a large community that has written several additional plugins that provide a wide-ranging set of features. If that isn't enough, you can always write your own plugin to accomplish what you need.

Apache Cordova didn't start as an Apache project. Initially, the project was named PhoneGap and was owned by Nitobi Software. In the early stages, it was distributed as project templates that could be used in Xcode or Eclipse to create hybrid apps. While it was easy to develop single-platform apps, it was more difficult to set up multi-platform apps (one had to create copies of the web portion and keep them in sync across projects). Even so, many production apps were developed and hosted on app stores.

In 2011, Adobe purchased Nitobi Software. As part of the acquisition, the PhoneGap code was contributed to Apache as open source, and was renamed to Apache Callback and then to Apache Cordova (when the prior name was considered too generic). Adobe kept the PhoneGap name, and maintained a fork of Apache Cordova's code. The version was upped to 2.x. Most of the time, the two were largely identical (with only minor variations). Because the project templates of the prior era were often problematic, project creation transitioned to a command-line interface. Multi-platform development was somewhat easier, though not ideal.

Apache Cordova 3.x was released in July 2013. It provided a new command-line interface that dramatically simplified multi-platform development while also making plugin installation easier and less problematic than before. It also split out all the core features (beyond the native packaging) and distributed them as core plugins. This allows users to pick and choose what plugins they need rather than taking them out later (which was often difficult). This means that apps written with 3.x only ask for the permissions they actually use, whereas under 2.x, an app would often ask for permissions it never needed.

At the very beginning, the only way to use PhoneGap was to compile your project on your own development machine. This meant that you needed a machine capable of supporting the specific development environment for the platforms you supported. Setting up and maintaining this environment can be time consuming and difficult, and so PhoneGap Build was released as a cloud-based development method.

PhoneGap Build allows developers to write their apps on their machines, and then upload those apps to the cloud for compilation and packaging. This means that there is no need to set up and maintain a fully developed environment, a text editor is sufficient. There are some platforms that require additional steps before the results can be tested or deployed (Apple requires various certificates and provisioning), but for the first time, it made it possible for less-technical web designers to begin making hybrid apps that could be sold on the App Store.

Whether you use Apache Cordova or Adobe PhoneGap is up to you; we'll use Apache Cordova 3.x. It provides a set of APIs that permit your project to access the native features of the mobile device, such as the accelerometer and the camera, and much more. Using these APIs, it is possible to create an app that runs on mobile devices that has native functionality, along with HTML, CSS, and JavaScript. Where necessary, Cordova also provides the necessary expansion to create additional plugins to support features that the core API doesn't support, which means the possibilities are truly endless.

Adobe PhoneGap 3.x is a distribution of Apache Cordova 3.x. Generally, these can be thought of as the same thing, but PhoneGap integrates closely with Adobe's PhoneGap Build offering, which allows developers to compile their apps without having a complete platform SDK on their computer. It's quite possible that Adobe will bring other enhancements to this distribution that aren't part of Cordova.

Adobe PhoneGap 3.x is a distribution of Apache Cordova 3.x. Generally, these can be thought of as the same thing, but PhoneGap integrates closely with Adobe's PhoneGap Build offering, which allows developers to compile their apps without having a complete platform SDK on their computer. It's quite possible that Adobe will bring other enhancements to this distribution that aren't part of Cordova.

Which one you use is up to you; we'll go over the installation instructions for both, how to use each (generally, the commands are the same), and where they differ. For the rest of the book, we'll be using the Apache Cordova distribution, but you are welcome to use the Adobe PhoneGap distribution as well.

What do we build?

In this project, we'll go through the steps necessary to install a Cordova/PhoneGap distribution, and we'll then create your very first project.

What does it do?

Cordova/PhoneGap 3.x has grown up; it's a mature tool with a suggested workflow that is largely command-line based. While PhoneGap 1.x is largely focused on providing templates that could be used within each platform's IDE, it was quickly becoming apparent that this didn't provide a great experience when building cross-platform apps. (One usually ended up having multiple copies of their code in various places.) PhoneGap 2.x introduced a new way of creating these projects using the command line, but it was still largely platform-specific, and each project created was initialized with all the available core plugins. This sometimes created difficulty when releasing to app stores since these plugins required permissions the app may never have used. In 3.x, the command-line method has been greatly refined and provides a simpler method for cross-platform management. What once was a template created from within Xcode or Eclipse is now a cross-platform tool that can create and compile the entire project without ever entering the IDE while also creating lightweight projects that only use the plugins and permissions they need.

The project we create in this chapter is nothing amazing; consider it your Hello World app. However, it will ensure that you've got everything set up in a way that will enable you to create cross-platform apps.

Why is it great?

Once you've created this first project, you'll be able to continue with the projects in this book as well as create your own projects. You'll know that your development machine is properly configured, and you'll be able to compile and test your projects.

How are we going to do it?

One thing the old 1.x versions had going for them is that they were nearly painless to install. You just had to download the template and create a project from within the IDE and you were ready to go. But for cross-platform development, it was far from simple, and when the time came to upgrade from one version to the next, it was even worse.

The new command-line method requires a little more work to set up and install, but in the long run, it's worth it. I promise!

Here's what we'll do:

- ▸ Install node.js and configure SDKs
- ▸ Install Cordova/PhoneGap
- ▸ Create your first project

- ▸ Manage your project's platforms
- ▸ Manage your project's plugins
- ▸ Build your project
- ▸ Deploy your project to the simulator/device

What do I need to get started?

Before you continue, it's worth noting that iOS app development (and Windows Phone app development) will not work on just any OS. For iOS, you'll need a Mac with a recent version of Mac OS X 10.8.4 or higher (and Xcode 5 or higher), and for Windows Phone development, you'll need a Windows PC with Windows 8 (and the Visual Studio IDE). Android development is largely platform agnostic—that is, it can be done on Mac, Windows, and Linux.

If you use PhoneGap Build, some of the hardships can be avoided since you don't have to rely on your local development environment to build the app. But a Mac is required to generate the certificates necessary for iOS app signing (even with PhoneGap Build) and is definitely required for deployment to the App Store. The same is true for Windows; you need to deploy to the App Store from Windows only.

This book will focus solely on those platforms that use WebKit (and related browsers) to power their built-in web views. This includes iOS and Android (and though it isn't supported, it should extend to BlackBerry 10). This does not include Windows Phone (the web view is based on Trident), nor does it include the Firefox mobile OS (which is based on Gecko). Most of the code will translate easily, but not all of it (especially where vendor prefixes are used or where the event mechanisms are different). If you want to build apps for those platforms, you will need to feel free to adapt the code as necessary, but that isn't the focus of this book.

You'll need to ensure that you have installed the following before you continue:

- ▸ The platform SDK for each platform you want to support, as follows:
  - ❑ **For iOS:**Xcode 5 or higher on OS X 10.8.4 or higher; for OS X 9, Ant 1.8 or higher on Mac OS X
  - ❑ **For Android**: Eclipse or Android Studio on Mac OS X / Windows / Linux, the Android SDK, and Ant (if not already installed)
  - ❑ **For Windows Phone**: Visual Studio Express on Windows 8
- ▸ A fantastic code editor that understands HTML, JavaScript, and CSS. You might want to consider one of the following:
  - ❑ Sublime Text Editor (commercial)
  - ❑ JetBrains WebStorm (commercial)
  - ❑ Eclipse or Android Studio
  - ❑ Pico/Vim/Emacs

Installing Node.js and configuring SDKs

Cordova/PhoneGap depend upon node.js to be installed, and therefore, you need to install it first on your system. This is true whether or not you intend on using PhoneGap Build.

Getting on with it

Navigate to `http://www.nodejs.org` in your preferred browser. You'll be greeted with a page that looks somewhat like this:

Assuming the site has correctly detected your OS, click on **Install**, and a download of the correct installation package should begin. If the site doesn't correctly detect your OS, or if you would like to see the other options available, click on **Download** and then proceed with the file of your choice.

Note to Mac Users

If you have homebrew installed, you can use that to install node.js instead by typing `brew install node` in your Terminal app. If you don't have it installed and want to learn more, visit `http://brew.sh`.

Installing node.js

Once the package has been downloaded, find it in your download manager or file browser and execute it to start the installation package. Depending on what OS you are running on, the process will be slightly different, but the instructions on each screen are standard and self-explanatory. The installer will notify you about where it is installing node and npm; make note of this path because you'll need it in the next step.

For example, the following series of screens results from installing node.js on a Mac:

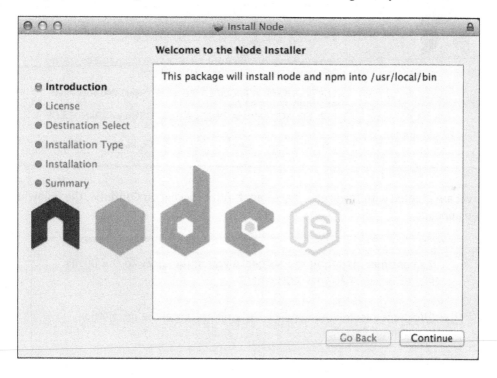

After clicking on **Continue**, your screen should look similar to what is shown in the following screenshot:

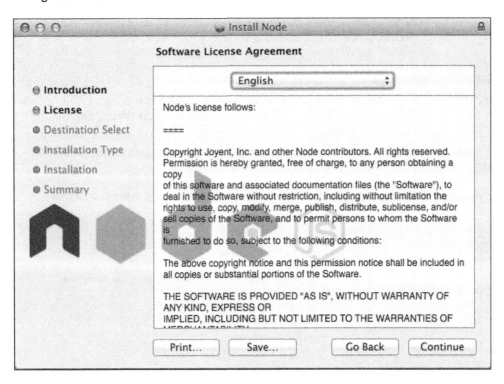

Now we are greeted with the license agreement. After clicking on **Continue**, the following screen appears:

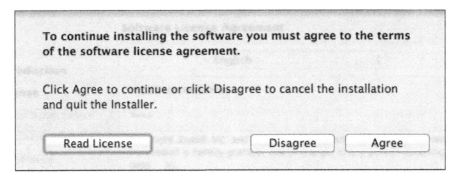

Upon clicking on **Agree**, we're notified about how much space the application will take:

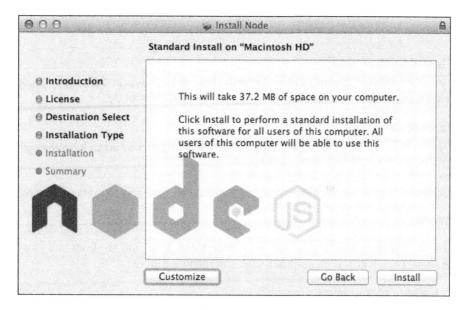

Once we click on **Install**, we're asked for our administrative password, and then the installation process kicks off. When it is complete, the following screen is presented:

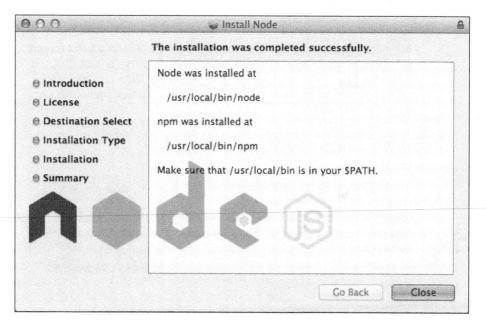

At this point, make note of the path requirement. This will be different for each platform, but for Mac, we will need to add `/usr/local/bin` to our path. Once you've made a note of the directory, you can close the installer.

Configuring your path

Unfortunately, configuring your path is platform specific. For Linux and Mac, the process will be nearly identical, but for Windows, it is done completely differently.

For Mac/Linux

Although you can perform these steps using the GUI, it's easiest to do so with the command line.

First, determine if your path is already set up. Open a terminal and type the following:

```
echo $PATH
```

If you see the directory specified in the installation steps, *stop*! You're all set and you can go to the next section. If not, then continue with the following steps:

1. Navigate to your home directory:

    ```
    cd ~
    ```

2. Next, determine your profile:

    ```
    ls .*profile*
    ```

 It's entirely possible that you don't have a profile, and if so, you won't see any files listed. In that case, you'll have to go with the defaults. For Mac OS X, this is typically `.profile` or `.bash_profile`, and for Linux (assuming you use the Bash shell), it's typically `.bash_profile`. Consult your shell's man page if you are unsure.

3. Once you determine your profile, you'll want to edit it:

    ```
    pico .profile
    ```

 Honestly, it doesn't matter what editor you use. Pico is generally installed everywhere and is a simple terminal-based editor that most people can get used to easily.

On a Mac, `open .profile` should open the file in TextEdit if you would prefer to use a GUI application.

4. Now that you've got an open file, navigate to the bottom (assuming there is anything in it) and add the following lines:

```
# for NODE
PATH="${PATH}:/usr/local/bin"
export PATH
```

 Be sure to use the exact path noted during the node.js installation process. Also, be sure to type everything exactly as written; otherwise, things won't work correctly and you may receive errors when you log in to the terminal in the future.

5. When done, save the file (Pico uses *Ctrl + O*) and exit the editor (Pico uses *Ctrl + X*).

6. To be sure the changes have taken, you can either close the terminal and log back in or source your profile:

```
. .profile
```

7. If you get errors, go back and edit the profile and make sure you've done everything correctly. Once you are error free, check to make sure that the directory is in your path by typing the following command:

```
echo $PATH
```

You should see the directory path in the output. If not, stop and go over the instructions again. Do not continue until your path is correct.

For Windows 8

First, verify that your path is already set up by opening a command prompt and typing the following command:

```
echo %PATH%
```

If the directory specified by node.js is displayed, you're good; stop and go to the next step. If not, continue with the following steps:

1. Close the command window you just opened and open the Control Panel. Open the search panel from the charms and type `Path`. Select **Edit the system environment variables**. A window should appear with **Path** in the list. Click on that row and click on **Edit**.

2. Navigate to the end of the field and add (replace "path-specified-by-installer" with the actual path):

```
;path-specified-by-installer
```

3. Click on **OK** and then on **OK** again. Open up another command prompt and verify that the path is correct by typing the following command:

```
echo %PATH%
```

If the path is not correct, stop and review the installation instructions, fixing any mistakes. Do not continue until your path is correct.

Configuring your platform SDKs (if not using PhoneGap Build)

As part of the installation process, Cordova/PhoneGap will check to ensure that your platform SDKs are correctly configured. In order to avoid error messages, it's best to take care of that now.

iOS development (Xcode)

First, make sure you've got Xcode 5 installed. Once that's taken care of, start it up, and then open the Xcode menu and click on **Preferences...**. Click on the **Downloads** tab and find the **Command Line Tools** option. If it's not installed, click on the icon to the right of **Command Line Tools** to download it. Now, go get a cup of coffee; this takes a little while.

> You may receive an error indicating that you need to add an account to Xcode 5 prior to downloading the command-line tools. Just click on **Open Accounts...** in the error message. Then, click on the **+** icon in the lower-left corner of the window and click on **Add Apple ID...**. Enter your developer credentials and then click on **Add** (or if you aren't signed up yet, click on **Join Program...**). Once done, try to download the tools again.

When finished, your display should look like this:

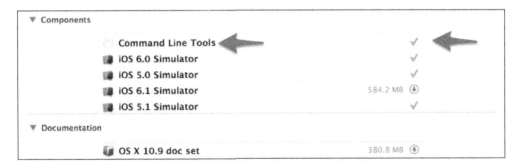

OS X 10.9 / Xcode 5.0.1

Apple decided to make things just a little more difficult for us. There's no UI to install the command-line tools anymore, so just type `xcode-select --install` at the command prompt instead. You'll be asked to accept the license, and then it will go and download everything for you.

Next, open a terminal and type the following command:

```
sudo xcodebuild -license accept
```

When prompted, enter your password.

Keep in mind that whenever Xcode is updated, you may need to rerun this command. If you get funny errors from Xcode, try running this first, just in case.

If you get an error notice when doing this, try closing your terminal session and starting a new one. Chances are you installed the command-line tools but didn't restart your terminal session to get all the new environment settings.

Android development

Make sure you've installed the Android SDK. If you haven't already, grab it from `http://developer.android.com/sdk/index.html`. If you already have the SDK installed, make sure you have a recent version, or things are apt to go awry.

If you don't have Java installed yet, install Java 6 or better. Make sure you install a JDK, not a JRE, otherwise things won't work. Once installed, you'll need to configure your `JAVA_HOME` environment variable. This is different for each OS.

For Mac, open your profile (the same file used in the prior section), and add the following to the bottom (be sure to type a backtick instead of a quote):

```
# for JAVA_HOME
export JAVA_HOME=`/usr/libexec/java_home`
```

For Linux, the process is much the same, but you will need to first locate where Java was installed. Then add this to the bottom of your profile:

```
# for JAVA_HOME
export JAVA_HOME='path-to-your-java-install'
```

For Windows, the process is much the same as adding to your system path. Open the search panel from the charms, and type `Path`. Select **Edit the system environment variables**. A window should appear with `Path` in the list. Now click **New**, and enter the variable name as `JAVA_HOME`. Enter the path in the next box. Click **OK** and **OK** again. Re-open any open command prompts to reload the environment settings.

Next, make sure you have the Android tools in your path. For Mac/Linux, add the following snippet to your profile:

```
# for Android
PATH="${PATH}:/Path-To-Android-SDK/tools:/Path-To-Android-SDK/platform-
tools"
export PATH
```

For Windows 8, follow the same instructions for adding node.js to the path, adding the Android SDK directories to the path instead.

It's also critically important to install Ant. Some Mac OS X versions (10.8.x or lower) come with it preinstalled, but later versions do not. Windows does not have it installed by default.

For Mac OS X, the easiest method to install it is to use homebrew. First, you need to install it (learn more by visiting `http://brew.sh`) using the following command:

```
ruby -e "$(curl -fsSL https://raw.github.com/mxcl/homebrew/go)"
```

Then, run `brew doctor` as follows:

```
brew doctor
```

Then, you can install Ant as follows:

```
brew install ant
```

For Windows, download Ant from Apache's website (`http://ant.apache.org/bindownload.cgi`) and follow the installation instructions at `http://ant.apache.org/manual/install.html`.

What did we do?

So far, all we've done is get your machine ready for development. You've downloaded and installed node.js, which is required for Cordova/PhoneGap. You've downloaded your development SDKs and configured them appropriately unless you're going to use PhoneGap Build. At this point, we're actually ready to install Cordova/PhoneGap.

What else do I need to know?

Keep in mind that if you're going to do iOS development, you'll need a Mac and the latest version of Xcode, whether or not you intend on using PhoneGap Build. At a minimum, Xcode is required to submit the app to the App Store and a Mac is required in order to generate the certificates necessary to sign the app.

Installing Cordova/PhoneGap

Now that the prerequisites have been taken care of, we can install Cordova/PhoneGap. You can install one or the other, or both, on your system. To help you make that decision, let's go over some of the differences.

It's possible to do mobile app development using only the Cordova **command-line interface** (**CLI**). This requires the platform SDKs to be installed and properly configured.

Adding the PhoneGap CLI enables the use of Adobe's remote building capabilities, which means you don't need to have the platform SDKs installed in order to build your app. (There are caveats here; it is best to refer to the PhoneGap Build website at `http://build.phonegap.com` for more information.)

Installing the PhoneGap CLI will also install the Cordova CLI since it relies on this for most of its functionality. The PhoneGap CLI does not understand the same commands, but since it works with the Cordova CLI, it's possible to use the Cordova CLI when the PhoneGap CLI doesn't offer to do all the same funcitonality things.

If you intend to do all your development locally, you only need to worry about the Cordova CLI. If you need the flexibility to do remote builds without having platform SDKs installed on your machine, install the PhoneGap CLI.

Getting ready

It is important to note that the installation process requires that your computer be connected to the Internet as we will use npm to download the required packages.

Getting on with it

Based on your earlier decision as to which command line to install, refer to the appropriate section, shown as follows to install Cordova / PhoneGap.

Downloading the example code

You can download the example code files for all Packt books you have purchased from your account at http://www.packtpub.com. If you purchased this book elsewhere, you can visit http://www.packtpub.com/support and register to have the files e-mailed directly to you.

Installing Cordova (if not installing PhoneGap)

To begin, open up your terminal or command prompt.

If you're running Mac OS X or Linux, type the following command:

```
sudo npm install -g cordova
```

If you're running Windows, make sure you're running as an administrative account and type this:

```
npm install -g cordova
```

If prompted, enter your password.

You should see output that looks similar to the following. It won't be exactly the same, but the important thing is that you shouldn't see any errors.

```
npm http GET https://registry.npmjs.org/cordova

npm http 200 https://registry.npmjs.org/cordova

npm http GET https://registry.npmjs.org/cordova/-/
  cordova-3.1.0-0.1.0.tgz

npm http 200 https://registry.npmjs.org/cordova/-/
  cordova-3.1.0-0.1.0.tgz

...
/usr/local/bin/cordova -> /usr/local/lib/
  node_modules/cordova/bin/cordova

cordova@3.1.0-0.1.0 /usr/local/lib/node_modules/cordova

├── ncallbacks@1.0.0

└── plugman@0.13.0 (ncallbacks@1.1.0, osenv@0.0.3,
  bplist-parser@0.0.4, semver@2.0.11, underscore@1.4.4,
  xcode@0.6.1, nopt@1.0.10, dep-graph@1.1.0, rc@0.3.0,
  tar.gz@0.1.1, npm@1.3.4)
```

To make sure that you can correctly access Cordova from the command line, type this:

```
cordova --version
```

You should see output similar to this:

```
3.1.0-0.1.0
```

 If your installation of Cordova hangs during the process (perhaps due to a network connectivity issue), just break the process (*Ctrl* + *C*) and try again.

Installing PhoneGap (if not installing Cordova)

Open your terminal or command prompt. If you're running Mac OS X or Linux, type this:

```
sudo npm install -g phonegap
```

If you're running Windows (as an administrative user), type this:

```
npm install -g phonegap
```

If prompted for your password, enter it.

You should see output that looks like this:

```
npm http GET https://registry.npmjs.org/phonegap

npm http 200 https://registry.npmjs.org/phonegap

npm http GET https://registry.npmjs.org/phonegap/
  -/phonegap-3.1.0-0.15.0.tgz

npm http 200 https://registry.npmjs.org/phonegap/
  -/phonegap-3.1.0-0.15.0.tgz

npm http GET https://registry.npmjs.org/node-static/0.7.0

npm http GET https://registry.npmjs.org/phonegap-build/0.8.4

...

/usr/local/bin/phonegap -> /usr/local/lib
  /node_modules/phonegap/bin/phonegap.js

phonegap@3.1.0-0.15.0 /usr/local/lib/node_modules/phonegap

├── pluralize@0.0.4

└── cordova@3.1.0-0.1.0 (ncallbacks@1.0.0, colors@0.6.2,
  open@0.0.3, mime@1.2.11, follow-redirects@0.0.3,
  shelljs@0.1.2, glob@3.2.6, xcode@0.5.1, elementtree@0.1.5,
  tar@0.1.18, prompt@0.2.7, request@2.22.0, express@3.0.0,
  ripple-emulator@0.9.18, npm@1.3.11, plist@0.4.3, plugman@0.13.0)
```

When complete, test whether you can access PhoneGap by typing this:

```
phonegap --version
```

You should see output similar to this:

```
3.1.0-0.15.0
```

 As with installing Cordova, if your installation hangs, just break it (*Ctrl + C*) and redo the installation.

What did we do?

In this section, we successfully installed the Cordova CLI and, if you chose to, the PhoneGap CLI on your machine. Your machine is now ready for Cordova/PhoneGap development.

What else do I need to know?

It's possible that you'll see various errors or notices in the output of the install process. Generally, **WARN** and **304** notifications aren't cause for alarm, but if you see anything more serious, you may need to retry the install or address the underlying cause.

It's also possible that if your platform SDK is improperly set up, you'll get errors during the installation process. These should indicate the platform SDK in question.

Creating your first project

A project contains your code, other platform-specific code, and other assets required to generate an app ready for you to run on a simulator or device. All of this information is stored within a project directory. When you create a project, the command-line interface generates this directory structure for you and generates a basic app, which allows you to verify that you can get a *Hello World* style app built.

Getting ready

It is important to note that the installation process requires that your computer be connected to the Internet as the project creation step may need to download information.

Getting on with it

Creating a project is really simple regardless of which command-line interface is being used. Let's create a project first with the Cordova command line.

Creating a project with the Cordova CLI

First, open your terminal or command prompt and navigate to wherever you want to store your project.

 I highly suggest that you create your projects in a directory where there are no spaces in the path. For example, storing all your projects in /users/ yourname/my projects/ would be a bad idea since the CLIs tend to have problems handling paths with spaces in them.

Then, type the following command:

```
cordova create ./HelloWorld com.phonegaphotshot.helloworld HelloWorld
```

The first parameter indicates to Cordova that it should create a project in specific directory specified by the second parameter. The third parameter is the project's ID ; these should always be unique and specified in reverse domain name order. The final parameter is the name of the project.

This command may take a few seconds to complete if anything needs to be downloaded, but when done, you should see something like this:

```
Creating a new cordova project with name "HelloWorld" and id "com.
phonegaphotshot.helloworld" at location "/Users/You/HelloWorld".
```

Once done, though, you should have a new project in the HelloWorld directory and you should have several new folders and files in that directory. While each is important, we will only really focus on the merges and www directories in this book.

Creating a project with the PhoneGap CLI

To create a project with the PhoneGap CLI, open your command prompt or terminal, navigate to the location you want your project to be stored, and type this:

```
phonegap create ./PGHelloWorld com.phonegaphotshot.pghelloworld
PGHelloWorld
```

As with the Cordova CLI, the first parameter indicates that a project should be created in a directory specified by the second parameter. The third parameter is the project ID, which must be unique and should be specified in reverse domain-name order. The final parameter is the name of the project.

 I highly suggest that you create your projects in a directory where there are no spaces in the path. For example, storing all your projects in /users/ yourname/my projects/ would be a bad idea since the CLIs tend to have problems handling paths with spaces in them.

The PhoneGap CLI is a little more verbose than the Cordova CLI, and so you should see output similar to the following:

```
[phonegap] missing library phonegap/www/3.1.0
[phonegap] downloading https://github.com/phonegap/
  phonegap-app-hello-world/archive/3.1.0.tar.gz...
[phonegap] created project at /Users/You/.../PGHelloWorld
```

If you compare the two structures, you'll find that they are very similar. Because they share the same structure, it's fully possible to use the Cordova CLI within this book's project.

What did we do?

In this step, we created two projects, one using the Cordova CLI and the other using the PhoneGap CLI. We compared the structures created by both and found them similar.

What else do I need to know?

It's possible that at some point the PhoneGap distribution will deploy different sample code than the Cordova distribution. As such, the structures under the www folder may not always be identical.

Managing your project's platforms

We've created our first projects, but we haven't specified the platforms that the projects support. We'll add the iOS and Android platforms in this step and also show you how to manage the available platforms in your project.

Getting ready

It's important for your computer to be connected to the Internet as, while adding platforms, you may need to download platform-specific code.

Getting on with it

After creating your project, the next step usually involves adding the platforms the project will support. However, it's important to remember that you can also manage these platforms at any time. You can remove platforms, update platforms (in the case of an update to Cordova), and list out the supported platforms.

Adding platforms

To add the iOS and Android platforms (regardless of which CLI you used to create your project), open your terminal or command prompt, navigate to your project's directory, and type this:

```
cordova platform add ios android
```

Windows / Linux Users

You won't be able to add the `ios` platform, so just use `cordova platform add android`.

There may be a delay since each Cordova platform may need to download various platform files from the Internet. If you want to add other platforms, you can follow this pattern:

```
cordova platform add platform-name
```

Here, `platform-name` is any of the supported platforms, including the following:

- `ios`: The iOS platform
- `android`: The Android platform
- `blackberry10`: The BlackBerry 10 OS platform
- `firefoxos`: The Firefox OS platform
- `wp7`: The Windows Phone 7 platform
- `wp8`: The Windows Phone 8 platform
- `windows 8`: The Windows 8 platform

In order to build or deploy a project for a given platform, you need to have the appropriate platform SDK installed and properly configured. If not, you may receive errors.

Lots of new files have been added in the **merges**, **platforms**, and **plugins** folders. These are the platform-specific portions of your project.

Listing the available platforms

At some point in the future, you may want to ask Cordova which platforms your project is configured to support. To find out, just type the following command:

```
cordova platform ls
```

You'll see output similar to this:

```
Installed platforms: android, ios
Available platforms: blackberry10, firefoxos
```

Removing platforms

To remove a platform, just type this:

```
cordova platform remove platform-name
```

This will remove the appropriate directories and files from your project.

Updating platforms

If you update Cordova, you may want to update your project's platforms as well. To do so, update Cordova first (`sudo npm update -g cordova`) and then type this:

```
cordova platform update platform-name
```

What did we do?

In this section, you added the iOS and Android platforms to your Hello World project. You also learned how to add additional platforms, list the installed and available platforms, remove platforms, and update platforms.

Managing your project's plugins

Plugins are the mechanism Cordova uses to provide native functionality to your app. There is a set of core plugins that used to be provided to each app by default in the 2.x days. Now they have been unbundled and need to be installed separately if you want to use them. While a little more labor intensive, it also solves the problem of apps requesting more permissions than they actually need.

Plugins can be installed from several different sources, and the CLIs provide mechanisms that make it easy to add plugins from your local machine, from a Git repository, or from the plugin repository at `http://plugins.cordova.io`. If the plugin you need is available in the plugin repository, this is probably the easiest way since you just need to know the plugin's identifier rather than a long path or URL. All the plugins in this book should be available via Git or the plugin repository.

To simplify the addition of plugins, there is a plugin registry that allows you to specify plugins by name in reverse-domain notation.

Advanced Readers

Plugins must conform to a specification in order to be added to your projects. If you're interested in how this works, see `http://cordova.apache.org/docs/en/edge/guide_hybrid_plugins_index.md.html#Plugin%20Development%20Guide`.

Getting ready

You'll need to be connected to the Internet in order to install plugins from the plugin registry since their content needs to be downloaded before it can be installed in your project.

Getting on with it

Plugins can be managed using either the Cordova CLI or the PhoneGap CLI (which ends up using the Cordova CLI in the background). The important detail to remember when you use the PhoneGap CLI is that plugins must be installed locally (not remotely).

Managing plugins with the Cordova CLI

First, open your command prompt or terminal and navigate to your project directory. From here, you can install plugins, remove plugins, and list the available plugins in your project.

Installing plugins

To install a plugin, use a command with the following pattern:

```
cordova plugin add plugin-name
```

If the plugin is local, use the path to the plugin instead of the plugin name. If the plugin is hosted on a Git repository, use the URL to the Git repository. Otherwise, just use the plugin ID from the registry.

To install all of the core plugins, you can use the following command (as of 3.1.x):

```
cordova plugin add org.apache.cordova.device
org.apache.cordova.network-information org.apache.cordova.battery-
status org.apache.cordova.device-motion org.apache.cordova.device-
orientation org.apache.cordova.geolocation org.apache.cordova.camera
org.apache.cordova.media org.apache.cordova.media-capture
org.apache.cordova.file org.apache.cordova.file-transfer
org.apache.cordova.dialogs org.apache.cordova.vibration
org.apache.cordova.contacts org.apache.cordova.globalization
org.apache.cordova.splashscreen org.apache.cordova.inappbrowser
org.apache.cordova.console
```

You won't normally want to install each core plugin, as this means your app will need far more permissions on the device than necessary.

If you want to know what each plugin does, see http://cordova. apache.org/docs/en/edge/cordova_plugins_ pluginapis.md.html#Plugin%20APIsZ

Give the command a few seconds to complete; it will need to download the plugins from the registry, and after a few seconds, you should be returned to the prompt.

Listing plugins

To check whether the plugins were indeed added, you can use a simple command:

```
cordova plugin list
```

You should see the following output, assuming you added all the core plugins:

```
[ 'org.apache.cordova.battery-status',
  'org.apache.cordova.camera',
  'org.apache.cordova.console',
  'org.apache.cordova.contacts',
  'org.apache.cordova.device',
  'org.apache.cordova.device-motion',
  'org.apache.cordova.device-orientation',
  'org.apache.cordova.dialogs',
  'org.apache.cordova.file',
  'org.apache.cordova.file-transfer',
  'org.apache.cordova.geolocation',
  'org.apache.cordova.globalization',
  'org.apache.cordova.inappbrowser',
  'org.apache.cordova.media',
  'org.apache.cordova.media-capture',
  'org.apache.cordova.network-information',
  'org.apache.cordova.splashscreen',
  'org.apache.cordova.vibration' ]
```

Removing plugins

You can remove any plugin you want by following this pattern:

```
cordova plugin remove plugin-name
```

For example, let's remove the globalization and contacts plugins:

```
cordova plugin remove org.apache.cordova.globalization
org.apache.cordova.contacts
```

Now, if you list the plugins, you should see this:

```
[ 'org.apache.cordova.battery-status',
  'org.apache.cordova.camera',
  'org.apache.cordova.console',
  'org.apache.cordova.device',
  'org.apache.cordova.device-motion',
  'org.apache.cordova.device-orientation',
  'org.apache.cordova.dialogs',
  'org.apache.cordova.file',
  'org.apache.cordova.file-transfer',
  'org.apache.cordova.geolocation',
  'org.apache.cordova.inappbrowser',
  'org.apache.cordova.media',
  'org.apache.cordova.media-capture',
  'org.apache.cordova.network-information',
  'org.apache.cordova.splashscreen',
  'org.apache.cordova.vibration' ]
```

Managing plugins with the PhoneGap CLI

The PhoneGap CLI requires that you install plugins locally, and as such, it uses a slightly different syntax. With that said, the same operations are available as with the Cordova CLI.

Installing plugins

To install a plugin, you use a command with the following pattern:

```
phonegap local plugin add plugin-name
```

If the plugin is a local plugin, use the path to the plugin instead of `plugin-name`. If the plugin is hosted on a Git repository, use the URL to the Git repository. Otherwise, just use the plugin ID from the registry.

To install all of the core plugins, you can use the following commands (as of 3.1.x):

- ▶ `phonegap local plugin add org.apache.cordova.device`
- ▶ `phonegap local plugin add org.apache.cordova.network-information`
- ▶ `phonegap local plugin add org.apache.cordova.battery-status`

- `phonegap local plugin add org.apache.cordova.device-motion`
- `phonegap local plugin add org.apache.cordova.device-orientation`
- `phonegap local plugin add org.apache.cordova.geolocation`
- `phonegap local plugin add org.apache.cordova.camera`
- `phonegap local plugin add org.apache.cordova.media`
- `phonegap local plugin add org.apache.cordova.media-capture`
- `phonegap local plugin add org.apache.cordova.file`
- `phonegap local plugin add org.apache.cordova.file-transfer`
- `phonegap local plugin add org.apache.cordova.dialogs`
- `phonegap local plugin add org.apache.cordova.vibration`
- `phonegap local plugin add org.apache.cordova.contacts`
- `phonegap local plugin add org.apache.cordova.globalization`
- `phonegap local plugin add org.apache.cordova.splashscreen`
- `phonegap local plugin add org.apache.cordova.inappbrowser`
- `phonegap local plugin add org.apache.cordova.console`

 You won't normally want to install each core plugin, as this means your app will need far more permissions on the device than necessary. If you want to know what each plugin does, see `http://cordova.apache.org/docs/en/edge/cordova_plugins_pluginapis.md.html#Plugin%20APIsZ`

You'll see the following output from each command:

```
[phonegap] adding the plugin: org.apache.cordova.device
[phonegap] successfully added the plugin
```

Listing plugins

To check whether the plugins were indeed added, you can use a simple command:

```
phonegap local plugin list
```

You should see the following output, assuming you added all the core plugins:

```
[phonegap] org.apache.cordova.battery-status
[phonegap] org.apache.cordova.camera
[phonegap] org.apache.cordova.console
[phonegap] org.apache.cordova.contacts
[phonegap] org.apache.cordova.device
[phonegap] org.apache.cordova.device-motion
```

```
[phonegap] org.apache.cordova.device-orientation
[phonegap] org.apache.cordova.dialogs
[phonegap] org.apache.cordova.file
[phonegap] org.apache.cordova.file-transfer
[phonegap] org.apache.cordova.geolocation
[phonegap] org.apache.cordova.globalization
[phonegap] org.apache.cordova.inappbrowser
[phonegap] org.apache.cordova.media
[phonegap] org.apache.cordova.media-capture
[phonegap] org.apache.cordova.network-information
[phonegap] org.apache.cordova.splashscreen
[phonegap] org.apache.cordova.vibration
```

Removing plugins

You can remove any plugin you want by following this pattern:

```
phonegap local plugin remove plugin-name
```

For example, let's remove the globalization and contacts plugins:

```
phonegap local plugin remove org.apache.cordova.globalization
phonegap local plugin remove org.apache.cordova.contacts
```

You should see a notice like this:

```
[phonegap] removing the plugin: org.apache.cordova.globalization
[phonegap] successfully removed the plugin
```

Now, if you list the plugins, you should see the following output:

```
[phonegap] org.apache.cordova.battery-status
[phonegap] org.apache.cordova.camera
[phonegap] org.apache.cordova.console
[phonegap] org.apache.cordova.device
[phonegap] org.apache.cordova.device-motion
[phonegap] org.apache.cordova.device-orientation
[phonegap] org.apache.cordova.dialogs
[phonegap] org.apache.cordova.file
[phonegap] org.apache.cordova.file-transfer
[phonegap] org.apache.cordova.geolocation
[phonegap] org.apache.cordova.inappbrowser
```

```
[phonegap]  org.apache.cordova.media
[phonegap]  org.apache.cordova.media-capture
[phonegap]  org.apache.cordova.network-information
[phonegap]  org.apache.cordova.splashscreen
[phonegap]  org.apache.cordova.vibration
```

What did we do?

In this section, we used both CLIs to add, list, and remove plugins.

What else do I need to know?

The plugin registry will typically be your first stop when you look for new plugins. Most plugin developers will use this, but there may always be a few out there that are hosted only on Git repositories. If you create your own plugin, it may be hosted solely on your machine. The process for adding these plugins will be the same; point to the path or URL instead of using the plugin name. Once added, you can remove them using the reverse-domain notation.

While the core plugins generally support each platform, there are always exceptions. It's a good idea to look closely at the documentation for each plugin in order to determine whether it supports all the platforms you need in your project (or whether you need to add additional plugins to cover any gaps).

Building your project

All we've done so far is created a project, added some platforms to it, and added several of the core plugins. We've not actually attempted to build a project.

Building involves compiling all the native code using the platform SDKs on your machine and then packaging your HTML, JavaScript, and CSS (and any assets) with this code so that it can be deployed to a simulator or device.

There are many steps involved when you actually build your project, but thankfully, the CLIs make it very easy to get something that can go on your device.

Getting ready

If you intend on using PhoneGap Build to build your project, you'll need to be connected to the Internet, and you'll need a PhoneGap Build account. You can get one at http://build.phonegap.com. You'll also need to set up your signing and provisioning certificates, which is beyond the scope of this book.

Getting on with it

Building your project can be done with either of the CLIs, and the PhoneGap CLI also provides remote building (which doesn't require your machine to have a platform SDK installed). As such, the syntax is a little different for each CLI, but both accomplish the same thing.

Building your project using the Cordova CLI

To build your project for all platforms, you can just open a command prompt or terminal, navigate to your project directory, and type this:

```
cordova build
```

Give the command some time to complete, as the project must be compiled for each platform, and ideally, you should have no output. If you do receive errors, it may indicate a problem with your platform SDK configuration or a problem with some native code (which shouldn't happen yet, since we've not changed or written any).

If you just want to build for one particular platform (or multiple but not all), just use the following command:

```
cordova build platform
```

To solely build for iOS, for example, you could use the following command:

```
cordova build ios
```

Building your project using the PhoneGap CLI

To build your project for a specific platform, you can open your command prompt or terminal, navigate to your project directory, and type the following command:

```
phonegap local build platform-name
```

You can only build one platform at a time; if you need to build multiple platforms, you'll need to specify each one. For Android, you'd type this:

```
phonegap local build android
```

For iOS, you'd type this:

```
phonegap local build ios
```

You should get output similar to this:

```
[phonegap] compiling iOS...
[phonegap] successfully compiled iOS app
```

Give this some time to complete, as the compilation steps do quite a bit of work underneath the hood. If you get errors, chances are good that you've got an error in your native code (which shouldn't happen at this point as we haven't changed any native code), or there's a problem in the configuration of your platform SDK.

To build your project remotely using PhoneGap Build, it's just about as easy, but you do need to have an account on PhoneGap Build and have all the necessary certificates and provisioning files set up.

To build a platform remotely, type this:

```
phonegap remote build platform-name
```

If you haven't previously logged in to PhoneGap Build from your command line, you'll probably be asked for your username and password.

Your project will then be uploaded to the cloud, where it will be compiled. This may take a few moments depending on your bandwidth.

You should see output similar to this:

```
[phonegap]  PhoneGap/Build Login
[phonegap]  Sign up at build.phonegap.com
 [warning]  GitHub accounts are unsupported
  [prompt]  enter username: username
  [prompt]  enter password: password
[phonegap]  logged in as username
[phonegap]  compressing the app...
[phonegap]  uploading the app...
[phonegap]  building the app...
[phonegap]  Android build complete
```

At this point, you'll need to actually navigate to `http://build.phonegap.com` in order to see the results.

 If you receive an error message during this process, ensure that there is a `config.xml` file in the www directory. If you are using the code package for this book, the `config.xml` file lives above the www directory. Also, if you'll want to add any plugins your project uses (if any) to the `config.xml` file, as noted at `http://docs.build.phonegap.com/en_US/configuring_plugins.md.html#Plugins`.

What did we do?

In this section, we successfully built the project for each platform using the Cordova CLI and local and remote PhoneGap CLIs.

What else do I need to know?

Building remotely using PhoneGap Build is a little different from building locally since you may not see the results of the build instantly; the service will build the code as soon as it has a chance. The only way to verify that things went as expected is to log on to your account at `http://build.phonegap.com` and verify the results.

Deploying your project to a simulator/device

Once you've built a project, the next logical step is to actually test it. To do this, you can deploy the code to a simulator (which is handy for debugging on your machine) or deploy the code to a device (which is a must to get a feel for how the app performs on a real device). You can do both using either CLIs, depending upon what the platform SDK supports. (For example, some platform SDKs may only support deploying to a simulator.)

Getting ready

If you need to deploy to the iOS simulator, you may need to install programs called `ios-sim` and `ios-deploy`.

To install both, just use the following commands from your command-line or terminal (wait for the first to complete before attempting the second):

```
sudo npm install -g ios-sim
sudo npm install -g ios-deploy
```

Getting on with it

Both CLIs can deploy your code to a device or simulator. If you need to test on iOS, keep in mind that iOS only permits deploying to the simulator as of Cordova 3.1. If you need to test on Android, it will normally depend on whether or not you have a device plugged in with USB debugging enabled and whether you are deploying the app to the simulator or a device.

Deploying using the Cordova CLI

The simplest method is to use the following pattern:

```
cordova emulate platform
```

To test on the Android simulator, you can type this:

```
cordova emulate android
```

To test on the iOS simulator, you can type this:

```
cordova emulate ios
```

Both options should launch the respective simulators and then launch the app. If you need to launch in a specific simulator, it's best to open the simulator manually and then deploy to the simulator.

You'll know things are working properly when you can see the app in the simulator. It should look something like this:

 The **Device is Ready** indicator should pulse on the simulator or device.

If you want to deploy to your Android device, plug it in first and then type the following command:

```
cordova run android
```

Wait a few moments and your device should begin running the app.

Deploying using the PhoneGap CLI

To deploy using the PhoneGap CLI, it's important to remember that this only works for local builds. If you built remotely, you need to navigate to `http://build.phonegap.com` and install from there.

To deploy to the iOS simulator, type this:

```
phonegap local install ios
```

To deploy to your Android device (be sure to plug it in) or simulator, type this:

```
phonegap local install android
```

You should see output similar to the following:

```
[phonegap] trying to install app onto device
[phonegap] no device was found
[phonegap] trying to install app onto emulator
[phonegap] successfully installed onto emulator
```

If everything goes as it should, you should see the following image:

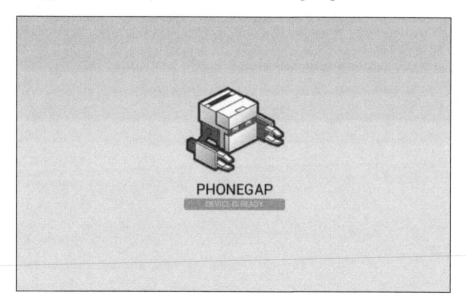

 The **Device is Ready** indicator should pulse on the simulator or device.

What did we do?

In this task, we deployed the app to a simulator or your device using the Cordova CLI and the PhoneGap CLI.

It's also important to note that as of Cordova 3.1, deploying directly to your iOS device (as in `cordova run ios`) is not supported.

Game Over..... Wrapping it up

It's taken a bit of work, but you were successfully able to install node.js, configure your platform SDKs, install the Cordova and/or PhoneGap CLIs, and optionally install `ios-sim` and `ios-deploy`. You created your first project using either one of the CLIs, added platforms to it, added the core plugins, and then built it and deployed it to your simulator or device.

Can you take the HEAT? The Hotshot Challenge

We will be focusing heavily on Android and iOS mobile application development. However, you might want to deploy to another platform. Try your hand at adding another platform, say BlackBerry 10 or Firefox OS or Windows Phone 8, to your project, and see if you can build and deploy it to the simulator or device.

Project 2

Localization and Globalization

"Localization and globalization" isn't a glamorous term by any means, and it's often neglected until the final stages of a product—if it is paid any attention at all. As it is unlikely we will ever live in a world where everyone speaks the same language, localization and globalization will continue to be critical to expanding the reach of your application. Without it, your app is restricted to those who can understand a specific language, and this may limit the appeal of your app.

There are two factors to consider: one is the translation of text from one language to the other, and the other is translation of formats. For example, currency is often rendered very differently from area to area, and it is important to display information in the form that your users will understand. Failing to do so can lead to fundamental misunderstandings by your users, for example, does 5/10/2013 refer to May 10, 2013, or does it refer to October 5? Is 145,322 a large number (hundreds of thousands) or a small number (just in the hundreds)?

Thankfully, the formatting of numbers, dates, and such is made easier by lots of great frameworks (such as jQuery/globalize) that make it easy to globalize your app by inserting the right code around user-facing data. For example, one might use something like `format(3459.23, 'c2')` to generate the correctly localized currency (for the US, $3,459.23).

The hard part comes when you need to translate the text of your app. While various automatic translators appear to reduce the complexity somewhat, they do not come close to approaching the ability of a native speaker who is familiar with idioms, turns of phrase, cultural attachments to various words and phrases, and more. It's unlikely to hurt your app a lot if you just make your users laugh—assuming they get the intended meaning. What's worse is if you offend your users somehow. It might then have been better to have not translated at all. Because of this, it is difficult and often expensive, to properly convert from one language to another. Even so, there's no reason not to globalize your app so that it can accommodate a translation; so that even if you don't add an alternate language now, you still have the ability to do so easily in the future.

If you wait too long to consider all of these issues, your app will end up being very hard to localize because you'll have to go back and identify every piece of text, every number, every date, and so on, and add code to each place to handle translation and formatting. At that point, you'll be wishing you had started your app with a framework already in place, and that's where we begin.

What do we build?

In this project, we're not building anything terribly fancy yet. Think of this as a "getting your hands wet" project. What we will be doing is working through various examples of localization and globalization.

The app will support several localizations: English (American and British) and Spanish (American and Spain). We can support any number of languages. For example, we could have used just French or added French to the list of existing languages. The point here is to show you how the mechanisms work and how you can apply them to future projects.

What does it do?

When you've completed this project, you'll have been introduced to several important ideas. You'll be able to create a new project by using an existing template, you'll be introduced to YASMF v0.4 (the framework we're using for this book), and most importantly, you'll have a good idea about how to localize text and numbers.

Why is it great?

Although the app doesn't really do anything useful, it is absolutely critical. Localization should never be brought in after a project is complete; instead, it should exist in your projects from day one. (Trust me. It's very hard to come back and put localization code into a project just before shipping it.)

How are we going to do it?

Normally, we'd start out by going over the app's user interface and model designs. Since this app is essentially a demonstration app that exists only for playing around with localization, we'll skip that particular step for now.

Instead, we'll go over the following topics:

- ▸ Creating the template
- ▸ Creating a new project based on an existing template
- ▸ Introducing the YASMF v0.4 framework
- ▸ Determining the user's locale
- ▸ Formatting numbers and dates
- ▸ Translating text

What do I need to get started?

You should already have installed the Cordova CLI and the requisite platform SDKs if you intend on building your application locally. If you intend on building with PhoneGap Build, make sure you've installed the PhoneGap CLI.

You should also download the code package for this book. It's available on Packt Publishing's website and also on GitHub (`https://github.com/kerrishotts/PhoneGap-HotShot-3-x-Code-Bundle`). There is a template folder within the package that will serve as the basis for all our projects.

Creating the template

In the previous chapter, we discussed how to use the Cordova CLI in order to create new projects and manage the platforms and plugins within each project. This works well, except for one thing: the www folder in your project is already pre-populated with files that need replacing. Wouldn't it be great if you could create a new Cordova project with all the files you needed in the www folder instead? In order to do this, we need to create a template that holds the files we actually want to have in our projects.

It should be noted that if you don't want to go through the work of creating a template, you can download the code package for this book and use ours instead.

Getting on with it

A template project lives in its own directory, so you'll need to create a new directory for the template to reside in. Since we'll be passing this directory to Cordova on the command line, it would be advisable for you to avoid paths with spaces in them.

Then, you'll need to mirror the following structure:

```
/template
  /www
    /css
    /html
    /img
    /js
      /app
        /factories
        /models
        /views
      /lib
        /cultures
```

Then, download the following files and place them where indicated:

- **RequireJS:** Download either the minified or commented version from `http://requirejs.org/docs/download.html#requirejs` to `/www/js/lib/require.js`

- **RequreJS text plugin**: Download `text.js` from `https://github.com/requirejs/text` to `/www/js/lib/text.js`.

- **jQuery/globalize**: A new version is undergoing extensive redevelopment. The current version, however, lacks many needed features, and so we use the last stable version. For whatever reason, the old version is only available at this link:

  `https://github.com/jquery/globalize/tree/79ae658b842f75f58199d6e9074e01f7ce207468/lib`

  You will need to download `globalize.js` to `/www/js/lib/globalize.js`. Then, download the following files from the repo's `culture` directory to `/www/js/lib/cultures`:

  - `globalize.culture.en-US.js`
  - `globalize.culture.es-US.js`
  - `globalize.culture.en-GB.js`
  - `globalize.culture.es-ES.js`

- ▶ **Q**: Stable releases are available at `http://q-releases.s3-website-us-west-1.amazonaws.com`. Download `q.min.js` to `/www/js/lib/q.js`.

- ▶ **YASMF (Yet Another Simple Mobile Framework)**: Download the entire directory (including subdirectories) from `https://github.com/photokandyStudios/YASMF-Next/tree/master/dist` and place it in `/www/js/lib`. If you've downloaded it correctly, `/www/js/lib/yasmf`-assets should include many different icon files that we can use in later projects.

What did we do?

In this section, we created a template `www` folder that we can instruct Cordova to use when we create our projects in future. In the next section, we'll create a project based on this template.

Creating a new project based on an existing template

Now that we have a template, we need to create a project based on it. Note that we'll be using the Cordova CLI in this section.

> At the time of writing this book, the PhoneGap CLI did not support creating projects based on templates, so if you plan on using the PhoneGap CLI, you'll need to create your project, remove the content you don't want from the `www` directory, and copy the files in your template directory to your project's `www` folder.

Getting on with it

First, open your terminal app or command prompt and navigate to the location where you want to store your project files. Be sure to avoid paths that have spaces in them (depending on the platform and Cordova version, spaces can sometimes break things).

Then, use the following command:

```
create ./localizationdemo com.packtpub.phonegaphotshot.localizationdemo
LocalizationDemo --copy-from /path/to/code/package/template/www
```

Change into the project directory (`cd localizationdemo`) and then add the iOS and Android platforms:

```
cordova platform add ios android
```

Once that's done, you should be able to view the `www` directory and find that it is pre-populated with various libraries (in `www/js/lib`). This is the project structure we'll be following for the remainder of the book:

```
/localizationdemo
    /merges         -- files specific to each platform; we don't
        -- use this directory in this book.
    /www
      /css       -- project-specific styles
      /html      -- HTML for views, templates, etc.
      /img       -- images
      /js        -- Javascript
        /app           -- App-specific
          /factories  -- Factory code (object creation)
          /models     -- Data Models
          /views      -- User Interface
        /lib           -- Libraries
          /cultures    -- jQuery/Globalize cultures
              -- Our template has four: en-US
              -- es-US, en-GB, es-ES
```

Finally, we need to adjust the `config.xml` file in the `www` directory to set various parameters that control how the app functions on the device, in addition to changing the title and description in the app. Ours are shown as follows (the preferences at the bottom are the most important changes):

```
<?xml version='1.0' encoding='utf-8'?>
<widget id="com.packtpub.phonegaphotshot.localizationdemo"
  version="1.0.0" xmlns="http://www.w3.org/ns/widgets"
  xmlns:cdv="http://cordova.apache.org/ns/1.0">
  <name>LocalizationDemo</name>
  <description>
    PhoneGap HotShot 3.x Mobile Application Development,
      Localization Demo
  </description>
  <author email="kerrishotts@gmail.com"
    href="http://www.photokandy.com/books/pghs3">
    Kerri Shotts
  </author>
  <content src="index.html" />
  <access origin="*" />
```

```
    <preference name="fullscreen" value="false" />
    <preference name="webviewbounce" value="false" />
    <preference name="DisallowOverscroll" value="true"/>
    <preference name="HideKeyboardFormAccessoryBar" value="false"/>
    <preference name="Orientation" value="default" />
    <preference name="BackgroundColor" value="0xfff1eee5" />
</widget>
```

Let's just go over each preference before we move on:

- `fullscreen`: This determines whether the app should occupy the whole screen or not. On iOS 7, this doesn't mean much—apps take up the whole screen (whether or not the status bar is present is a different issue), but on Android, this can determine whether the status bar is present or not. Since we want it present, we set the value to `false`.

- `webviewbounce`: This determines whether the web view should bounce when the user scrolls and reaches the bounds of the container. This option is superseded by the next property, but it was generated by the CLI, and so we set the value to `false` (to prevent the bounce).

- `DisallowOverscroll`: This determines whether the web view should bounce when the user reaches the bounds of the container. We don't want this to occur because it doesn't typically feel "natural" for an app to have its contents bouncing around. It wouldn't be so bad if this just meant lists and other internal scrolling containers would bounce, but this includes the navigation bar and toolbars and other important elements. Since we want to disable the feature, we set it to `true`.

- `HideKeyboardFormAccessory`: This determines whether the keyboard on iOS should show the accessory bar above the keyboard. This bar usually contains the "next", "previous", and "done" buttons, and some people don't like it. However, it can cause layout issues if it is turned off, and so we'll leave this value set to `false`.

- `Orientation`: This determines what orientations are supported by the app. We set it to `default` here, indicating that we support the default orientations. (This varies by platform.) Valid options are `default`, `landscape`, and `portrait`.

- `BackgroundColor`: This determines the background color of the web view. The format is not your typical HTML color, but a 4-byte color including the alpha channel. So if we want the background color to be #F1EEE5, the value used is `0xfff1eee5`, indicating an opaque color.

If you want to know more about the various preferences that can be specified, see `http://cordova.apache.org/docs/en/edge/config_ref_index.md.html#The%20config.xml%20File`.

What did we do?

In this section, we created a new project using our template. We also modified the config.xml file for our project.

Introducing the YASMF v0.4 framework

YASMF v0.4 (also known as YASMF-Next) is a simple framework designed to make mobile development simpler and faster. It is short for **Yet Another Simple Mobile Framework**. It provides utility functions that work with: the **document object model** (**DOM**), the filesystem, and a single-inheritance object model. It also provides user interface methods that manage views and animations between them.

This version of the framework is actually a newer version of the framework we used in the previous edition of this book. It has taken the best things from that version, left a few less useful or obsolete items on the cutting-room floor, and expanded on the old version by adding useful new features. Even though it's a new version with the same name, it really is a different framework and is incompatible with prior versions of YASMF.

There are many well-established frameworks available for you to use to build a mobile app, including jQuery Mobile, Sencha Touch, Ionic, M-Project, Intel App Framework, Zepto.JS, Kendo UI, and more. For that matter, you could build an app without any framework; just HTML, CSS, and JavaScript will do.

So, with so many good frameworks available, why YASMF? YASMF is small, which means there's not a lot of intimidating code should you wish to explore the internals yourself. YASMF also allows us to focus more on the HTML, CSS, and vanilla JavaScript than some other frameworks.

Ultimately, the concepts learned from any framework readily apply to other frameworks, much as learning the syntax of one programming language assists the learning of another language that much faster. Some of the syntax in this book may be different, but the concepts can be applied universally to any framework. Where a framework doesn't supply a concept, it's usually simple enough to supply your own implementation (or use YASMF as a base).

So what does this have to do with localizing text and formatting? YASMF provides a very simple translation matrix for text and utilizes jQuery/globalize to format numbers, percentages, currency, and dates. The translation matrix is easy enough to implement solely on your own if you don't want to be beholden to any framework, but formatting numbers and dates is not so easy, and I'd be lying if I said it was something I would ever want to do from scratch.

One final thing to note is that, in code, YASMF is rarely ever spelled out. Instead, you'll often see _y.

Determining the user's locale

A locale indicates the formatting preferences and language that the user prefers. In order to display numbers and text in the way that the user expects, it is critical that we be able to determine this value.

Getting on with it

A locale can consist of a two-character language code, or it can consist of both a two-character language code and a two-character region code. They typically look like this: en (English), es (Spanish), en-US (American English), es-MX (Spanish in Mexico), and so on. YASMF can support any locale for text translation (though you must specify the translations), but it can only support the locales supported by jQuery/globalize for number and date formatting. You can see the list of supported locales at https://github.com/jquery/globalize/tree/79ae658b842f75f58199d6e9074e01f7ce207468/lib/cultures.

You might think that the best way to obtain the locale is any one of these promising properties on the navigator object: language, browserLanguage, systemLanguage, or userLanguage. You might write something like the following:

```
var userLocale = navigator.language || navigator.browserLanguage ||
navigator.systemLanguage || navigator.userLanguage;
```

Unfortunately, this is wrong. Although many browsers report the user's locale with these properties, sometimes they report incorrect values. For example, Android always reports en-US, no matter the user's current locale.

A workaround is to detect whether the device is an Android device and then look at navigator.userAgent:

```
var userLocale = "en-US";
if ( navigator.userAgent.toLowerCase().indexOf ("android") > -1 )
{
  var userAgent = navigator.userAgent;
  // inspired by http://stackoverflow.com/a/7728507/741043
  var tempLocale = userAgent.match(/Android.*([a-zA-Z]{2}-[a-zA-
    Z]{2})/);
  if (tempLocale) {
    userLocale = tempLocale[1];
  }
}
```

```
else
{
  userLocale = navigator.language || navigator.browserLanguage ||
    navigator.systemLanguage || navigator.userLanguage;
}
```

All this is well and good, but it fails on Android 4.4, which doesn't report this value in the user agent, and continues to report `en-US` for `navigator.language`.

Unfortunately, when on the desktop, this is about as good as we can get. There's no 100 percent guaranteed method that you can use to determine the user's preferred locale without asking them directly.

However, on a mobile device, we have one more ace up our sleeve: we can use a plugin to ask the system what the user's preferred locale really is.

To do this, we'll first need to add a plugin to our project:

```
cordova plugin add org.apache.cordova.globalization
```

Now, we can write the following code:

```
var userLocale = "en-US";
navigator.globalization.getLocaleName (
  function (locale) {
    userLocale = locale.value;
  },
  function () {
    // error
  });
```

This works, but the primary problem is that the locale is now determined asynchronously and also requires the plugin to be present and initialized. If we call `navigator.globalization.getLocalName` before the plugin has initialized, we'll have a problem. Furthermore, even if the function works, we have to delay any translation or formatting until the asynchronous result is received. On the desktop, however, we have another problem: we'll get an error the moment we even try this code.

Desktop? Aren't we building mobile apps?

Yes, absolutely. However, it is immensely useful to be able to test your code in a WebKit browser on the desktop (remote debugging is also very useful, but you have to redeploy your app to your device each time you test; on the desktop, one can simply refresh the page). Furthermore, you may desire your app to be useful as a web app for desktop applications, but you may also want to take advantage of native features available on a mobile device.

Handling the plugin requirement is pretty simple; we can simply detect whether `navigator.globalization.getLocalName` exists, and if it doesn't, use `navigator.language` or `navigator.userAgent`. It won't be perfect, but it's better than nothing. We can do this:

```
if (typeof navigator.globalization !== "undefined")
{
  if (typeof navigator.globalization.getLocaleName !==
    "undefined") {
    // call navigator.globalization.getLocalName()
  }
}
```

On the other hand, there's only one way to know that the plugin has been initialized in the following code snippet. We have to wait for the `deviceready` event:

```
var userLocale = "en-US";
function startApp()
{
  // do translations, format numbers, etc.
}
function getLocaleAndStartApp()
{
  navigator.globalization.getLocaleName (
    function (locale) {
      userLocale = locale.value;
      startApp();
    },
    function () {
      // error; start app anyway
      startApp();
    });
}
document.addEventListener ( "deviceready", getLocaleAndStartApp,
false);
```

There's only one real problem with all of this: the moment we wait on `deviceready`, we again eliminate the desktop browser since this event is specific to Cordova. There's no great way to handle this. The easiest method is simply to have two lines of code: one that starts if working on a desktop and one that starts if working on a mobile device, and then comment them out as appropriate. Of course, this is only suitable during testing.

The only other mechanism is to listen for `deviceready`, and if it doesn't occur within a short amount of time, assume that we aren't running within Cordova. This isn't ideal since it means the desktop experience will pause for a second while trying to determine whether the event is ever going to fire, but it's really the only other option. The code looks like this:

```
function executeWhenReady ( callback ) {
  var executed = false;
  document.addEventListener ( "deviceready", function () {
    if (!executed) {
      executed = true;
      if (typeof callback === "function") {
        callback();
      }
    }
  }, false);
  setTimeout ( function () {
    if (!executed) {
      executed = true;
      if (typeof callback === "function") {
        callback();
      }
    }
  }, 1000 );
};
executeWhenReady ( function() { getLocaleAndStartApp(); } );
```

At this point, we've got the user's preferred locale (as best as we can determine it, based on the browser we're using), and can actually start translating text and formatting numbers and dates.

That said, all of this is rather tedious, and YASMF takes care of this for us. The following is what it looks like instead:

```
_y.executeWhenReady ( function () { _y.getDeviceLocale (startApp); }
);
```

If you want proof that YASMF is indeed doing everything we just did, take a look at the code: `https://github.com/photokandyStudios/YASMF-Next/blob/master/lib/yasmf/util/core.js`.

What did we do?

In this section, we learned how best to (and how difficult it is to) determine the user's preferred locale.

What else do I need to know?

The locale returned by the globalization plugin is of the form `la_RE` (language followed by an underscore followed by the region). YASMF, on the other hand, uses a dash instead. In case the value is somehow missing any separator, YASMF also adds one for us. It also handles short locales that only specify the language (omitting the region). This is done in a function called `normalizeLocale`, and it looks like the following:

```
function normalizeLocale ( theLocale ) {
  var theNewLocale = theLocale;
  if (theNewLocale.length < 2) {
    throw new Error ("Fatal: invalid locale; not of the format
      la-RE.");
  }
  var theLanguage = theNewLocale.substr(0,2).toLowerCase();
  var theRegion = theNewLocale.substr(-2).toUpperCase();
  if (theNewLocale.length < 4) {
    theRegion = ""; // there can't possibly be a valid region on a
      3-char string
  }
  if (theRegion !== "") {
    theNewLocale = theLanguage + "-" + theRegion;
  } else {
    theNewLocale = theLanguage;
  }
  return theNewLocale;
}
```

Formatting numbers and dates

Formatting numbers and dates is, to put it mildly, insanely difficult. Thankfully, jQuery/globalize (and YASMF's wrapper) make it very easy to support.

Getting ready

Let's create a shell `www/index.html` so that we can fill it in as we progress through the remaining sections. As you proceed, you can run the app and see the results:

```
<!DOCTYPE html>
<html>
  <head>
    <meta charset="utf-8" />
    <meta name="apple-mobile-web-app-capable" content="yes" />
```

```
      <meta name="viewport" content="width=device-width, maximum
        -scale=1.0" />
      <meta name="format-detection" content="telephone=no" />
      <link rel="stylesheet" type="text/css"
        href="js/lib/yasmf.css"/>
      <title>Localization Demo</title>
  </head>
  <body>
    <div id="output">Results of localizations:</div>
    <script type="text/javascript" src="cordova.js"></script>
    <script type="text/javascript"
      src="js/lib/globalize.js"></script>
    <script type="text/javascript" src="js/lib/yasmf.js"></script>
    <script type="text/javascript"
      src="js/lib/cultures/globalize.culture.en-US.js"></script>
    <script type="text/javascript"
      src="js/lib/cultures/globalize.culture.es-US.js"></script>
    <script type="text/javascript"
      src="js/lib/cultures/globalize.culture.en-GB.js"></script>
    <script type="text/javascript"
      src="js/lib/cultures/globalize.culture.es-ES.js"></script>

    <script>
      function print ( s ) {
        document.getElementById("output").innerHTML += "<p>" + s +
          "</p>";
      }
      function doLocalizationDemos() {
        print ( "------------------------------------------------
          --" );
        print ( "Locale: " + _y.currentUserLocale );
        print ( "------------------------------------------------
          --" );

        // add new demos here

        print ( " " );
        print ( " " );
        print ( " " );
      }
      function startApp () {
        // use current locale first
        doLocalizationDemos();
        _y.currentUserLocale = "en-US";
        doLocalizationDemos();
```

```
        _y.currentUserLocale = "es-US";
        doLocalizationDemos();
        _y.currentUserLocale = "en-GB";
        doLocalizationDemos();
        _y.currentUserLocale = "es-ES";
        doLocalizationDemos();
      }
      _y.executeWhenReady ( function () { _y.getDeviceLocale(
        startApp ); } );
    </script>
  </body>
</html>
```

All we've done is create a `print` method that will display the results of our localization in the `output` div. We also defined a shell `doLocalizationDemos` function. Right now, it only displays the current locale, but that'll fill in later. We call this five different times: first with the default user locale (which should match the device's locale) and then with four specific locales.

What does all the other code mean?

Essentially, the `meta` tags in the `head` tag set various properties in the mobile browser. These control how the page displays when it is run on a mobile device. We'll go over what each one of these does in a later project.

Getting on with it

jQuery/globalize defines a `format` method that can be used to format numbers and dates, but YASMF goes a step further; it defines a method for each kind of value we might want to format: numbers, currency, percentages, and dates. This keeps code readable without requiring the reader to memorize what specific format codes mean, and YASMF's method names also have the advantage of being shorter.

To format a number, call `_y.N` (go ahead and add this to the `doLocalizationDemos` function as well):

```
// no format
print ( "314159.14159 (d): " + _y.N(314159.14159) );
// 4 decimal places
print ( "314159.14159 (4): " + _y.N(314159.14159, "4") );
// negative; 2 decimals
print ( "-314159.14159 (2): " + _y.N(-314159.14159, "2") );
print ( " " );
```

The_y.N method takes three parameters: the number to format, the number of decimal places, and the locale. If no locale is specified, the current locale is used. If no decimal places are provided, no decimal places are printed, which could be problematic (3.5050 would round to 4). So, unless you know you are dealing with an integer, you should always specify the number of decimal places. Values are rounded as necessary, and the result is zero-padded to the number of decimal places provided.

The results should correlate to the following:

Number	.0	en-US	es-US	en-GB	es-ES
314159.14159	d	314,159	314,159	314,159	314.159
314159.14159	4	314,159.1416	314,159.1416	314,159.1416	314.159,1416
-314159.14159	2	-314,159.14	-314,159.14	-314,159.14	-314.159,14

To format currency, call _y.C:

```
print ( "$314159.14159 (d): " + _y.C(314159.14159) );
print ( "$314159.14159 (4): " + _y.C(314159.14159, "4") );
print ( "-$314159.14159 (2): " + _y.C(-314159.14159, "2") );
print ( " " );
```

The_y.C method takes the same parameters that _y.N takes. The difference is that, if no decimal places are specified, _y.C will render two decimal places by default. Rounding and padding occur as necessary. Some locales will format negatives by using parentheses instead of a negative sign, which is why we have a negative currency value here.

Don't forget the exchange rate!

Our example is pretty simple, but in a real-world scenario, $100 (USD) does not equal €100 (EUR). Money.js (http://josscrowcroft.github.io/money.js/) interfaces with the Open Exchange Rates project (https://openexchangerates.org) to provide real-time currency conversion. There are many other options as well, but this is the cheapest way to get started.

You should get results like the following:

Number	.0	en-US	es-US	en-GB	es-ES
314159.14159	d	$314,159.12	$314,159	£314,159	€314.159
314159.14159	4	$314,159.1416	$314,159.1416	£314,159.1416	€314.159,1416
-314159.14159	2	($314,159.14)	($314,159.14)	-£314,159.14	-€314.159,14

Percents are slightly more verbose; _y.PCT does the trick:

```
print ( ".0314159% (d): " + _y.PCT(.0314159) );
print ( ".0314159% (4): " + _y.PCT(.0314159, "4") );
print ( "-.0314159% (2): " + _y.PCT(-.0314159, "2") );
```

Like _y.N and _y.C, _y.PCT takes the same parameters. It will then multiply the value by 100 and display a percentage in the form the locale specifies (for example, in American English, 3.14 percent). If the number of decimal places isn't supplied, two is again assumed to be the default. Padding and rounding are again applied as necessary.

You should get results like the following:

Number	.0	en-US	es-US	en-GB	es-ES
.0314159	0	3.14 %	3.14 %	3.14 %	3,14 %
.0314159	4	3.1416 %	3.1416 %	3.1416 %	3,1416 %
-.0314159	2	-3.14 %	-3.14 %	-3.14 %	-3,14 %

Dates, on the other hand, are something else; there are a wide variety of format strings that are available for your needs. Add the following to your code:

```
print ( "Today's date, default: " + _y.D( new Date() ) );
print ( "Today's date, D: " + _y.D( new Date(), "D" ) );
print ( "Today's date, f: " + _y.D( new Date(), "f" ) );
print ( "Today's date, F: " + _y.D( new Date(), "F" ) );
print ( "Today's date, t: " + _y.D( new Date(), "t" ) );
print ( "Today's date, T: " + _y.D( new Date(), "T" ) );
print ( "Today's date, Y: " + _y.D( new Date(), "Y" ) );
print ( "Today's date, M: " + _y.D( new Date(), "M" ) );
print ( "Today's date, all: " + _y.D( new Date(),
   "d dd ddd dddd M MM MMM MMMM yy yyyy m mm h hh H HH s ss f ff
   fff t tt z zz zzz g gg" ) );
print ( " " );
```

The preceding examples use various date formats, including the default, if no format is specified (d). All but the last are shortcuts; a single character can specify quite a bit of formatting information. This information varies based on the locale, but the intent is largely the same. The last line lists out every possible option, but be careful when using this since you need to be more sensitive to how various cultures order date fields ("2/12/2014" can mean two very different dates: February 12, 2014 or December 2, 2014.)

At the time of writing this book, the following shortcuts are used:

Format	Meaning	en-US	es-US	en-GB	es-ES
f	Long date Short time	Wednesday, February 12, 2014 3:02 PM	miércoles, febrero 12, 2014 3:02 PM	12 February 2014 15:02	miércoles, 12 de febrero de 2014 15:02
F	Long date Long time	Wednesday, February 12, 2014 3:02:36 PM	miércoles, febrero 12, 2014 3:02:36 PM	12 February 2014 15:02:36	miércoles, 12 de febrero de 2014 15:02:36
t	Short time	3:02 PM	3:02 PM	15:02	15:02
T	Long time	3:02:36 PM	3:02:36 PM	15:02:36	15:02:36
d (default)	Short date	2/12/2014	2/12/2014	12/02/2014	12/02/2014
D	Long date	Wednesday, February 12, 2014	miércoles, febrero 12, 2014	12 February 2014	miércoles, 12 de febrero de 2014
Y	Month/year	2014 February	febrero de 2014	February 2014	febrero de 2014
M	Month/day	February 12	12 de febrero	12 February	12 febrero

The following format specifiers are also used:

Format	Meaning	en-US	es-US	en-GB	es-ES
d	Day of month	12	12	12	12
dd	Two-digit day of month (padded)	12	12	12	12
ddd	Day name (abbr)	Wed	mié	Wed	mié
dddd	Day name (full)	Wednesday	miércoles	Wednesday	miércoles
M	Month of year	2	2	2	2
MM	Two-digit month of year (padded)	02	02	02	02

Format	Meaning	en-US	es-US	en-GB	es-ES
MMM	Month name (abbr)	Feb	feb	Feb	feb
MMMM	Month name (full)	February	febrero	February	febrero
yy	Two-digit year	14	14	14	14
yyyy	Four-digit year	2014	2014	2014	2014
'literal'	Literal text	literal	literal	literal	literal
\'	Single quote	'	'	'	'
m	Minutes	2	2	2	2
mm	Two-digit minutes (padded)	02	02	02	02
h	Hours (12 hours)	3	3	3	3
hh	Hours (12 hours, padded)	03	03	03	03
H	Hours (24 hours)	15	15	15	15
HH	Hours (24 hours, padded)	15	15	15	15
s	Seconds	36	36	36	36
ss	Two-digit seconds (padded)	36	36	36	36
f	Deciseconds	9	9	9	9
ff	Centiseconds	91	91	91	91
fff	Milliseconds	919	919	919	919
t	AM/PM (one letter)	P	P	P	(n/a)
tt	AM/PM	PM	PM	PM	(n/a)
z	Timezone (hours)	-6	-6	-6	-6
zz	Timezone (hours, leading zero)	-06	-06	-06	-06

Format	Meaning	en-US	es-US	en-GB	es-ES
zzz	Timezone (full)	-06:00	-06:00	-06:00	-06:00
g	Era	A.D.	d.C.	A.D.	d.C.
gg	Era	A.D.	d.C.	A.D.	d.C.

Note that some format specifiers may result in no output. Look in the `es-ES` column for `t` and `tt`; there's no output for these fields.

Personally, unless you need one particular field, it is usually better to use the shortcuts; otherwise, there is a great risk of ordering fields incorrectly. `MM/dd/yyyy` is not universally accepted as month-day-year when the day of the month is 12 or less.

There's one last format method that lets you specify any format you want that jQuery/globalize understands—`format`:

```
print ( "314159.14159 (d10): " + _y.format(314159.14159, "d10") );
print ( " " );
```

It takes the same parameters as all the functions so far, but it assumes no default formatting rules whatsoever. Furthermore, it doesn't assume specific types, either, which means you must specify the type of value you are formatting. The following are used:

Format	Type
n#	Number (# of decimals)
c#	Currency (# of decimals)
p#	Percentage (# of decimals)
d#	Decimal (# of digits, left-padded)
(any date format string)	Date

The only format that YASMF doesn't supply a wrapper for is the decimal format. This ignores any actual decimal places and always zero-pads the number to fill the specified digits. Therefore, in the preceding example, the result should be `0000314159`.

What did we do?

In this section, we covered the various number and date formatting routines available from jQuery/globalize and wrapped by YASMF.

Translating text

Adding translatable text to your app is, in some ways, much easier than handling all the various rules when formatting numbers and dates. There's only one function that is provided by YASMF to do any translation. The bigger problem comes into view when one realizes that various translations often have different length strings and, as such, can appear very different on the screen. Of course, the ultimate hurdle is often finding a native-language translator; Google Translate simply will not cut it for a production deployment.

Getting on with it

Fundamentally, the technology behind supporting multiple text translations is simple. All you need is a list of keys that represent words and phrases and the corresponding translations in each locale you intend to support. This is reasonably simple to implement. All you need is a dictionary of the following form:

```
{ "KEY": { "LOCALE1": "TEXT", "LOCALE2": "TEXT" [,…] } [,…] }
```

You can implement this by creating a new object and defining an `addTranslation` function:

```
var localizedText = {};
function addTranslation (locale, key, value) {
  if (self.localizedText[locale]) {
    self.localizedText[locale][key.toUpperCase()] = value;
  } else {
    self.localizedText[locale] = {};
    self.localizedText[locale][key.toUpperCase()] = value;
  }
};
// use like this:
addTranslation ( "en", "HELLO", "Hello" );
addTranslation ( "en-US", "HELLO", "Howdy" );
addTranslation ( "es", "HELLO", "Hola" );
```

This works fine for when you want to add a single translation, but what if you want to supply many translations at once? The following code is a little more concise:

```
function addTranslations ( o ) {
  for (var key in o) {
    if (o.hasOwnProperty (key)) {
      for (var locale in o[key]) {
        if (o[key].hasOwnProperty (locale)) {
          addTranslation (locale, key, o[key][locale]);
        }
```

```
        }
      }
    }
};

addTranslations ( { "HELLO": { "en": "Hello",
                              "en-US": "Howdy",
                              "es": "Hola" } } );
```

Now, how do we get a translation out? Let's handle looking up a translation for a single locale by defining a function called `lookupTranslation`:

```
function lookupTranslation (key, theLocale) {
  var upperKey = key.toUpperCase();
  if (typeof self.localizedText[theLocale] !== "undefined") {
    if (typeof self.localizedText[theLocale][upperKey] !==
      "undefined") {
      return self.localizedText[theLocale][upperKey];
    }
  }
  return void(0);
};

var s = lookupTranslation ( "en-US", "HELLO" );
// s = "Howdy"
```

The main problem here is that we get no value whatsoever back if we don't have a translation for a particular language or locale. Let's define a hierarchy instead:

```
locale-of-last-resort
  language-of-last-resort
    user's language
      user's locale
```

If a key is not found at the lowest level, we look higher until we find a match. It may not be perfect, but some text is always better than absolutely nothing. (Depending on the context, the user may even be able to guess the intent.)

To do this, let's define a translation method called `T`:

```
var localeOfLastResort = "en-US";
var languageOfLastResort = "en";
function T (key, locale) {
  var currentValue = "";
  if (typeof ( currentValue = self.lookupTranslation(key, locale))
    === "undefined") {
```

```
      userLocale = userLocale.substr(0, 2);
      if (typeof ( currentValue = self.lookupTranslation(key,
        locale)) === "undefined") {
        if (typeof ( currentValue = self.lookupTranslation(key,
          self.languageOfLastResort)) === "undefined") {
          if (typeof ( currentValue = self.lookupTranslation(key,
            self.localeOfLastResort)) === "undefined") {
            currentValue = key;
          }
        }
      }
    }
  return currentValue;
};

T("HELLO", "en-US"); // "Howdy"
T("HELLO", "en-GB"); // "Hello" (from "en")
T("HELLO", "es-ES"); // "Hola" (from "es")
T("MISSING", "en-US"); // "MISSING"
```

We're almost there. There's one extra feature we could add that would be very useful. When displaying output, we often need to render text intermixed with variables, like the following:

```
var x = T("FEBRUARY") + " 12";
```

Translations, however, throw a wrench into the works because the position of the variable may need to change based upon the grammar of the language. Instead, it would be nicer to be able to write something like the following:

```
var x = T("%MONTH%_%DAY%", { "MONTH": T("FEBRUARY"), "DAY": "12"
  });
```

Now, a translation matrix like the following one becomes possible:

```
addTranslations ( { "%MONTH%_%DAY%":
  { "en-US": "%MONTH% %DAY%",
  "es-US": "%DAY% de %MONTH%"}
} );


T("%MONTH%_%DAY%", { "MONTH": T("FEBRUARY"),
  "DAY": "12" }, "en-US") // February 12
T("%MONTH%_%DAY%", { "MONTH": T("FEBRUARY"),
  "DAY": "12" }, "es-US") // 12 de febrero
```

Of course, you should always use the date formatting routines to accomplish globalization, but the point made here is valid: the placement of our variables can change drastically depending upon the language.

Let's create a routine that performs variable replacement:

```
function replaceVariables(string, replacements) {
  var newString = string;
  for (var theVar in replacements) {
    if (replacements.hasOwnProperty (theVar)) {
      var thisVar = '%' + theVar.toUpperCase() + '%';
      while (newString.indexOf(thisVar) > -1) {
        newString = newString.replace(thisVar,
        replacements[theVar]);
      }
    }
  }
  return newString;
};
```

Then, we change `T`, shown as follows:

```
function T (key, replacements, locale) {
  ...
  return replaceVariables (currentValue, replacements);
};
```

At this point, you've got the exact behavior we were looking for earlier.

Now, all this is quite a bit of work on its own and, thankfully, YASMF provides all this so that we don't have to build it all ourselves. The code is also very similar (go to `https://github.com/photokandyStudios/YASMF-Next/blob/master/lib/yasmf/util/core.js`). Instead of the methods mentioned earlier, we can do something like the following:

```
_y.addTranslation ( "EN-US", "HELLO", "Howdy" );
_y.addTranslations ( { "%MONTH%_%DAY%":
  { "en-US": "%MONTH% %DAY%",
  "es-US": "%DAY% de %MONTH%"}
} );
_y.T("HELLO", "en-US"); // "Howdy"
_y.T("%MONTH%_%DAY%", { "MONTH": T("FEBRUARY"),
  "DAY": "12" }, "en-US") // February 12
```

Just so you can see everything in action, let's test several things out. Add the following to your `startApp` function:

```
_y.addTranslation ( "EN", "HELLO", "Hello" );
_y.addTranslation ( "ES", "HELLO", "Hola" );
_y.addTranslations ( {"GOODBYE": { "EN": "Goodbye",
  "ES": "Adios" },
  "HELLO_%NAME%": { "EN": "Hello %NAME%",
```

```
        "ES": "Hola %NAME%" },
    "ONLY_ONE_KEY": { "EN": "We only have an English translation" },
    "HIERARCHY": { "EN": "Generic English",
      "EN-US": "American English",
      "ES": "Generic Spanish",
      "ES-US": "Spanish (United States)" }
} );
```

Next, add the following to your `doLocalizationDemos` function:

```
print ( "HELLO: " + _y.T("HELLO") );
print ( "GOODBYE: " + _y.T("GOODBYE") );
print ( "HELLO_%NAME%: " + _y.T("HELLO_%NAME%", { "NAME": "Mary"
  }) );
print ( "ONLY_ONE_KEY: " + _y.T("ONLY_ONE_KEY") );
print ( "HIERARCHY: " + _y.T("HIERARCHY") );
print ( "MISSING_%KEY%: " + _y.T("MISSING_%KEY%", { "KEY":
  "Replacement" } ) );
print ( " " );
```

You should get results like those shown in the following table:

Value	en-US	es-US	en-GB	es-ES
HELLO	Hello	Hola	Hello	Hola
GOODBYE	Goodbye	Adios	Goodbye	Adios
HELLO_%NAME%	Hello, Mary	Hola Mary	Hello, Mary	Hola Mary
ONLY_ONE_KEY	We only have an English translation			
HIERARCHY	American English	Spanish (United States)	Generic English	Generic Spanish
MISSING_%KEY%	MISSING_ Replacement	MISSING_ Replacement	MISSING_ Replacement	MISSING_ Replacement

 YASMF internally stores translations with the locale in uppercase form. This means you can specify locales with en-us, en, EN-US, and EN. Since it also normalizes them, you could also use ENUS.

It's perfectly okay to use key words and phrases, but it's also important to understand that the translation might vary based on the context. As such, it isn't a bad idea to namespace your translations so it is very clear which one you are using. For example, `app.aView.SAVE` and `app.anotherView.SAVE` might, depending upon the context, have different translations.

There's absolutely no rule requiring the key and the translated text to match in any way, shape, or form. You could just number your keys sequentially, but it wouldn't be obvious from your code what the on-screen result might be. The only thing that must match exactly between key and translation are the replacement variables; beyond that, if you prefer a different method of namespacing (or not at all) or another method of organization, go for it.

Now that we've got the basics out of the way, we need to handle the fact that translated text may have a very different length than our native language. This has tripped many developers up simply because they didn't expect that a word or phrase in a different language might be much longer than they expected. As such, text is often truncated or oddly wrapped, or widgets may appear out of place.

The only real way to deal with this is to plan for it from the beginning. Since we're coding in HTML, we have an advantage: HTML has a layout engine that is very capable of dealing with varying text lengths. If we allow as much content to flow inline as possible, we gain quite a bit for free. (This isn't to say we won't run into places where we might have to truncate, but this is true in any language. Consider a title for a particular view; there's only so much screen space for any language, and so it must be truncated after a certain point since it can't run on down the screen.)

Sometimes, we need to position elements absolutely, and it is at this point that we lose the benefits of HTML. The only way to account for the width of an element in this case is to calculate its width (and/or height) directly. Note that, because these are CSS values, it's best to use `parseInt` to eliminate any units such as `px`:

```
var computedStyle = window.getComputedStyle ( element );
var widthOfElement = parseInt (computedStyle.getPropertyValue
    ("width"),10);
var heightOfElement = parseInt (computedStyle.getPropertyValue
    ("height"),10);
```

At this point, one can adjust other elements as needed to account for the space needed for the translated text.

Finally, there's a really important subject we haven't mentioned yet: that of actually translating the text in your app to another language. Google Translate, although we've used it in this book, really should only be used for internal testing purposes. If you're not well versed in a particular language but still want to ensure that you are properly handling how different translations might appear on screen, Google Translate is fine. But once you intend to deploy the app to production, you really need to find a native translator that understands technical jargon. Sometimes, you might be able to find a friend or college student who will help you out for little or nothing, but you'll often need to pay a company to do the work. Some examples of translators are as follows:

- ▸ **Google's App Translation Service** (for Android apps): This is used for commercial purposes

- ▸ **ICanLocalize** (`http://www.icanlocalize.com`): This is used for commercial purposes

- ▸ **AppLingua** (`http://www.applingua.com`): This is used for commercial purposes

- ▸ **Babble-on** (`http://www.ibabbleon.com`): This is used for commercial purposes

- ▸ **Ackuna** (`http://www.ackuna.com`): This is used for crowd-sourced translations

What did we do?

In this section, we discussed how to translate text, how to account for the different lengths of translated text, and how to find a translator.

What else do I need to know?

It really doesn't matter where you define your translations as long as they are available to the app when it starts. I like to keep the translations in the same files as my views (which keeps the translations close to the code that uses them), but you might prefer to have them in a single large script. Alternatively, if you only want to load the translations that are absolutely necessary, you could use **XHR** (**XMLHttpRequest**) to load the code dynamically.

Game Over..... Wrapping it up

That was a lot to cover, but it's all important. Getting your app ready for international use is absolutely critical if you want to have as large a market base as possible. Rather than putting it in just before you publish the app (or after), it's far better to build it in from the start. We'll be using many of these methods in our projects in the rest of this book, so even though it may not be the most exciting topic ever, it's terribly important to understand it before we move on.

Can you take the HEAT? The Hotshot Challenge

We've covered quite a bit about translation and localization. You might try to modify the project to add additional language support. If you're looking for a challenge, implement dynamic loading of translations using XHR.

Project 3

Mobile Application Design

While it is certainly possible to build a complex app without any specific design, this is not generally recommended. You will inevitably run into situations that your original code wasn't designed for, and may have to scrap and rewrite your code each time. It is simpler to just start with a good design before you begin coding, and that's what this chapter is about.

What do we build?

In this project (as well as in the next several upcoming projects), we're going to build a fairly simple productivity app, a note-taking app. Since it will be developed throughout several upcoming projects in this book, it also provides an excellent foundation for all the additional learning that's ahead—things such as interacting with the camera, videos, file storage, sharing, and so on. It also underscores the need for good design up front since we need a good foundation upon which to build.

What does it do?

This project will introduce you to mobile application design from start to finish, including designing the user interface and data models and writing code for models, factories, and views. All this is critical: the next several projects build on this app, so you should be certain you understand the concepts within this project before moving on.

You'll also learn about RequireJS—a framework that simplifies dependency management in JavaScript which provides mechanisms for loading scripts and other content based on your needs. You can certainly create apps without RequireJS, but you will hopefully see how the framework can significantly ease development when there are lots of dependencies.

You'll also be building a complete project that actually implements something useful. The final result will work on iOS, Android, and even the desktop (assuming it is a WebKit browser). Throughout this project, you'll see how to query the DOM for specific elements, how to work with HTML5/CSS features, and more, all of which will be important for your future application development.

Why is it great?

In this project, we'll focus on the text aspect of taking notes. We'll provide a storage mechanism using `LocalStorage` for now and will also work on the user interface. We'll also provide a good foundation for future note types (such as audio, images, and video).

How are we going to do it?

We'll start out by talking about the design of the application considering both the user interface and code aspects. We'll then implement each portion of the app. We'll specifically cover the following:

 ▸ Designing the user interface

 ▸ Designing the data model

 ▸ Implementing the Base Note data model

 ▸ Implementing the Note Storage model

 ▸ Implementing the note list view

 ▸ Implementing the text note edit view

 ▸ Implementing the CSS

 ▸ Putting it all together

What do I need to get started?

Create a new project based on the template you downloaded from us or that you created in the last chapter. Be sure to carry out the following steps:

 ▸ Add the globalization plugin (add the Cordova plugin from `https://cordova.apache.org/`)

 ▸ Alter the `config.xml` file by adding the same parameters we added in the last chapter

 ▸ Delete the `index.html` file; we'll rebuild it at the end of the chapter

Designing the user interface

Usually, the first step toward creating a new app is to sketch out the user interface and determine how it is expected to function. This can consist of high-resolution mockups or rough sketches. The various interactions may consist of simple annotations or arrows, or one might use tools that allow the mockup to be interactive (particularly useful when you are getting feedback from other individuals). Regardless of how you prefer to design, it does help determine the underlying code for our app and is therefore important.

Getting ready

Although we're ready to design our user interface, there's one more difficulty: our app will be run on more than one platform, and each platform has its own look and feel. There are several ways to approach this:

- Build the user interface for the platform the majority of users will be running, and use the same interface on all other platforms. On these other platforms, however, the app doesn't "fit in" and will lead to poor reviews. (Most users don't use apps that look like they were taken from other platforms with no attempt at fitting them in.)

- Customize the app's user interface for each platform in an attempt to feel *native*. The goal is to make the app feel like it was written using the platform's native UI frameworks. The problem is that this requires significant work to accomplish and to get the look and feel *just right*. It's also far too easy to end up in the *uncanny valley* of user interfaces where your UI looks and feels 99 percent like the real thing but doesn't quite go all the way. Users often expect certain behaviors that can be hard to duplicate perfectly in HTML, CSS, and JavaScript without also being privy to the underlying native code in the various user-interface frameworks. (Even with access to the native code, this can be difficult. Case in point: iOS 7's frosted-glass effect). Users are probably less worried about the exact look of an app (very few will notice a pixel difference here or there), but they will definitely notice how the app reacts to various touches and gestures. If the app responds in a way the user doesn't expect, they will certainly know it.

- ► Alternatively, you can aim for a platform-agnostic look and feel. This is the direction we'll take; the interface should seem at home (with minor adjustments) on iOS as well as Android devices. We'll use some elements that are familiar to iOS users and some that are familiar to Android users. This is not to say that the appearance will be identical across both devices; it won't. It will instead incorporate some of the platform-specific notions as well.

Don't forget form factors and orientations!

Most apps should be able to work in both portrait and landscape orientation, and they should also adapt to the large number of different screen sizes on the market. Think carefully about how your app will look in these situations; it would be a good idea to make several variations of your mockups to get a good feel for various orientations and form factors.

Getting on with it

We already know, without doing a mockup, that we'll need at least two views: one to show a list of notes that have been stored and another to edit a specific note.

Let's look at the design for the first view, what we call "note list view":

The screenshot on the left is what we want our app to look like. On the right, we've included some of the CSS classes that we're using for each section. This information proves useful while creating the view's HTML template (which you can see in `/www/html/noteListView.html`). The CSS classes for each part of a list item are also displayed (and you can see the template in `/www/html/noteListItem.html`).

Before we go any further, let's also mock up how our app will look on an Android device:

Note the differences between the two images: the icons are in a different location, the title on the navigation bar has a different alignment, and the colors are different. Although this is not always the case, usually this will suffice. It looks different enough that an Android user isn't going to instantly think that this app looks like an iOS app. It does require a different template, though. You can find it in `/www/html/noteListView_android.html`.

Let's define some of the interactivity; there's a toolbar that contains four icons. Tapping an icon should create a new note. (Note that for our purposes in this chapter, we'll only handle the first icon, which represents a text note.) Each row in the list should also be tappable and allow the user to edit the existing note.

We also need to determine our graphical assets, so it's also important that we cover an important topic: how to handle retina or high-DPI displays. Most of our app is purely text. There are really only six graphical assets in the entire application—five on this view, and the last one is on the next view (the **Back** button graphic). On this screen, note the chevron in each row. Although it's easy to draw this as a vector using SVG, not all platforms support using SVG as a mask (for example, Android doesn't), and so we supply a bitmap instead. The critical point is that the graphics need to be supplied in a format that supports images large enough to cover all the available pixels.

In general, a retina display will use what are called *logical pixels*. These aren't the real physical pixels on the device but a group of pixels that roughly approximate the size of a pixel on a non-retina device. This means that a 32 x 32 pixel icon will still take the same visual space on a retina display and a non-retina display. The problem is that this icon will actually need more pixels (on an iOS device, four times as many). To fix this, we can design the icon with 64 x 64 pixels but use CSS to scale the icon down to 32 x 32. This means that a non-retina device will see a 64 x 64 icon scaled down to 32 x 32 pixels, and a retina device will see a 64 x 64 icon with no scaling. If scaling isn't desired, there are other mechanisms (media queries are a good example) to render differently sized icons based on the screen size. Because most modern devices are now retina devices, I tend only to create the retina-sized icon and allow the scaling to handle non-retina devices, but if you want the sharpest results, you need to target to each device scaling in your target audience.

All that said, we don't actually have to create the chevron. YASMF has a few graphical assets that we can use that will work just fine. You can see them in the `yasmf-assets` directory.

Next, we need to define the properties and methods that will be present in our view:

noteListView (V1)	
p	_navigationBar
p	_scrollContainer
p	_listOfNotes
p	_newTextNoteButton
p	_newAudioNoteButton
p	_newImageNoteButton
p	_newVideoNoteButton
p	_createAndEditNote(noteType)
	createNewTextNote()
	editExistingNote (event)
	quitApp()
o	render()
o	renderToElement()
	renderList()
	onOrientationChanged()
o	init(parentElement)
o	initWithOptions(options)
o	destroy()

. property	r/w read/write	r/o read-only
p private	o override	↖ notification

Now, let's see the second view, named "text note edit view":

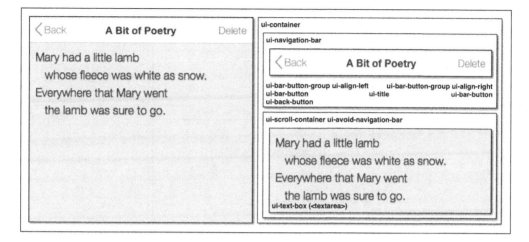

In the preceding screenshot, the left indicates how we want the view to appear, while on the right, we have the various CSS classes (the template is at /www/html/ textNoteEditView.html).

The interactions on this screen are a little more complicated than on the previous screen. If the user taps the **Back** button, the note should be saved, and the user should be returned to the previous view (the note list view). If the user taps on the **Delete** button, the note should be deleted. However, since it's been deleted, it shouldn't be visible anymore, and so the user must also be returned to the list view.

If the user taps on the title (the name of the note), it becomes editable. If the user taps on the text area, the contents become editable. When the user taps on **Back**, the note is saved.

If the user has changed something, the previous view should update to reflect the changes, whatever they may be (new notes, removed notes, extra lines, changed names, and so on).

Finally, let's define the properties and methods in this view:

textNoteEditView (V1)	
p	_backButton
p	_contentsEditor
p	_deleteButton
p	_nameEditor
p	_navigationBar
p	_note
p	_scrollContainer
	deleteNote()
	goBack()
	releaseBackButton()
o	render()
o	renderToElement()
	saveNote()
o	init(parentElement)
o	initWithOptions(options)
o	destroy()

. property	**r/w** read/write	**r/o** read-only
p private	**o** override	↖ notification

What did we do?

In this section, we've covered the user interface design and interactions. Once we define the models, we'll be ready to code!

What else do I need to know?

You aren't required to use YASMF's assets. Here are some other great asset collections that work well in mobile apps:

- **Essence icons for iOS 7 (commercial; $29.99)**: These can be found at `http://iconsandcoffee.com/essence/`.

- **Icons 8 icons for iOS 7 (free)**: These can be found at `http://icons8.com/free-ios-7-icons-in-vector/`. They also offer icons for Windows 8, as well as commercial options.

- **Glyphish Complete for iOS 7 (commercial; $99)**: These can be found at `http://www.glyphish.com`. It offers cheaper packages, as well as some for free.

- **Tabs icons (commercial; price varies)**: These can be found at `http://www.tabsicons.com`. These are not yet updated to match iOS 7, but these are still great resources.

- **Android developer icons (commercial; $25)**: These can be found at `http://www.androidicons.com`.

- ▸ **Android developer downloads (free)**: These can be found at `http://developer.android.com/design/downloads/index.html`.

- ▸ **IcoMoon (commercial/free, $Varies)**: These icons can be found at `http://icomoon.io`. These are font-based icons, so their use and support is a little different, but these are still awesome! What is even better is that there is no mucking about with multiple resolutions.

Now, if you take a look at the icons provided by YASMF (and many other collections), you might wonder where the color is coming from, since they are all black and transparent. We're actually taking advantage of the mask-image CSS feature in modern browsers that lets us use the image as a template of sorts to generate an icon with a specific color.

The mask indicates which portions of the icon to *exclude* or *cut out*. This means we can set the background color to the desired color (say, green), and then the background color is masked by the image. This leaves only the shape of the image visible to the user.

The process is as follows:

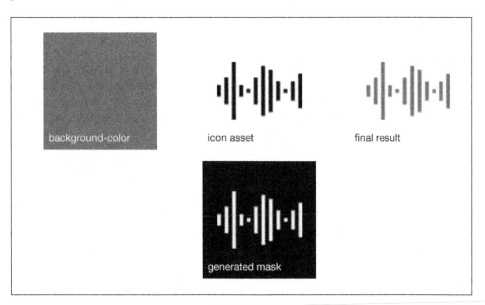

In general, any non-transparent color in the icon will react this way. If you load the asset in an editor, you'll find that the background is transparent, not white. The amount of transparency determines how much of the pixel is excluded, so it is also possible to get smooth lines and curves without "jaggies."

If another icon set uses the same method (and most do), then you're assured an easy method of changing the color of the icon visually without actually modifying the asset itself (or worse, creating multiple copies for different colors).

Here's how it looks in CSS:

```
height: 30px;
width: 30px;
background-color: #some-color;
mask-image: url(…);
mask-position: center center;
mask-repeat: no-repeat;
mask-size: 30px 30px;
```

Keep in mind that not every browser understands the non-prefixed styles, so you should add the vendor prefix (such as `-webkit-`) to ensure that it will work.

Designing the data model

Now that we've defined the user interface, we need to define the underlying data models. It's critical that we have a good idea of our desired data model now before we start to code; otherwise, a new feature we need later could require a significant rewrite.

Getting on with it

The chances are that you've already got a good idea of what data models we'll need. Even so, we need to plan for future expansion since we'll eventually need to handle multiple kinds of notes. We need a model for a single note, which we'll call the "base note model" and we'll also need a model for a collection of notes, which we'll call the "Note Storage model". The base note model knows about everything that makes up a note—the name, contents, length, and so on—and the Note Storage model knows everything about how to store and manage a collection of notes.

We'll also need to define a note factory, which we can use to create notes of various types. For now, it only needs to worry about text notes, but it will be important for future projects.

Here's the final model:

baseNote

r/w	.uid
r/w	.name
r/w	.textContents
r/w	.mediaContents
r/w	.unitValue
r/o	.formattedUnitValue
r/w	.unitLabels
r/o	.createdDate
r/o	.modifiedDate
r/o	.representation
r/o	.JSON
p	_serialize()
p	_deserialize(data)
o	init(UID)
	initWithJSON (JSON)
o	initWithOptions(options)
◥	uidChanged
◥	nameChanged
◥	textContentsChanged
◥	mediaContentsChanged
◥	unitValueChanged
◥	unitLabelsChanged

noteStorage

p	_notes
r/o	.collection
	loadCollection()
	saveCollection()
	createNote(noteType)
	getNote (UID)
	saveNote (note)
	removeNote (UID)
p	_collectionChangedListener
o	init()
◥	collectionChanged
◥	collectionLoading
◥	collectionLoaded
◥	collectionFailedLoading
◥	collectionSaving
◥	collectionSaved
◥	collectionFailedSaving
◥	noteChanged
◥	noteSaved
◥	noteFailedSaving
◥	noteRemoved
◥	noteFailedRemoving
◥	noteCreated

noteFactory

| | createNote(noteType) |
| | createAssociatedMediaFileName (noteType, uid) |

. property **r/w** read/write **r/o** read-only
p private **o** override ◥ notification

The base note model (`baseNote`) and Note Storage model (`noteStorage`) are the two models we need to create, and the note factory (`noteFactory`) is a special kind of object that knows how to create various kinds of notes. When we get to coding our models, they will each live in `/www/js/app/models`, whereas the factory will live in `/www/js/app/factories`. Therefore, the base note model will be located at `/www/js/app/models/note.js`. The Note Storage model will be located at `/www/js/app/models/noteStorage.js`. And finally, the note factory will be located at `/www/js/app/factories/noteFactory.js`.

The base note model has several properties. We've prefixed these with a dot (.) in the diagram.

▸ The `UID` property uniquely identifies our notes. While not truly unique, the date and time are good enough for our purposes since it's unlikely a person will ever create two notes in the same millisecond.

▸ The `"name"` and `"textContents"` properties should be self-explanatory. The `"mediaContents"` property is a little more obtuse since we currently only support text notes. In the future, we'll use this property to attach audio, images, and video.

▸ The `"unitValue"` and `"unitLabels"` properties work together to provide information about our note. For text notes, we'll count the number of lines. As such, the `"unitValue"` property will be the number of lines, and the `"unitLabels"` property will contain the singular and plural form of `"line"`. The `"formattedUnitValue"` property will provide easy access to a formatted combination of the `"unitValue"` and `"unitLabels"` properties.

▸ The `"createdDate"` and `"modifiedDate"` properties reflect the date the note was created and the date it was last modified, respectively.

▸ The `"representation"` property lets us indicate to the user what kind of note they are about to view. That means this property will indicate a specific icon to use to represent text notes (see the toolbar in the note list view for the icons we're using).

▸ Finally, the `"JSON"` property is possibly nonobvious at first glance. We need a way to store the note without all the extra baggage attached to the object, including methods and other internal properties. Therefore, we define a property, `"JSON"`; it lets us get a cleaned-up object that contains the note data but none of the code that goes along with the note.

Along with these properties, there are several methods:

▸ `"_serialize"` and `"_deserialize"` are methods that do the hard work of creating a clean object in the JSON format and parsing that format into a note again using the JSON library provided by JavaScript.

▸ The next three methods are all initialization methods: `"init"`, `"initWithOptions"`, and `"initWithJSON"`. The `"initWithJSON"` method is a little different from the others in that it is the frontend to the private `"_deserialize"` method. When we want to load a note from some JSON code, this is what we'll use.

Finally, there are several notifications that the model can send. Observers can be defined to listen for these particular notifications and then react accordingly. For example, some external object may want to do something specific when the text of the note is changed. Using notifications is a simple way to react to changes in the data model without having to actually inject code into the model itself.

Before we go on, we need to cover how YASMF implements objects. Each object inherits from `BaseObject`. This `BaseObject` provides a lot of functionality that you get for free, and this primarily boils down to three things: inheritance, tags, and notifications.

Inheritance allows us to create an object based on the definition of another object (or class). There are many different ways to implement this in JavaScript. We could utilize prototypal inheritance (which often seems counterintuitive at first glance), but frankly, I prefer the classical object-oriented inheritance model instead. Use whatever you prefer in your own projects.

One benefit of classical inheritance is that it permits the redefinition of methods while being able to call the overridden (or *super*) method. It's a powerful way to make code reusable.

Tags, as provided by YASMF, are a simple **key-value observing** (**KVO**) mechanism. We don't use them in this project at all, but they are useful as you can have as many tags as you like and then fire notifications off when a tag changes its value. This lets other objects subscribe to the tag so they can be notified when something has changed.

Notifications are a simplification and expansion of the KVO mechanism. Instead of sending a notification every time a property changes, we send notifications based on events. Sometimes, this has a direct correlation with KVO. The base note model does a lot of this; it can send several notifications, and each one is based on a property changing its value. But more importantly, notifications don't have to be limited to property changes. They can indicate state changes, errors, and more. Just like KVO, other objects can subscribe to the notifications and know when they should react based on the notifications our object sends.

Most frameworks provide the same functionality, though often in different ways. If you want to see how YASMF implements this, the code is available online (`https://github.com/photokandyStudios/YASMF-Next/blob/master/lib/yasmf/util/object.js`) or in the code package of this book (/framework/lib/yasmf/util/object.js.

Implementing notifications, KVO, and inheritance

Implementing these features isn't terribly difficult. Notifications are implemented using an array of listeners attached to a notification key. Tags and KVO are implemented similarly, though they also provide methods for getting and setting values (and when a value is set, all the observers in the list get notified). Object inheritance is also surprisingly easy because it has an internal class hierarchy that is maintained in an array; additionally, any overridden methods are stored in a private array. This means that an overridden method is still accessible.

Next, let's examine the Note Storage model. Oddly enough, there's only one public property—`"collection"`. This property is read-only in the sense that you can't create a new collection by changing it, but not in the sense that you can't change the notes inside.

Let's go through each of the methods:

- ► `"loadCollection"` and `"saveCollection"`: These deal with loading the collection from storage and saving it again. It's important to recognize what the collection in storage is: just a list of unique IDs and not actually the note itself. Think of this as a list of all the notes. Whenever we add, delete, or change a note, we need to make sure this list is up-to-date.

- ► `"createNote"`, `"getNote"`, `"saveNote"`, and `"removeNote"`: These deal with managing notes. Note that any time we create, save, or remove a note, the collection must be saved.

- ► `"_collectionChangedListener'`: This listens for a `"collectionChanged"` notification. We need to save the collection to storage any time it changes. (The registration of this method is actually handled in `"init"`.)

- ► `"init"`: This initializes the model.

Then, there's a long list of notifications. They should all be pretty self-explanatory, but it should also help illustrate the power of notifications.

Since future versions will support different kinds of notes, we need a mechanism to create any kind of note we need without involving a lot of duplicated code. We need to create a different note type in response to a tap on one of our icons, but we also need this functionality while loading a collection of notes. And while it might not seem obvious yet, we also need a way to determine which editing view to use.

We'll rely on the concept of a **generic factory**. The concept is simple: we want to prevent duplication of code (as in, **don't repeat yourself (DRY)**). It also provides a simple mechanism for expansion in the future.

We'll create two factories: one for notes (which we've previously indicated) and one for the views that are used to edit notes. Each one needs a `"create"` method that takes the type of note (or view) to create, which then instantiates the desired object. That means we can ask the factory for a new note instead of duplicating that code.

Our note factory has one additional method (`"createAssociatedMediaFileName"`) that creates the filenames for various types of media. We won't need a lot of code for this at the moment since text notes don't support additional media, but we'll be adding to it as we progress through the next several projects.

What did we do?

In this section, we defined the data models for notes and the collection of notes. Now that we've done this, it will be easy to write code that implements this functionality.

Implementing the Base Note data model

Now that we've got the model designed, it's time to implement it in code. This particular model will need to go in `/www/js/app/models/baseNote.js`.

Getting ready

Here's the code for the base note model. We've stripped a lot of the preamble and the comments as they appear in the code. In place of the stripped comments, we've added more in-depth commentary where necessary.

Let's start with the shell of the module. We do this by starting with `define`. This indicates to RequireJS that we're defining a module. The name of the module is inferred from the filename. We indicate that we'll need YASMF as a dependency. We also create a subclass of YASMF's `BaseObject` class. Note that we use `_className` here. YASMF objects maintain an internal class hierarchy, and this adds our class's name into that hierarchy. We use a private variable here simply because it's better than having to type it out several times (since this won't be the only time we'll need it).

```
define ( ["yasmf"], function ( _y ) {
    var _className = "BaseNote";
    var BaseNote = function () {
        var self = new _y.BaseObject();
        self.subclass ( _className );
        // the rest of the following code is inserted here.
        return self;
    };
    // translation matrices are inserted here.
    return BaseNote;
});
```

Next, add code to register all the notifications that the model can send. (If we don't, YASMF will complain when we try to send those notifications.) This needs to be added prior to the `return self` line in the preceding code.

```
self.registerNotification ( "uidChanged" );
self.registerNotification ( "nameChanged" );
self.registerNotification ( "textContentsChanged" );
self.registerNotification ( "mediaContentsChanged" );
self.registerNotification ( "unitValueChanged" );
self.registerNotification ( "unitLabelsChanged" );
```

Create the `UID` property. Note the pattern: a private backing variable, and then public-facing `get`/`set` functions, followed by the code to bind it all together as a property.

```
self._uid = undefined;
self.getUID = function () {
    return self._uid;
}
self.setUID = function ( theUID ) {
    self._uid = theUID;
    self.notify ( "uidChanged" );
}
Object.defineProperty ( self, "UID",
{get: self.getUID, set: self.setUID, configurable: true });
Object.defineProperty ( self, "uid", {get: self.getUID,
set: self.setUID, configurable: true });
```

Declare the properties for the date the note was created and the date it was modified. By providing only a `get` function, this property is considered *read-only*.

```
self._createdDate = undefined;
self.getCreatedDate = function () {
    return self._createdDate;
}
Object.defineProperty ( self, "createdDate",
{get: self.getCreatedDate, configurable: true });

self._modifiedDate = undefined;
self.getModifiedDate = function () {
    return self._modifiedDate;
}
Object.defineProperty ( self, "modifiedDate",
{get: self.getModifiedDate, configurable: true });
```

Declare the property for the visible name of the note. When the name is changed, the modification date is also changed.

```
self._name = "";
self.getName = function () {
    return self._name;
}
self.setName = function ( theName ) {
    self._name = theName;
    self._modifiedDate = new Date();
    self.notify ( "nameChanged" );
}
Object.defineProperty ( self, "name", {get: self.getName,
set: self.setName, configurable: true });
```

Next, we create the unitValue and unitLabels properties. Since we will have many different types of notes in the future, this provides a generic way to refer to different kinds of units (lines, seconds, and so on.). Here, unitValue is the number of lines, and unitLabels contains the zero, singular, and plural forms of the word *line*. We also create the formattedUnitValue property that combines both the unitValue and unitLabels properties to create a readable representation.

```
self._unitValue = 0;
self._unitLabels = [ "app.bn.LINES", "app.bn.LINE",
"app.bn.LINES" ];
self.getUnitValue = function () {
  return self._unitValue;
}
self.setUnitValue = function ( theValue ) {
  self._unitValue = theValue;
  self.notify ( "unitValueChanged" );
}
Object.defineProperty ( self, "unitValue", {
get: self.getUnitValue, set: self.setUnitValue,
configurable: true});

self.getUnitLabels = function () {
  return self._unitLabels;
}
self.setUnitLabels = function ( theLabels ) {
  self._unitLabels = theLabels;
  self.notify ( "unitLabelsChanged" );
}
Object.defineProperty ( self, "unitLabels", {
get: self.getUnitLabels, set: self.setUnitLabels,
configurable: true});

return _y.N(self.unitValue) + " " + _y.T(self.unitLabels[Math.
min((self.unitLabels.length-1),Math.round(self.unitValue))]);
}
Object.defineProperty ( self, "formattedUnitValue",
{get: self.getFormattedUnitValue, configurable: true});
```

Next, create the textContents property. If the contents change, update the modification date and the line count. (We restrict updating the unitValue to the BaseNote class so that other note types don't have to worry about their own unitValue class being overwritten when the text changes.)

```
self._textContents = "";
self.getTextContents = function () {
   return self._textContents;
```

```
    }
    self.setTextContents = function ( theContents ) {
        self._textContents = theContents;
        self._modifiedDate = new Date();
        if (self.class === "BaseNote") {
         self.unitValue = self._textContents.split("\n").length;
        }
        self.notify ( "textContentsChanged" );
    }
    Object.defineProperty ( self, "textContents", {
    get: self.getTextContents, set: self.setTextContents,
    configurable: true});
```

Next, create the property for `mediaContents`. Our text note doesn't really do anything with it, but it'll be there for future use.

```
    self._mediaContents = null;
    self.getMediaContents = function () {
      return self._mediaContents;
    }
    self.setMediaContents = function ( theContents ) {
      self._mediaContents = theContents;
      self._modifiedDate = new Date();
      self.notify ( "mediaContentsChanged" );
    }
    Object.defineProperty ( self, "mediaContents", {
    get: self.getMediaContents, set: self.setMediaContents,
    configurable: true});
```

Add the property for the note's `representation` method. For now, this is an icon that represents a page of text.

```
    self._representation = "page-text-new";
    self.getRepresentation = function () {
      return self._representation;
    }
    Object.defineProperty ( self, "representation", {
    get: self.getRepresentation, configurable: true});
```

Next, create the method that serializes the object into a JSON string ready for saving in storage:

```
    self._serialize = function () {
      return JSON.stringify ({
        "uid": self.uid,
        "createdDate" : self.createdDate,
        "modifiedDate" : self.modifiedDate,
```

```
            "name": self.name,
            "textContents": self.textContents,
            "mediaContents": self.mediaContents,
            "unitValue": self.unitValue,
            "unitLabels": self.unitLabels,
            "representation": self.representation
        });
    }
    Object.defineProperty ( self, "JSON", {
    get: self._serialize, configurable: true });
```

Now, we create the method that deserializes a JSON string and returns `true` if the string was deserialized or `false` if there was an error. Note the order of property assignments. It's critical that `modifiedDate` be assigned last since the previous lines will actually set `modifiedDate` to the current date and time.

```
    self._deserialize = function ( theSerializedObject ) {
        try {
            var aNote = JSON.parse (theSerializedObject);
            self.uid = aNote.uid;
            self._createdDate = new Date(aNote.createdDate);
            self.name = aNote.name;
            self.textContents = aNote.textContents;
            self.mediaContents = aNote.mediaContents;
            self.unitValue = aNote.unitValue;
            self._modifiedDate = new Date(aNote.modifiedDate);
            return true;
        }
        catch ( e ) {
            return false;
        }
    };
```

Next, we initialize the note. An optional parameter can specify the UID. Note the pattern utilized for overriding the data. First, we call `self.overrideSuper` with the `class` name, the name of the method, and a reference to the actual method we're overriding. Then we redefine the method. Our superclass (the base object) doesn't take any additional parameters, so we don't need to pass any additional values to `super`. Whatever you do, do not replace `_className` with `self.class` here; it won't work for child objects!

```
    self.overrideSuper ( self.class, "init", self.init );
    self.init = function ( theUID ) {
        self.super ( _className, "init" );
```

Assign the current date and time; if the note is deserialized later, it gets overwritten:

```
    self._createdDate = new Date();
    if ( typeof theUID !== "undefined" ) { self.uid = theUID; }
}
```

Next, we initialize the note with specific JSON:

```
self.initWithJSON = function ( theJSON ) {
    self.init ();
    if ( typeof theJSON !== "undefined" ) {
        return self._deserialize ( theJSON );
    }
    else {
        return false;
    }
}
```

Initialize the note with various options. We can use this pattern to avoid worrying about the parameter order, especially when there are a lot of options:

```
self.initWithOptions = function ( options ) {
    self.init();
    if ( typeof options !== "undefined" ) {
        if ( typeof options.uid !== "undefined" )
        { self.uid = options.uid; }
        if ( typeof options.createdDate !== "undefined" )
        { self._createdDate = options.createdDate; }
        if ( typeof options.name !== "undefined" )
        { self.name = options.name; }
        if ( typeof options.textContents !== "undefined" )
        { self.textContents = options.textContents; }
        if ( typeof options.mediaContents !== "undefined" )
        { self.mediaContents = options.mediaContents; }
        if ( typeof options.unitValue !== "undefined" )
        { self.unitValue = options.unitValue; }
        if ( typeof options.modifiedDate !== "undefined" )
        { self._modifiedDate = options.modifiedDate; }
    }
}
```

At the bottom of the module, just prior to the last `return` method, define the translations we need for localization:

```
_y.addTranslations ( {
    "app.bn.LINE":
    {
```

```
        "EN": "Line",
        "ES": "Línea"
    },
    "app.bn.LINES":
    {
        "EN": "Lines",
        "ES": "Líneas"
    }
});
```

We're done with the base note model, but we need to define the note factory. First, we define a new module that depends on YASMF and the note model we just created. Note that when we specify JavaScript dependencies, we don't attach the file extension. (You may wonder why we don't use the entire path. This is because of the way we configure RequireJS. We set it up later in this project so that we can save a few keystrokes each time we use a dependency.) In /www/js/app/factories/noteFactory.js, add the following code:

```
define ( ["yasmf", "app/models/baseNote"],
function ( _y, BaseNote) {
   var noteFactory = {};
   // the following code is inserted here.
   return noteFactory;
});
```

Now, define the various note types we'll eventually support. Base notes and text notes are the same, so they get the same value:

```
noteFactory.BASENOTE = "BASENOTE";
noteFactory.TEXTNOTE = "BASENOTE";
noteFactory.AUDIONOTE = "AUDIONOTE";
noteFactory.VIDEONOTE = "VIDEONOTE";
noteFactory.IMAGENOTE = "IMAGENOTE";
```

Next, we need to define the method for creating a note, based on the requested note type. For now, it's pretty simple: we can only return text notes.

```
noteFactory.createNote = function ( noteType ) {
   switch ( noteType.toUpperCase().trim() ) {
      case noteFactory.BASENOTE:
      case noteFactory.TEXTNOTE:
         return new BaseNote();
      default:
         throw new Error (
         "Note Factory doesn't understand a " + noteType );
   }
}
```

Finally, define a method that creates the file name for any media that we might attach to notes in the future. For text notes, it shouldn't do much, but the rest of the code is important because media types vary across platforms, and the file extensions vary as well (an extension being .wav, .3gp, .mov, and so on).

```
noteFactory.createAssociatedMediaFileName =
function (noteType, uid) {
  var newFileName;
  var extension = {};
  switch (noteType.toUpperCase().trim()) {
    case noteFactory.BASENOTE:
    case noteFactory.TEXTNOTE:
      newFileName = "";
      break;
    default:
      throw new Error(
      "Note Factory doesn't understand a " + noteType);
  }
  if (newFileName !== "") {
    var newFileExtension = (typeof
    extension[_y.device.platform()] !== "undefined") ?
        extension[_y.device.platform()]
      : extension["default"];
    newFileName = newFileName + uid + "." +
    newFileExtension;
  }
  return newFileName;
};
```

What did we do?

If you're not familiar with RequireJS, you may be wondering about the define statement wrapping the entire piece of code. This simply defines a module (the module name is inferred from the filename) and declares that it needs the YASMF framework, which will be passed in to the inner block of code as _y (the shorthand name for the framework). When other code needs to use our code, they'll use a define model (depending on the situation) that includes the name of our model.

Everything inside the define block can use _y without worrying about whether or not it's been loaded into memory. This solves a critical problem in JavaScript, namely that it has no include statement and no dependency management. For a simple app such as ours, it would be reasonably easy to ensure that every dependency is satisfied, but we'd need several SCRIPT tags in our index.html file and we'd need to have them in the correct order.

Once inside the `define` statement, we define the `BaseNote` object based on an instance of YASMF's `BaseObject` class. Most object inheritance frameworks provide an `extends` method to extend one object from another. YASMF provides the `subclass` method instead. The only parameter is the name of the class—`BaseNote`, in our case (from `_className`).

Note the pattern we use when overriding methods. Each framework that provides classical inheritance does this in different ways—YASMF chooses to make the override very obvious. What's going on behind the scenes when an override occurs is simple: the previous version is simply stored in an internal dictionary.

This pattern will be repeated with each override, and it's important to get it just right, or the inheritance chain may be corrupted in future subclasses. Whatever you do, do *not* replace `_className` with `self.class`. You'll end up in a painful situation when you start making other objects that inherit from this one.

After we define all our properties and methods, we return the object. One thing to note is that we've been referring to it as `self` all this time and not `this`. Others may use `me` or `that`, but the purpose is the same, that is, we can't rely on `this` to always point to what we expect it to point to.

The last line in the `define` block then returns the function that creates a note object. Essentially, it returns the blueprint for a base note object.

We also wrote the code for the note factory, which allows us to request new notes of any supported type. Right now, it seems like a lot of code for no benefit, but further down the road it will be very important.

Implementing the Note Storage model

Now that we've defined the model for a note, we need to define the storage mechanism for maintaining a collection of notes. This file will be at `/www/js/app/models/noteStorage.js`.

Getting on with it

Like the last model, we start off by defining the module (note the dependencies; we depend on the Q tag here, but we won't actually use that until the next project):

```
define ( ["yasmf", "Q", "app/factories/noteFactory"], function (
  _y, Q, noteFactory ) {
```

Next, we define a private convenience method for generating a reasonably unique identifier based on the date and time:

```
var _generateUID = function ()
{
    return _y.datetime.getUnixTime();
};
```

Then, we define the class itself:

```
var _className = "NoteStorage";
var NoteStorage = function ()
{
    var self = new _y.BaseObject();
    self.subclass ( _className );

    self.registerNotification ( "collectionChanged" );
    self.registerNotification ( "collectionLoading" );
    self.registerNotification ( "collectionLoaded" );
    self.registerNotification ( "collectionFailedLoading" );
    self.registerNotification ( "collectionSaving" );
    self.registerNotification ( "collectionSaved" );
    self.registerNotification ( "collectionFailedSaving" );
    self.registerNotification ( "noteChanged" );
    self.registerNotification ( "noteSaved" );
    self.registerNotification ( "noteFailedSaving" );
    self.registerNotification ( "noteRemoved" );
    self.registerNotification ( "noteFailedRemoving" );
    self.registerNotification ( "noteCreated" );
```

Up next, let's look at the collection of notes; the collection itself is read-only, though the contents are read-write. Though it's technically an object, we tend to subscript it like an array later.

```
self._notes = {};
self.getCollection = function () {
    return self._notes;
}
Object.defineProperty ( self, "collection", {
get: self.getCollection, configurable: true });
```

Next, we define the method that loads the collection from `localStorage` (we expect it to be an array of objects of the form—`UID: noteUID, type: noteType`). We load each one in turn (each note is stored in `localStorage` under the key `"note"+UID`) and notify any listeners when we're done (or if a failure occurred).

```
self.loadCollection = function () {
    self.notify ( "collectionLoading" );
    try {
        var allNoteIDsJSON = localStorage.getItem ( "notes" );
        if ( allNoteIDsJSON !== null ) {
            self._notes = {};
            var allNoteIDs = JSON.parse (allNoteIDsJSON );
            allNoteIDs.forEach ( function (theNote) {
                var aNoteJSON = localStorage.getItem (
                "note" + theNote.UID );
                var aNote = noteFactory.createNote (
                theNote.type );
                if ( aNote.initWithJSON ( aNoteJSON ) ) {
                    self._notes [theNote.UID] = aNote;
                }
                else {
                    self.notify ( "collectionFailedLoading" );
                    return;
                }
            });
            self.notify ( "collectionLoaded" );
        }
        else {
            self._notes = {};
            self.notify ( "collectionLoaded" );
        }
    }
    catch ( e ) {
        self.notify ( "collectionFailedLoading",
        [e.message] );
    }
}
```

Next, we define how to save the collection to storage. Note that we aren't saving the individual notes, just the collection. Any `null` notes we come across, we'll exclude, since these are deleted notes. In order to store anything in `localStorage`, it has to be a string, so we use `JSON.stringify` to convert our data into a form that can be saved.

```
self.saveCollection = function () {
    self.notify ( "collectionSaving" );
```

```
        try {
            var allNoteIDs = [];
            var aNote;
            for ( var aNoteUID in self._notes ) {
                if (self._notes.hasOwnProperty(aNoteUID)) {
                    aNote = self._notes[aNoteUID];
                    if ( aNote !== null ) {
                        allNoteIDs.push ( {
                        UID: aNote.UID, type: aNote.class} );
                    }
                }
            }
            var allNoteIDsJSON = JSON.stringify ( allNoteIDs );
            localStorage.setItem ( "notes", allNoteIDsJSON );
            self.notify ( "collectionSaved" );
        }
        catch ( e ) {
            self.notify ( "collectionFailedSaving", [e.message] );
        }
    }
```

Creating a single note is pretty easy. First, we ask our factory for a new text note. After we get the new note, we need to generate a new UID, get any media file name (which doesn't apply to text notes), and assign some default content. Then, we add it to the collection and save the note (which saves the collection as well).

```
self.createNote = function ( noteType ) {
    var aNote = noteFactory.createNote ( noteType ||
    noteFactory.TEXTNOTE );
var noteUID = _generateUID();
var newMediaFileName = noteFactory.createAssociatedMediaFileName
( noteType || noteFactory.TEXTNOTE,noteUID );
aNote.initWithOptions ( { "uid": noteUID,
                          "name": _y.T("app.ns.A_NEW_NOTE"),
                          "textContents": _y.T(
                          "app.ns.WHATS_ON_YOUR_MIND"),
                          "mediaContents": newMediaFileName
                        } );
self._notes [ aNote.uid ] = aNote;
    self.notify ( "noteCreated", [ aNote.uid ] );
    self.saveNote ( aNote );
    return aNote;
};
```

Returning a specific note is very simple:

```
self.getNote = function ( theUID ) {
    return self._notes [ theUID ];
}
```

Saving a specific note isn't too hard, either. We get the serialized JSON and then store it in `localStorage` using `"note"+UID`:

```
self.saveNote = function ( theNote ) {
    try  {
        var theJSON = theNote.JSON;
        localStorage.setItem ( "note" + theNote.uid, theJSON );
        self.notify ( "noteSaved", [ theNote.uid ] );
        self.notify ( "collectionChanged" );
    }
    catch ( e ) {
        self.notify ( "noteFailedSaving", [ theNote, e.message ]
);
    }
}
```

Next, we define how to remove a specific note:

```
self.removeNote= function ( theUID ) {
    try {
        localStorage.removeItem ( "note" + theUID );
        self._notes [ theUID ] = null;
        self.notify ( "noteRemoved", [ theUID ] );
        self.notify ( "collectionChanged" );
    }
    catch ( e ) {
        self.notify ( "noteFailedRemoving", [ theUID, e.message ]
);
    }
}
```

We define a handler that listens for changes in the collection, and when they occur, it saves the collection:

```
self._collectionChangedListener = function () {
    self.saveCollection();
}
```

Our `init` method attaches the preceding listener to the `collectionChanged` notification:

```
        self.overrideSuper ( self.class, "init", self.init );
        self.init = function () {
            self.super ( _className, "init" );
            self.addListenerForNotification (
            "collectionChanged", self._collectionChangedListener );
        };
        return self;
    }
```

Finally, add our translations to the global translation matrix:

```
    _y.addTranslations ( {
        "app.ns.A_NEW_NOTE" : {
            "en" : "A New Note",
            "es" : "Una Nota Nueva"
        },
        "app.ns.WHATS_ON_YOUR_MIND" : {
            "en" : "What's on your mind?",
            "es" : "¿Que pasa por tu mente?"
        }
    });

    return NoteStorage;
});
```

What did we do?

So far, we've created the code for the Note Storage model. We're not quite done yet, though. There's one more thing we need to do, and it involves a separate, short little snippet of code. We want to make sure we only ever have one collection of notes in our app, so we need a **singleton**. A singleton is essentially object-oriented programming's answer to global variables. You may argue about whether this is good or not; I like them, but others don't.

To define the singleton, we just need a short model in `/www/js/app/models/noteStorageSingleton.js`. It looks like this:

```
define ( ["app/models/noteStorage"], function ( NoteStorage )
{
    var noteStorage = new NoteStorage();
    noteStorage.init ();
    return noteStorage;
});
```

All we do in this code is call the `NoteStorage` factory that we just defined and initialize it. We then return that object. Since this snippet isn't a factory—it just returns an instance of a class—it will be unique across the application, no matter how many times it is requested.

Implementing the note list view

Now that we've implemented the models, we can focus on the views. We'll start with the note list view, which should be defined in `/www/js/app/views/noteListView.js`. We'll also define three HTML snippets in `/www/html/noteListView.html`, `/www/html/noteListView_android.html`, and `/www/html/noteListItem.html`.

Getting ready

Before we do any of that, we need one additional piece of code: the note view factory. Just like we need a note factory to create notes of a specific type, we also need a note view factory to create the various editing views for each type of note. This is defined in `www/js/app/factories/noteViewFactory.js`, as follows:

```
define ( ["app/views/textNoteEditView", "app/factories/noteFactory"],
function ( TextNoteEditView, noteFactory ) {
   var noteViewFactory = {};
   noteViewFactory.createNoteEditView = function ( noteType ) {
      switch ( noteType.toUpperCase().trim() ) {
         case noteFactory.BASENOTE:
            return new TextNoteEditView();
         default:
            throw new Error ( "Note View Factory doesn't understand a
" + noteType );
      }
   }
   return noteViewFactory;
});
```

Getting on with it

Let's start with defining the templates. The reason we keep these in their own HTML files is that of convenience. It's easier to put HTML in text files than it is to hard-code them using JavaScript where you have to worry about quotes and line endings.

The first snippet is for the main view, in `/www/html/noteListView.html`:

```
<html>
<body>
<div class="ui-navigation-bar">
```

```
<div class="ui-title">%APP_TITLE%</div>
</div>
<div class="ui-scroll-container">
<ul class="ui-list ui-avoid-navigation-bar ui-avoid-tool-bar">
</ul>
</div>
<div class="ui-tool-bar">
<div class="ui-bar-button-group ui-align-center">
<div class="ui-bar-button ui-background-tint-color ui-glyph
ui-glyph-page-text-new"></div>
<div class="ui-bar-button ui-background-tint-color ui-glyph
ui-glyph-sound-wave"></div>
<div class="ui-bar-button ui-background-tint-color ui-glyph
ui-glyph-camera"></div>
<div class="ui-bar-button ui-background-tint-color ui-glyph
ui-glyph-camera-video"></div>
</div>
</div>
</body>
</html>
```

This is fairly standard HTML, but the important thing to note is that there are `%...%` substitution variables throughout. These will be replaced by more appropriate values when the template is rendered by our code.

Because we have different layouts for our two supported platforms, we need another template that supplies the layout for Android, in `/www/html/noteListView_android.html`. Pay careful attention to where the icons appear in this template:

```
<html>
  <body>
    <div class="ui-navigation-bar">
      <div class="ui-title">%APP_TITLE%</div>
        <div class="ui-bar-button-group ui-align-right">
            <div class="ui-bar-button ui-background-tint-color ui-
glyph ui-glyph-page-text-new"></div>
            <div class="ui-bar-button ui-background-tint-color ui-
glyph ui-glyph-sound-wave"></div>
            <div class="ui-bar-button ui-background-tint-color ui-
glyph ui-glyph-camera"></div>
            <div class="ui-bar-button ui-background-tint-color ui-
glyph ui-glyph-camera-video"></div>
        </div>
    </div>
    <div class="ui-scroll-container">
```

```
          <ul class="ui-list ui-avoid-navigation-bar">
          </ul>
      </div>
    </body>
  </html>
```

The next snippet is for each list item in /www/html/noteListItem.html:

```
<html>
<body>
<div class="ui-list-item-contents" data-uid="%UID%">
<div class="ui-glyph note-representation ui-glyph-%REPRESENTATION%"></
div>
<div class="ui-label note-name">%NAME%</div>
<div class="ui-label note-modified-date">%MODIFIED%</div>
<div class="ui-label note-info">%INFO%</div>
<div class="ui-indicator ui-arrow-direction-right"></div>
</div>
</body>
</html>
```

Again, it's nice and simple, and it's easier than packing it in a JavaScript string. Furthermore, it separates the layout from the code. We could change the order of elements and such without having to alter any JavaScript code.

Next, we define the code for the view in /www/js/app/views/nodeListView.js. We start by listing all the dependencies, and there are quite a few. Note that we include our HTML templates by using the special form text!html/filename.html!strip. This uses the Text plugin in the project template to load these templates into memory, as shown in the following code:

```
define ( ["yasmf",
          "app/models/noteStorageSingleton",
          "text!html/noteListView.html!strip",
          "text!html/noteListView_android.html!strip",
          "text!html/noteListItem.html!strip",
          "app/factories/noteFactory",
          "app/factories/noteViewFactory"],
function ( _y, noteStorageSingleton, noteListViewHTML,
noteListViewAndroidHTML,
          noteListItemHTML, noteFactory, noteViewFactory )
{
    var _className = "NoteListView";
    var NoteListView = function () {
      var self = new _y.UI.ViewContainer ();
```

```
        self.subclass ( _className );
        // the following code inserted here
        return self;
    };
    // translations inserted here
    return NoteListView;
});
```

In the preceding code, our view descends from a simple `ViewContainer` object, which is a simple object that YASMF provides to do some very simple view handling. It defines basic methods for inserting a view into the DOM and rendering it. If you want to see the code behind this object, look at `/framework/lib/yasmf/ui/viewContainer.js` in the code package for this book. (If you prefer online, visit `https://github.com/photokandyStudios/YASMF-Next/blob/master/lib/yasmf/ui/viewContainer.js`.

Next, we declare private variables that we will use to hold references to various DOM elements:

```
        self._navigationBar = null;
        self._scrollContainer = null;
        self._listOfNotes = null;
        self._newTextNoteButton = null;
        self._newAudioNoteButton = null;
        self._newImageNoteButton = null;
        self._newVideoNoteButton = null;
```

When the left-most icon in the toolbar is tapped, we need to create a text note. But first, we should define a generic method that can create any kind of note and display its associated view (passing our parent element to the new view is how it can attach itself to the DOM):

```
        self._createAndEditNote = function (noteType) {
            var aNewNote = noteStorageSingleton.
createNote(noteType);
            var aNoteEditView = noteViewFactory.
createNoteEditView(noteType);
            aNoteEditView.initWithOptions({note: aNewNote, parent:
self.parentElement});
        };
```

Now, we can create a simple method that creates a new text note:

```
        self.createNewTextNote = function () {
          self._createAndEditNote(noteFactory.TEXTNOTE);
        };
```

When a row is tapped, the user wants to edit an existing note. To do that, we get the row that was tapped from the event and convert it into a simpler event model (we'd cover this event model in more detail, but we'll be switching to a more comprehensive touch and gesture library in *Project 5, Working with Audio*). We then get the UID from an attribute on the row and get the desired note from Note Storage. Once we have the note, we can request a new view from the Note View factory and then display it on screen by attaching it to our parent element in the DOM.

```
self.editExistingNote = function ( e ) {
    var theEvent = _y.UI.event.convert ( this, e );
    var theUID = theEvent.target.getAttribute("data-uid");
   var aNote = noteStorageSingleton.getNote(theUID);
   var aNoteEditView = noteViewFactory.createNoteEditView(aNote.
class);
    aNoteEditView.initWithOptions({note: aNote, parent: self.
parentElement});
    }
```

If the user hits the physical **Back** button, we should quit the app:

```
self.quitApp = function () {
    navigator.app.exitApp();
}
```

When the view is displayed, it will need our HTML templates. We'll use the `template` method to replace the substitution variables with the correct values. Note how we determine which template to utilize by checking the platform of the device.

```
self.overrideSuper ( self.class, "render", self.render );
    self.render = function () {
return _y.template(_y.device.platform()==="android" ?
noteListViewAndroidHTML : noteListViewHTML, {
                     "APP_TITLE": _y.T("APP_TITLE") });
    }
```

Next, we define `renderToElement`. This asks YASMF to attach the rendered HTML to the DOM by calling our `super` method. Then, we are responsible for locating all the elements we need and attach any event handlers necessary to those elements. We also register a listener to handle the physical **Back** button being pressed.

```
self.overrideSuper (
self.class, "renderToElement", self.renderToElement );
self.renderToElement = function () {
    self.super ( _className, "renderToElement" );
    self._navigationBar = self.element.querySelector (
    ".ui-navigation-bar" );
```

```
                    self._scrollContainer = self.element.querySelector (
                    ".ui-scroll-container" );
                    self._listOfNotes = self.element.querySelector (
                    ".ui-list" );
                    var newButtons = self.element.querySelectorAll (
                    ".ui-bar-button" );
                    self._newTextNoteButton = newButtons[0];
                    self._newAudioNoteButton = newButtons[1];
                    self._newImageNoteButton = newButtons[2];
                    self._newVideoNoteButton = newButtons[3];
                    _y.UI.event.addListener ( self._newTextNoteButton,
                    "click", self.createNewTextNote );
                    _y.UI.backButton.addListenerForNotification (
                    "backButtonPressed", self.quitApp );
                }
```

To actually see the list of notes on the screen, we need to render the list. We could do it in the preceding method, but that's only called once during the view's lifetime. We need this to be called whenever the collection actually changes. So we'll define a method to render the list and will later register it so that it is notified when the collection of notes changes.

```
            self.renderList = function () {
                var notes = noteStorageSingleton.collection;
                var fragment = document.createDocumentFragment();
                for (var note in notes) {
                    if ( notes.hasOwnProperty ( note ) ) {
                        if (notes[note] !== null) {
                            var e = document.createElement ( "li" );
                            e.className = "ui-list-item";
                            e.setAttribute ( "data-uid", notes[note].uid );
                            e.id = "note_item_" + notes[note].uid;
                            e.innerHTML = _y.template ( noteListItemHTML, {
                              "UID": notes[note].uid,
                              "NAME": notes[note].name,
                              "REPRESENTATION":
                              notes[note].representation,
                              "MODIFIED":
                              _y.D(notes[note].modifiedDate,"D"),
                                            "INFO": "" +
                              _y.N(notes[note].formattedUnitValue)
                              } );
                            _y.UI.event.addListener ( e, "click", self.
                            editExistingNote );
                            fragment.appendChild ( e );
                            }
```

```
        }
      }
      self._listOfNotes.innerHTML = "";
      self._listOfNotes.appendChild ( fragment );
    }
```

There's a particular iOS bug that may prevent the list from scrolling. We'll listen for orientation changes so that we can fix the bug, but we need to define the handler first. Unfortunately, this forces the list to flicker, but it's the only way to fix the bug.

```
      self.onOrientationChanged = function () {
        if (_y.device.platform() == "ios")
        {
          self._scrollContainer.style.display = "none";
          setTimeout(function () {
          self._scrollContainer.style.display = ""; }, 0);
        }
      };
```

Next, we need to override the init method so that we can register for changes in the Note Storage collection and so that we can actually load the notes for the first time. We'll also attach the previous handler to the orientation change event. The super method actually creates a DIV element for us with the desired classes of noteListView and ui-container and attaches it to the passed-in element.

```
      self.overrideSuper ( self.class, "init", self.init );
      self.init = function ( theParentElement ) {
        self.super ( _className, "init", [undefined, "div",
        "noteListView ui-container", theParentElement] );
        noteStorageSingleton.addListenerForNotification (
        "collectionChanged", self.renderList );
        noteStorageSingleton.addListenerForNotification (
        "collectionLoaded", self.renderList );
        noteStorageSingleton.loadCollection ();
        _y.UI.orientationHandler.addListenerForNotification(
        "orientationChanged", self.onOrientationChanged);
      }
```

Next, we also define a corresponding initWithOptions object:

```
      self.overrideSuper ( self.class, "initWithOptions", self.init );
      self.initWithOptions = function ( options ) {
        var theParentElement;
        if ( typeof options !== "undefined" ) {
            if ( typeof options.parent !== "undefined" ) {
    theParentElement = options.parent; }
```

```
        }
        self.init ( theParentElement );
    }
```

We should always properly clean up after ourselves when we're no longer needed. This has the side effect of removing us from the DOM when asked.

```
    self.overrideSuper ( self.class, "destroy", self.destroy );
    self.destroy = function () {
    _y.UI.orientationHandler.removeListenerForNotification(
    "orientationChanged", self.onOrientationChanged);
        self._navigationBar = null;
        self._newTextNoteButton = null;
        self._newAudioNoteButton = null;
        self._newVideoNoteButton = null;
        self._newImageNoteButton = null;
        self._scrollContainer = null;
        self._listOfNotes = null;
        self.super ( _className, "destroy" );
    }
```

Last but not least, be sure to add the translations:

```
    _y.addTranslations (
    {
        "APP_TITLE": { "EN": "Filer" },
        "BACK": { "EN": "Back",
                  "ES": "Volver" }
    });
```

What did we do?

In this section, we've written the code for the note list view. Let's go over a few important details before moving on.

The `renderToElement` method does the hard work of rendering the view by first calling its `super` method. This inserts our template into the DOM by attaching it to a specific container. For the first view in our app, this is `rootContainer`.

Once the template is in the DOM, we search the DOM for certain elements using the `querySelector` method. This looks up an item by using CSS selectors.

 Why not `getElementById`? Although we don't do it in this app, it's possible to have the same view in the DOM multiple times, perhaps editing different notes. If we used an ID, we'd have problems finding the right DOM item, because IDs are supposed to be unique across the entire DOM.

We then add event listeners to the icons using `_y.UI.event.addListener`. This method is essentially the same as `object.addEventListener`, but it maps touch events to mouse events when on the desktop (which is useful for testing).

We use the `click` event here for now, but in later projects, we'll modify this to be more performant on mobile devices.

 We also add a listener for the `backButton` notification. YASMF helpfully adds this listener automatically and lets the most recent listener know when the user has pressed it. This is only for the physical Back button, not a **Back** button on the screen. The code is not complex, but take note of the section that ensures that we don't register multiple presses of the Back button in quick succession.

```
UI._BackButtonHandler = function () {
  var self = new BaseObject();
  self.subclass("BackButtonHandler");
  self.registerNotification("backButtonPressed");
  self._lastBackButtonTime = -1;
  self.handleBackButton = function () {
    var currentTime = (new Date()).getTime();
    if (self._lastBackButtonTime < currentTime - 1000) {
      self._lastBackButtonTime = (new Date()).getTime();
      self.notifyMostRecent("backButtonPressed");
    }
  };
  document.addEventListener(
  'backbutton', self.handleBackButton, false);
  return self;
};
UI.backButton = new UI._BackButtonHandler();
```

We also defined some code that deals with a particularly painful iOS bug in which a scrollable view sometimes becomes nonscrollable after a change in device orientation. This code relies on an orientation handler provided by YASMF. The code for this is also relatively simple, but note that it does quite a bit more than simply detect orientation; it also allows us to write CSS styles based on that orientation, the device, form factor, and OS version:

```
UI._OrientationHandler = function () {
  var self = new BaseObject();
  self.subclass("OrientationHandler");
  self.registerNotification("orientationChanged");
  self.handleOrientationChange = function () {
    var curDevice;
```

```
            var curOrientation;
            var curFormFactor;
            var curScale;
            var curConvenience;
            curDevice = _y.device.platform();
            if (curDevice == "ios")
            {
               if (navigator.userAgent.indexOf("OS 7") > -1) {
                  curDevice += " ios7"; }
               if (navigator.userAgent.indexOf("OS 6") > -1) {
                  curDevice += " ios6"; }
               if (navigator.userAgent.indexOf("OS 5") > -1) {
                  curDevice += " ios5"; }
            }
            curFormFactor = theDevice.formFactor();
            curOrientation = theDevice.isPortrait() ?
            "portrait" : "landscape";
            curScale = theDevice.isRetina() ? "hiDPI" : "loDPI";
            curConvenience = "";
            if (theDevice.iPad()) { curConvenience = "ipad"; }
            if (theDevice.iPhone()) { curConvenience = "iphone"; }
            if (theDevice.droidTablet()) {
            curConvenience = "droid-tablet"; }
            if (theDevice.droidPhone()) {
            curConvenience = "droid-phone"; }
            document.body.setAttribute(
            "class", curDevice + " " + curFormFactor + " " +
            curOrientation + " " + curScale + " " + curConvenience);
            self.notify("orientationChanged");
         };
      window.addEventListener(
      'orientationchange', self.handleOrientationChange, false);
      self.handleOrientationChange();
      return self;
   };
UI.orientationHandler = new UI._OrientationHandler();
```

Implementing the text note edit view

We need to implement our last view, the text note edit view. It should be defined in
/www/js/app/views/textNoteEditView.js. The associated template should be
defined in /www/html/textNoteEditView.html.

Getting on with it

First, we define the template (in `/www/html/textNoteEditView.html`):

```html
<html>
<body>
<div class="ui-navigation-bar">
<div class="ui-title" contenteditable="true">%NOTE_NAME%</div>
<div class="ui-bar-button-group ui-align-left">
<div class="ui-bar-button ui-tint-color ui-back-button">%BACK%</div>
</div>
<div class="ui-bar-button-group ui-align-right">
<div class="ui-bar-button ui-destructive-color">%DELETE_NOTE%</div>
</div>
</div>
<div class="ui-scroll-container ui-avoid-navigation-bar">
<textarea class="ui-text-box" >%NOTE_CONTENTS%</textarea>
</div>
</body>
</html>
```

Note that the title has the `contenteditable` attribute set to `true`. This means that the element is editable, which makes sense, because the note's title is editable. It's an alternative to using the `INPUT` elements, though you can't use it everywhere. Note also that we used a `textarea` tag for the contents of the note. The `contenteditable` DOM elements don't always get the same editing behaviors that the `INPUT` and `textarea` elements get for free (such as scrolling properly while selecting content).

Next, we define the code in `/www/js/app/views/textNoteEditView.js`. Most of the preamble should be pretty familiar by now.

```javascript
define ( ["yasmf", "app/models/noteStorageSingleton",
          "text!html/textNoteEditView.html!strip"],
         function ( _y, noteStorageSingleton,
         textNoteEditViewHTML ) {
   var _className = "TextNoteEditView";
   var TextNoteEditView = function () {
      var self = new _y.UI.ViewContainer ();
      self.subclass ( _className );
      self._navigationBar = null;
      self._nameEditor = null;
      self._scrollContainer = null;
      self._contentsEditor = null;
      self._backButton = null;
      self._deleteButton = null;
      self._note = null;
```

When we need to save the note, we copy the name and contents from the DOM and request our Note Storage singleton to save the note:

```
self.saveNote = function () {
    self._note.name = self._nameEditor.innerText;
    self._note.contents = self._contentsEditor.value;
    noteStorageSingleton.saveNote ( self._note );
}
```

When the user taps the **Delete** button, ask storage to remove the note and then destroy ourselves in order to return to the previous view. Note that the user is given no warning; we'll fix this in *Project 7, Capturing Video*.

```
self.deleteNote = function () {
    noteStorageSingleton.removeNote ( self._note.uid );
    self.destroy();
}
```

When the physical or onscreen Back button is pressed, save the note and go back to the previous view:

```
self.goBack = function () {
    self.saveNote();
    self.destroy();
}
```

Next, we render the HTML template and replace any substitution variables:

```
self.overrideSuper ( self.class, "render", self.render );
self.render = function () {
    return _y.template ( noteEditViewHTML,
                         {
                             "NOTE_NAME": self._note.name,
                             "NOTE_CONTENTS":
                             self._note.textContents,
                             "BACK": _y.T("BACK"),
                             "DELETE_NOTE":
                             _y.T("app.nev.DELETE_NOTE")
                         });
}
```

As in the prior task, `renderToElement` does the hard work of searching the DOM and linking up all the elements we need to keep track of:

```
self.overrideSuper ( self.class, "renderToElement",
self.renderToElement );
self.renderToElement = function () {
```

```
        self.super ( _className, "renderToElement" );
        self._navigationBar = self.element.querySelector (
        ".ui-navigation-bar" );
        self._nameEditor = self.element.querySelector (
        ".ui-navigation-bar .ui-title" );
        self._backButton = self.element.querySelectorAll (
        ".ui-navigation-bar .ui-bar-button" )[0];
        self._deleteButton = self.element.querySelectorAll (
        ".ui-navigation-bar .ui-bar-button" )[1];
        self._scrollContainer = self.element.querySelector (
        ".ui-scroll-container" );
        self._contentsEditor = self.element.querySelector (
        ".ui-text-box" );

        _y.UI.event.addListener (
        self._backButton, "click", self.goBack )
        _y.UI.event.addListener (
        self._deleteButton, "click", self.deleteNote );

        _y.UI.backButton.addListenerForNotification (
        "backButtonPressed", self.goBack );
    }
```

Next, we override the `init` method. We'll be passed the UID of the note we're to edit, so we'll ask our storage singleton to return the actual note. Then, we create the DIV element for our view (but we classify it with both a generic `noteEditView` class and our actual class, which will be different for different types of notes):

```
        self.overrideSuper ( self.class, "init", self.init );
        self.init = function ( theParentElement, theUID ) {
            self._note = noteStorageSingleton.getNote ( theUID );
            self.super ( _className, "init", [undefined, "div",
            self.class + " noteEditView ui-container",
            theParentElement] );
        }
```

Provide a suitable `initWithOptions` method since we have to pass the note around:

```
        self.overrideSuper ( self.class, "initWithOptions",
        self.init );
        self.initWithOptions = function ( options ) {
            var theParentElement;
            var theUID;
            if ( typeof options !== "undefined" ) {
                if ( typeof options.parent !== "undefined" ) {
                theParentElement = options.parent; }
```

```
                    if ( typeof options.uid !== "undefined" ) {
                    theUID = options.uid; }
                }
            self.init ( theParentElement, theUID );
        }
```

As always, we clean up after ourselves. We also stop listening for physical **Back** button events:

```
        self.releaseBackButton = function () {
            _y.UI.backButton.removeListenerForNotification (
            "backButtonPressed", self.goBack );
        }
        self.overrideSuper ( self.class, "destroy", self.destroy );
        self.destroy = function () {
            self.releaseBackButton ();
            self._navigationBar = null
            self._backButton = null;
            self._deleteButton = null;
            self._scrollContainer = null;
            self._nameEditor = null;
            self._contentsEditor = null;
            self.super ( _className, "destroy" );
        }
        return self;
    };
```

Add any necessary translations:

```
    _y.addTranslations (
    {
        "app.nev.DELETE_NOTE":
        {
            "EN": "Delete",
            "ES": "Eliminar"
        }
    });
    return TextNoteEditView;
});
```

What did we do?

In this section, we wrote the code for the text note edit view. Most of the code should be fairly self-explanatory at this point. However, take a look at the saveNote method, which gets called whenever we hit the Back button (physical or onscreen). We set the name and contents based on the values of the DOM elements.

For the name, we use the `innerText` property since `contenteditable` creates the DOM elements while the user is editing the text and we don't want them in our name. The `innerText` property strips these out and returns only the text. For the title, we use the value of the `textarea` property, which is also plain text. Once copied to the note, we ask the storage singleton to save it.

The next interesting method is `deleteNote`, which is called whenever the remove button is pressed. We ask storage to remove the note, and then we destroy it ourselves. This has the effect of removing our view from the DOM. (It also does this instantly. We'll get into animations in *Project 5, Working with Audio*.)

In `renderToElement`, we call `super` again to add the template in the DOM. We then seek out the DOM elements we need. We use `querySelector` for all but the two buttons because the two buttons have similar classes. For those we use `querySelectorAll`, returns a list of matching DOM elements, and we know that the **Back** button is the first and the **Remove** button is the second.

Implementing the CSS

YASMF provides some default styling in `www/js/lib/yasmf.css`, and we'll be taking a look at the foundation it provides. In this section, we'll override these styles using `www/css/style.css` to assign our desired look and feel.

Getting ready

Let's look into the CSS provided by YASMF for a few moments since it provides the foundation for our styles. You'll want to open `/www/js/lib/yasmf.css` in an editor and follow along. If you prefer SASS stylesheets, you can look at `/framework/lib/yasmf.scss` in the code package for this book.

The first and most important detail is that we reset the styles of several elements using Eric Meyer's famous reset code (`http://cssreset.com`). This helps ensure consistency between different browsers and platforms when we apply our own styles.

Next, the `BODY` element is styled with various properties and fonts, but the important items are the `tap-highlight-color`, `user-select`, and `outline` styles. The first item prevents any element from being highlighted when tapped, which is fine in a browser but not in an app. The `outline` style also prevents the browser from outlining the element when it is selected. The `user-select` style prevents text selection in the app. Generally, we don't want the user to select just any text on the screen. For editable controls, this can be overridden.

The `text-rendering` property is also important as it enables kerning and ligatures on platforms that support it. It exhibits undesirable behavior on some platforms, though (mainly Android), and so it is disabled on Android devices.

In the *Implementing the note list view* section, we talked about an iOS bug dealing with orientation and showed you the code for handling orientation events. This code also puts various classes in the `BODY` tag, one of which is the platform. This allows YASMF (and us, by extension) to have different styles applied based on the platform. YASMF detects the platform largely by looking at the user agent string (which we covered to some degree in the previous chapter).

The `DIV` elements are also styled to ensure that background images are positioned with consistency and, more importantly, to ensure that we use the `border-box` sizing model. This ensures that borders and padding are included within the size of the element instead of outside of it (which is the norm).

Next up is the `ui-container` class; this is the class we use to wrap all our full-screen elements. It's designed to fill the screen, so it's positioned absolutely. It also has a 3D transform on it; this is important for animation when we come to it in *Project 5, Working with Audio*.

The next section dealing with split view containers is safe to skip for now. We'll come back to it in *Project 9, Devices of Different Sizes*.

The classes following the split view container classes are related to the concept of using a key color to identify interactive elements. We also define a *background* version to use the `background-color` style instead of the `color` style in CSS. (This becomes important when you want to use icon masks to render icons of the desired tint.)

A destructive color is also defined so that we can identify items that are destructive in nature (such as deleting a note).

The next section focuses on the navigation bar (`ui-navigation-bar`) for each OS. The important point is that we need to handle various sizes: one size for Android (48 px), one for iOS 6 (44 px), and one for iOS 7 (64 px including 20 px top padding). The differences for iOS 7 are due to the status bar overlapping the WebView. The other important detail is that we can't duplicate iOS 7's frosted glass effect in CSS, and so we use a linear gradient instead. (Note that the base styles are meant for iOS by default; you will have to use overrides for Android styles.) This was used based on inspiration from Thomas Fuch's website from an article about CSS styles for iOS 7 (`http://mir.aculo.us/2013/09/16/how-to-create-a-web-app-that-looks-like-a-ios7-native-app-part-1/`).

Up next are the styles that handle the toolbar (`ui-tool-bar`). These are similar to navigation bars, but they are positioned at the bottom of the view.

Following

Following this are several styles that deal with tab bars. We don't use these in this book, but you can use them to render tab bars that display in the appropriate position for the platform (at the bottom of the view for iOS and near the top of the view for Android).

Next come the bar button styles. These can be used on navigation bars and toolbars and provide mechanisms for grouping multiple buttons together with left, center, and right alignments.

Classes that handle avoiding the navigation and toolbars come next. These ensure that our content stays out of the way of these widgets (although content is allowed to scroll underneath them).

By default, containers prevent scrolling, so there's a `ui-scroll-container` class, which is a fullscreen view that allows scrolling. We use this to wrap our scrollable elements in our templates.

There are also items that control how lists and their items are displayed (`ui-list` and `ui-list-item`) as well as the indicators that usually appear inside (`ui-indicator`).

After the list section, there's a section that covers how icons are rendered by using icon masks (as described previously).

There are other styles as well, and we'll get to those over the next projects. For now, it's time to override these styles with our own.

Getting on with it

Our styles are defined in `www/css/style.css`:

```
body {
  background-color: #f1eee5;
}
body.android {
  background-color: #e7ece6;
}

.ui-tint-color {
  color: #45bc64;
}
.android .ui-tint-color {
  color: #484848;
}
.ui-tint-color:active {
  color: rgba(69,188,100,0.5);
}
.android .ui-tint-color:active {
  color: rgba(72,72,72, 0.5);
```

```
  }

  .ui-background-tint-color {
    background-color: #45bc64;
  }
  .android .ui-background-tint-color {
    background-color: #484848;
  }

  .ui-background-tint-color:active {
    background-color: rgba(69,188,100,0.5);
  }
  .android .ui-background-tint-color:active {
    background-color: rgba(72,72,72, 0.5);
  }

  .ui-navigation-bar {
    border-bottom: 1px solid rgba(87, 52, 32, 0.25);
  }
  .android .ui-navigation-bar {
    -webkit-box-shadow: 0px 2px 5px rgba(0,0,0,0.2);
    -moz-box-shadow: 0px 2px 5px rgba(0,0,0,0.2);
    -ms-box-shadow: 0px 2px 5px rgba(0,0,0,0.2);
    box-shadow: 0px 2px 5px rgba(0,0,0,0.2);
    border-bottom: 0;
    background-color: #d7dcd6;
  }
  .ui-tool-bar {
    border-top: 1px solid rgba(87, 52, 32, 0.25);
  }
  .android .ui-tool-bar {
    border-top: 0;
    -webkit-box-shadow: 0px -2px 5px rgba(0,0,0,0.2);
    -moz-box-shadow: 0px -2px 5px rgba(0,0,0,0.2);
    -ms-box-shadow: 0px -2px 5px rgba(0,0,0,0.2);
    box-shadow: 0px -2px 5px rgba(0,0,0,0.2);
    background-color: #d7dcd6;
  }

  .android .ui-container.left-side {
    border-right: 1px solid #484848;
  }

  .ui-back-button::before {
    background-color: #45bc64;
  }
```

```css
.android .ui-back-button::before {
  background-color: #484848;
}
.android .ui-back-button {
  color: transparent;
}


.noteListView, .noteEditView {
  background-color: #f1eee5;
  color: #573920;
}
.android .noteListView, .android .noteEditView {
  background-color: #e7ece6;
  color: #484848;
}
.noteListView { z-index: 10; }
.noteEditView { z-index: 20; }


.noteListView .ui-list-item {
  overflow: auto; /* so we don't have to clear */
  border-bottom: 1px solid rgba(87,52, 32, 0.25);
}
.android .noteListView .ui-list-item {
  border-bottom: 1px solid rgba(72, 72, 72, 0.25);
  z-index: 1;
}
.noteListView .ui-list-item-contents {
  background-color: #f1eee5;
}
.android .noteListView .ui-list-item-contents {
  background-color: #e7ece6;
}


.noteListView .ui-list-item:active,
.noteListView .ui-list-item-contents:active {
  background-color: rgba(58, 97, 154, 1);
}
.android .noteListView .ui-list-item:active,
.android .noteListView .ui-list-item-contents:active {
  background-color: #f7fcf6;
}


.noteListView .ui-list-item .note-representation {
  background-color: rgba(87,52, 32, 0.5);
```

```
    float: left;
    height: 30px;
    width: 30px;
}
.android .noteListView .ui-list-item .note-representation {
    background-color: #484848;
}

.noteListView .ui-list-item:active .note-representation {
    background-color: rgba(255, 255, 255, 0.5);
}
.android .noteListView .ui-list-item .note-representation {
    background-color: #484848;
}
.android .noteListView .ui-list-item
.note-representation.ui-glyph-page-text-new {
    background-color: #33B5E5;
}
.android .noteListView .ui-list-item
.note-representation.ui-glyph-sound-wave {
    background-color: #AA66CC;
}
.android .noteListView .ui-list-item
.note-representation.ui-glyph-photo {
    background-color: #FFBB33;
}
.android .noteListView .ui-list-item
.note-representation.ui-glyph-film {
    background-color: #99CC00;
}

.noteListView .ui-list-item .note-name {
    font-size: 25px;
    line-height: 30px;
    font-weight: 200;
    margin-right: 35px;
    margin-left: 40px;
}
.noteListView .ui-list-item:active .note-name {
    color: #FFFFFF;
}

.android .noteListView .ui-list-item:active .note-name {
    color: #242424;
}
```

```
.noteListView .ui-list-item .note-modified-date {
  font-size: 16px;
  line-height: 20px;
  font-weight: 300;
  color: rgba(87, 52, 32, 0.5);
  float: left;
}
.android .noteListView .ui-list-item .note-modified-date {
  color: #606060;
}
.noteListView .ui-list-item:active .note-modified-date,
.noteListView .ui-list-item:active .note-info {
    color: rgba(255,255,255,0.5);
}
.android .noteListView .ui-list-item:active .note-modified-date,
.android .noteListView .ui-list-item:active .note-info {
  color: #242424;
}


.noteListView .ui-list-item .note-info {
  font-size: 16px;
  line-height: 20px;
  font-weight: 300;
  color: rgba(87, 52, 32, 0.5);
  float: right;
}
.android .noteListView .ui-list-item .note-info {
  color: #606060;
}


.noteListView .ui-list-item .ui-indicator {
  background-color: rgba(87,52, 32, 0.5);
}
.android .noteListView .ui-list-item .ui-indicator {
  background-color: #484848;
}
.noteListView .ui-list-item:active .ui-indicator {
  background-color: #FFFFFF;
}
.android .noteListView .ui-list-item:active .ui-indicator {
  background-color: #242424;
}
```

```css
.noteEditView .ui-navigation-bar .ui-title, .noteEditView .ui-text-box
{
  -webkit-user-select: text;
  user-select: text;
}


.noteEditView .ui-navigation-bar .ui-title {
  left: 70px;
  right: 70px;
  overflow: hidden;
  white-space: nowrap;
}
.android .noteEditView .ui-navigation-bar .ui-title {
  left: 20px;
}


.noteEditView .ui-back-button::before {
  background-color: #45bc64;
}
.android .noteEditView .ui-back-button::before {
  background-color: #484848;
}
.android .ui-back-button {
  color: transparent;
}


.noteEditView .ui-text-box {
  min-height: 100%;
  line-height: 1.25em;
  display:block;
  border:0;
  background-color:transparent;
  padding:10px;
  margin:0;
  box-sizing:border-box;
  width:100%;
  font-family: -apple-system-font,
 "Helvetica Neue", Helvetica, Arial, Sans-Serif;
  font-size:20px;
  -webkit-appearance: none;
  -moz-appearance: none;
  -ms-appearance: none;
  appearance: none;
  color: #573920;
```

```
    line-height: 1.5em;
    font-weight: 200;
    height: 100%;
    border-radius: 0;
}
.android .noteEditView .ui-text-box {
    font-family: "Roboto", "DroidSans",
  Helvetica, Arial, Sans-Serif;
    color: #484848;
}
```

What did we do?

The first several styles override the colors inherited from YASMF (which are otherwise fairly monochrome). Our iOS version gets a cream-colored background with a green tint, and our Android version gets a light Holo theme. We also redefine some of the colors used when interactive elements are touched. These affordances help the user know that their touch has been registered.

The interesting styles start as we define the colors and styles for each view. The important part is that we assign each a z-index property. Until we get into animating the views, we need to worry about their order onscreen. Since the text note edit view will always be topmost, we make sure of that by giving it a higher z-index value.

We then set up the styles for our list items, which include the positioning of the name of the note, the date it was modified, and the number of lines. We also set up the affordance for changing the colors of the list item when it is touched by a user.

The next styles control the layout of the note edit view. We have to enable a user-select item for the title in the navigation bar so that contenteditable will work properly. We also specify the styling for the textarea property so that it renders the text like we want it to (including the font and line spacing to prevent it from looking overcrowded).

Putting it all together

We're almost there! We just need to put everything together with a couple of glue scripts, and then you can enjoy the app on your device!

Getting on with it

We need to define a few more short files to fill out the app, but once done, we'll have something that's ready to be built and deployed.

First, we need to define /www/js/app/main.js, as follows:

```
define ( ["yasmf", "app/views/noteListView"], function (
  _y, NoteListView ) {
    var APP = {};
```

Load the first view and initialize it (this will show the list of notes):

```
    APP.start = function () {
```

Find the rootContainer DOM element. YASMF always creates this for us, and it acts as the topmost element in the DOM hierarchy:

```
        var rootContainer = _y.ge("rootContainer");
        var noteListView = new NoteListView ();
```

Tell it to attach itself to the rootContainer element:

```
        noteListView.init( rootContainer );
        // store this for future reference
        APP.noteListView = noteListView;
    }
    return APP;
});
```

Next, define www/js/app.js:

```
requirejs.config({
```

Our libraries live in baseURL:

```
    baseUrl: './js/lib',
```

Specify where our app code lives, where our HTML templates live, and also any aliases (I like to refer to Q with an uppercase "Q", but it is typically lowercased on the file system):

```
    paths: {
      'app': '../app',
      'html': '../../html',
      'Q': 'q'
    },
```

The following is great for development. It ensures that the cache is never referenced, which always gets in the way when you need to debug something. You can remove this in production-level apps:

```
urlArgs: "bust=" + (new Date()).getTime(),
```

Define dependencies; the culture files require the jQuery/Globalize library to be loaded, and YASMF requires Q. We also declare that we aren't using Q like a regular module. It will instead define a global variable named Q. This line lets us use it like a regular module, though.

```
shim: {
    "cultures/globalize.culture.en-US": ["globalize"],
    "cultures/globalize.culture.es-US": ["globalize"],
    "Q": { exports: "Q" },
    "yasmf": ["Q"]
  }
});
```

Next, we start the application once all the necessary prerequisites are met. Note that not every required module requires a matching item in the parameter list.

```
require(['yasmf', 'app/main',
         'Q',
         'cultures/globalize.culture.en-US',
         'cultures/globalize.culture.es-US'], function ( _y, APP )
  {
```

For future reference, add _y and APP to the global object, which is useful for debugging. Then start!

```
  window._y = _y;
  window.APP = APP;
  _y.executeWhenReady ( function () { _y.getDeviceLocale( APP.start )
} );
});
```

Finally, we need to define the index.html file in /www/index.html:

```
<!DOCTYPE html>
<html>
<head>
<meta charset="utf-8" />
<meta name="apple-mobile-web-app-capable" content="yes" />
<meta name="viewport" content="width=device-width,
maximum-scale=1.0" />
<meta name="format-detection" content="telephone=no" />
<link rel="stylesheet" type="text/css" href="js/lib/yasmf.css" />
```

```
<link rel="stylesheet" type="text/css" href="css/style.css" />
<title>Filer v1</title>
</head>
<body>
<script type="text/javascript" src="cordova.js"></script>
<script type="text/javascript" src="js/lib/require.js"
data-main="js/app.js"></script>
</body>
</html>
```

What did we do?

We defined our index.html file at the very end, but it's the first thing that actually gets loaded by Cordova. Take a look at the META tag; there are some important details you need to know.

```
<meta name="viewport" content="width=device-width,
maximum-scale=1.0" />
```

The properties on this tag specify that the width of the page should be the width of the device (this is important so that the mobile browser doesn't attempt to scale the page) and that the maximum zoom is 1x (to ensure that the user can't pinch and zoom the page). Native apps don't normally allow this by default.

There's another META tag that's important: the format-detection META tag. This disables the formatting of telephone numbers in the app, which is something we want to avoid (since we would like to control these ourselves). It also prevents the browser from guessing incorrectly, which is even worse.

Inside the BODY tag, we have two SCRIPT tags. The first loads the cordova.js file, which is necessary if we want to access any native device features or use Cordova's plugins.

The second tag loads RequireJS. The data-main tag indicates which file to load when it starts, which points at our app.js file.

In app.js, we configure RequireJS, load our initial libraries, and then call APP.start, which is defined in main.js.

The `main.js` file creates a new note list view and attaches it to the DOM. All of this together bootstraps our app.

Before we finish things off, let's go over the RequireJS configuration items:

- ▸ `baseUrl`: This indicates where all the other references should begin. Usually, this points at a library directory, as it does here.

- ▸ `paths`: This indicates how to find other directories that are related to the `baseUrl` item. This frees us from having to use relative paths in every `require` and `define` statement. We point `app` to `../app`, which is really `www/js/app`. We point `html` to `../../html`, which is really just `www/html`. We also point Q to `q` (the `.js` extension is implied).

- ▸ `urlArgs`: This is used to bust the cache. Most browsers have the annoying habit of caching script files, which can be frustrating during testing. You don't need this in production code, however.

- ▸ `shim`: This is there to ensure that jQuery/globalize's culture files depend on the library; otherwise, they might load out of order. It's also there to let RequireJS know that the Q library exports a global variable named Q. Without it, RequireJS would expect it to load in a different manner and things wouldn't work correctly. Finally, we indicate that YASMF depends on Q so that it gets loaded in the correct order.

What else do I need to know?

Mobile devices have a soft keyboard that appears during text editing (assuming a physical keyboard isn't present). This wreaks havoc with our layout onscreen. On Android devices, Cordova shrinks the WebView to fit within the reduced space, but on iOS devices, this doesn't occur. As a result, scrolling feels very unnatural. To fix this, we can add a plugin:

```
cordova plugin add org.apache.cordova.keyboard
```

We also need to add a property to the project's `config.xml` file:

```
<preference name="KeyboardShrinksView" value="true"/>
```

Game Over..... Wrapping it up

That was quite a bit of work, but it was necessary to prepare for the next several projects where we build on this project to handle images, audio, and video. When you run the app on your device (or in your browser), it should look like the mockups at the start of this chapter.

 There's one last detail you need to know. Our use of `localStorage` in this project is simply a means to an end (that is, a shorter project even if it doesn't feel like it). Do *not* use `localStorage` if you need to store a large amount of data — the amount of data you can store in `localStorage` is limited by the browser and the platform (usually 5GB). `localStorage` is fine for user preferences and such, but for large amounts of data, it's better to use persistent storage, which do by introducing you to the File API in the next project..

Can you take the HEAT? The Hotshot Challenge

Because we've kept our templates and code separate, it is easy to change the look of the app. Why don't you try your hand at changing the layout to something of your design? Before attempting the challenge, be sure to create a duplicate of the project to use for future projects since they all build on each other.

Project 4
The File API

One critical feature of applications is that they usually need to store the user's data persistently. Until now, we've been using `localStorage` for our application, but it would be even better if we could use the device's actual filesystem.

This is where the File API comes in. It's actually not specific to Cordova; there are several browsers that support the File API (to varying degrees). The specification itself is defined by the W3C (`http://www.w3.org/TR/FileAPI/` and `http://www.w3.org/TR/file-system-api/`).

The File API gives you the ability to access your app's sandboxed filesystem. That means you can create folders and files, move them around, copy them, edit them, and delete them, just like you can with native code.

There's only one downside: the API itself is largely asynchronous, which usually means venturing into "callback hell"; not a very fun place to be. It can be incredibly difficult to debug a callback chain or prevent such a chain from devolving into spaghetti code. There's simply got to be a better way. That would be Promises. Promises are essentially a mechanism to handle dealing with "callback hell", which also means they are great to use to work with the File API. Even better, YASMF provides a wrapper around the File API that provides Promise support.

What do we build?

We'll be working on Version 2 of our Filer app. Visually, it won't look any different, but behind the scenes, we want to move away from storing notes in `localStorage` and use the filesystem instead.

What does it do?

The changes we make to the project will allow it to access the app's sandboxed file system, just like native code does. While this may not seem like a huge deal initially—after all `localStorage` worked fine—it actually helps us out a great deal down the road. For one, we're going to need access to the filesystem when it comes to adding different kinds of notes (video, audio, and so on). For another, some app stores are a bit persnickety when it comes to approving non-native apps, and they often want apps to use native features. (This is a common reason for rejection by Apple.) Although one might not immediately think of the filesystem as a native feature, it is, and it can improve the chances of an app being accepted.

Why is it great?

We'll be covering several technologies in this project: the File API, the concept of Promises, and then the YASMF's `FileManager` implementation. It's not required that you use the latter, but it saves you the pain of wrapping the File API yourself. There are other libraries that attempt to wrap the File API; some use Promises and some don't. The benefit of using Promises, however, is it makes our code so much easier to read, follow, and understand.

How are we going to do it?

This will be a short project, especially when compared with the previous project. The following is what we'll be doing:

- ▸ Covering the File API
- ▸ Covering Promises and Q.js
- ▸ Covering YASMF's `FileManager` file
- ▸ Changing the `NoteStorage` model

What do I need to get started?

If you successfully finished the previous project, you've got everything you need. If you want, you can continue to work in the same project directory, or if you want to create a new project, you can do that as well. If you create a new project, don't forget to add the plugins from the last project. Be sure to update your `config.xml` and `index.html` files as well.

Covering the File API

There are many different implementations of the File API, but Cordova's is the one we're primarily concerned with. That said, should you want to test your code in a browser, Google Chrome (v30 or higher) is a good option. It has some crucial differences too, but those are really only involved at the very beginning; after that, everything works the same way.

Getting ready

In order to use the File API in our app, we need to first add it as a plugin. Use the following command to add it:

```
cordova plugin add org.apache.cordova.file
```

If you fail to add the plugin, then the code will mysteriously fail to work when you run the app.

Getting on with it

The concept of a File API should already be familiar to you. Most environments have some access to the file system, usually through a library. This API is no different, but its implementation is somewhat onerous.

Should you ever need more information than what is in this chapter about the File API, please visit the following sites:

- http://www.w3.org/TR/file-system-api/
- http://www.w3.org/TR/FileAPI/
- https://github.com/apache/cordova-plugin-file/blob/dev/doc/index.md
- http://www.html5rocks.com/en/tutorials/file/filesystem/

Asynchronous callbacks

One of the most difficult facets of the File API is the asynchronous nature of most methods and the use of callbacks. This means that one can't perform a file operation and immediately depend on the results; it may not be done yet. This is unlike most file-handling libraries where your code waits on the result of a file-handling request.

We might have written something like the following:

```
var aFileHandle = navigator.persistentFileSystem.getFile ("example.
txt", {create: true});
aFileHandle.truncate();
```

```
aFileHandle.write ("This is some text.");
aFileHandle.close();
```

Instead, we have to write something ridiculous, such as:

```
window.requestFileSystem(LocalFileSystem.PERSISTENT,
  gotFS, fail);
function gotFS ( fs ) {
  fs.root.getFile("example.txt","', {create: true},
    gotFileEntry, fail );
}
function gotFileEntry ( fileEntry ) {
  fileEntry.createWriter ( gotFileWriter, fail );
}
function gotFileWriter ( writer ) {
  writer.onwrite = function  ( e ) {
    writer.onwrite = function ( e ) {
      weAreFinished();
    }
    writer.write ("("Some Text");");
  }
  writer.truncate();
}
function fail (e) {
  console.log ( e.code );
}
function weAreFinished () {
  console.log ( ""Hi! We wrote a file!"!" );
}
```

Two different filesystems

At an operating-system level, it's possible to have many different filesystems. Importantly, these filesystems are usually expected to be persistent. That is, the data on them is expected to be reasonably permanent (not withstanding damage, corruption, or a virus that wipes out the drive).

The File API has a persistent filesystem, but it also has a temporary filesystem. This temporary filesystem is similar to temporary directories on most modern operating systems (such as /tmp), while we don't expect the data to immediately disappear, we can't expect the data to be permanent either. How temporary the data actually is depends on a large number of factors (including the implementation of the API), but one should never trust that data saved to a temporary filesystem persists for very long.

For our purposes in this chapter, we'll only be worrying about the persistent filesystem, but it is important that you understand the temporary filesystem is there and will be used in future projects.

Requesting a quota

A quota allows you to ask the filesystem for a given amount of storage space for your data. If sufficient space is available, you'll usually get what you asked for, but it's possible you'll receive less. When using Cordova, it's important to recognize that requesting a quota is not necessary, but if you're writing code that needs to work in a browser, a quota is required.

When you ask for a quota, you need to know what filesystem you're using since you might need a large amount of temporary storage space but only a much smaller amount of persistent storage space.

In order to ask Chrome for some persistent storage, we can use the following:

```
navigator.webkitPersistentStorage.requestQuota ( theBytesWeNeed,
    success, failure );
```

The amount of storage we need is expressed in bytes, so if we expect to only need a megabyte of data, we can pass `1024 * 1024`. If we need five megabytes, we can pass `5 * 1024 * 1024`. You can, of course, calculate the actual number, but it is often easier to read in this form.

Should the quota be granted, the `success` method will be called with the granted amount of storage. This may be a different amount, so it's important to take note of the value. Should the quota be refused, the `failure` method will be called with an error code indicating what went wrong.

It's important to note that the user may be asked about the quota, so you can't assume it will be granted immediately. By the time the user responds to the request, several seconds may have passed, and if you've not waited for that response, your code has generated errors.

The user may refuse the quota, in which case you need to have a strategy to handle the refusal. It might be something like displaying an alert, or the app could fall back on some other storage mechanism.

Requesting a filesystem

Once a quota has been requested and approved, we can ask the browser for the actual filesystem. This is necessary to get access to methods that work on the filesystem, including reading or writing files, creating folders, and so on.

While one wouldn't normally ask for a quota using Cordova, it is required that you ask for a filesystem in both Cordova and desktop browsers.

When asking for a filesystem, we pass the granted quota along with the request. In Cordova, this will generally be zero, but in a web browser, it will be the amount of storage we are permitted to use.

The following shows how we can ask for a filesystem in Chrome:

```
window.webkitRequestFileSystem ( PERSISTENT, quota, success, failure
);
```

In Cordova, we can ask for it in the following way:

```
window.requestFileSystem ( LocalFileSystem.PERSISTENT, quota, success,
failure );
```

If the request works, the `success` method will be called with the filesystem as a parameter. From that point on, our code can use the filesystem to manage files and directories. Should the request fail, however, the `failure` method will be called with an appropriate error message.

The differences in the preceding code are:

- Chrome puts a `webkit` prefix in front of `requestFileSystem`
- Chrome defines `PERSISTENT` and `TEMPORARY` globally, whereas Cordova defines them on the `LocalFileSystem` object

To support both cases, we can do something like the following:

```
var PERSISTENT = (typeof LocalFileSystem !== "undefined") ?
LocalFileSystem.PERSISTENT : window.PERSISTENT;
var requestFileSystem = window.webkitRequestFileSystem || window.
requestFileSystem;
requestFileSystem ( PERSISTENT, quota, success, failure );
```

A `fileSystem` object contains a very important property: `root`. It gives us access to the root directory of the filesystem. Now, in no way does this give your app access to the root directory on your computer or mobile device as the File API is always sandboxed. Thus, even if you delete everything in the returned filesystem, you can't hurt your device or your computer if something goes wrong.

What the root directory does give us is a starting point for all our other operations, whether they be creating, reading, or writing files; creating directories; and so on.

Android is an exception

Android tends to store the files on the SD card (or the emulated SD card on those devices without expandable storage). This means that it really is possible to wipe out parts of the SD card. If you aren't sure of your code, put in a newly formatted SD card while testing; that way, you don't obliterate any of your important data.

Directory entries

The `root` property of `fileSystem` is considered a `DirectoryEntry` object. Any directory, even a subdirectory, has a `DirectoryEntry` object. If your filesystem is empty, the only `DirectoryEntry` object is the `root` directory.

Getting the `root DirectoryEntry` is easy:

```
var rootDirectoryEntry = fileSystem.root;
```

Getting a subdirectory, on the other hand, isn't quite as simple:

```
fileSystem.root.getDirectory ( "example", options, success,
    failure );
```

The preceding code would pass `DirectoryEntry` to the `success` method, assuming there is an `example` directory in the `root` directory. If there isn't, the `failure` method will be called with an error (the errors code should be `FileError.NOT_FOUND_ERR`).

Note that you can provide a path relative to `DirectoryEntry` if you want, for example:

```
fileSystem.root.getDirectory ( "artists/JohnDoe", options,
    success, failure );
```

The `options` parameter is an object consisting of two optional properties:

▸ `create`: If `true`, this creates the directory. If the directory doesn't exist and the value is `false`, the function will fail.

▸ `exclusive`: If `true` (and used with the preceding property set to `true`), this creates the directory only if the directory didn't already exist. If the directory exists and both properties are `true`, the function fails.

`DirectoryEntry` has a lot of properties and methods that are important. We won't cover every one, but a good list is given next. Be sure to consult the specification and Cordova documentation as well, as these may have changed. (Technically, the `success` and `failure` parameters are optional, but this is not encouraged for production apps.)

▸ `isFile: false`

▸ `isDirectory: true`

- ▸ `fullPath`: This gives the absolute path of the directory (from the root `DirectoryEntry`) such as, `/example` or `/artists/JohnDoe`

- ▸ `name`: This gives the name of the directory (`example` or `JohnDoe` as we just saw)

- ▸ `copyTo( targetDirectoryEntry, [newName], success, failure )`: This copies the directory to a different `DirectoryEntry` file with an optional new name

- ▸ `createReader()`: This creates a `DirectoryReader` object (to get a list of files and directories within `DirectoryEntry`)

- ▸ `getDirectory( path, options, success, failure )`: This gets `DirectoryEntry`, relative to this `DirectoryEntry`

- ▸ `getFile( path, options, success, failure )`: This gets `FileEntry`, relative to this `DirectoryEntry`

- ▸ `getMetadata( success, failure )`: This gets metadata about this `DirectoryEntry` file

- ▸ `getParent( success, failure )`: This gets the parent `DirectoryEntry` object

- ▸ `moveTo( targetDirectoryEntry, [newName], success, failure )`: This moves `DirectoryEntry` to a different `DirectoryEntry` object

- ▸ `remove( success, failure )`: This removes `DirectoryEntry` (it must be empty)

- ▸ `removeRecursively( success, failure )`: This removes `DirectoryEntry` (and all its contents)

- ▸ `setMetadata( success, failure, metadata )`: This sets metadata about this `DirectoryEntry`

- ▸ `toURL()`: This returns a URL representation of the `DirectoryEntry` path (`cdvfile://localhost/persistent/example`)

File entries

Like `DirectoryEntry`, each file in the filesystem has a `FileEntry`. This can be retrieved by asking `DirectoryEntry` for the file using `getFile()`. If you don't have a `DirectoryEntry` object, use the filesystem's root `DirectoryEntry`:

```
aDirectoryEntry.getFile ("file.txt", options, success, failure );
```

We can also specify a path to the file, relative to `DirectoryEntry`:

```
aDirectoryEntry.getFile ("path/to/file.txt", options, success,
  failure );
```

The `options` parameter here is just like the one used to get `DirectoryEntry`.

If the file can be retrieved (or created), the `success` method is called with a `FileEntry` object. If it can't be retrieved (or created), the `failure` method is called with an error code. Inspect the error code as it will indicate why the failure occurred.

`FileEntry` has a lot of useful properties and methods listed as follows (be sure to check the specification and Cordova documentation in case these have changed since the writing of this does not make sense):

- `isFile`: `true`
- `isDirectory`: `false`
- `fullPath`: The absolute path from the root `DirectoryEntry` to this file
- `name`: The name of the file (minus the path)
- `copyTo( targetDirectoryEntry, [newName], success, failure )`: This copies the file to another `DirectoryEntry` (with an optional new name)
- `createWriter()`: This creates a `FileWriter` object (used to write data to a file)
- `file( success, failure )`: This creates a `File` object (suitable to read data from a file)
- `getMetadata( success, failure )`: This gets metadata for the `FileEntry` object
- `getParent( success, failure )`: This gets the parent `DirectoryEntry`
- `moveTo( targetDirectoryEntry, [newName], success, failure )`: This moves the file to another `DirectoryEntry` (with an optional new name)
- `remove( success, failure )`: This removes `FileEntry`
- `setMetadata( success, failure, metadata )`: This sets metadata for the `FileEntry` object
- `toURL()`: This gets a URL representation of the `FileEntry` path

Reading the contents and properties of a file

`FileEntry` itself does not provide much information about the file or the data contained within the file. For example, `FileEntry` does not tell you anything about the size of the file, the type of the file, or when it was last modified. To get that information or to read the data from it, we have to get a `File` object.

To get a `File` object, we first need a `FileEntry` object. Then we can do the following:

```
aFileEntry.file( success, failure );
```

Unless something goes horribly awry, the `success` method will be called with the `File` object. If the `failure` method is called, it will be called with an error code indicating why it failed.

Once you have the `File` object, you can get information about the file using the following properties:

- `name`: This gives the name of the file
- `fullPath`: This gives the absolute path to the file
- `lastModifiedDate`: This gives the last modification date
- `size`: This gives the size of the file (in bytes)
- `type`: This gives the MIME type of the file

A `File` object also has one method, `slice()`, which returns a new `File` object. It's useful for reading only a portion of a file, but we won't be using it in our projects.

To actually read a file, we have to make a `FileReader` object and pass the file along for the ride. Once we have that, we need to subscribe to various events in order to know what is going on and whether or not we're done.

For example, have a look at the following code:

```
var reader = new FileReader ();
reader.onload = function ( e ) {
  var fileContents = e.target.result;
}
reader.onerror = function ( e ) {
  // error is e.code
}
reader.readAsText ( theFile );
```

Where we've always had a `success` and a `failure` method, this time we have events and have to listen to them. The following are the events a `FileReader` object can have:

- `onloadstart`: This is fired when the load begins
- `onload`: This is fired when the read is successful
- `onabort`: This is fired when the read is aborted
- `onerror`: This is fired if an error occurs
- `onloadend`: This is fired when the read is complete (whether successful or not)

A `FileReader` object also has various properties that you can query:

- ▶ `error`: This gives the contents of an error (if one has been generated)
- ▶ `readyState`: This has one of three possible states: DONE, EMPTY, and LOADING
- ▶ `result`: This gives the contents of the file (assuming it's been read)

The `FileReader` object has the following methods:

- ▶ `abort()`: This stops the reading of a file
- ▶ `readAsArrayBuffer( file )`: This reads the file as an array buffer
- ▶ `readAsBinaryString( file )`: This reads the file as a binary file (not a text file)
- ▶ `readAsDataURL( file )`: This reads the file and gets the data as a base64-encoded data URL
- ▶ `readAsText( file )`: This reads the file and gets the data as plain text

Writing data to a file

To write data to a file, we need a `FileWriter` object, which we can only create from a `FileEntry` object. As with a `FileReader` object, we need to subscribe to events in order to know whether things have worked or not. For example, consider the following code:

```
function gotWriter ( writer) {
  writer.onwrite = function ( e ) {
    writer.onwrite = function ( e ) {
      // the file has been written
    }
    writer.write ( new Blob (["Some contents"],
    {type: 'plain/text'}) );
    }
    writer.onerror = function ( e ) {
      // error is e.code
    }
    writer.truncate (0);
  }
aFileEntry.createWriter(gotWriter, failure);
```

A `FileWriter` object has the following events:

- ▶ `onwritestart`: This is fired when the write begins
- ▶ `onwrite`: This is fired when a write completes successfully
- ▶ `onabort`: This is fired when a write is aborted
- ▶ `onerror`: This is fired when there is an error
- ▶ `onwriteend`: It is fired when the operation is complete (whether successfully or not)

The `FileWriter` object has the following properties:

- ▸ `fileName`: This gives the name of the file
- ▸ `length`: This gives the length of the file
- ▸ `position`: This gives the current position in the file
- ▸ `readyState`: This can have one of three possible states: DONE, INIT, WRITING

The `FileWriter` object has the following methods:

- ▸ `abort()`: This stops the writing of the file
- ▸ `seek( toPosition )`: This moves the file pointer to the specified position (in bytes)
- ▸ `truncate( bytes )`: This truncates the file to the specified size (in bytes)
- ▸ `write( data )`: This writes the data to the file

Be certain to truncate!

When writing to a file, be sure to truncate it first; otherwise, depending on the browser you are using, you may see data from previous writes in the file.

Getting the entries in DirectoryEntry

Many times, you need to know the actual content of `DirectoryEntry`. Much like reading a file, we need `DirectoryReader` to accomplish this. We can only get a `DirectoryReader` object from a `DirectoryEntry`.

For example, consider the following code:

```
var directoryReader = theDirectoryEntry.createReader();
var entries = [];
function readEntries() {
  directoryReader.readEntries (
    function success ( theEntries ) {
      if (!theEntries.length) {
        // entries has all the directory and file entries
      }
      else {
        entries = entries.concat ( Array.prototype.slice.call (
          theEntries || [], 0 ) );
        readEntries();
      }
```

```
        },
        function failure (e) { }
        );
    }
    readEntries();
```

Depending on the implementation, the `readEntries()` method may or may not return all the entries in one go. Therefore, it's important for you to know that you may see several lists of entries. If you do, concatenate them like we did earlier. Because the list of entries isn't a proper JavaScript array, you can convert it into one using `Array.prototype.slice.call()`.

Copying and moving

Copying and moving files and directories is simple, especially when compared to reading and writing files. All we need is a `FileEntry` file that represents the file we want to copy, and a `DirectoryEntry` file that represents the target directory. Of course, this means multiple levels of callbacks, like so:

```
var sourceFileEntry;
function success () {…}
function failure( e ) {…}
function gotDirectoryEntry ( theDirectoryEntry ) {
  sourceFileEntry.copyTo ( theDirectoryEntry, null, success,
  failure );
}
function gotFileEntry ( theFileEntry ) {
  sourceFileEntry = theFileEntry;
  theFileSystem.root.getDirectory ( "some/other/directory", {},
    gotDirectoryEntry, failure );
}
theFileSystem.root.getFile ( "some/path/to/file.txt", {},
gotFileEntry, failure );
```

Copying a directory works the same way, except we need two directory entries. Moving works similarly (just use `moveTo`).

Both methods support the copy/move operation with a new name. Simply pass a new name in the second parameter:

```
aFileEntry.moveTo ( anotherDirectoryEntry, "newName.txt", success,
failure );
```

Removing files and directories

Removing files and directories is also pretty simple. You need the corresponding `FileEntry` or `DirectoryEntry` entries, and then simply call `remove()`:

```
theFileEntry.remove( success, failure );
```

When you call `remove()` on a directory, the directory must be empty or the operation will fail. If you want to remove a directory without it needing to be empty, call `removeRecursively()`.

There's even more...

There's quite a bit more we can do with the filesystem, including handling metadata, file transfers, and such, but for now, this is sufficient. If you want to look up additional information, use the links provided at the beginning of this section.

What did we do?

In this section, we covered some of the more commonly used features in the File API. If you had any difficulty thinking about all those callbacks and how far they really can (and often do) nest, then you're not alone. There's simply got to be a better way, and thankfully, there is!

What else do I need to know?

The W3C specifications are still in flux, as are the implementations of the specification. If you find out that some portion of code is failing or notice that a property or method has a new name, don't fret. This is normal. There's usually a list of changes in new updates that indicate how older code should be modified in order for it to work correctly with the newer File API. Although this is technically one of the dangers browser developers face when they implement APIs that aren't yet finalized, it's far too useful an API to ignore, especially given that `localStorage` isn't guaranteed to be persistent.

Covering Promises and Q.js

As we said before, there's simply got to be a better way to deal with the callback hell that the File API has caused us to suffer. There is, but it takes a little bit of work to get there. For very simple operations, it might not always be worth it, but when you need to chain many operations together, having Promises really pays off.

Getting on with it

You've seen a glimpse of what callback hell looks like. It can get far, far worse. If you'll pardon the pun, Promises promise to alleviate the headache.

For the low-down on this, you might want to take a look at the Promises/A+ specification at `http://promises-aplus.github.io/promises-spec/`. Note that it doesn't provide any code; the specification leaves it up to other libraries to implement the specification. Q.js is but one; there are many others you can use. Generally, as long as they indicate they implement the specification, they can all be used in very similar ways (though each may have their own additional features).

A Promise is a representation of an eventual value returned by a method that might take an undetermined amount of time, such as when dealing with asynchronous methods. A Promise returned from a function indicates "I have to do this asynchronously; here's a Promise that I'll eventually return a result."

It would be great, then, if we could rewrite some of our file-handling code to something more like the following:

```
window.requestFileSystem ( PERSISTENT, 1024*1024 )
.then ( function ( fileSystem ) {
  return fileSystem.getFileEntry ("/some/file.txt", {}); }
.then ( function ( fileEntry ) {
  return fileEntry.readFileContents(); }
.then ( function ( theContents ) {
  console.log ( theContents ); }
.catch ( function ( e ) {
  console.log ( e ); }
.done ();
```

While not the most beautiful code, it's much improved over the callback hell we've been working with, isn't it?

Wrapping the File API

The only downside is that browsers don't come with native support for Promises (yet), and nor does the File API. This means we have to wrap the File API.

To do this, we can create a method that returns a Promise for each File API method. Let's use getting a `FileEntry` object as an example:

```
function getFileEntry ( theParentDirectoryEntry, theFileName,
  options ) {
  var deferred = Q.defer();
```

```
theParentDirectoryEntry.getFileEntry ( theFileName, options,
    function success ( theFileEntry ) { deferred.resolve (
        theFileEntry ); },
    function failure ( anError ) { deferred.reject ( anError );  }
);
return deferred.promise;
}
```

There are two ways to make a Promise: `Q()` and `Q.defer()`. You can use `Q()` when the Promise will return immediately, but this doesn't work for the File API. Instead, `Q.defer()` works for asynchronous methods when we aren't sure when the result will be known.

Once we create it, we call our asynchronous method in the usual manner. We need to handle the `success` and `failure` methods as well, but unlike before, all we need to do is specify whether we're resolving or rejecting the Promise. By calling `resolve()`, we can specify the return value of the method (in this case, `FileEntry`), and by calling `reject()`, we can specify why the Promise was rejected.

At the end of the method, we return the Promise. In actual practice, the control flow will return this Promise before the File API has had a chance to generate a success or failure, and so control to the calling method is also returned well before a `FileEntry` object has been returned or not. This doesn't seem to do us any good, except that we can use the `then` method of the returned Promise to indicate that we need to wait for a return value and then call something else with it. It's a roundabout way of inverting the callback tree if you really want to look at it that way, but it's a lot easier to follow this way. So now, if we needed to do something that depended on our Promise, we could write the following:

```
getFileEntry ( theParentDirectoryEntry, "aFile.txt", {} )
.then ( // do something with it )
.catch ( function ( e ) { // do something with the error } )
.done ();
```

The `catch` method is useful in that it traps any thrown errors in the chain, which makes error handling simple. It's equivalent to a `try { ... } catch { ... }` block. There's also a `finally` method that is useful for handling clean-up code that needs to be executed whether or not the chain succeeds or fails.

Finally, `done` at the bottom, signals to Q that the chain is finished. While not ideal, it's wise to have it at the end of a chain for now. (Q.js is looking at a way to avoid this in the future.)

So far, all our Promises have been dealing with single parameters in the chain. What if you needed two, perhaps to copy a file to a directory? We can use `spread` for that:

```
getFileSystem ( PERSISTENT, 1024 * 1024 )
.then ( function ( fileSystem ) {
    return [fileSystem.root.getFileEntry( "path/to/file.txt", {} ),
```

```
        fileSystem.getDirectoryEntry ( "path/to/directory", {} )] }
    .spread ( function ( fileEntry, directoryEntry ) {
        return copyFileToDirectory (fileEntry, directoryEntry); }
    .catch ( function ( e ) { console.log (e.code); } )
    .done ();
```

If you ever need to return multiple Promises at the beginning of a chain, you can do so using `Q.all ( [Promise1, Promise2]] )`.

Now, if only there was a library out there that wrapped the File API up into nice Promises for us, right? It turns out that YASMF has one, and we'll go over that in the next section.

There are many, many other features and possibilities that come with using Q.js. I urge you to check out the documentation at `https://github.com/kriskowal/q`.

What did we do?

In this section, you learned about Promises and how they make the control flow of asynchronous programming easier to read and follow. You also learned how to wrap methods from the File API up into Promises.

Covering YASMF's FileManager file

YASMF's `FileManager` file simply wraps the File API using Promises (and Q.js specifically). It simplifies some of the API calls as well by maintaining the idea of a current working directory (much like your command line or terminal does). Although nothing says you have to use YASMF in your code, you might want to consider at least using the `FileManager` file. You can get a script that has minimal dependencies from YASMF's site.

Getting ready

If you want to view the code behind YASMF's `FileManager` file, visit `https://github.com/photokandyStudios/YASMF-Next/blob/master/lib/yasmf/util/fileManager.js`. You should be able to notice the similarities between the way in which we wrapped the File API in the previous section with how the code is written.

Getting on with it

YASMF's `FileManager` file provides a simpler way to deal with the File API using Promises. First, one instantiates a new `FileManager` and then initializes `FileManager` by asking for a filesystem and a quota:

```
var fm = new _y.FileManager();
fm.init ( fm.PERSISTENT, 1024 * 1024 )
```

Because init() returns a Promise, you can then attach then, catch, and finally to the chain and that code will wait until the File API has been initialized.

It also abstracts out the need to figure out which PERSISTENT object to use; do we use LocalFileSystem.PERSISTENT or just window.PERSISTENT? YASMF figures that out for us. Also abstracted out is whether or not we need to ask for a quota; if a quota is required, it will ask for it, and if a quota isn't required, it won't.

> That's not to say the quota isn't important. It is, and if you want to figure out what the returned quota actually is, you can look at the value in fm.actualQuota.

Now that everything is initialized, it becomes easy to do work on the filesystem. For example, if we want to enumerate the entries in a directory, we just do the following:

```
fm.init ( fm.PERSISTENT, 1024 * 1024 )
  .then ( function () { return fm.readDirectoryContents (
fm.fileSystem.root, {} ); }
  .then ( function ( theEntries ) { console.log (theEntries); }
  .done();
```

The following are some useful properties of FileManager:

▸ PERSISTENT, TEMPORARY: These are constants for the persistent and temporary filesystems

▸ FILETYPE: This contains TEXT, DATA_URL, BINARY, and ARRAY_BUFFER

▸ fileSystemType: This gives the type of filesystem requested at init() time

▸ requestedQuota: This gives the quota requested at init() time

▸ actualQuota: This gives the quota actually granted at init() time

▸ cwd / currentWorkingDirectory: These give the current working directory (by default, root)

FileManager has the following proxies to the File API, all of which return Promises:

▸ getFileURL (path) / getDirectoryURL (path): These return a URL that refers to the file or directory. Here, path is relative to the current working directory.

▸ resolveFileSystemURL (theURL): This returns the file entry that maps to the specified URL. It is used when we are given a full path to a file from a plugin but don't know how it maps to our filesystem.

▸ getFileEntry (path) / getDirectoryEntry (path): These return the actual FileEntry or DirectoryEntry object. Here, path is relative to the current working directory.

- getFileURL (path) / getDirectoryURL (path): These return a URL string that represents the path of the file or directory (for example, cdvfile:// localhost/persistent/path/to/file.txt).

- changeDirectory (path): This changes the current working directory to the path specified; path is relative to the current working directory.

- readFileContents (path, options, kind): This reads the file specified by path (relative to the current working directory) using the specified options (or { } if not specified). Use FILETYPE constants for the kind.

- readDirectoryContents (path, options): This reads the directory entries at the path (relative to the current working directory, so use "." if you want to read the current working directory's entries) using the specified options. The entries are returned as an array of FileEntries and DirectoryEntries.

- writeFileContents (path, options, data): This writes the data to the file at path (relative to the current working directory) using the specified options. The type of file written depends on the type of data passed; typically, you would pass the data in Blob.

- createDirectory (path): This creates a directory relative to the current working directory.

- copyFile (pathToFile, pathToDirectory, newName): This copies a file (specified via pathToFile) to a directory (specified by pathToDirectory). If newName is specified, it also gets a new name. To duplicate a file in the current working directory, use ".", for example, copyFile ("fileA.txt", ".", "fileB.txt").

- moveFile (pathToFile, pathToDirectory, newName): This moves a file to a directory with an optional new name. To rename a file in the current directory, use moveFile ("fileA.txt", ".", "fileB.txt").

- copyDirectory (sourceDirectory, targetDirectory, newName): Instead of copying a file, it copies a directory. The directory is copied recursively.

- moveDirectory (sourceDirectory, targetDirectory, newName): Instead of moving a file, it moves a directory. The directory is copied recursively.

- deleteFile (pathToFile): This deletes the file from the system (path is relative to the current working directory).

- removeDirectory (pathToDirectory, recursively): This removes the directory. If the second parameter is true, it is removed recursively. If it is false, the directory is removed only if it is empty.

Not every feature of the File API is wrapped, unfortunately, but most of them are. When you encounter one that isn't, you can wrap it with a Promise using instructions from the previous section.

Just so you know...

Most of the APIs that accept paths also accept the `FileEntry` and `DirectoryEntry` objects. This means we don't require an intervening call to try and dig out the full path from an entry just to do something with it.

What did we do?

In this section, you learned about YASMF's integrated support for wrapping the File API with Promises.

Changing the Note Storage model

Now that we've gone through the File API, Promises, and YASMF's `FileManager`, it's time to update our `NoteStorage` model to support the new storage mechanism. Almost nothing else needs to change. The look and feel of the app will still function in the same way, but it will use the filesystem for storing notes instead of `LocalStorage`.

Getting ready

Android versions prior to 4.4 (KitKat) don't natively support easy creation of `Blob`—what we use to save files to storage. In order to fix this, we need to create a polyfill that will provide this support without having to make changes to the rest of our code.

To do this, create a new file at `www/js/lib/Blob.js`:

```
// Copyright (c) 2013 The Chromium Authors. All rights reserved.
// Use of this source code is governed by a BSD-style license that can
be
// found in the LICENSE file.
// last line modification by Kerri Shotts for PhoneGap Hotshot
try {
  new Blob([]);
} catch (e) {
  var nativeBlob = window.Blob;
  var newBlob = function(parts, options) {
    if (window.WebKitBlobBuilder) {
      var bb = new WebKitBlobBuilder();
      if (parts && parts.length) {
```

```
      for (var i=0; i < parts.length; i++) {
        bb.append(parts[i]);
      }
    }
    if (options && options.type) {
      return bb.getBlob(options.type);
    }
    return bb.getBlob();
  }
}
newBlob.prototype = nativeBlob.prototype;
window.Blob = newBlob; // clobber the global
}
```

This should be identical to the file at `https://github.com/MobileChromeApps/chrome-cordova/blob/master/plugins/polyfill-blob-constructor/Blob.js`, save for the last line. This clobbers the original `Blob` type (which doesn't work) and assigns the new `Blob` object (that does work). It's not a complicated polyfill, and on any other platform, it does nothing; however, without it, Android 4.3 and lower fail to work.

We're almost done, but we also need to add a line (highlighted in the following code) to `index.html` to load this script so it's ready to work on Android devices:

```
...
<body>
  <script type="text/javascript" src="cordova.js"></script>
  <script type="text/javascript" src="js/lib/Blob.js"></script>
  <script type="text/javascript" src="js/lib/require.js" data
    -main="js/app.js"></script>
</body>
...
```

Getting on with it

Change the `noteStorage.js` file at `www/js/app/models` as follows. First, we need to add a section of code to create a property for our `FileManager`:

```
self._fileManager = null;
self.getFileManager = function () {
  return self._fileManager;
}
Object.defineProperty ( self, "fileManager", {get:
  self.getFileManager, configurable: true});
```

Next, add a method that initializes `FileManager` when needed. Note that it also creates an internal directory called `com.packtpub.phonegaphotshot.filer`. This keeps us from putting files into the root directory on an SD card when this is running on an Android device:

```
self._initializeFileManager = function () {
  if (self._fileManager === null) {
    var deferred = Q.defer();
    var fm   = new _y.FileManager();
    self._fileManager = fm;
    fm.init ( fm.PERSISTENT, 1024*1024 )
    .then ( function () { return fm.createDirectory (
      "com.packtpub.phonegaphotshot.filer" ); } )
    .then ( fm.changeDirectory )
    .then ( function ()     { deferred.resolve(); } )
    .catch ( function ( e ) { deferred.reject ( e ); } )
    .done();
    return deferred.promise;
  }
  else {
    return Q(); // already initialized
  }
}
```

Next, we need to indicate how to parse the contents of a note, given some JSON:

```
self._parseNoteContents = function ( theNoteType, aNoteJSON ) {
  var aNote = noteFactory.createNote ( theNoteType );
  if ( aNote.initWithJSON ( aNoteJSON ) ) {
    self._notes [aNote.uid] = aNote;
    return;
  }
  else {
    throw new Error ( "Couldn't initWithJSON" );
  }
}
```

Now we need to parse the contents of a collection once it is loaded (note the use of `Q.all` to return each Promise for every note in the collection):

```
self._parseCollectionContents = function ( allNoteIDsJSON ) {
  var fm = self._fileManager;
  self._notes = {};
  if ( allNoteIDsJSON !== null ) {
    try {
      var allNoteIDs = JSON.parse (allNoteIDsJSON );
```

```
          var allNotePromises = [];
          allNoteIDs.forEach ( function (theNote) {
            allNotePromises.push (
              fm.readFileContents ( "note" + theNote.UID + ".txt", {},
                fm.FILETYPE.TEXT)
            .then ( function ( theNoteJSON ) { return [ theNote.type,
              theNoteJSON ]; } )
              .spread ( self._parseNoteContents )
          );
        });
      return Q.all(allNotePromises);
    }
    catch ( e ) {
      self.notify ( "collectionFailedLoading", [e.message] );
      throw e;
    }
    }
    else {
      return Q();
    }
  }
```

A small change needs to be made to `loadCollection()` as well:

```
  self.loadCollection = function () {
    self.notify ( "collectionLoading" );
    self._initializeFileManager()
    .then ( function fileSystemInited() {
      var fm = self._fileManager;
      return fm.readFileContents ( "notes.txt", {},
        fm.FILETYPE.TEXT);
    } )
    .then ( self._parseCollectionContents )
    .then ( function notifyComplete () { self.notify
      ("collectionLoaded"); return; } )
    .catch ( function anErrorHappened ( anError ) {
      self.notify ( "collectionFailedLoading", [anError.message] );
      return;
    })
    .done ();
  }
```

Of course, we need to modify `saveCollection()` appropriately as well (the changed portion is highlighted):

```
self.saveCollection = function () {
  self.notify ( "collectionSaving" );
  try {
    var allNoteIDs = [];
    var aNote;
    for ( var aNoteUID in self._notes ) {
      if (self._notes.hasOwnProperty(aNoteUID)) {
        aNote = self._notes[aNoteUID];
        if ( aNote !== null ) {
          allNoteIDs.push ( {UID: aNote.UID, type: aNote.class} );
        }
      }
    }
    var allNoteIDsJSON = JSON.stringify ( allNoteIDs );
    self._initializeFileManager ()
    .then ( function fileSystemInited() {
      var fm = self._fileManager;
      return fm.writeFileContents ( "notes.txt", { create: true,
        exclusive: false},
        new Blob ( [allNoteIDsJSON], {type: 'text/plain'} ));
      })
    .then ( function colletionSaved() {
      self.notify ("collectionSaved");
      return;
    } )
    .catch ( function anErrorHappened (anError)  {
      self.notify ("collectionFailedSaving", [anError.message] );
      return;
    } )
    .done ();
  }
  catch ( anError )
  {
    self.notify ("collectionFailedSaving", [anError.message] );
  }
}
```

We also need to change `createNote()` (so that we are ready for future note types). Again, the highlighted content is the portion that has changed. Note that where we used to return the actual note, we now return a Promise. This is to account for the possibility that we might need to create a media file in the future:

```
self.createNote = function ( noteType ) {
  var aNote = noteFactory.createNote ( noteType ||
    noteFactory.TEXTNOTE );
  var noteUID = _generateUID();
  var newMediaFileName = noteFactory.createAssociatedMediaFileName
    ( noteType || noteFactory.TEXTNOTE,
    noteUID );
  aNote.initWithOptions ( { "uid": noteUID,
    "name": _y.T("app.ns.A_NEW_NOTE"),
    "textContents": _y.T("app.ns.WHATS_ON_YOUR_MIND"),
    "mediaContents": newMediaFileName
  } );
  self._notes [ aNote.uid ] = aNote;

  var fm = self.fileManager;
  var deferred = Q.defer();
  if (newMediaFileName !== "") {
    fm.getFileEntry ( newMediaFileName, {create: true, exclusive:
      false} )
    .then ( function gotFile ( theFile )
    { aNote.mediaContents = theFile.fullPath;
    self.notify ( "noteCreated", [ aNote.uid ] );
    self.saveNote ( aNote );
    deferred.resolve (aNote);
    })
    .catch ( function ( anError ) { deferred.reject ( anError ); }
      )
    .done ();
  }
  else {
    deferred.resolve (aNote);
    self.notify ( "noteCreated", [ aNote.uid ] );
    self.saveNote ( aNote );
  }
  return deferred.promise;
};
```

We also need to be able to save a single note to persistent storage:

```
self.saveNote = function ( theNote ) {
  try {
    var theJSON = theNote.JSON;
    self._initializeFileManager()
    .then ( function fileSystemInited()
      { var fm = self._fileManager;
      return fm.writeFileContents ( "note" + theNote.uid + ".txt",
        { create: true, exclusive: false },
        new Blob ( [theJSON], {type: 'text/plain' } ) );
      })
    .then ( function noteSaved() {
      self.notify ( "noteSaved", [ theNote.uid ] );
      self.notify ( "collectionChanged" );
      return;
    })
    .catch ( function anErrorHappened ( anError ) {
      self.notify ( "noteFailedSaving", [ theNote, anError.message
        ] );
      return;
    })
    .done();
  }
  catch ( e ) {
    self.notify ( "noteFailedSaving", [ theNote, e.message ] );
  }
}
```

Lastly, when we remove a note, we want to remove the file, so we need to adjust `removeNote()` as well (note that the media file is also removed if it exists).

```
self.removeNote= function ( theUID ) {
  try {
    self._initializeFileManager()
    .then ( function fileSystemInited() {
      var fm = self._fileManager;
      return fm.deleteFile ( "note" + theUID + ".txt" );
    })
    .then ( function fileDeleted() {
      var fm = self._fileManager;
      var aNote = self.getNote ( theUID );
      self._notes [ theUID ] = null;
      self.notify ( "noteRemoved", [ theUID ] );
      self.notify ( "collectionChanged" );
```

```
      if (aNote.mediaContents !== null ) {
        return fm.deleteFile ( aNote.mediaContents );
      }
      return;
    } )
    .catch ( function anErrorHappened ( anError ) {
      self.notify ( "noteFailedRemoving", [ theUID,
        anError.message ] );
      return;
    })
    .done ();
  }
  catch ( e ) {
    self.notify ( "noteFailedRemoving", [ theUID, e.message ] );
  }
}
```

There's only one other thing we must do; now that `createNote` returns a Promise, we must also alter `_createAndEditNote()` in `noteListView` (www/js/app/views/noteListView):

```
self._createAndEditNote = function (noteType) {
  noteStorageSingleton.createNote(noteType)
  .then(function (aNewNote) {
    var aNoteEditView =
      noteViewFactory.createNoteEditView(noteType);
    aNoteEditView.initWithOptions({note: aNewNote, parent:
      self.parentElement});
  })
  .catch(function (anError) { console.log(anError) })
  .done();
}
```

What did we do?

In this section, we successfully modified our `NoteStorage` model to use the File API. We also modified the `noteListView` file as needed to correctly interface with the change in the model.

One thought about how we create the `FileManager` object: there's no need to initialize it more than once (although it wouldn't hurt), and so we create a deferred Promise around the initialization of `FileManager` if it hasn't previously been created. If it has been created, we just return a blank Promise using `Q()`. As part of the initialization, we create a new directory for our files. This is not necessary on iOS but is critical on Android (otherwise, we might store the content in the root of an SD card). Since it doesn't hurt iOS to have it, we don't make the distinction.

What else do I need to know?

If the collection is empty, the collection actually fails to load, and so we don't generate a template in our `noteListView` file. That's okay, because the list should be empty anyway. It is just something to be aware of, however, in case you were doing other things (such as displaying something else if the collection was empty).

There's also one other detail you need to be aware of. The File API plugin that Cordova uses has a setting that determines where the persistent filesystem is actually stored. By default, this points to the SD card (if available; otherwise, it points to the internal storage) on Android, and on iOS, it points to the app's sandboxed `Documents` directory.

This isn't always where you should store data. For example, iOS makes a distinction between user-generated content and content that can be regenerated (typically, cached information, but this may also be preloaded information that comes with your app). On Android, you can forcibly indicate that the data should be stored internally rather than on the SD card (especially if you want to ensure no other programs are looking at your data on non-rooted devices).

The Android preference is called `AndroidPersistentFileLocation` and can take one of two values:

- `Internal`: This will store the persistent filesystem on internal storage
- `Compatibility`: This will store the persistent filesystem on the SD card, if available or under `/data/data` if that isn't available

The iOS preference is called `iOSPersistentFileLocation` and can take one of two values:

- `Library`: This will store the persistent filesystem in the `Library` directory (which is where content that can be regenerated should be stored)
- `Compatibility`: This will store the persistent filesystem in the `Documents` directory (which is where user-generated content should be stored)

These preferences can be added to the `config.xml` file. For example, for our app, you'd probably want to use the following:

```
<preference name="iosPersistentFileLocation" value="Compatibility" />
<preference name="AndroidPersistentFileLocation" value="Compatibility"
/>
```

Since these are the defaults, we didn't specify them in our own project, but it is possible that, at some point in the future, it will become a requirement to indicate which location the persistent filesystem should live in.

Game Over..... Wrapping it up

While we didn't have to do nearly as much in this chapter as in the last chapter, it still required us to deal with callback hell and the File API. We also learned about how Promises help mitigate the pain a bit by allowing us to chain calls together instead of having callbacks strewn everywhere. We then looked at YASMF's implementation of the File API using Promises. Finally, we updated our `NoteStorage` model to use persistent storage.

Can you take the HEAT? The Hotshot Challenge

It might be cool to add support for multiple collections to the app. This would require you to add an extra view (in front of the `NoteList` view) so that you can display the available collections. This would also eliminate the use of `NoteStorageSingleton`; you'd be able to have as many `NoteStorage` objects as you wanted. Although you don't have to use folders, it wouldn't hurt to make each collection its own folder.

Project 5
Working with Audio

The media capabilities of our mobile devices are amazing, especially when you consider where we were just a few years ago. The first mass-produced MP3 player was the *SaeHan/ Eiger MPMan* introduced in 1997. The device had 32 MB of storage, enough for roughly 6-7 songs. While this may seem severely limited by today's standards, it was a revolution and offered a new way to listen to music. The history of portable media players is fascinating. For more information, you can refer to `http://en.wikipedia.org/wiki/Portable_media_player`.

Today's devices are capable of so much more. Portable entertainment devices can play games, video, and all sorts of audio. Although not absolutely required, many apps use sound to some degree, especially if it is to call attention to something important. *TweetBot* is a classic example of an app that is enhanced by the sound it produces via the user's interactions.

Today's devices can also record audio for a variety of purposes, whether for a reminder later, a speech or meeting, or something else entirely. There are a lot of apps that don't require this functionality, but for a certain segment of apps, it's important that you know how to record.

What do we build?

So far, our Filer app can only handle one kind of note: a text note. In this project, we'll expand its capabilities to include audio recordings as well as text notes. We'll include both recording and playback.

We'll also work with gestures and animations in our app so our app will start to feel more native. We'll specifically talk about *fast clicks* (a way to respond to touch events as they occur), and we'll implement the common swipe-to-delete gesture so that the user can delete notes in the note list view. We'll also talk about how to animate the appearance and disappearance of views and the animation of the swipe-to-delete gesture.

If you're not familiar with the swipe-to-delete gesture, a user can swipe in a certain direction (usually right-to-left) on a table cell in order to tell the app they'd like to delete the row. A delete or trash button appears, which they can then tap to finalize the operation. The following image should help you see what happens:

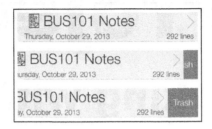

What does it do?

In this project, you'll learn how to interact with the Media API provided by Cordova/PhoneGap and learn to record audio and play it back. You'll also learn what audio formats iOS and Android support.

Misnamed API

The Media API is, to a large extent, misnamed. It only handles audio, not any type of media. As such, think of this API more as an Audio API that permits recording and playback, but nothing more. We'll work with videos and images in *Project 6, Working with Still Images* and *Project 7, Capturing Video*.

You'll also learn about `Hammer.js`, which is a library offering near-effortless gesture support to our app. It can also detect touch events very quickly. Not only will it serve to intercept every tap a user might make in our app, it is also crucial to implementing the swipe-to-delete gesture.

And finally, you'll learn about view management and a typical implementation of a view stack. You'll learn about pushing and popping views and what that really means regarding how and when views appear and disappear.

Why is it great?

Introducing this new note type is a perfect demonstration of the utility of object-oriented programming, when it comes to making extensible models and views, since we can build upon the code we've already written.

It's also important to learn more about the view lifecycle and the management of views—how views appear and disappear and how they are rendered on screen. Some apps can get away with only one or two views, but most apps require many more views, and it is critical that you know how to manage these views appropriately.

Gesture support is also something we've learnt to take for granted on our mobile devices. It often comes free with the native SDK. It's usually only a couple of lines of code to detect a swipe or zoom gesture. With JavaScript, we lose that free gesture support, but thankfully, there are libraries out there that make our lives significantly easier.

How are we going to do it?

Our process in this project is much the same as in prior projects, so this is what we'll be doing:

- Covering the Media API
- Designing the user interface
- Designing the data model
- Implementing the data model
- Covering Hammer.js
- Covering the view stack
- Implementing the user interface
- Putting it all together

What do I need to get started?

If you were able to successfully finish the previous project, you've got everything necessary for this next project. If you wish, you can continue to work in the same project folder, or you can create a new project and copy the contents. Don't forget to add the file, globalization, and keyboard plugins to your new project as well.

Covering the Media API

In this task, you'll be introduced to the Media API and will create a class that our audio notes can use to interact with the Media API. We'll call this a media manager.

Getting ready

Before going any further, you should add the Media plugin to the project:

```
cordova plugin add org.apache.cordova.media
```

Although we'll be covering the majority of the Media API, it's always best to consult the Cordova documentation to ensure you're seeing the most up-to-date information. You should be able to see the documentation on the Media API at
`https://github.com/apache/cordova-plugin-media/blob/dev/doc/index.md`.

Getting on with it

As with the File API, the Media API is based on callbacks, though thankfully, not to the same extent. We can interact with most of the API in a synchronous fashion, but there are a few areas that work asynchronously.

To instantiate a `Media` object, you can do the following:

```
var myMedia = new Media ( pathToFile, success, error, status );
```

Let's look at each of these parameters:

- ▶ `pathToFile`: This is a reference to the desired file. It might be a reference to a remote file or, in our case, a local file.

- ▶ `success`: This is the method that is called whenever a play, record, or stop operation is completed.

- ▶ `error`: This is the method that is called whenever an error occurs.

- ▶ `status`: This is the method called whenever the status of the `Media` object changes. Possible values are: `Media.MEDIA_NONE (0)`, `Media.MEDIA_STARTING (1)`, `Media.MEDIA_RUNNING (2)`, `Media.MEDIA_PAUSED (3)`, and `Media.MEDIA_STOPPED (4)`.

For iOS and Android, the Media API can play various types of files, including those in the MP3 format. Recording, however, is a very different matter. Android can only record using a variable bitrate, and the extension for the file should be `.3gp`. iOS, on the other hand, can only record using the WAV format, and the extension must be `.wav`.

Supported audio playback formats

For Android, visit `http://developer.android.com/guide/appendix/media-formats.html`. For iOS, visit `https://developer.apple.com/library/ios/documentation/audiovideo/conceptual/multimediapg/usingaudio/usingaudio.html`.

For iOS, the following information applies to file paths:

- ▶ If the path refers to a web resource (starting with `http://` or `https://`), the audio is streamed. Recording is not supported.

- ▶ If the path starts with `documents://`, the location is assumed to be relative to the application's `Documents` folder.

- ▶ If the path starts with `cdvfile://`, the location is assumed to be relative to the specified filesystem. For example, `cdvfile://localhost/persistent/` would refer to the persistent filesystem, and `cvvfile://localhost/temporary/` would refer to the temporary folder for the app.

▸ If the path is an absolute file path, recording will record to a file at that location, and playback will play from that location.

▸ If the path is a relative file path, recording will record to the app's temporary folder. Playback will first look in the app's www folder for the file and will then look at the temporary folder.

For Android, the following applies to file paths:

▸ If the path refers to a web resource (starting with `http://` or `https://`), the audio is streamed. Recording is not supported.

▸ If the path starts with `cdvfile://`, the location is assumed to be relative to the specified file system. For example, `cdvfile://localhost/persistent/...` would refer to the persistent file system, and `cvvfile://localhost/temporary/...` would refer to the location of the temporary file system.

▸ Recording is always done to a temporary file and moved (if possible) to the file path specified. If the rename fails, the temporary file will remain on the file system.

▸ If the path is an absolute path, playback will occur from the specified location and recording will move the temporary file to the location specified.

▸ If the path is relative, recording will check to see if an SD card is mounted, and if it is, will move the recorded file to a location relative to the SD card. If the SD card is not mounted, a location relative to the app's cache folder (`/data/data/package-name/cache/`) is used to move the file.

▸ If the path begins with `/android_asset/`, playback occurs from the app's assets. Recording is not permitted.

Once you have a `Media` object, you gain access to several parameters and methods. These are as follows:

▸ `position`: This is used to denote the current position of audio playback in seconds. (It is not continuously updated.)

▸ `duration`: This is used to denote the duration of the audio in seconds.

▸ `getCurrentPosition()`: Call this to ask for the `position` property to be updated. It also calls a callback with the audio position.

▸ `getDuration()`: This calls a callback with the duration of the audio. It also sets the `duration` property.

▸ `play()`: This starts playback; if paused, it resumes playback.

▸ `pause()`: This pauses playback.

▸ `seekTo()`: This changes the audio position to a given time specified in milliseconds.

▸ `startRecord()`: This starts a recording session.

> ▸ `stopRecord()`: This stops a recording session.

> ▸ `stop()`: This stops playback.

> ▸ `setVolume()`: This sets the playback volume.

> ▸ `release()`: This releases system audio resources. (This is especially important on Android.)

Let's go over some key methods:

> ▸ `play()`, `pause()`, or `stop()`: These three methods work in concert to facilitate audio playback.
>
> For example, have a look at the following code:
>
> ```
> var aSong = new Media (
>  "http://www.example.com/music.mp3",
>  mediaSuccess, mediaError );
> aSong.play();
> setTimeout ( aSong.pause, 1000 ); // pause after a second
> setTimeout ( aSong.play, 2000 );
> // play a second after pausing
> setTimeout ( aSong.stop, 3000 );
> // stop completely after 3 seconds
> ```
>
> The `mediaSuccess` argument is called whenever the play operation is successful or when it is forcibly stopped. This enables us to be notified when a song has ended (without having to guess based on the duration).

> ▸ `startRecord()`/`stopRecord()`: These are used to start or stop recordings. Recording requires certain types of files for it to work correctly. For iOS, WAV files are the only option. For Android, variable bitrate (`.3gp`) files are the only option.
>
> When a recording session starts, the specified file is created, if possible. This means that the full path to the file must exist. Once recording has stopped, the file can be played back if desired.
>
> The following is an iOS example (Android would use a `.3gp` extension):
>
> ```
> var aRecorder = new Media (
>  "cdvfile://localhost/persistent/recording.wav",
>  mediaSuccess, mediaError );
> aRecorder.startRecord();
> setTimeout ( aRecorder.stopRecord, 10000 );
> // stop recording after 10 seconds
> ```
>
> As with playback, the `mediaSuccess` method will be called when recording is stopped. You should be careful, however, of allowing unbounded recording in a production app. You could easily fill up the user's space if the recording process never stopped.

▶ `seekTo()`/`Position` and `Duration`: Because the files that the Media API deals with may not be local, it may not be possible to instantly return the duration of the file. The API also doesn't calculate the position of playback continuously, and so this must be requested explicitly.

To ask for the position in a file, one can use this:

```
var aSong = new Media (
  "http://www.example.com/song.mp3",
  mediaSuccess, mediaError );
aSong.play();
aSong.getCurrentPosition ( function ( position ) {
    if (position > -1) { … }
} );
```

The asynchronous `getCurrentPosition` **method**
Don't assume that the value of the position property is immediately updated after the call. If you do, you may actually see a prior value for the property rather than the expected value.

It's possible to receive a value of `-1` if the position isn't known. If you're updating some other variable with the position within the file, it would be wise to ignore `-1` positions.

To ask for the duration of a file, you can do the following:

```
var duration = aSong.getDuration();
```

That's easy, right? Except for the fact that the duration may not yet be known—especially if streaming a remote file. Instead, you need to check it periodically until the value is something other than `-1`:

```
var dur = -1;
var aTimer = setInterval ( function () {
    var tempDur = aSong.getDuration();
    if ( tempDur > 0 ) {
        clearInterval (aTimer);
        dur = tempDur;
    }
}, 1000 );
```

This has an issue. It will continuously ask for the duration indefinitely, so it would be wise to add a limiter as appropriate. For example, you could give up requesting the duration after 20 seconds if nothing is returned.

Duration and position have been, so far, reported in seconds. `seekTo` needs its position in milliseconds:

```
aSong.seekTo (1000); // a second into the song.
```

▸ `release()`: Releasing the audio resources when no longer needed is critical, especially on certain platforms such as Android where there are a limited number of audio resources. Once the resource is no longer required, `release` should be called:

```
aSong.play();
setTimeout (aSong.stop, 10000); // stops after 10 seconds
setTimeout (aSong.release, 11000);
// releases after 11 seconds
```

It's particularly critical to release any resources prior to a recording attempt, especially on the Android platform. Failure to release the resources so may cause recording to fail.

MediaError

When an error occurs, the `error` method is called, it was defined when the `Media` object was created. A parameter will be passed to indicate the error. Look at the error's `code` property in the following to see what happened:

```
function mediaError ( anError ) {
    console.log (anError.code);
}
```

The possible errors are:

▸ `MediaError.MEDIA_ERR_ABORTED`

▸ `MediaError.MEDIA_ERR_NETWORK`

▸ `MediaError.MEDIA_ERR_DECODE`

▸ `MediaError.MEDIA_ERR_NONE_SUPPORTED`

Creating a media manager

Now that we've covered the API, it's time to create our `MediaManager` class. Create the module shell in `mediaManager.js` under `www/js/app/models/`. Note that we add some useful constants near the end of the module definition in the following code:

```
define ( ["yasmf"], function ( _y )
{
    var _className = "MediaManager";
    var MediaManager = function ()
    {
```

```
        var self = new _y.BaseObject();
        self.subclass ( _className );
        // insert code here
        return self;
    };
    MediaManager.STATE_NONE = 0;
    MediaManager.STATE_PAUSED = 1;
    MediaManager.STATE_STOPPED = 2;
    MediaManager.STATE_PLAYING = 3;
    MediaManager.STATE_RECORDING = 4;
    return MediaManager;
});
```

Add the following notifications to the module after the `self.subclass` statement:

```
        self.registerNotification ( "playingStarted" );
        self.registerNotification ( "playingPaused" );
        self.registerNotification ( "playingStopped" );
        self.registerNotification ( "recordingStarted" );
        self.registerNotification ( "recordingStopped" );
        self.registerNotification ( "positionUpdated" );
        self.registerNotification ( "durationUpdated" );
        self.registerNotification ( "error" );
        self.registerNotification ( "statusUpdated" );
        self.registerNotification ( "mediaAllocated" );
        self.registerNotification ( "mediaDestroyed" );
```

Now, we need a place to store the `Media` object returned by the Media API:

```
        self._media = null;
```

We need two properties: one for the current playback position and one for the duration of the file. If the value for either property is less than zero, we'll report zero instead. In order to be consistent with the `seekTo()` Media API method, we'll report these values in milliseconds.

The two properties assume that they are being updated on a continuous basis (we'll write that code in a second). Also of note is that the position property is assignable; changing the value will invoke a seek operation:

```
        self._position = -1;
        self.getPosition = function () {
            return self._position >= 0 ? self._position : 0;
        }
        self.setPosition = function ( thePosition ) {
            if (self._media !== null) {
```

```
            self._media.seekTo ( thePosition );
            self.notify ( "positionUpdated" );
        }
        else {
            throw new Error ("Can't seek to a position without
            initialized Media." );
        }
    }
    Object.defineProperty ( self, "position", {
    get: self.getPosition, set: self.setPosition,
    configurable: true } );
    self._duration = -1;
    self.getDuration = function () {
        return self._duration >= 0 ? self._duration : 0;
    }
    Object.defineProperty ( self, "duration", {
    get: self.getDuration, configurable: true} );
```

Next, we need to manage our state—whether we are recording, playing, stopped, or just paused:

```
        self._state = MediaManager.STATE_NONE;
        self.getState = function () {
          return self._state;
        }
        Object.defineProperty ( self, "state", {
        get: self.getState, configurable: true } );
```

In order to make code more readable, however, we can add some convenience code so that we can ask our code if it is doing a specific operation:

```
        self.getIsPlaying = function () {
            return self._state === MediaManager.STATE_PLAYING;
        }
        Object.defineProperty ( self, "isPlaying", {
        get: self.getIsPlaying, configurable: true } );

        self.getIsRecording = function () {
            return self._state === MediaManager.STATE_RECORDING;
        }
        Object.defineProperty ( self, "isRecording", {
        get: self.getIsRecording, configurable: true } );

        self.getIsPaused = function () {
            return self._state === MediaManager.STATE_PAUSED;
        }
        Object.defineProperty ( self, "isPaused", {
```

```
        get: self.getIsPaused, configurable: true } );

    self.getIsStopped = function () {
      return self._state === MediaManager.STATE_STOPPED;
    }
    Object.defineProperty ( self, "isStopped", {
    get: self.getIsStopped, configurable: true } );
```

Next, let's write the method that updates our position and duration. This will be called on a continuous basis (roughly every second). We only need to update the playback position during playback; recording doesn't support a playback position. Also note that we convert the time from seconds to milliseconds:

```
        self._intervalId = null;
        self._updateStatus = function () {
          if (self._media !== null) {
            if ( self.isPlaying ) {
              self._media.getCurrentPosition ( function ( position ) {
                self._position = position * 1000; // milliseconds
                self.notify ( "positionUpdated" );
                                        } );
            }
            var minDurationAllowed = -100;
            if ( self._duration > minDurationAllowed &&
            self._duration < 0 ) {
              var d = self._media.getDuration();
              if (d > -1) {
                self._duration = d * 1000; // milliseconds
                self.notify ( "durationUpdated");
              }
              else {
                if (self._duration > minDurationAllowed ) {
                  self._duration--; // this will eventually give up
                }
              }
            }
          }
```

Before we wrap this method up, let's add some basic duration information while recording:

```
        if ( self.isRecording ) {
          self._duration += 1000;
          self.notify ( "durationUpdated");
        }
      }
    }
```

Next, we need to write the method to be called whenever a play or record operation completes. Note that we reset the position to zero and release the underlying resources.

```
self._mediaSuccess = function () {
  self._position = 0;
  self.notify ( "positionUpdated" );
  if (self.isPlaying) { self.notify ( "playingStopped" ); }
  if (self.isRecording) { self.notify ( "recordingStopped" ); }
  self._state = MediaManager.STATE_STOPPED;
  self._media.release();
}
```

We also need a way to handle errors, so let's add that method as well as a supporting property:

```
self._lastError = null;
self.getLastError = function () {
   return self._lastError;
}
Object.defineProperty ( self, "lastError", {
get: self.getLastError, configurable: true});

self._updateMediaError = function ( anError ) {
   self._lastError = anError;
   console.log ( "Media Error: encountered " +
   anError.code + ". Current status is " + self.status);
   self.notify ( "error" );
}
```

It's conceivable that external code might want to have access to the internal state of the `media` object as reported by the Media API. Let's provide an easy method of access:

```
self._mediaStatus = -1;
self.getMediaStatus = function () {
   return self._mediaStatus;
}
Object.defineProperty ( self, "mediaStatus", {
get: self.getMediaStatus, configurable: true});

self._updateMediaStatus = function ( aStatus ) {
   self._status = aStatus;
   self.notify ( "statusUpdated" );
}
```

When external code asks us to play or record a song, we need to create the underlying `media` object using the following code:

```
self._createMediaObjectIfNecessary = function () {
   if (self._media === null) {
      self._media = new Media (
      self.src, self._mediaSuccess, self._updateMediaError,
      self._updateMediaStatus );
      self._intervalId = setInterval (
      self._updateStatus, 1000 );
      self._state = MediaManager.STATE_STOPPED;
      self.notify ( "mediaAllocated");
   }
}
```

When we're done with the `media` object, we need to get rid of it and stop any status updates:

```
self._destroyMediaObjectIfNecessary = function () {
   if (self._media !== null) {
      self._media.release();
   }
   if (self._intervalId !== null ) {
      clearInterval ( self._intervalId );
      self._intervalId = null;
   }
   self._media = null;
   self._state = MediaManager.STATE_NONE;
   self.notify ("mediaDestroyed");
}
```

Next, we need a property that stores the audio filename:

```
self._src = null;
self.getSrc = function () {
   return self._src;
}
self.setSrc = function ( newSrc ) {
   self._destroyMediaObjectIfNecessary();
   if (typeof newSrc !=="undefined") {
     self._src = newSrc;
     self._createMediaObjectIfNecessary();
   }
   else {
    self._src = null;
   }
}
```

```
Object.defineProperty ( self, "src", {
get: self.getSrc, set: self.setSrc, configurable: true } );
```

At this point, we can create the routine for playback. Note that if we're already doing something, we need to stop that first.

```
self.play = function () {
   self._createMediaObjectIfNecessary();
   if (self.isRecording || self.isPlaying ) {
      self.stop();
   }
   self._media.play();
   self._state = MediaManager.STATE_PLAYING;
   self.notify ( "playingStarted" );
}
```

We should implement a way to pause playback as well (note that pausing isn't supported for recording):

```
self.pause = function () {
   self._createMediaObjectIfNecessary();
   if (self.isPlaying) {
      self._media.pause();
      self._state = MediaManager.STATE_PAUSED;
      self.notify ( "playingPaused" );
   }
   else if (self.isRecording) {
     console.log (
     "Media Error: can't pause during recording.")
   }
}
```

Next, let's implement the code that starts recording. Note that we reset the position and duration; they will be invalidated by the record operation. By starting the recording, the _updateStatus method will add a second to our duration as the recording progresses, and if we didn't reset the duration, we might add on to the duration from a prior recording attempt:

```
self.record = function () {
  self._createMediaObjectIfNecessary();
  if (self.isPlaying || self.isRecording ) {
    self.stop();
  }
  self._media.startRecord();
  self._position = 0;
```

```
        self._duration = 0;
        self._state = MediaManager.STATE_RECORDING;
        self.notify ( "recordingStarted" );
        self.notify ( "durationUpdated" );
        self.notify ( "positionUpdated" );
    }
```

We need to add some code so that we can stop playback or recording. Note the immediate play/stop combination after we're done recording. This is to ensure that the Media API recalculates the duration of the newly recorded file. Setting the duration to -1 also ensures that _updateStatus will pick up the changed duration:

```
    self.stop = function () {
        self._createMediaObjectIfNecessary();
        if (self.isRecording) {
            self._state = MediaManager.STATE_STOPPED;
            self._media.stopRecord();
            self.notify ( "recordingStopped" );
            self._media.release();
            self._duration = -1;
            self._media.play();
            self._media.stop();
            self._media.release();
        }
        else if (self.isPlaying || self.isPaused ) {
            self._state = MediaManager.STATE_STOPPED;
            self._media.stop();
            self._position = 0;
            self.notify ( "positionUpdated" );
            self.notify ( "playingStopped" );
            self._media.release();
        }
    }
```

We're almost done! We need to override the init method so we can specify the audio file immediately once we've created it:

```
    self.overrideSuper ( self.class, "init", self.init );
    self.init = function ( theSource ) {
        self.super ( _className, "init" );
        if (typeof theSource !== "undefined") { self.src = theSource;
    }
    }
```

Finally, we need to clean up after ourselves:

```
self.overrideSuper ( self.class, "destroy", self.destroy );
self.destroy = function ()
{
    self._destroyMediaObjectIfNecessary();
    self.super ( _className, "destroy" );
}
```

What did we do?

First, we covered the Media API. Then, we created a `MediaManager` class to wrap these into a convenient handler.

Designing the user interface

Because we're reusing our user interface for this project, we only need to consider the user interface for an audio note. As part of this, we need to implement a simple recording and playback mechanism.

Getting on with it

Our project will now have three views in it: the note list view, the text note edit view, and the audio note edit view. The text note edit view and note list view are visually unchanged from the prior version, so we won't go over any changes for it, but we do need to cover the audio note edit view.

Essentially, we need to determine how we want to allow the user to edit an audio note. We could make an initial view that only displays the text and could present a button that displays another view for recording/playing audio, but this introduces too many taps for the feature. A user wanting to create an audio recording may need to do so as quickly as they can, and introducing unnecessary steps into the process will only slow them down and may cause the loss of invaluable data. Instead, we'll display a simple control at the top of the view that allows recording and playback. Then, we can leave the remainder of the view for the text area. Take a look at the following screenshot:

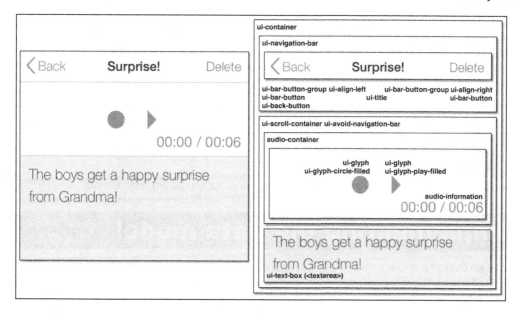

What did we do?

In this task, we created the user interface for the audio note edit view.

Designing the data model

In order to take advantage of the support we built into our app for multiple note types, we need to design the model for an audio note. Because of our foundation, however, we can base this model on our base note, which means we can avoid needless repetition of code.

Getting on with it

Let's take a look at the model for an audio note:

audioNote (+baseNote)	
r/o	.media
p	_updateUnit()
p	_updateModificationDate)
o	setMediaContents (filename)
o	destroy()

. property	**r/w** read/write	**r/o** read-only		
p private	**o** override	⬎ notification		

The `audioNote` object extends (inherits from) `BaseNote` (denoted by the **+** sign in the `audioNote` model) and adds a new property, `media`. This property will hold our media manager. This is what will let us play and record audio. There are a couple of additional private methods that are added to support the updating of `unitValue` and `modifiedDate` when the audio changes. The other overrides are in place to let the `audioNote` object handle the `mediaContents` property and to properly dispose of any resources allocated for audio processing.

What did we do?

In this task, we extended our base note model to create our audio note model.

Implementing the data model

Let's go over the implementation of our audio note model. There's not a large amount of code to cover, but as you read through the section, try to imagine the code for our base note model working together with this new code to produce new behavior without lots of duplicated code.

Getting on with it

First, we need to create the module's shell at www/js/app/models/audioNote.js:

```
define ( ["yasmf","app/models/baseNote", "app/models/mediaManager"],
function ( _y, BaseNote, MediaManager ) {
   var _className = "AudioNote";
   var AudioNote = function () {
      var self = new BaseNote();
      self.subclass ( _className );
      // insert code here
      return self;
   }
   // translations are inserted here
   return AudioNote;
});
```

Then, we need to add a property that stores a media manager:

```
self._media = null;
self.getMedia = function () {
   return self._media;
}
Object.defineProperty ( self, "media", {
get: self.getMedia, configurable: true});
```

We also need to override the visual representation for this note type. Let's use a sound wave:

```
self._representation = "sound-wave";
```

Of course, using lines for units doesn't make sense when you talk about audio. Let's use seconds instead:

```
self.unitLabels = [
"app.an.SECONDS", "app.an.SECOND", "app.an.SECONDS" ];
```

In a text note, the unit value is updated whenever the text content changes by themselves. Now, we need a mechanism to change the unit value when the audio has changed. (The division by 1000 in the following code is simply because the duration is represented by milliseconds.)

```
self._updateUnit = function () {
    self.unitValue = self._media.duration / 1000;
}
```

We also need a way to update the modification date when the audio changes, so let's write a method for that as well:

```
self._updateModificationDate = function () {
    self._modifiedDate = new Date();
}
```

Because our audio note also supports media in addition to text, we need to override the setter for the `mediaContents` property. Once overridden, we have to redeclare the property so that it acts as desired.

We also need to initialize our media manager; thankfully, the Media API supports the `cdvfile` scheme that is used by the File API. Since we know we're storing everything in the persistent file system, we hardcode that here:

```
self.overrideSuper ( self.class, "setMediaContents",
self.setMediaContents );
self.setMediaContents = function ( theMediaContents ) {
    self.super ( _className, "setMediaContents", [
    theMediaContents ] );
    if (self._media !== null) {
        self._media.destroy();
        self._media = null;
    }
    self._media = new MediaManager();
    self._media.init (
    "cdvfile://localhost/persistent/" + theMediaContents );
    self.notify ( "mediaContentsChanged" );
    self._media.addListenerForNotification (
```

```
            "durationUpdated", self._updateUnit );
            self._media.addListenerForNotification (
            "recordingStopped", self._updateModificationDate );
        }
        Object.defineProperty ( self, "mediaContents", {
        get: self.getMediaContents, set: self.setMediaContents,
        configurable: true});
```

Finally, as always, we need to clean up after ourselves:

```
        self.overrideSuper ( self.class, "destroy", self.destroy);
        self.destroy = function () {
            self._media.destroy();
            self._media = null;
            self.super ( _className, "destroy" );
        }
```

Let's not forget, though, that we need proper translations for our new unit value:

```
    _y.addTranslations ( {
        "app.an.SECOND": { "EN": "second",
                           "ES": "segundo" },
        "app.an.SECONDS": { "EN": "seconds",
                            "ES": "segundos" }
    });
```

Because we've added a new note model, we also need to update our note factory so that it can create a new audio note. In `www/js/app/factories/noteFactory.js`, add the following to the `switch` statement, above the `default` case in the `createNote` method:

```
        case noteFactory.AUDIONOTE:
            return new AudioNote();
```

Then, in the `createAssociatedMediaFileName` method, add the following to the `switch` statement, above the `default` case:

```
        case noteFactory.AUDIONOTE:
            extension = { "ios": "wav", "android": "3gp" };
            newFileName = "audio";
            break;
```

What did we do?

We implemented the code for the audio note and updated the note factory so that it could create a new audio note and create a filename with the appropriate extensions for an audio file.

Covering Hammer.js

Native-code SDKs have amazing gesture support built in. Even complicated gestures can be recognized with surprisingly little code. But when we enter the world of JavaScript, all that disappears. Gesture support has to be detected based on touch event coordinates, and that quickly becomes very complicated. There's got to be a better way!

Enter Hammer.js.

Getting ready

To install Hammer.js for the project, visit `http://eightmedia.github.io/hammer.js/` and click on the large **Download** button. You'll be taken to a portion of their code repository; download the `hammer.min.js` or `hammer.js` file. Whichever one you download, name it `hammer.js` and save it to `www/js/lib`. If you're using the template provided in the code package for the book when creating projects, `hammer.js` is already downloaded for you.

Getting on with it

We're not going to cover every aspect of Hammer.js; that would consume several chapters full of demonstrations. What we are going to cover is related to two things we need to deal with: our slow tap response and implementing swipe-to-delete.

First, let's see how to detect a gesture:

```
var anElement = document.getElementById ("someElement");
hammer(anElement).on ("tap", tappedAnElement);
hammer(anElement).on ("swipe", swipedAnElement);
```

In this example, if the element were tapped (a tap consists of a `touchstart` and a `touchend` event), the `tappedAnElement` method would be called. Likewise, if a swipe were to occur on the element, `swipedAnElement` would be called.

Our taps are slow

Many browsers do some gesture detection in order to emulate mouse events. For example, we can have the `click` and `dblclick` event handlers attached to an element. In order to properly detect both, there needs to be a slight delay between when a click is detected and when a double-click is detected. On mobile devices, this is a long delay—around 300 milliseconds, which is very noticeable, especially when most native controls react immediately.

Hammer.js speeds this process up by not waiting for the second tap or click prior to sending the first one. Therefore, we get an immediate tap as soon as the user's finger leaves the screen. Then, and only then, if the user taps again might we see a double-tap. But Hammer.js also does one more thing by default: even if that double-tap is sent, a tap is also sent, so interactions always feel faster.

It also does mean that we might have to occasionally take care to turn this behavior off if a tap and a double-tap could be confused. In our case, we don't have that issue; we want all taps to count.

When we implement the user interface, watch for these to be used frequently instead of the previous `click` events. It really does help make the app feel snappier.

Need an instant response?

If we don't want to wait for the user to lift their finger, we can use the `touch` event instead. It is triggered the moment the user touches the screen with their finger.

Swipe-to-delete

Swipe-to-delete isn't a difficult gesture to recognize when using native SDKs, but without Hammer.js, it wouldn't be simple to recognize in JavaScript. A proper implementation isn't terribly easy even with Hammer.js, but we can approximate the desired effect using the following code:

```
Hammer(anElement).on("swipeleft", swipeToDelete);
Hammer(anElement).on("swiperight", hideDeleteButton);
```

It's never that simple

In the interests of space, we're taking the easy way out here. This doesn't implement a swipe-to-delete in the way iOS behaves. Typically, on iOS, any touch after the initial left swipe will cause the row to slide back over any action buttons. The code for this is somewhat difficult, but if you want to take a further look, be sure to look at the `noteListView.js` file for this chapter.

Now that we know how to listen for gestures, how do we actually implement the feature?

The easiest mechanism to use is to have the table row slide left, exposing the action underneath. We can accomplish this like so:

```
<div class="ui-list-item-contents" data-uid="%UID%">
    ...
</div>
<div class="ui-list-action-group">
```

```
    <div class="ui-list-action ui-background-destructive-color"
    data-uid="%UID%"><div>%TRASH%</div></div>
</div>
```

The `ui-list-item-contents` class must then have a higher value for `z-index` than `ui-list-action-group`. It also needs a `background-color` property so that you can't see the delete button underneath. These are defined in YASMF's base stylesheet, but you can accomplish it with the following styles:

```
.ui-list-item .ui-list-item-contents {
  z-index: 3; }
.ui-list-item .ui-list-action-group {
  background-color: #CCC;
  position: absolute;
  right: 0;
  top: 0;
  bottom: 0;
  z-index: 2; }
.ui-list-item .ui-list-action-group .ui-list-action {
  height: 100%;
  min-width: 44px;
  text-align: center;
  display: inline-table; }
.ui-list-item .ui-list-action-group .ui-list-action div {
  display: table-cell;
  vertical-align: middle;
  padding: 10px; }
```

When a left swipe is detected, we can animate the `ui-list-item-contents` DIV element to the left, which will expose the delete button. And when a right swipe is detected, we can slide the contents back over the delete button.

But how does one get the width of the delete button? We could hardcode it, of course, but that doesn't work when we consider different languages. We can use something like the following instead:

```
var amountToMove = getComputedStyle ( theULElement.querySelector (
  ".ui-list-action" ) ).getPropertyValue ( "width" );
```

Now that we have the width, how do we reveal the button? We could simply modify the element to be at the new position instantly, but it's better to animate it. To do that, we can use the `transition` property, as follows:

```
transition: transform 0.3s ease-in-out
```

And then, whenever the `transform` property changes, we get a nice animation. For example, use the following code:

```
transform: translateX(-70px)
```

This will result in a nice, smooth animation.

Don't forget the prefixes

If only we lived in a world where every system browser (which is where your code is being rendered by Cordova/PhoneGap) understood modern CSS. Since we don't live in that world, we still need to worry about users on an older device that may only handle `-webkit-` prefixed styles. In the previous example, you can use `-webkit-transform: translateX(-70px)` to support older devices. Of course, if the device is too old, there's nothing you can do, but this allows you to provide nice animations on as many devices as possible.

What did we do?

In this section, we covered the use of Hammer.js to speed up tap detection, and we also implemented a very simple swipe-to-delete mechanism, which we'll use later.

What else do I need to know?

Of course, there's more in regards to gesture detection than what we covered here. I urge you to check out the code and documentation for Hammer.js. It's not terribly great documentation—you'll have to experiment a good deal—but as a library, it is a lifesaver.

Covering the view stack

So far, we've been ignoring the concept of a view stack, even though we have already dealt with it implicitly. Remember back in *Project 3, Mobile Application Design*, when we assigned `z-index` to each view? This was to ensure they always stacked in the proper order when on screen.

Thankfully, most UI frameworks eliminate this tedium, and YASMF is no different. It provides a simple solution to having hardcoded z-index for our views.

Getting on with it

The view stack (or view hierarchy) is simply a representation of the visible and hidden views active in the DOM. So far, we've only had to deal with one view being on top of another, but in complex apps, you can imagine that it would be possible to have several views on the stack. In order to handle them all, it is better to manage them programmatically rather than manually.

Something else you've no doubt noticed is that our app doesn't have any animation between views. Typically, mobile apps perform some animation between views, whether a panning motion, a fade, or something else. We've been switching instantly between views, and it's not a native sensation.

Most UI frameworks also provide this sort of animation for free when you move between views on the stack, and YASMF is no exception. By using the view stack, we get nice, smooth animations between views, which helps our app feel closer to a native app.

So how does the view stack work? Typically, views are controlled by a navigation controller; this is a special view that knows about the view stack and all the views within it. When we want to display a view, we push it onto the navigation controller's view stack. When we want to remove the view, we pop it from the navigation controller's view stack.

Each navigation controller also has a root view—the first view on the stack. To prevent a horrible animation at the start of the app (apps don't generally start with their first view flying in from offscreen), the root view must be created first and given to the navigation controller when it is created. This displays the root view without any animation. Subsequent views that need to be added to the stack can be created and then pushed, and an animation will occur.

For example, let's use the following code:

```
var aView = new _y.UI.ViewContainer();
aView.init (…);
var aNavController = new _y.UI.NavigationController();
aNavController.initWithOptions ( { rootView: aView; parent:
someElement } );
```

At this point, `aView` is the top view on the stack and is the visible view. Let's say we then push another view:

```
var bView = new _y.UI.ViewContainer();
bView.init (…);
aNavController.pushView ( bView );
```

Now, `bView` is the top view on the stack; `aView` has animated offscreen to the left. What happens when we pop the top view?

```
aNavController.popView ();
```

This pops `bView` off the stack, animating it to the right, and presents `aView` again. The `bView` object is now free to be destroyed if we want to.

Let's see what the stack looked like at each step:

At creation	After push	After pop
`aView` (visible)	`aView` (invisible)	`aView` (visible)
	`bView` (visible)	

So far this is great, but views often also need to respond to their appearance (or disappearance) on screen. YASMF handles this by sending specific notifications when the view is about to appear and when it has finished appearing. (The same is true for disappearing.)

The following are some of the notifications that can be sent to the view:

▶ `viewWasPushed`: This is used to notify that the view has been pushed onto a view stack. The view isn't yet on screen.

▶ `viewWillAppear`: This is used to notify the properties that the view is about to appear on screen. Keep any DOM changes here to a minimum, or you risk the animation stuttering.

▶ `viewDidAppear`: This is used to notify the properties that the view is on screen .

▶ `viewWillDisappear`: This is used to notify the properties that the view is about to go off screen . Keep any DOM changes to a minimum lest the animation stutter.

▶ `viewDidDisappear`: This is used to notify the properties that the view is off screen.

▶ `viewWasPopped`: This is used to notify that the view has been popped from a view stack; the view is off screen. The view can be disposed of at this point, if desired.

There's more to a navigation controller than just this simple example, but it's enough to give our app some nice animation and an easier way to handle displaying and removing views.

So if you're not using YASMF, how do you manage the view stack and add animations between view changes?

Basically, you need an array in which you can manage all the views on the stack. To push a view on the stack, you can call the array's `push` method with the view. To pop a view, just call the array's `pop` method. In order to provide animation and insert the view into the DOM, however, you need to provide your own `pushView` and `popView` methods. For example, the following code is a simplified version of YASMF's `pushView` method. Note that `UI.styleElement` and `UI.styleElements` are convenience methods for setting styles on DOM elements:

```
self.pushView = function ( aView ) {
    var theHidingView = self.topView;
    var theShowingView = aView;
    var animationDelay = 0.3;
    var animationType = "ease-in-out";
    // add the view to our array, at the end
    self._subviews.push ( theShowingView );
    theShowingView.navigationController = self;
    theShowingView.notify ( "viewWasPushed" );
    // get each element's z-index, if specified
    var theHidingViewZ = parseInt(
    getComputedStyle(theHidingView.element).getPropertyValue(
    "z-index") || "0",10),
        theShowingViewZ= parseInt(getComputedStyle(
        theShowingView.element).getPropertyValue(
        "z-index") || "0",10);
    if (theHidingViewZ >= theShowingViewZ) {
      theShowingViewZ = theHidingViewZ + 10;
    }
    // then position the view so as to be off screen, with
    the current view on screen
    UI.styleElement ( theHidingView.element, "transform",
    "translate3d(0,0," + theHidingViewZ + "px)");
    UI.styleElement ( theShowingView.element, "transform",
    "translate3d(100%,0," + theShowingViewZ + "px)");
    // set up an animation
      UI.styleElements ( [theShowingView.element,
      theHidingView.element], "transition", "transform " +
      animationDelay + "s " + animationType);
    }
    // and add the element with us as the parent
    theShowingView.parentElement = self.element;
    setTimeout ( function ()
    {
        // tell the topView to move over to the left
        UI.styleElement ( theHidingView.element, "transform",
        "translate3d(-50%,0," + theHidingViewZ + "px)");
        // and tell our new view to move as well
        UI.styleElement ( theShowingView.element, "transform",
        "translate3d(0,0," + theShowingViewZ + "px)");
        // tell the view it's about to show...
        theHidingView.notify ( "viewWillDisappear" );
        theShowingView.notify ( "viewWillAppear" );
        // tell anyone who is listening who got pushed
        self.notify ( "viewPushed", [theShowingView] );
```

```
            // tell the view it's visible after the animation
            delay has passed
            setTimeout ( function () {
                theHidingView.element.style.display = "none";
                theHidingView.notify ( "viewDidDisappear" );
                theShowingView.notify ( "viewDidAppear" );
                }, animationDelay * 1000 );
        }, 50);
    }
```

Popping a view is essentially using the code in the reverse order. If you want to see the full code for YASMF's navigation controller, see `/framework/lib/yasmf/ui/navigationController.js` in the code package for this book, or if you want to see the code online, visit `https://github.com/photokandyStudios/YASMF-Next/blob/master/lib/yasmf/ui/navigationController.js`.

You also need a mechanism for setting the root view. This is the same as pushing a view onto the view stack, except that no animation occurs and the view stack is cleared if the root view is changed.

What did we do?

In this task, we were introduced to the view stack and YASMF's implementation of it. We learned how to push and pop views and create an instance of a `NavigationController` object.

What else do I need to know?

All the animation is performed by the GPU for smooth animation (on most modern mobile devices, anyway).

But WebKit has a bug in that it tends to forget about any carefully placed Z indexes during the animation (and sometimes after). There's a fix, which YASMF has, but I wanted to let you know about it in case you were using some other framework that didn't account for it.

The fix is simply that each item with a `z-index` property should also have an equivalent `translateZ()` transform style applied. Check the styling of the navigation and tool bars in `yasmf.css`. You'll notice that YASMF applies a `translateZ()` method there as well. This ensures that they stay above any elements in the view (assuming they don't have a `z-index` or `translation` property). If this isn't done, the contents of the view often appear above the navigation toolbar during the animation and then pop back under when the animation is complete. It looks ugly, and so if it occurs, just be sure to add an equivalent `translateZ()` transform style to your element styles.

Implementing the user interface

We've done a lot so far and are not quite done. We still need to implement a couple of changes in the note view factory, alter the note list view, and implement the new audio note edit view.

Getting on with it

The first thing we need to do is alter our note view factory in `www/app/js/noteViewFactory.js`. Add the following to the `switch` statement prior to the `default` case:

```
case noteFactory.AUDIONOTE:
    return new AudioNoteEditView();
```

Next, let's make the requisite changes to the note list view in `www/js/app/noteListView.js`. We need to add a method to create a new audio note and hook that up with an event listener to the sound wave icon on the toolbar. We also need to replace our previous event handlers with Hammer.js gesture support. We also need to add swipe-to-delete support. Finally, we need to use YASMF's navigation controller for view management.

The following is what our revised model looks like (new methods in bold):

```
┌──────────────────────────────────────────────────┐
│  ┌──────────────────────────────────────────────┐ │
│  │              noteListView (V3)                │ │
│  ├──────────────────────────────────────────────┤ │
│  │ p   _navigationBar                            │ │
│  │ p   _scrollContainer                          │ │
│  │ p   _listOfNotes                              │ │
│  │ p   _newTextNoteButton                        │ │
│  │ p   _newAudioNoteButton                       │ │
│  │ p   _newImageNoteButton                       │ │
│  │ p   _newVideoNoteButton                       │ │
│  ├──────────────────────────────────────────────┤ │
│  │ p   _createAndEditNote( noteType )            │ │
│  │     createNewTextNote()                       │ │
│  │     createNewAudioNote()                      │ │
│  │     deleteExistingNote()                      │ │
│  │     editExistingNote ( event )                │ │
│  │     exposeActionForNote ()                    │ │
│  │     hideActionForNote ()                      │ │
│  │     quitApp()                                 │ │
│  │ o   render()                                  │ │
│  │ o   renderToElement()                         │ │
│  │     renderList()                              │ │
│  │     onOrientationChanged                      │ │
│  │ o   init( parentElement )                     │ │
│  │ o   initWithOptions( options )                │ │
│  │ o   destroy()                                 │ │
│  └──────────────────────────────────────────────┘ │
│                                                    │
│   .  property   r/w read/write   r/o read-only     │
│   p private     o    override    ↖ notification    │
└──────────────────────────────────────────────────┘
```

First, we added a reference to Hammer.js in the `define` statement at the top of the file:

```
define ( ["yasmf",
          "app/models/noteStorageSingleton",
          "text!html/noteListView.html!strip",
          "text!html/noteListView_android.html!strip",
          "text!html/noteListItem.html!strip",
          "app/factories/noteFactory",
          "app/factories/noteViewFactory",
          "hammer"],
  function ( _y, noteStorageSingleton, noteListViewHTML,
  noteListViewAndroidHTML, noteListItemHTML, noteFactory,
  noteViewFactory, Hammer ) {
```

We need to edit `_createAndEditNote` to push the editing view onto the stack; the difference is highlighted in the following code:

```
self._createAndEditNote = function (noteType) {
    noteStorageSingleton.createNote(noteType)
      .then(function (aNewNote) {
          var aNoteEditView =
          noteViewFactory.createNoteEditView(noteType);
          aNoteEditView.initWithOptions({note:
          aNewNote});
          self.navigationController.pushView(aNoteEditView);
            })
      .catch(function (anError) { console.log(anError) })
      .done();
    }
```

Next, let's add a method to create a new audio note:

```
self.createNewAudioNote = function () {
  self._createAndEditNote(noteFactory.AUDIONOTE);
};
```

We also need to change `editExistingNote`:

```
self.editExistingNote = function (e)
{
  var theUID = this.getAttribute("data-uid");
  var aNote = noteStorageSingleton.getNote(theUID);
  var aNoteEditView =
  noteViewFactory.createNoteEditView(aNote.class);
  aNoteEditView.initWithOptions({note: aNote });
  self.navigationController.pushView(aNoteEditView);
};
```

Next, we need to supply a mechanism for sliding a row to the left when it is swiped; this will expose the underlying **Trash** button.

 The `styleElement` method is a convenience function provided by YASMF to apply styles to elements. We'll cover this in a bit.

```
self.exposeActionForNote = function (e) {
  _y.UI.styleElement(this, "transition",
  "%PREFIX%transform 0.3s ease-in-out");
  var amountToTranslate =
  getComputedStyle(self._listOfNotes.querySelector(
  ".ui-list-action")).getPropertyValue("width");
  _y.UI.styleElement(this, "transform", "translateX(
  -" + amountToTranslate + ")");
};
```

Next, we need the mechanism to slide the row back over the **Trash** button:

```
self.hideActionForNote = function (e) {
  _y.UI.styleElement(this, "transition",
  "%PREFIX%transform 0.3s ease-in-out");
  _y.UI.styleElement(this, "transform",
  "translateX(0px)");
};
```

We need to edit `renderToElement` to add the event listener for the purpose of creating a new audio note and to switch over to Hammer.js gestures; the differences are highlighted:

```
self.overrideSuper(self.class, "renderToElement",
self.renderToElement);
self.renderToElement = function () {
  self.super(_className, "renderToElement");
  self._navigationBar =
  self.element.querySelector(".ui-navigation-bar");
  self._scrollContainer =
  self.element.querySelector(".ui-scroll-container");
  self._listOfNotes = self.element.querySelector("
  .ui-list");
  var newButtons = self.element.querySelectorAll("
  .ui-bar-button");
  self._newTextNoteButton = newButtons[0];
  self._newAudioNoteButton = newButtons[1];
  self._newImageNoteButton = newButtons[2];
  self._newVideoNoteButton = newButtons[3];
```

```
                    Hammer(self._newTextNoteButton).on("tap",
                    self.createNewTextNote);
                    Hammer(self._newAudioNoteButton).on("tap",
                    self.createNewAudioNote);
          _y.UI.backButton.addListenerForNotification("backButtonPressed",
          self.quitApp);
                    };
```

In order to implement our swipe-to-delete gesture (and to add Hammer.js taps to each row), we need to edit `renderList`:

```
            self.renderList = function () {
                var notes = noteStorageSingleton.collection;
                var fragment = document.createDocumentFragment();
                for (var note in notes) {
                    if ( notes.hasOwnProperty ( note ) ) {
                        if (notes[note] !== null) {
                            var e = document.createElement ( "li" );
                            e.className = "ui-list-item";
                            e.setAttribute ( "data-uid", notes[note].uid );
                            e.id = "note_item_" + notes[note].uid;
                            e.innerHTML = _y.template ( noteListItemHTML,  {
                                "UID": notes[note].uid,
                                "TRASH": _y.T("TRASH"),
                                "NAME": notes[note].name,
                                "REPRESENTATION":
                                notes[note].representation,
                                "MODIFIED":
                                _y.D(notes[note].modifiedDate,"D"),
                                "INFO": "" +
                                _y.N(notes[note].formattedUnitValue)
                                } );
                            var contentsElement = e.querySelector (
                            ".ui-list-item-contents"),
                            actionElement  = e.querySelector (
                            ".ui-list-action" );

                            Hammer ( contentsElement ).on (
                            "tap", self.editExistingNote );
                            Hammer ( contentsElement, {
                            swipe_velocity:0.1} ).on
                            ("swipeleft", self.exposeActionForNote );
                            Hammer (
                            contentsElement, {swipe_velocity:0.1 } ).on (
                            "swiperight", self.hideActionForNote );
```

```
                Hammer ( actionElement    ).on (
                "tap", self.deleteExistingNote );
                fragment.appendChild ( e );
              }
            }
          }
          self._listOfNotes.innerHTML = "";
          self._listOfNotes.appendChild ( fragment );
        }
```

And finally, we need to add a translation to the module for our **Trash** button:

```
    _y.addTranslations ( {
       ...
      "TRASH": { "EN": "Trash",
                 "ES": "Borrar" }
    } );
```

With all the other views out of the way, let's focus on the audio note edit view. First, let's look at the view's model:

audioNoteEditView (+textNoteEditView)	
p	_recordAudioButton
p	_playAudioButton
p	_audioInformation
o	render()
o	renderToElement()
	onAudioStopped()
	onRecordAudio()
	onPlayAudio()
	updateAudioInformation()
o	init(parentElement)
o	destroy()

. property	**r/w** read/write	**r/o** read-only
p private	**o** override	↖ notification

Now, create the audio note edit view template in `www/html/audioNoteEditView.html`:

```
<html>
  <body>
    <div class="ui-navigation-bar">
      <div class="ui-title"
contenteditable="true">%NOTE_NAME%</div>
      <div class="ui-bar-button-group ui-align-left">
```

```
                <div class="ui-bar-button ui-tint-color
    ui-back-button">%BACK%</div>
            </div>
            <div class="ui-bar-button-group ui-align-right">
                <div class="ui-bar-button ui-destructive-color">
    %DELETE_NOTE%</div>
            </div>
        </div>
        <div class="ui-scroll-container ui-avoid-navigation-bar">
            <div class="audio-container">
                <div class="ui-glyph ui-background-tint-color
    ui-glyph-circle-filled"></div>
                <div class="ui-glyph
    ui-background-tint-color ui-glyph-play-filled"></div>
                <div class="audio-information">--:-- / --:--</div>
            </div>
            <textarea class="ui-text-box" >%NOTE_CONTENTS%</textarea>
        </div>
    </body>
</html>
```

Next, create the module shell in www/js/app/views/audioNoteEditView.js:

```
define ( ["yasmf", "app/models/noteStorageSingleton",
          "text!html/audioNoteEditView.html!strip",
          "app/views/textNoteEditView", "hammer"],
function ( _y, noteStorageSingleton, audioNoteViewHTML,
           TextNoteEditView, Hammer ) {
    var _className = "AudioNoteEditView";
    var AudioNoteEditView = function () {
        var self = new TextNoteEditView();
        self.subclass ( _className );
        // insert code here
        return self;
    }
    return AudioNoteEditView;
});
```

Then add some properties to hold references to the record and play buttons as well as to the audio information (indicating playback position and duration):

```
        self._recordAudioButton = null;
        self._playAudioButton = null;
        self._audioInformation = null;
```

We need to override `render`. If we used our `super` method's version, it would use the template for a text note, not an audio note:

```
self.overrideSuper ( self.class, "render", self.render );
self.render = function () {
    return _y.template ( audioNoteViewHTML, {
                         "NOTE_NAME": self._note.name,
                         "NOTE_CONTENTS":
                          self._note.textContents,
                         "BACK": _y.T("BACK"),
                         "DELETE_NOTE":
                          _y.T("app.nev.DELETE_NOTE")
                        });
}
```

We also need to override `renderToElement` (note that we inherit the functionality of our `super` method, which handles the text area portion of the view):

```
self.overrideSuper ( self.class, "renderToElement",
self.renderToElement );
self.renderToElement = function () {
 self.super ( _className, "renderToElement" );

 var audioButtons = self.element.querySelectorAll (
 ".audio-container .ui-glyph");
 self._recordAudioButton = audioButtons [0];
 self._playAudioButton = audioButtons [1];
 self._audioInformation = self.element.querySelector(".audio-
 information");
 Hammer(self._recordAudioButton).on("tap", self.onRecordAudio);
 Hammer(self._playAudioButton).on(
"tap", self.onPlayAudio);
 };
```

Let's add a method that updates the current playback position and duration (`getPartsFromSeconds` is a convenience method that we'll cover in a moment):

```
self.updateAudioInformation = function () {
    var durationParts = _y.datetime.getPartsFromSeconds (
self._note.media.duration == 0 ? self._note.unitValue :
self._note.media.duration/1000, _y.datetime.PRECISION_MINUTES),
        positionParts = _y.datetime.getPartsFromSeconds (
self._note.media.position/1000, _y.datetime.PRECISION_MINUTES);
    self._audioInformation.innerHTML = _y.template (
"%MM1%:%SS1% / %MM2%:%SS2%",
                                                  {
```

```
      "SS1": _y.format(positionParts.seconds, "d2"),
      "MM1": _y.format(positionParts.minutes, "d2"),
      "SS2": _y.format(durationParts.seconds, "d2"),
      "MM2": _y.format(durationParts.minutes, "d2") });
        }
```

Next, let's add the handler for the play button (note that the square-filled glyph that we use represents a stop icon):

```
        self.onPlayAudio = function () {
          if (!self._note.media.isPlaying) {
            self._note.media.play();
            self._playAudioButton.classList.remove(
            "ui-glyph-play-filled");
            self._playAudioButton.classList.add(
            "ui-glyph-square-filled");
            self._note.media.addListenerForNotification(
            "playingStopped", self.onAudioStopped);
            self._note.media.addListenerForNotification(
            "positionUpdated", self.updateAudioInformation);
          }
          else {
            self._note.media.stop();
            self._note.media.removeListenerForNotification(
            "playingStopped", self.onAudioStopped);
            self._note.media.removeListenerForNotification(
            "positionUpdated", self.updateAudioInformation);
            self._playAudioButton.classList.remove(
            "ui-glyph-square-filled");
            self._playAudioButton.classList.add(
            "ui-glyph-play-filled");
          }

          self._recordAudioButton.classList.remove(
            "ui-glyph-square-filled");
          self._recordAudioButton.classList.add(
            "ui-glyph-circle-filled");
        };
```

We also need to add the handler used to press the record button:

```
        self.onRecordAudio = function () {
          if (!self._note.media.isRecording) {
            self._note.media.record();
            self._recordAudioButton.classList.remove(
            "ui-glyph-circle-filled");
```

```
      self._recordAudioButton.classList.add(
      "ui-glyph-square-filled");
      self._note.media.addListenerForNotification(
      "recordingStopped", self.onAudioStopped);
    }
    else {
      self._note.media.stop();
      self._note.media.removeListenerForNotification(
      "recordingStopped", self.onAudioStopped);
      self._recordAudioButton.classList.remove(
      "ui-glyph-square-filled");
      self._recordAudioButton.classList.add(
      "ui-glyph-circle-filled");
    }

    self._playAudioButton.classList.remove(
      "ui-glyph-square-filled");
    self._playAudioButton.classList.add(
      "ui-glyph-play-filled");
};
```

When playback ceases naturally, we need to reset the visible states of the playback and record buttons and remove any listeners:

```
self.onAudioStopped = function () {
    self._playAudioButton.classList.remove (
    "ui-glyph-pause-filled" );
    self._playAudioButton.classList.add (
    "ui-glyph-play-filled" );
    self._recordAudioButton.classList.remove (
    "ui-glyph-pause-filled" );
    self._recordAudioButton.classList.add (
    "ui-glyph-circle-filled" );
    self._note.media.removeListenerForNotification (
    "recordingStopped", self.onAudioStopped );
    self._note.media.removeListenerForNotification (
    "playingStopped", self.onAudioStopped );
    self._note.media.removeListenerForNotification
      ("positionUpdated", self.updateAudioInformation);
}
```

Since we need to listen for changes to the duration of our audio file, we need to override the init method so that we can attach a listener when the view is pushed and dispense with that listener when the view is popped:

```
self.overrideSuper(self.class, "init", self.init);
self.init = function ( theParentElement, theNote ) {
  self.super(_className, "init", [theParentElement, theNote]);
```

```
      self.addListenerForNotification ( "viewWasPushed", function ()
{
        self._note.media.addListenerForNotification("durationUpdated",
        self.updateAudioInformation);
        self.updateAudioInformation();
      });
      self.addListenerForNotification ( "viewWasPopped", function ()
{
        self._note.media.removeListenerForNotification("durationUpdat
ed", self.updateAudioInformation);
      });
    }
```

As always, we also need to clean up after ourselves:

```
      self.overrideSuper(self.class, "destroy", self.destroy);
      self.destroy = function () {
        self._recordAudioButton = null;
        self._playAudioButton = null;
        self._audioInformation = null;
        self._note.media.removeListenerForNotification("recordingStopp
        ed", self.onAudioStopped);
        self._note.media.removeListenerForNotification("playingStopp
        ed", self.onAudioStopped);
        self._note.media.removeListenerForNotification("positionUpdat
        ed", self.updateAudioInformation);
        self._note.media.removeListenerForNotification("durationUpdat
        ed", self.updateAudioInformation);
        self._note.media.stop();
        self.super(_className, "destroy");
      };
```

What did we do?

We modified the note view factory so that it could create a new audio note view. We then modified the note list view to support swipe-to-delete, and we also switched our touch handling to Hammer.js. Finally, we created the audio note view's template and code.

What else do I need to know?

Let's go over a few convenience methods used in the preceding code. First, `styleElement` and `styleElements` simplify applying styles to DOM elements, especially when we might have to worry about vendor prefixes.

The code is as follows:

```
UI.styleElement = function (theElement, theStyle, theValue)
{
  var prefixes = ["-webkit-","-moz-","-ms-","-o-",""];
  for (var i=0; i<prefixes.length; i++) {
    var thePrefix = prefixes[i];
    var theNewStyle = thePrefix + theStyle;
    var theNewValue = theValue.replace("%PREFIX%",thePrefix);
    theElement.style.setProperty (theNewStyle, theNewValue);
  }
};

UI.styleElements = function (theElements, theStyle, theValue) {
  var i;
  for (i = 0; i < theElements.length; i++) {
    UI.styleElement(theElements[i], theStyle, theValue);
  }
};
```

Normally, we only need to worry about vendor prefixes on the CSS style name, but occasionally, we need to worry about them on CSS values as well. The preceding code will replace `%PREFIX%` with the specific vendor prefix, if it is specified in `theValue`. This simply reduces the amount of code we have to write.

 Although we only need to worry about WebKit vendor prefixes, YASMF can run on many other platforms, and so it needs to have support for several other vendor prefixes.

The `styleElements` method is simply a convenience method when we need to apply the same style to a list of elements. Again, we're trying to reduce code repetition.

The next major convenience method we use is `getPartsFromSeconds`. It's part of YASMF's `datetime` namespace and provides a useful feature; when given a number of seconds, it can split them into the corresponding number of hours, minutes, and seconds. For example, 125 seconds is 2 minutes and 5 seconds. The `getPartsFromSeconds` method can go a bit further; it can break things down by days, weeks, and years, too.

Because our audio information view only supports minutes and seconds, we pass a second parameter to `getPartsFromSeconds` to indicate how far it should split things out; in our case, this is `PRECISION_MINUTES`.

The code looks like the following:

```
PRECISION_SECONDS: 1,
PRECISION_MINUTES: 2,
PRECISION_HOURS: 3,
PRECISION_DAYS: 4,
PRECISION_WEEKS: 5,
PRECISION_YEARS: 6,
getPartsFromSeconds: function ( seconds, precision ) {
  var partValues = [ 0, 0, 0, 0, 0, 0, 0 ];
  var modValues = [ 1, 60, 3600, 86400, 604800,
  31557600];
  for (var i = precision; i>0; i--) {
    if (i==1) {
      partValues[i-1] = seconds % modValues[i-1];
    }
    else {
      partValues[i-1] = Math.floor(seconds % modValues[
        i-1]);
    }
    partValues[i] = Math.floor(seconds / modValues[i-1]);
    seconds = seconds - partValues[i] * modValues[i-1];
  }
  return { fractions: partValues[0],
           seconds:   partValues[1],
           minutes:   partValues[2],
           hours:     partValues[3],
           days:      partValues[4],
           weeks:     partValues[5],
           years:     partValues[6]  };
}
```

Putting it all together

There are only a couple of details left—modifying the app's styling and changing www/js/ app/main.js—and then you can build and run your app!

Getting on with it

First, let's update our styles in www/css/style.css; add the following code to the end of the file:

```
.android .noteEditView .ui-text-box {
  font-family: "Roboto", "DroidSans", Helvetica, Arial,
    Sans-Serif;
  color: #484848;
```

```
}
.AudioNoteEditView .ui-text-box {
  height: calc(100% - 100px);
}
.AudioNoteEditView .audio-container {
  text-align: center;
  background-color: #FFF;
  border-bottom: 1px solid rgba(87, 52, 32, 0.25);
  height: 100px;
}
.android .AudioNoteEditView .audio-container {
  background-color: #e7ece6;
  border-bottom: 2px solid #484848;
}
.AudioNoteEditView .audio-container div {
  display: inline-block;
  min-width: 44px;
  min-height: 44px;
}
.AudioNoteEditView .audio-information {
    position: absolute;
    right: 10px;
    bottom: 10px;
    min-height: 0 !important;
    opacity: 0.5;
}
```

 We're using `calc()` to simplify some of our layout. iOS 6 needs a `-webkit-` prefix in order for this to work. Android <4.4 will not understand the rule at all, but in this case, it doesn't affect the usability of the app.

Now, we need to update www/js/app/main.js to use YASMF's navigation controller:

```
define ( ["yasmf", "app/views/noteListView"], function ( _y,
NoteListView )
{
    var APP = {};
    APP.start = function () {
        var rootContainer = _y.ge("rootContainer");
        var noteListView = new NoteListView ();
        noteListView.init( );
        var navigationController = new _y.UI.NavigationController();
        navigationController.initWithOptions ( { rootView: noteListView,
        parent: rootContainer } );
    }
    return APP;
});
```

What did we do?

Let's go through our styles first, and then we'll finish up with `main.js`.

The first rule sets the height of `ui-text-box` to `calc(100%-100px)`. This ensures that the textbox fills the rest of the view. We can't use `100%`, because the `audio-container` object takes up 100 px, but that pixel value isn't a percentage, which means we can't use some other percentage. So we use the relatively new `calc()` feature. Not all browsers support it, but most modern ones can handle it without an issue.

The `audio-container` method is then given a `100px` size and appropriate coloring. The `DIV` objects inside are displayed inline so that they float next to each other. (These are the record and play buttons.) The `audio-information` `DIV` element is positioned absolutely in the lower-right corner of the `audio-container` object.

For `main.js`, the first thing we had to change was to prevent the `noteListView` object from attaching to the `rootContainer` object when we created it. We did this by passing nothing to `init`.

We then created a new navigation controller and passed the `noteListView` object as the root view. The controller will attach itself to the specified `parent` object, which is `rootContainer`.

Game Over..... Wrapping it up

And there you have it; the project is complete. You should be able to build and deploy the project to your device and create a new audio note. You should also be able to use swipe-to-delete to delete notes.

 You may not be able to test this app on your simulator/emulator due to the audio recording feature. It's better to run this app on a real device.

Can you take the HEAT? The Hotshot Challenge

There are so many ways you could take this to the next level. Why don't you try a few?

▸ We didn't switch our text note edit view to Hammer.js gesture support. Why don't you follow our example in the audio note edit view and see if you can do that yourself? You can check yourself against the code package for the book.

▸ Spruce up the audio note edit view's audio recording and playback section. Perhaps add an animation that lets the user know when something is playing or recording. If you want to get *really technical*, write a plugin that lets the app monitor the microphone levels, and generate an animation that accurately reflects the volume of the recording. Do the same for playback.

▸ Change the units for an audio note to reflect the size of the audio file, or to better represent the duration (such as hours:minutes:seconds).

▸ Improve our swipe-to-delete mechanism so that any visible **Trash** buttons go away if a tap or gesture is detected anywhere else. The code package has our implementation; try your hand at it first, prior to looking at our implementation.

▸ Make a new kind of note that records when the user enters text while a recording is in progress. Then, allow them to play back their recording and show the text being entered at the same pace as during recording.

Project 6

Working with Still Images

Our modern mobile devices often have good—even excellent—cameras. Now more than ever, users expect to be able to take pictures at any time. This helps explain the plethora of apps that deal specifically with capturing and editing images. However, an app can use the camera without restricting itself to be an image-capturing app and/or image-editing app. In this project, we'll allow users to add photo notes to our app.

What do we build?

Our Filer app can now handle text and audio notes. In this project, we'll extend it to handle photo notes. We'll interact with the device's camera in order to allow the user to take a picture and attach it to their notes.

What does it do?

The primary focus for this project is interacting with the Camera API provided by Cordova/PhoneGap. You'll learn how to capture images and how to adjust various options in order to achieve the kinds of images you need for your app.

Why is it great?

Because we've designed our app to support multiple types of notes, it's going to be incredibly easy to add image support to our app. Even so, we'll cover some of the potential issues that come with working with the camera. We'll also talk a little about performance while displaying many thumbnails at once.

How are we going to do it?

We'll follow the same process we've been using thus far. This is what we'll be doing:

- ▸ Designing the user interface
- ▸ Designing the data model
- ▸ Covering the Camera API
- ▸ Implementing the data model
- ▸ Implementing the user interface
- ▸ Putting it all together

Designing the user interface

In a way, we already designed the user interface for this project when we designed the interface for the audio note edit view. Instead of a small control widget at the top that permits recording and playback, we'll display the image at the top of the view and have a button that permits image capture.

Getting on with it

Our project will have four views in it: the note list view, the text note edit view, the audio note edit view, and the image note edit view. The latter view is the only new view; everything else stays the same. As such, we only need to design the UI for one view!

Let's see what the UI design looks like for this view:

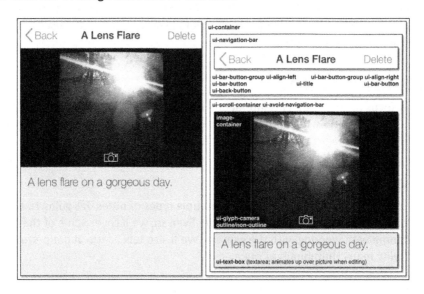

Our view is structured similarly to an audio note edit view, but instead of audio controls at the top, we have a picture at the top of the view in addition to a camera icon (which allows the user to take a new picture).

 The camera icon has an outline around it to help distinguish it from the surrounding image content. At the bottom of the view, we have the text for the note. Due to space constraints on a mobile device, this text area needs to slide up over the image while the soft keyboard is visible.

What did we do?

In this section, we defined the look and feel of the new image note edit view.

What else do I need to know?

It's hard to notice in the previous image, but our camera icon has an outline around it. In most cases, we color an icon with a tint and let it go at that. This time, however, we've colored it white. Since this is hard to see against white photos, we have also added a black outline to the icon. There's no easy way to do this and continue to use *mask-image* in CSS, because masks can only communicate two colors (the background color and the transparent color).

As such, we'll have two elements visible onscreen, and both will be the same icon. One will be colored white and the other black. The black icon will be slightly offset from the white icon, which will create an outline effect so that the icon can still stand out on white images.

Defining the data model

We only have one new data model, much like the previous chapter. In this case, we need to create a model for an image note.

Getting on with it

Like the audio note we defined in the previous project, we will be inheriting the functionality from BaseNote for the image note. This is what the model looks like:

imageNote (+baseNote)	
r/o	.camera
p	_updateUnit()
p	_updateModificationDate)
o	getFormattedUnitValue()
o	setMediaContents (filename)
o	destroy()

Like the audio note, there's not a lot that needs to be done because the BaseNote class does most of our work. Let's go over the changes:

- ▸ A camera property will store a reference to a CameraManager instance. We'll define this in the next section; it lets us talk to the Camera API. It serves the same purpose as the media property on an audio note.

- ▸ _updateUnit will calculate the size of the image.

- ▸ _updateModificationDate will update the modification date after an image is taken.

- ▸ getFormattedUnitValue will override the version of BaseNote. To make things a little easier to read, we'll convert the file size to kilobytes or megabytes if the file is large enough (rather than showing "1,048,576 bytes", we can show "1 MB").

- ▸ setMediaContents will override the BaseNote object's version of CameraManager. It is similar to setMediaContents of the audio note. It will create a new CameraManager object when the property changes.

- ▸ destroy will release the camera object.

What did we do?

In this section, we defined the data model for an image note and covered how it is different from BaseNote.

Covering the Camera API

The Camera API is what permits us to capture images and to access the user's saved photo library. While we'll cover a lot of the API in this task, if you want to see the most up-to-date documentation for it, visit `https://github.com/apache/cordova-plugin-camera/blob/dev/doc/index.md`.

Getting ready

Before continuing, be sure to add the camera plugin to your project:

```
cordova plugin add org.apache.cordova.camera
```

Getting on with it

Taking a picture is easy, especially when compared with prior APIs we've dealt with. You can simply use this:

```
navigator.camera.getPicture ( success, error [, options] );
```

The Camera API will then open in the device and the user can take a picture. Once they are done and approve the picture as taken, the `success` function will be called with the image. If an error occurs (or the user rejects the image), the `error` function will be called.

The `options` parameter is a dictionary that consists of several properties that control the image source (the camera or the user's photo gallery) and the resulting image. The properties are as follows:

- ▸ `quality`: This determines the quality of the image. A smaller number results in a smaller image (more compression) but more visual artifacts. A larger number results in a larger image (less compression) but fewer visual artifacts. For older devices, you may need to target 50 or fewer in order to deal with memory constraints. For our purposes, we'll be using 75 to get a good-quality image.

- ▸ `destinationType`: This indicates how our image should be passed to the `success` method. If this value is `Camera.DestinationType.DATA_URL`, the `success` method will receive base64-encoded image data. If the value is `Camera.DestinationType.FILE_URI`, the path to the image is passed instead (such as `file://path/to/image.jpg`). If this value is `Camera.DestinationType.NATIVE_URL`, the native path to the image is passed (for example, on iOS this might be `assets-library://`). The option most typically used is the middle option. It's the easiest to use and doesn't incur the extra memory overhead of the first option.

- ▶ `sourceType`: This indicates where the image should come from. If this value is `Camera.PictureSourceType.CAMERA`, the camera is used to obtain a picture. If `Camera.PictureSourceType.PHOTOLIBRARY` or `Camera.PictureSourceType.SAVEDPHOTOALBUM` is used, the image is obtained from the user's photo library. On iOS, a different portion of the library is shown for each value, but Android simply shows the same library for each.

- ▶ `allowEdit`: This determines whether an image can be edited prior to returning it to our `success` method. The interface for image editing (if editing is even possible) is platform dependent. Note that this interface is not supported by Android.

- ▶ `encodingType`: This indicates the image type. `Camera.EncodingType.JPEG` will save a file in JPEG format, and `Camera.EncodingType.PNG` will save it in PNG format. PNG is lossless but isn't really suitable for photos as it can't compress well without having lots of similar colors in a row. JPEG is the preferred format for photos as it has good quality and small file sizes.

- ▶ `targetWidth`: This determines the width of the image when specified. Cameras have lots of megapixels, and so the final file size can be quite large. If you only need to use a certain size in your app that is less than the original resolution, you can reduce the file size of the image by reducing the width. It must be used in tandem with `targetHeight` and will maintain the image's aspect ratio.

- ▶ `targetHeight`: This determines the height of the image when specified. It must be used in tandem with `targetWidth` and maintains the aspect ratio of the image.

- ▶ `mediaType`: This indicates what kind of media to include while displaying the user's photo library. Valid options are `Camera.MediaType.PICTURE`, `Camera.MediaType.VIDEO`, and `Camera.MediaType.ALLMEDIA`. Typically, one will use `Camera.MediaType.PICTURE` when the app can only handle images.

- ▶ `correctOrientation`: (If this is true) this makes sure the image matches the orientation of the user's device when the image was captured. That is, if the image was taken in portrait orientation, the image will be in portrait orientation as well. If false, the image may not match the device's orientation at the time of capture.

- ▶ `saveToPhotoAlbum`: (If this is true) this will also save the captured image to the user's photo library.

- ▶ `popoverOptions`: This is for iOS only and controls the location of the photo library popover when used on an iPad. It can also control the direction of the arrow. If you're submitting apps to Apple that work on the iPad, you must use this, or the app may be rejected.

- ▶ `cameraDirection`: This indicates which camera to use. Many devices have a front-facing and a rear-facing camera, and using this, we can indicate which one we want to use. Valid options are `Camera.Direction.BACK` and `Camera.Direction.FRONT`. Note that for Android, specifying either value will use the back-facing camera.

When it comes to capturing images on iOS, it is important to note that if you use the `destinationType` property of `Camera.DestinationType. FILE_URI`, the file is stored in the app's temporary storage. This can be cleaned up at any time by issuing the following command:

```
navigator.camera.cleanup ( success, error );
```

Heads up!

Both Android and iOS store captured images in locations that you might not expect. On iOS, the image is stored in a temporary folder in the app's directory, whereas on Android, it will probably end up in the `DCIM` folder on the device's SD card. This means that to save the file, we have to move it from this location into our own app's persistent storage.

In order to make working with the Camera API a little easier (and to handle the various glitches, such as temporary files, that the various platforms have), we'll create a model called `CameraManager`. It's analogous to the `MediaManager` object in the previous project, and the concept is the same as the `FileManager` object in Version 2 of this app.

Creating a camera manager

First, let's define the data model for a `CameraManager` object:

cameraManager		
r/w	.alsoSaveToPhotoAlbum	= false
r/w	.cameraDirection	= BACK
r/w	.cameraSource	= CAMERA
r/w	.editingAllowed	= false
r/w	.encodingType	= JPEG
r/w	.mediaFilter	= PICTURE
r/w	.quality	= 75
r/w	.src	
r/w	.targetSize ({width:, height:})	
r/w	.useCorrectOrientation	= true
p	_buildCaptureOptions()	
p	_captureImage()	
	takePicture()	
	doesPhotoExist()	
o	init()	
↖	photoCaptured	

. property   **r/w** read/write   **r/o** read-only
p private   **o** override   ↖ notification

Now that we've defined the data model, let's implement the code in www/js/app/models/ cameraManager.js.

First, create the shell of the model as follows:

```
define ( ["yasmf", "Q"], function ( _y, Q )
{
    var _className = "CameraManager";
    var CameraManager = function () {
        var self = new _y.BaseObject ();
        self.subclass ( _className );

        // insert code below here
        return self;
    };

    return CameraManager;
});
```

Next, add the lone notification that we support:

```
        self.registerNotification ( "photoCaptured" );
```

Now, add all the properties. Most of these are simple properties (that is, they don't do anything when set), so the same pattern can be used for each. As such, we've omitted a good portion of the code that is similar (you can look at the code package for the entire code if you would like).

```
        self._quality = 75;
        self.getQuality = function () {
            return self._quality;
        }
        self.setQuality = function ( theQuality ) {
            self._quality = theQuality;
        }
        Object.defineProperty (self, "quality", {
        get: self.getQuality, set: self.setQuality,
        configurable: true });

        ...
        Object.defineProperty ( self, "cameraSource", {
        get: self.getCameraSource, set: self.setCameraSource,
        configurable: true });

        ...
        Object.defineProperty ( self, "editingAllowed", {
        get: self.getEditingAllowed, set: self.setEditingAllowed,
        configurable: true });
```

```
...
Object.defineProperty ( self, "encodingType", {
get: self.getEncodingType, set: self.setEncodingType,
configurable: true });


...
Object.defineProperty ( self, "mediaFilter", {
get: self.getMediaFilter, set: self.setMediaFilter,
configurable: true });


...
Object.defineProperty ( self, "useCorrectOrientation", {
get: self.getUseCorrectOrientation,
set: self.setUseCorrectOrientation, configurable: true });


...
Object.defineProperty ( self, "alsoSaveToPhotoAlbum", {
get: self.getAlsoSaveToPhotoAlbum,
set: self.setAlsoSaveToPhotoAlbum, configurable: true });


...
Object.defineProperty ( self, "cameraDirection", {
get: self.getCameraDirection,
set: self.setCameraDirection, configurable: true });


...
Object.defineProperty ( self, "src", {
get: self.getSrc, set: self.setSrc, configurable: true });
```

The `targetSize` property is a little different. We need to create a dictionary of the form `{width: #, height: #}`:

```
self._targetSize = null;
self.getTargetSize = function () {
   return self._targetSize;
}
self.setTargetSize = function ( targetWidth, targetHeight ) {
  if (typeof targetWidth === "object") {
    self._targetSize = targetWidth;
  }
  else {
    self._targetSize = { width: targetWidth,
    height: targetHeight };
  }
}
```

```
Object.defineProperty ( self, "targetSize", {
get: self.getTargetSize, set: self.setTargetSize,
configurable: true });
```

We need a method that can take all these properties and construct an options dictionary for the Camera API. Only if a property is set should it appear in the dictionary.

```
self._buildCaptureOptions = function () {
    var captureOptions = {};
    if (typeof self.quality !== "undefined" && self.quality
    !== null)
        { captureOptions.quality = self.quality; }
    if (typeof self.cameraSource !== "undefined" &&
    self.cameraSource !== null )
        { captureOptions.sourceType = self.cameraSource; }
    if (typeof self.editingAllowed !== "undefined" &&
    self.editingAllowed !== null )
        { captureOptions.allowEdit = self.editingAllowed; }
    if (typeof self.encodingType !== "undefined" &&
    self.encodingType !== null)
        { captureOptions.encodingType = self.encodingType; }
    if (typeof self.targetSize !== "undefined" &&
    self.targetSize !== null)
    {
        if (typeof self.targetSize.width !== "undefined" &&
        self.targetSize.width !== null)
        {
            captureOptions.targetWidth = self.targetSize.width;
        }
        if (typeof self.targetSize.height !== "undefined" &&
        self.targetSize.height !== null)
        {
            captureOptions.targetHeight =
            self.targetSize.height;
        }
    }

    if (typeof self.mediaFilter !== "undefined" &&
    self.mediaFilter !== null)
        { captureOptions.mediaType = self.mediaFilter; }
    if (typeof self.alsoSaveToPhotoAlbum !== "undefined" &&
    self.alsoSaveToPhotoAlbum !== null )
        { captureOptions.saveToPhotoAlbum =
        self.alsoSaveToPhotoAlbum; }
    if (typeof self.cameraDirection !== "undefined" &&
    self.cameraDirection !== null )
```

```
                { captureOptions.cameraDirection =
                self.cameraDirection; }
            if (typeof self.useCorrectOrientation !== "undefined" &&
            self.useCorrectOrientation !== null )
                { captureOptions.correctOrientation =
                self.useCorrectOrientation; }
            captureOptions.destinationType =
            Camera.DestinationType.FILE_URI;
            return captureOptions;
        }
```

Next, we need a method that wraps the Camera API so that we can return a promise while capturing an image:

```
        self._captureImage = function ()
        {
            var deferred = Q.defer();
            try {
                navigator.camera.getPicture ( function (imageURI) {
                deferred.resolve (imageURI); },
                function (anError) {deferred.reject (anError); },
                self._buildCaptureOptions() );
            }
            catch ( anError ) {
                deferred.reject (anError.message);
            }
            return deferred.promise;
        }
```

Now that we've wrapped the Camera API method, we can write a method to take a picture and copy it to the desired location (regardless of where the API might put the image, such as a temporary directory). Note that the path has the very first character eliminated (which is always a slash); without this, the File APIs tend to fail.

```
        self.takePicture = function ()
        {
          var fm = new _y.FileManager();
          var targetPath =
          _y.filename.getPathPart(self.src).substr(1);
          var targetName = _y.filename.getFilePart(self.src);
          return fm.init(fm.PERSISTENT, 0)
            .then(function () { return self._captureImage(); })
            .then(function (theURI) {
                  return fm.resolveLocalFileSystemURL(theURI);
                })
```

```
            .then(function (fileEntry) { fm.moveFile(fileEntry,
        targetPath, targetName); })
            .then(function () {
                    self.notify("photoCaptured");
                    return;
                });
        };
```

We also need a mechanism to determine whether an image file exists. If it does, we want the `File` object for the image so that we can determine the size.

```
self.doesPhotoExist = function ()
  {
    var fm = new _y.FileManager();
    var deferred = Q.defer();
    var img = self.src;
    if (_y.device.platform() === "android")
      { img = img.substr(1,img.length); }
    fm.init ( fm.PERSISTENT, 0 )
      .then ( function () { return fm.getFile (img, {} ); })
      .then ( function ( theFile ) { deferred.resolve ( theFile ); })
      .catch ( function ( anError ) { deferred.resolve ( null ); })
      .done();
    return deferred.promise;
  };
```

Finally, we need to define the `init` method as follows:

```
        self.overrideSuper ( self.class, "init", self.init );
        self.init = function ( theSource )
        {
          self.super ( _className, "init" );
          if (typeof theSource !== "undefined") {
        self.src = theSource; }
        }
```

What did we do?

First, we covered the Camera API. Then we created a `CameraManager` class to wrap the API into a convenient handler. Let's go over what we wrote.

First, after subclassing the `BaseObject` class, we created a new notification: `photoCaptured`. This allows us to send a notification whenever a photo has been captured by the camera.

Next, we defined several properties that mirror those properties in the `options` object that we pass to `navigator.camera.getPicture`. The properties are as follows:

- ▸ `quality`: This defaults to 75.
- ▸ `cameraSource`: This defaults to using the camera to take a picture, rather than the photo library.
- ▸ `editingAllowed`: This indicates whether editing can be performed on an image before it is returned to us. It has the same platform restrictions as `allowEdit` does. Valid options are `true` and `false`. The default is `false`.
- ▸ `encodingType`: This determines the file type as JPEG or PNG. The default is JPEG.
- ▸ `targetSize`: This is an object of the form {`width: #, height: #`}. It determines the size of the image after capture. Aspect ratios are maintained.
- ▸ `mediaFilter`: This defaults to allow only pictures in the photo library picker. This works for iOS only.
- ▸ `useCorrectOrientation`: This defaults to `true`.
- ▸ `alsoSaveToPhotoAlbum`: This defaults to `false`.
- ▸ `cameraDirection`: This defaults to the back-facing camera.
- ▸ `src`: This indicates the filename that we should use to capture an image. This usually means that the captured image will first be written to temporary storage (or another location) and then moved to the specified location. It's also used when we want to check for the existence of a photo at this location.

`_buildCaptureOptions` is the method that actually takes all of the preceding options and puts them together in a format that the Camera API understands. It properly handles the object when any property is not defined or is null, which explains some of the bulk of the code. Note that we always assume a `FILE_URI` manager by default. This manager doesn't support base64 or native URIs at all. This is all we need for our app.

Next, `_captureImage` is what actually takes a picture. As with the `FileManager` object, it uses promises to return the captured image URI or the appropriate error. `takePicture` does the hard work of calling `_captureImage` and then moving the files around. Since these images are initially saved elsewhere, we need to move them to the `src` parameter. We use `resolveLocalFileSystemURL` to map the original path to our app's filesystem first, and then we can use `moveTo` to complete the move.

`doesPhotoExist` is a useful convenience method that checks whether a file exists at `src`, and if it does, it returns the `File` object, which is an easy way to get the size and other metadata about the file. If it doesn't exist, null is returned instead.

What else do I need to know?

If you want to display the captured image in your HTML, it's pretty straightforward. You can pass the FILE_URI manager to the src property on an IMG tag, or you can assign it to the any of the styles that support images. Once you move the image into persistent storage, you can also reference it with the cdvfile URL scheme (for example, cdvfile://localhost/persistent/path/to/image.png).

For example, use the following code:

```
var cm = new CameraManager();
cm.init ( "image1234.jpg" );
cm.takePicture()
    .then ( function (theURI) {
        document.getElementById(
        "the-image").style.backgroundImage = "url(
        " + theURI + ")";
    } )
    .catch (…)
    .done();
```

Handling base64-encoded images

If the result is a base64-encoded image, you need to append data:image/jpeg;base64 to the incoming image data. (Use image/png if the image is PNG instead of JPEG.) That said, if you can avoid it, you should avoid using base64-encoded images as this consumes considerably more memory than using file URIs.

Keep in mind that the image displayed will be the original image. This means it could be quite large, especially if the camera has many megapixels. You can, of course, use CSS or IMG attributes to scale the image down, but the mobile device still has to process all that data.

If possible, use targetWidth and targetHeight (or targetSize in the CameraManager object) to downsize the final image to the maximum resolution you need. For example, many social media sites will downsample the image anyway, so there's no need for your app to store and display the full original image if that's all it's ever going to be used for.

If you need to display multiple images (say, a grid of thumbnails), then you need to worry about how much you are downsampling your images for display. Each downsampling operation takes a considerable amount of time, and any scrolling operations slow to a crawl.

The solution to this problem is drawing your image to a canvas that has the dimensions of your thumbnail. Canvases retain their image content even during scrolling, and so you only have to worry about loading the image data once. That means it'll still be slow the first time those images are displayed, but once they're all loaded in, scrolling will be very fast.

To do this, you need some HTML and some JavaScript code. Let's imagine you've defined a CANVAS tag as follows:

```
<canvas width=84 height=84></canvas>
```

The width and height parameters indicate the size of the thumbnail you want. Although it will be reset later on, it's important to define it now (otherwise, the contents of the page will jump around as images are loaded). Now, repeat the use of the CANVAS tag as many times as you need to populate your grid in a manner similar to the way we populate our note list view. You'll need to use querySelectorAll or getElementsByTagName in order to find them and loop through them in the next step.

Once you have the list of canvases, you can use the following method to draw to each one in series (this assumes an 84 x 84 thumbnail):

```
function drawImageToCanvas ( theCanvas, imageSrc ) {
  var img = new Image();
  img.onload = function () {
    var newWidth = 84;
    var newHeight = (this.height / this.width) * 84;
    if (newHeight > 84) {
      newHeight = 84;
      newWidth = (this.width / this.height) * 84;
    }
    var newLeft = 42 - (newWidth/2);
    var newTop = 42 - (newHeight/2);
    theCanvas.setAttribute (
    "width", newWidth * window.devicePixelRatio);
    theCanvas.setAttribute (
    "height",newHeight * window.devicePixelRatio);
    theCanvas.style.width = ""+newWidth+"px";
    theCanvas.style.height = ""+newHeight+"px";
    theCanvas.style.left  = ""+newLeft +"px";
    theCanvas.style.top = ""+newTop+"px";
    var theCanvasCtx = theCanvas.getContext("2d");
    theCanvasCtx.save();
    theCanvasCtx.scale (window.devicePixelRatio,
    window.devicePixelRatio);
    theCanvasCtx.imageSmoothingEnabled = false;
    theCanvasCtx.drawImage (this, 0, 0, newWidth, newHeight);
    theCanvasCtx.restore();
  }
  img.src = imageSrc;
}
```

You can use it like this:

```
var imagePaths = [ array of image paths ];
var canvases = someElement.getElementsByTagName("canvas");
for (var i=0; i<canvases.length; i++)
{
   drawImageToCanvas ( canvases[i], imagePaths[i] );
}
```

If you want to allow some processing time for user interaction, it might be best to use `setTimeout` and draw one or a few images every few milliseconds. (Otherwise, the app will most likely pause while the preceding code is working.)

Implementing the data model

Now that we've handled the camera interaction, we need to implement the image note so that it can take advantage of the `CameraManager` object.

Getting on with it

Let's create the image note model in `www/js/app/models/imageNote.js`. Start by creating the shell:

```
define ( ["yasmf","app/models/baseNote", "app/models/cameraManager"],
function (
 _y, BaseNote, CameraManager ) {
   var _className = "ImageNote";
   var ImageNote = function () {
      var self = new BaseNote();
      self.subclass ( _className );
      return self;
   }

   return ImageNote;
});
```

Next, we need to create a property to hold the camera manager:

```
      self._camera = null;
      self.getCamera = function () {
         return self._camera;
      }
      Object.defineProperty ( self, "camera", {
      get: self.getCamera, configurable: true});
```

As with our prior note, we need to override the representation of this note type:

```
self._representation = "photo";
```

We also need to set the appropriate units. Here, we've set labels that might be common when working with images. The labels are for images that are 0 bytes, 1 byte, 2-1023 bytes, 1-1023 kilobytes, and 1 megabyte or higher, respectively.

```
self.unitLabels = [ "bytes", "byte", "bytes", "KB", "MB" ];
```

It's not very user friendly to indicate that an image is 1,048,576 bytes large. It would make better sense to indicate 1 MB. To do this, we need to override getFormattedUnitValue to support the preceding labels, as follows:

```
self.overrideSuper ( self.class, "getFormattedUnitValue",
self.getFormattedUnitValue );
self.getFormattedUnitValue = function () {
  if ( self.unitValue < 1024 ) {
    return _y.N(self.unitValue) + " " +
    _y.T(self.unitLabels[Math.min(2,self.unitValue)]);
  }
  else {
    if (self.unitValue < (1024*1024)) {
      return _y.N(self.unitValue / 1024) +
      _y.T(self.unitLabels[ 3 ])
    }
    else {
      return _y.N(self.unitValue / (1024*1024) ) +
      _y.T(self.unitLabels[ 4 ])
    }
  }
}
Object.defineProperty ( self, "formattedUnitValue", {
get: self.getFormattedUnitValue, configurable: true});
```

When a photo is taken, we need to obtain the file size information from it. We can use doesPhotoExist for this, as follows:

```
self._updateUnit = function ()
{
  self._camera.doesPhotoExist()
      .then ( function ( theFile ) {
              self.unitValue = theFile.size;
            } )
      .catch ( function (anError ) {
              console.log ( anError );
```

```
                    } )

        .done ();
    }
```

We also need to update the modification date when a photo is taken, as follows:

```
self._updateModificationDate = function () {
    self._modifiedDate = new Date();
}
```

When the `mediaContents` property is set, we need to create a new `CameraManager` object. To do this, we need to override `setMediaContents`. Also note that we register for the `photoCaptured` notification so that we can update the modification date and the unit value.

```
self.overrideSuper ( self.class, "setMediaContents", self.
setMediaContents );
    self.setMediaContents = function ( theMediaContents )
    {
        self.super ( _className, "setMediaContents", [
        theMediaContents ]);
        if (self._camera !== null) {
            self._camera.destroy();
            self._camera = null;
        }
        self._camera = new CameraManager();
        self._camera.init ( theMediaContents );
        self.notify ( "mediaContentsChanged" );
        self._camera.addListenerForNotification (
        "photoCaptured", self._updateUnit );
        self._camera.addListenerForNotification (
        "photoCaptured", self._updateModificationDate );
    }
    Object.defineProperty ( self, "mediaContents", {
    get: self.getMediaContents, set: self.setMediaContents,
    configurable: true});
```

As always, we clean up after ourselves:

```
self.overrideSuper ( self.class, "destroy", self.destroy);
self.destroy = function () {
    self._camera.destroy();
    self._camera = null;
    self.super ( _className, "destroy" );
}
```

What did we do?

In this section, we created a model for an image note.

Implementing the user interface

The user interface will be quite similar to the audio note edit view, with a couple crucial differences. Let's get started.

Getting on with it

First, we need to create the template in `www/html/imageNoteEditView.html`. I've marked the differences between the templates used for the audio note edit view and the image note edit view. Let's start by using the following code:

```html
<html>
  <body>
    <div class="ui-navigation-bar">
      <div class="ui-title"
      contenteditable="true">%NOTE_NAME%</div>
      <div class="ui-bar-button-group ui-align-left">
        <div class="ui-bar-button ui-tint-color
        ui-back-button">%BACK%</div>
      </div>
      <div class="ui-bar-button-group ui-align-right">
        <div class="ui-bar-button ui-destructive-color">
        %DELETE_NOTE%</div>
      </div>
    </div>
    <div class="ui-scroll-container ui-avoid-navigation-bar">
      <div class="image-container">
        <div class="ui-glyph ui-background-tint-color
        ui-glyph-camera outline"></div>
        <div class="ui-glyph ui-background-tint-color
        ui-glyph-camera non-outline"></div>
      </div>
      <textarea class="ui-text-box"
      onblur="this.classList.remove('editing');"
      onfocus="this.classList.add('editing');">
      %NOTE_CONTENTS%</textarea>
    </div>
  </body>
</html>
```

Next, we need to create the code in www/js/app/views/imageNoteEditView.js, starting with the shell:

```
define ( ["yasmf", "app/models/noteStorageSingleton",
          "text!html/imageNoteEditView.html!strip",
          "app/views/textNoteEditView", "hammer"],
function ( _y, noteStorageSingleton, imageNoteViewHTML,
           TextNoteEditView, Hammer ) {
    var _className = "ImageNoteEditView";
    var ImageNoteEditView = function () {
        var self = new TextNoteEditView();
        self.subclass ( _className );

        return self;
    }
    return ImageNoteEditView;
});
```

Next, we need to keep track of the button that will take a picture as well as an image container:

```
self._takePictureButton = null;
self._imageContainer = null;
```

Override render so that we can indicate the correct template:

```
self.overrideSuper ( self.class, "render", self.render );
self.render = function () {
    return _y.template ( imageNoteViewHTML,
                            {
                                "NOTE_NAME": self._note.name,
                                "NOTE_CONTENTS":
                                 self._note.textContents,
                                "BACK": _y.T("BACK"),
                                "DELETE_NOTE":
                                _y.T("app.nev.DELETE_NOTE")
                            });
}
```

Next, when a photo is taken (or when the note is displayed), we need to update the image container with the appropriate image. We can do this by setting the background-image style to a URL of the form cdvfile://localhost/persistent/path/to/file. We also need to *bust the cache* so that the browser is forced to reload the image, which is important if the image has changed.

```
self.updatePhoto = function () {
    _y.UI.styleElement(self._imageContainer,
    "background-image", "inherit");
```

```
var template =
"url(cdvfile://localhost/persistent%URL%?%CACHE%)";
setTimeout(function () {
  var cacheBust = Math.floor(Math.random() * 100000);
  var newBackground = _y.template ( template, {
  "URL": self._note.mediaContents, "CACHE": cacheBust} );
  _y.UI.styleElement(self._imageContainer,
  "background-image", newBackground);
}, 100);
}
```

When a photo is captured, we remove our listener and ask to update the photo in the view. We can use the following code for this purpose:

```
self.onPhotoCaptured = function () {
  self._note.camera.removeListenerForNotification (
  "photoCaptured", self.onPhotoCaptured );
  self.updatePhoto();
}
```

To take a picture, we register a listener for photoCaptured so that we can update the view after a picture is taken. We then invoke takePicture on our CameraManager object:

```
self.takePicture = function () {
  self._note.camera.addListenerForNotification (
  "photoCaptured", self.onPhotoCaptured );
  self._note.camera.takePicture()
      .catch ( function ( anError ) {
              self._note.camera.removeListenerForNotification
              ( "photoCaptured", self.onPhotoCaptured);
              console.log (anError );
            })
      .done();
}
```

As with any view, we need to override renderToElement so that we can find and attach events to the DOM elements we care about. We also call updatePhoto to force the view to show the picture for the note when it is loaded:

```
self.overrideSuper ( self.class, "renderToElement",
self.renderToElement );
self.renderToElement = function () {
  self.super ( _className, "renderToElement" );
  self._takePictureButton = self.element.querySelector (
  ".image-container .ui-glyph.non-outline");
  self._imageContainer = self.element.querySelector
  (".image-container" );
```

```
              Hammer ( self._takePictureButton ).on("tap",
              self.takePicture);
              self.updatePhoto ();
          }
```

And, as always, we clean up after ourselves:

```
          self.overrideSuper ( self.class, "destroy", self.destroy );
          self.destroy = function () {
              self._takePictureButton = null;
              self._imageContainer = null;
              self._note.camera.removeListenerForNotification (
              "photoCaptured", self.onPhotoCaptured );
              self.super ( _className, "destroy" );
          }
```

What did we do?

First, we defined the template for the image note edit view. The only difference from the audio note edit view's template was the code near the bottom. All we did was define two `Camera DIV` elements. One indicates that it is outlined (this is the black shadow), and the other indicates that it isn't (this is the white version on top). The one that isn't outlined is the one we attach an event handler to so that the user can tap it and take a picture.

Notice the `onblur` and `onfocus` event handlers. When fired, they add or remove the `editing` class from the element whenever the element receives (or loses) focus. This is important because we need the `textarea` element to slide up when the soft keyboard appears. When the keyboard appears, we'll use a simple animation to slide it up and over the image. This is attached to the `editing` class in our CSS (which we define in the next section).

Finally, we wrote the code for the image note edit view. One portion should have caught your eye: we're using the `cdvfile` URL scheme. This is specific to Cordova. On a desktop browser, you could use `filesystem` to accomplish the same thing. This allows us to access images within persistent (or temporary) storage without having to know the physical path on the device. It works great for images but not for audio or video, which is why this is the only time we can use it.

The format of the CDVFile/filesystem scheme

The format of a path is as follows:

`scheme://hostname/storage-type/path/to/file.`

To access a file in temporary storage on a mobile device, use `cdvfile://localhost/temporary/path/to/file`. For persistent storage, use `cdvfile://localhost/persistent/path/to/file`.

What else do I need to know?

Our image note edit view doesn't support taking images from the user's photo library, but it would be something you could add quite easily. You could simply ask your user what they want to do each time they tap the Camera button, or you could add a second button that would use the photo library.

Another important issue is that of security. On most devices, your app will need permission to use the camera. On iOS, this might manifest as a message box asking the user for permission. Your code needs to handle the delay that might occur while the user reads and acts on the message, which is why we used promises in our code. Your code should also handle the unlikely event that the user rejects the request.

Putting it all together

We're almost there. We just need to add some styles, edit a couple of files with minor adjustments, and we'll be done!

Getting on with it

If you were to run the app now, it would work, but you wouldn't actually be able to create image notes, which defeats the purpose of what we've done so far. The reason the app fails is because we haven't updated our factories or our note list view.

In www/js/app/factories/noteFactory.js, we update the factory so that it can return an image note and an appropriate filename. Use the following code to update the factory:

```
define ( ["app/models/baseNote", "app/models/audioNote",
  "app/models/imageNote"],
function ( BaseNote, AudioNote, ImageNote )
{

    noteFactory.createNote = function ( noteType ) {
    …
        case noteFactory.IMAGENOTE:
            return new ImageNote();

    …
    }

    noteFactory.createAssociatedMediaFileName = function (
    noteType, uid) {
    …
            case noteFactory.IMAGENOTE:
```

```
                                extension = { "default": "jpg" };
                                newFileName = "image";
                                break;
        …
        }
    …
    });
```

In `www/js/app/factories/noteViewFactory.js,` use the following code:

```
define ( ["app/views/textNoteEditView",
  "app/views/audioNoteEditView", "app/views/imageNoteEditView",
  "app/factories/noteFactory"],
function ( TextNoteEditView, AudioNoteEditView, ImageNoteEditView,
  noteFactory )
{
…
    noteViewFactory.createNoteEditView = function ( noteType )
    {
    …
            case noteFactory.IMAGENOTE:
                return new ImageNoteEditView();
    …
        }
    …
    });
```

At this point, the app can create the image note and its associated view, but we need to update the note list view so that it actually tries to create an image note. To that end, use the following code in `www/js/app/views/noteListView.js`:

```
define ( ["yasmf",
            "app/models/noteStorageSingleton",
            "text!html/noteListView.html!strip",
            "text!html/noteListItem.html!strip",
            "app/factories/noteFactory",
            "app/factories/noteViewFactory",
            "hammer"],
function ( _y, noteStorageSingleton, noteListViewHTML,
  noteListItemHTML,
            noteFactory, noteViewFactory, Hammer )
{
…
        // after createNewAudioNote
        self.createNewImageNote = function () {
```

```
        self._createAndEditNote(noteFactory.IMAGENOTE);
      };
  …
      self.renderToElement = function ()
      {
      …
        Hammer ( self._newTextNoteButton ).on (
        "tap", self.createNewTextNote );
        Hammer ( self._newAudioNoteButton ).on (
        "tap", self.createNewAudioNote );
        Hammer ( self._newImageNoteButton ).on (
        "tap", self.createNewImageNote );
      …
      }
  …
  });
```

Now, let's define the styles we need to make the view look nice. In `www/css/style.css`, add the following code:

```css
.ImageNoteEditView .ui-text-box
{
  height: calc(100% - 200px);
  -webkit-transition: margin 0.3s ease-in-out,
  height 0.3s ease-in-out;
  transition: margin 0.3s ease-in-out,
  height 0.3s ease-in-out;
  background-color: #f1eee5;
}
.android .ImageNoteEditView .ui-text-box
{
  background-color: #000;
}


.ImageNoteEditView .ui-text-box.editing
{
  height: 100%;
  -webkit-transform: translateZ(1px);
  transform: translateZ(1px);
  margin-top: -200px;
}
```

```css
.ImageNoteEditView .image-container
{
  text-align: center;
  background-color: #000;
  border-bottom: 1px solid rgba(87, 52, 32, 0.25);
  height: 200px;
  background-position: center center;
  background-size: contain;
  position: relative;
}
.android .ImageNoteEditView .image-container
{
  background-color: #000;
  border-bottom: 2px solid #669900;
}
.ImageNoteEditView .image-container div
{
  position: absolute;
  top: 0;
  left: 0;
  right: 0;
  bottom: 0;
  -webkit-mask-position-y: 100%;
  -moz-mask-position-y: 100%;
  -ms-mask-position-y: 100%;
  mask-position-y: 100%;
  background-color: white;
}

.ImageNoteEditView .image-container div.outline
{
  position: absolute;
  top: 0;
  left: 0;
  right: 0;
  bottom: 0;
  -webkit-mask-position-y: calc(100% + 1px);
  -moz-mask-position-y: calc(100% + 1px);
  -ms-mask-position-y: calc(100% + 1px);
  mask-position-y: calc(100% + 1px);
  background-color: black;
}
```

What did we do?

First, we updated our factories so that they could create image notes and image note edit views. Then, we updated the note list view so that it can create a new image note.

Finally, we updated our styles. Let's go over them to see what's going on.

The first interesting part is on `.ImageNoteEditView .ui-text-box`; we've defined a transition for `margin` and `height`. We've also added a `background-color` attribute. Now look a little further down the code at `.ImageNoteEditView .ui-text-box.editing`. Here, the `height` attribute becomes `100%` and `margin-top` becomes `-200px`.

This means that, by default, the text area below the photo sits below the photo and takes up the rest of the screen (100 percent: 200 px). However, this space isn't sufficient when we start typing, because the soft keyboard comes up and obstructs most of our view. To combat this, the element adds the `editing` class to itself (remember the image note edit view template in the last task?), which changes the `height` and `margin-top` attributes. The `margin-top` attribute raises the text area above the photo. This is why we have a `background-color` attribute; to keep the photo from showing through. The value of `height` changes to `100%` so that it now fills our view. When the keyboard is dismissed, or when the user navigates away from the text area, the `editing` class is removed and the process is reversed.

Typically, in native apps, you would simply allow the photo and the text area to scroll together. But on both platforms, the scrolling is a little fussy when it comes to the multiple scroll areas presented by text areas and the entire view. On iOS, this often simply breaks down entirely, leaving a virtually nonscrollable text area.

The only other interesting portion of the styling is at the bottom, where we define the two `Camera` icons and how they are positioned. Note that we set the `outline` property of the camera to 1 px below the nonoutline camera (the non-outline camera is at `100%` and the outline is at `100% + 1 px` vertically) and give it a different color. This is what creates the *shadow* or *outline* effect and allows it to be visible even on white photos.

Game Over..... Wrapping it up

In this project, you were introduced to the Camera API and created a `CameraManager` object to handle some of the quirks that some of the platforms have. You created the user interface for the image note edit view and implemented it. You also handled the issues present when there's not enough space to type when the soft keyboard is visible.

 You won't be able to capture images using this app on the iOS simulator due to the lack of camera support. Run this app on a real device instead.

Can you take the HEAT? The Hotshot Challenge

There are many ways this project could be extended. Why don't you try a few?

- Display the actual photo (as a thumbnail in a CANVAS tag) in the note list view instead of the simple photo icon. For a larger challenge, support the caching of thumbnails so that they don't have to be regenerated each time the view appears.

- Allow the app to use the user's photo library in addition to taking a picture with the camera.

- If the user taps on the image (not the icons), display a new view that shows the image at full size. If you want a bigger challenge, allow the user to interact with the image by supporting pinch-to-zoom. If you want even more adventure, support rotation as well.

Project 7
Capturing Video

Once cameras on mobile devices came about, it didn't take very long for someone to ask the question, "What about video?" Initially, video recording, storage, and playback were hampered by the space and hardware limitations on mobile devices. It is one thing to snap a few JPEG files, which might be a few hundred kilobytes, but it is another thing to record a video longer than a few seconds, which does add up to a large file size. Furthermore, video has to be encoded and compressed while recording, and decompressed and decoded while playing. Needless to say, the early attempts were not something we would look back at now and think, *that's amazing*! That said, it was pretty amazing at the time.

When video recording and playback did become practical, it changed the way we perceived the world. It was now possible to have footage of news occurrences from anywhere there was a mobile phone, which was practically everywhere. What's more, it wasn't limited to "news-worthy" events—many record memories of their family's everyday lives. Video recording has changed the way we remember things.

What do we build?

Our Filer app has become reasonably complicated and useful. Let's make it even more useful by recording video notes. We'll have to interact with the device's camera again, which sounds similar to the previous project, but we'll do it in a slightly different manner. We'll also add a data-saving confirmation message when someone deletes a note within a note edit view.

What does it do?

The primary focus for this project is to interact with the Capture API provided by Cordova/PhoneGap. We'll learn how to capture a video and play it back. We'll also cover how to generate native and native-like alert messages and the benefits of both.

Why is it great?

Although a lot of apps don't necessarily require video capture capabilities, there are enough use cases where it's an important tool. More and more apps need to display confirmation and alert messages, and we'll cover how to use that feature as well.

How are we going to do it?

Similar to the previous projects, we'll cover the following:

- ▸ Designing the user interface
- ▸ Covering the Capture API
- ▸ Covering native, native-like, and non-native alerts
- ▸ Implementing the data model
- ▸ Implementing the user interface
- ▸ Putting it all together

Designing the user interface

By this point, you can probably guess how the user interface will appear for this particular project. Even so, let's get started.

Getting on with it

Our project will now have five views: the note list view, the text note edit view, the audio note edit view, the image note edit view, and now the video note edit view. The last view is the only new view, just like the previous project, and the UI is very familiar.

Let's look at the following screenshot that shows what the UI looks like:

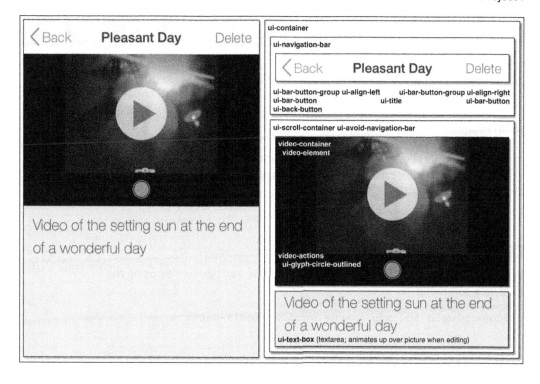

Our view is structured similar to both the audio note edit view and the image note edit view. We have a view at the top that will hold the video for playback, and below it, we have a single record control (the outlined circle as shown in the previous image).

An example of the asset we'll use on the note list view is shown in the following screenshot:

Note the new film strip icon; this is what we'll use to represent video notes.

What did we do?

In this task, we defined the user interface for the video note edit view.

Covering the Capture API

The Capture API, in some ways, duplicates some of the functionalities that the Camera API and the Media API provide. That said, the Capture API tries to be a little more general; its sole purpose is to capture media, whether that is images, sound, or video. Although I prefer the other APIs to take pictures or record audio, this API is the only one that supports video capturing.

As such, we'll only cover the portion of the API that works with video. If you want to see the other capture documentation, or if you just want the most up-to-date documentation for the entire API, visit `https://github.com/apache/cordova-plugin-media-capture/blob/dev/doc/index.md`.

Getting ready

Before continuing, add the media capture plugin to your project by using the following command:

```
cordova plugin add org.apache.cordova.media-capture
```

Getting on with it

It's easy to record a video, especially when you think about everything the device has to do. You can simply use the following command:

```
navigator.device.capture.captureVideo ( success, error [, options]
);
```

The device will then open the video recording view, and the user can start capturing a video. The interface presented is platform dependent. Once the user is done recording, they can approve the video or retake it. Once they approve the video, the success function will be called with a list of video files (in our case, this will always be one video file, but some devices permit capturing multiple video clips in sequence). If the video is rejected or some other error occurs, the error function is called.

Like the previous project, you can specify some options that control the video recording session, but unlike the previous project, there are only two properties:

> ► `duration`: This indicates the maximum duration for a video. Video files consume a lot of space, especially when compared with sounds and images, and as such, it might be wise to place an upper limit. The duration is specified in seconds. Not all platforms display this option, so consider it a suggestion.

▸ limit: This indicates how many video clips can be taken in sequence. To be honest, I've never really seen the need for taking more than one video at once, but some platforms support it. Notably, iOS does not, so it's wise to avoid using any value other than 1.

When the success method is called, it is passed a list of video files. In our case, we will always see only one item in that list, but if you use a different number for the limit, you will see several files.

Each video in the list contains useful information, such as the following:

▸ fullPath: This specifies the full path to the file

▸ lastModifiedDate: This is the the date the file was last modified

▸ name: This denotes the name of the file (without the path)

▸ size: This indicates file size, in bytes

▸ type: This is the mime type

For each video, one can request additional information using the following:

```
video.getFormatData ( success [, error] );
```

If the information can be retrieved, the success method will be called with an object containing the following properties:

▸ codecs: This is not supported on any platform

▸ bitrate: This is not supported on any platform, except iOS 4 for audio files

▸ height and width: This represents the height and width of the video

▸ duration: This represents the length of the file, in seconds

As in prior projects, we'll make a simple model that makes it easier to work with the API. We'll call it the video manager.

Creating a video manager

Before we create the code for our video manager, let's look at the model. Note that it looks quite a bit like our camera manager model, albeit with fewer configurable options.

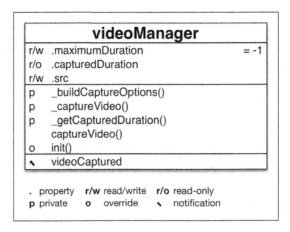

Now, let's define our module shell in `www/js/app/models/videoManager.js` as shown in the following code:

```
define ( ["yasmf", "Q"], function ( _y, Q ) {
    var _className = "VideoManager";
    var VideoManager = function () {
        var self = new _y.BaseObject ();
        self.subclass ( _className );
        // the following code is inserted here
        return self;
    }
    return VideoManager;
});
```

First, we define our single notification that we can send:

```
        self.registerNotification ( "videoCaptured" );
```

Let's add the code for the `maximumDuration` property. We'll default its value to `-1`, so videos will have no limit unless specifically overridden. Given the amount of space videos require, it might not be a bad idea to come up with a reasonable limit in your apps. So, use the following code:

```
        self._maximumDuration = -1;
        self.getMaximumDuration = function () {
```

```
        return self._maximumDuration;
    }
    self.setMaximumDuration = function ( theDuration ) {
        self._maximumDuration = theDuration;
    }
    Object.defineProperty ( self, "maximumDuration", {
    get: self.getMaximumDuration,
        set: self.setMaximumDuration,
            configurable: true } );
```

As in our other manager objects, we need to specify the location of the video, so we need to add a property called `src`:

```
        self._src = null;
        self.getSrc = function () {
            return self._src;
        }
        self.setSrc = function ( theSource ) {
            self._src = theSource;
        }
        Object.defineProperty ( self, "src", {
        get: self.getSrc, set: self.setSrc,
        configurable: true } );
```

Another useful property is the length of the video. It's only valid after a record operation though, and gives us only read-only access. Let's define it in the following code:

```
        self._capturedDuration = -1;
        self.getCapturedDuration = function () {
            return self._capturedDuration;
        }
        Object.defineProperty ( self, "capturedDuration", {
        get: self.getCapturedDuration, configurable: true } );
```

If you remember our camera manager, we defined a `_buildcaptureOptions` method to aggregate the public-facing properties in the manager into an object that can be passed to the Capture API. We need to do the same here, though there are fewer options, as seen in the following code:

```
        self._buildCaptureOptions = function () {
            var captureOptions = {};
            if (typeof self.maximumDuration !== "undefined" &&
                self.maximumDuration !== null &&
                self.maximumDuration >= 0) {
                captureOptions.duration = self.maximumDuration;
            }
```

```
            captureOptions.limit = 1; //
            we only support one video at a time
            return captureOptions;
        }
```

Capturing a video is an asynchronous operation—we need to wrap it with a promise, as is used in the following code:

```
        self._captureVideo = function () {
            var deferred = Q.defer();
            try {
                navigator.device.capture.captureVideo
                (
                    function ( mediaFiles ) { deferred.resolve (
                    mediaFiles ); },
                    function ( anError ) { deferred.reject ( anError );
                    },
                    self._buildCaptureOptions()
                );
            }
            catch ( anError ) {
                deferred.reject ( anError );
            }
            return deferred.promise;
        }
```

Getting the duration of a specific media file is also an asynchronous operation, and it is only valid after the file has been recorded. We'll wrap it in a promise as well, as shown in the following code:

```
        self._getCapturedDuration = function ( theMediaFile ) {
            var deferred = Q.defer();
            try {
                theMediaFile.getFormatData ( function (theFormatData)
                { deferred.resolve ( theFormatData ); },
                function (anError) {
                    deferred.reject ( anError ); } );
            }
            catch (anError) {
                deferred.reject (anError);
            }
            return deferred.promise;
        }
```

Now, let's do the real work—capture our video. First we split the value in our `src` property into its corresponding path and filename components. Then we call `_captureVideo` (defined in the preceding code) to capture the video. When the video has been captured, we get `fullPath` from the recorded video file and then call `_getCapturedDuration` to get the duration of the video. Once we have the duration, we ask our `FileManager` object to map the physical file path to a filesystem using `resolveLocalFileSystemURL`. Once we have a path mapping, we copy the video from the original location (which may be a temporary file) to the persistent filesystem. Add the following code snippet to the project:

```
self.captureVideo = function () {
    var fm = new _y.FileManager();
    var targetPath = _y.filename.getPathPart
    (self.src).substr(1);
    var targetName = _y.filename.getFilePart (self.src);
    var sourcePath;
    return fm.init ( fm.PERSISTENT, 0 )
        .then ( function () { return
    self._captureVideo(); })
            .then ( function (theMediaFiles ) {
                if (theMediaFiles.length == 1) {
                    sourcePath = theMediaFiles[0].fullPath;
                    return self._getCapturedDuration (
                    theMediaFiles[0] );
                }
                else {
                    throw new Error ( "Number of videos
                    returned is not 1." );
                }
            })
            .then ( function (theMediaFileData ) {
                self._capturedDuration =
                theMediaFileData.duration;
                return fm.resolveLocalFileSystemURL (
                sourcePath );
            })
            .then ( function (theFileEntry ) {
                return fm.moveFile ( theFileEntry,
                targetPath, targetName ) ;
            })
            .then ( function ( ) { self.notify
            ("videoCaptured"); return; });
    }
```

Finally, we need to add an `init` method:

```
self.overrideSuper ( self.class, "init", self.init );
self.init = function ( theSource ) {
    self.super ( _className, "init" );
    if (typeof theSource !== "undefined") {
    self.src = theSource; }
}
```

What did we do?

First we covered the Capture API itself as it pertains to capturing the video. Then we created a `VideoManager` class to wrap it into a convenient handler.

What else do I need to know?

It's a small point, but it's important to know that each of the various platforms record in different video formats, and that it is important to use the right extension when referencing video files.

For iOS, use `.mov` as the file extension. For Android, use `.3gp`.

Covering native, native-like, and non-native alerts

So far, our app has been pretty lax when it comes to deleting notes, that is, we do it immediately without any question. In some cases, this is expected—why would we tap **Delete** if we didn't mean to delete the note, right? You could argue that this is the expectation when using swipe-to-delete. But in each note edit view, the **Delete** button is pretty easy to tap by accident, and it would be frustrating to lose the note without ever being asked if that's really what we intended to do.

In this section, we'll examine the various mechanisms you can use to trigger alerts for the user. If you're familiar with JavaScript, you might be inclined to use `alert` and `prompt`, but these often include a very non-native title. Since this identifies our app as a non-native app immediately to the user, we need to avoid this. To do so, we can use native alerts (provided by a plugin) or native-like alerts provided by a framework (in our case, YASMF).

Getting on with it

It would be nice if we could get away with using JavaScript's `alert` method—it's easy to use, and something you're probably already familiar with. Unfortunately, it comes with a downside: it often shows `index.html` or some variation as the `alert` method's title. For simple apps that no one else will see (or to debug), this is fine. But for professional apps, we need something better. This can be in the form of native alerts or native-like alerts.

Native alerts can be triggered by first adding a plugin to your project:

```
cordova plugin add org.apache.cordova.dialogs
```

At this point, the `navigator.notification` object becomes available. It has four methods you can use to trigger various alerts:

- `alert( message, callback, [title], [button] )`: This generates a one-button alert. The `title` argument, if not specified, defaults to `Alert`, and if no button is specified, `OK` is the default.

- `confirm( message, callback, [title], [buttons] )`: This generates a confirmation with multiple buttons. The `callback` method receives a parameter indicating the button that is pressed. If `title` is omitted, `confirm` is used. If no buttons are specified, `[OK, Cancel]` is used as the default. If several buttons are displayed, they may be displayed vertically rather than in a row.

- `prompt( message, callback, [title], [buttons], [defaultText] )`: This generates a prompt with multiple buttons. The `callback` method receives the text entered as well as which button is pressed. If `title` is not specified, `Prompt` is the default. If no buttons are specified, `[OK, Cancel]` is used.

- `beep( numberOfBeeps )`: This plays a beep for a specified number of times.

Let's try a simple alert using the following code:

```
function alertDismissed () { // called when dismissed }
navigator.notification.alert ( "Your internet is offline",
alertDismissed, "Connection Lost", "OK" );
```

The preceding code displays the following alert on the screen:

Let's try something more complicated:

```
function alertDismissed ( buttonIndex ) {
  // buttonIndexes are one-based, not zero-based
  if (buttonIndex === 1) { // delete the item
  }
}
navigator.notification.confirm ( "Are you sure you want to delete
this?", alertDismissed, "Confirmation", ["Delete", "Don't
Delete"]);
```

The preceding code displays the following alert:

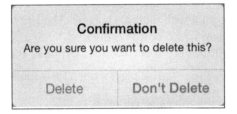

For good measure, let's try a prompt:

```
function promptDismissed ( results ) {
  if (results.buttonIndex === 2) {
    thePlayersName = results.input1;
  }
}
navigator.notification.prompt ( "What's your name?", promptDismissed,
"Player Setup", ["Don't Save", "Save"], "Player1" );
```

This renders the following prompt:

In general, native alerts really work quite well. However, there may be times when they don't offer quite enough functionality.

You may have noted in the preceding screenshot that there's always one button that is bolder than the rest. On iOS, this is typically reserved for the cancel button (the least destructive action). Furthermore, iOS has the notion of destructive buttons when displaying an action sheet—the destructive button is often colored red.

Alternatively, you may need more control over how the alert displays (or when it disappears). You may even need to update the text or title of the alert even after the alert has been displayed. If you want to have this level of control, you may need to build your own native-like alerts.

YASMF provides a simple library that simplifies native-like alerts. While these alerts are not actually native alerts, they come pretty close, and most users would be hard pressed to tell the difference.

An alert is created as shown in the following code:

```
var anAlert = new _y.UI.Alert();
```

At this point, we can call either `init` or `initWithOptions`—the latter is the preferred mechanism because it lets us declare the alert's title, text, and buttons all in one go. Here's how a simple `OK`/`Cancel` alert might be initialized—note how we can specify which button has bold texts:

```
anAlert.initWithOptions (
        { title:    "Notice!",
          text:     "Press OK or Cancel",
          buttons: [ _y.UI.Alert.button ( "OK" ),
                     _y.UI.Alert.button ( "Cancel", { type: "bold",
    tag: -1 } )
                   ] } );
```

Pretty easy to understand what's going on, right? And, you can probably imagine what it will look like, but here's the actual result (assuming an iOS device, YASMF will adapt the alert to mimic the native alert style depending on the platform):

Let's cover what's going on with the buttons, however, there are some complex things going on underneath the surface.

All alerts have at least one button—most have two or three, but even more are supported by YASMF. If two or three buttons are provided, they are displayed in a single row with equal width so that **Ok/Cancel** or **Yes/No/Cancel** can be displayed together. If only one button is provided, or if more than three are provided, they are displayed with one button per row. You do need to be careful here: there is no mechanism provided to handle the possibility of an alert having so many buttons that it might go offscreen, so keep the number of buttons to a minimum.

Each button can have various properties as follows:

- ▶ `type`: This indicates the button's type. All buttons are of `normal` type by default, but can also be `bold` (typically used for **Cancel** buttons) or `destructive`. The latter is used only for buttons that would perform a destructive action (such as deleting something).

- ▶ `tag`: This indicates the return value for the button. By default, buttons are assigned tags in the defined order, starting at zero. That means, the first button has a tag of `0`, and the second button has a tag of `1`, and so on. The **Cancel** buttons, however, are special—`-1` is used to indicate them. Since `-1` is out of order, we have to specify the tag directly. Of course, you could specify a tag for every button if the ascending order wasn't desired.

To show an alert, you only needs to use the following method:

```
anAlert.show();
```

However, what if you need to respond to the button that is tapped? There are two methods—the first is to listen for a notification:

```
anAlert.addListenerForNotification ( "buttonTapped",
function logTappedButton ( sender, notice, data ) {
```

```
        var buttonIndex = data[0];
        console.log ("Button tapped in alert
        (" + sender.title + "): " + buttonIndex);
    });
```

In some ways, however, this could lead back toward the callback hell, especially if we needed to present several alerts in a row that all depended on the user's previous choices.

The second method is using promises. When using `initWithOptions`, there is an additional property that we didn't show in the preceding example: `promises`. If set to `true`, the `show` method will return a promise, which is something we can then chain, like the following code:

```
anAlert.show()
        .then ( function (idx) {
           console.log ("Button tapped: " + idx); } )
        .catch ( function ( e ) {
           console.log ( "Cancelled: " + e); } )
        .done();
```

Should an alert need to be dismissed programmatically (say, after a specific length of time), the `hide` method can be called:

```
setTimeout ( function () { anAlert.hide(); }, 10000);
// hide after ten seconds
```

When an alert is forcibly hidden, the alert still sends a notification that a button was tapped. In all cases, this is assumed to be the cancel button.

Although it's not necessarily common, it's possible to change the title, text, and even the buttons after the initialization of the alert, and have those changes appear even after the alert was first shown.

Where this might be of use is in a countdown. An example is shown in the following code:

```
var countup = 0;
function increaseCountUp() {
    countup++;
    anAlert.text = "" + countup + " second(s) elapsed";
}
setInterval ( IncreaseCountUp, 1000 );
```

The alert will resize appropriately to accommodate any new title, text, or button, but as always, you do need to try to keep the messaging as short and succinct as possible while being unambiguous.

[
🔦 **What about prompts in YASMF?**

YASMF doesn't currently support a prompt-style alert. If you need this for your app, you'll need to use the native `navigator.notification.prompt` or non-native `prompt` method.
]

What did we do?

In this section, we covered the use of the native alerts provided by Cordova as well as the Alert module provided by YASMF. We also covered why using JavaScript's `alert` method is less than ideal.

What else do I need to know?

Crafting useful alert messages that are short yet unambiguous is like an art form. For example, try to avoid asking OK/Cancel questions; instead, use actions such as Delete/Don't Delete to clarify what each button is going to do when tapped.

Keep the number of buttons to the absolute minimum. Although YASMF's native-like alerts and Cordova's native alerts will adjust to accommodate any number of buttons, no affordance is made for whether content might go offscreen. As such, the practical limit is probably four or five for small screens, and only few more for large screens. To be honest, if you need that many buttons, rethink your user interface.

Native and non-native alerts usually stack so that only the latest alert is visible. As alerts are responded to, they disappear only to display the previous alert. YASMF's alert system does not do this. If more than one alert is triggered, they are both displayed. There is a sense of visual hierarchy, but in general, it's a bit messy. In general, you should avoid displaying more than one alert at once.

Building native-like alerts isn't terribly difficult. YASMF creates several `DIV` elements with specific classes (the styling comes from `yasmf.css`) and inserts these `DIV` elements into the DOM. YASMF also animates these `DIV` elements to give the alert some life using the `transform: scale3d()` style.

The following diagram shows how the alert is structured in the DOM:

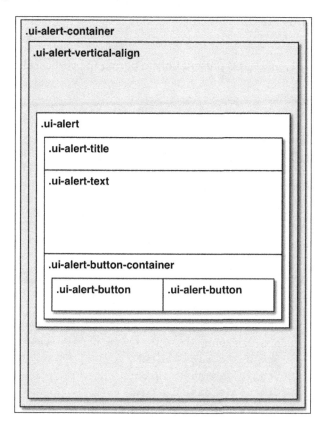

There's quite a few styles that are applied to these DOM elements. First, `ui-alert-container` fills the entire screen and is designed to be partially opaque so that the underlying content is visible. The `opacity` property is animated so that the alert background fades in when it is displayed. The `opacity` property is initially set to `0`; however, this is because the element isn't visible until we change the opacity to `1`. The `z-index` value assures that the alert appears over everything else. Using `display:table` ensures that we can vertically align the alert without needing to know its actual height. One other reason we have this `DIV` element is to ensure that the user can't touch anything outside of the alert; otherwise, the rest of the app would remain interactive. The styles for `ui-alert-container` are as follows:

```
position: absolute;
background-color: rgba(0, 0, 0, 0.25);
top: 0; left: 0; right: 0; bottom: 0;
width: 100%; height: 100%;
```

```
opacity: 0;
transition: opacity 0.25s ease-in-out;
z-index: 9999999;
display: table;
```

The `ui-vertical-align` class is present only to permit the vertical alignment of the alert on the screen:

```
display: table-cell;
vertical-align: middle;
```

The `ui-alert` class receives the majority of styling based on the platform it is emulating. It also has animations on the transform and position of the alert so that changes in size or scale are smoothly animated:

```
position: relative;
min-width: 260px; max-width: 420px;
margin: 0 auto;
background-color: white;
text-align: center;
opacity: 0;
transition: transform 0.125s ease-in-out,
            opacity 0.25s ease-in-out,
            top 0.25s ease-in-out, left 0.25s ease-in-out,
            right 0.25s ease-in-out,
            bottom 0.25s ease-in-out,
            width 0.25s ease-in-out,
            height 0.25s ease-in-out;
transform: scale3d(1, 1, 1);
box-shadow: 0px 0px 40px rgba(0, 0, 0, 0.5);
border-radius: 6px;
```

The `ui-alert-title` and `ui-alert-text` styles deal solely with the positioning and styling of text—this largely depends on your taste (and how faithful one wishes to remain to the native alert appearance).

The `ui-alert-button-container` and `ui-alert-buttons` styles are treated as a table and table cells, respectively. `ui-alert-button-container` has the `display:table` style, and `ui-alert-button` has `display:table-cell` style. This allows the buttons to appear in a horizontal layout (rather than vertical). `ui-alert-buttons` also have various padding and border styles to more closely match the native styling. Should a `ui-alert-button` need to be displayed without any other button on the same line, a `wide` class can be added, which uses `display:block`, as shown in the following code:

```
.ui-alert-button-container {
  position: relative;
```

```
    line-height: 2em;
    height: auto;
    font-size: 16pt;
    font-weight: normal;
    color: #333;
    width: 100%;
    border-collapse: collapse;
    display: table; }
.ui-alert-button-container .ui-alert-button {
    position: relative;
    display: table-cell;
    background-clip: padding-box;
    padding-left: 20px; padding-right: 20px;
    border: 1px solid rgba(0, 0, 0, 0.125);
    border-bottom: 0;
    width: 50%;
    font-weight: normal;
    color: #40B0FF; }
.ui-alert-button-container .ui-alert-button.wide {
    display: block;
    border: 0;
    border-top: 1px solid rgba(0, 0, 0, 0.125);
    border-bottom: 1px solid rgba(0, 0, 0, 0.125);
    line-height: 2em;
    height: 2em;
    width: 100%; }
```

There are a few additional styles in `yasmf.css`, of course, that render Android-style alerts and handle destructive and bold buttons (these just deal with color styles). If you want to see all of the styling, feel free to look in `yasmf.css`.

The styles provide nearly all the visual appearance, but there's one portion they don't provide: the initial bounce animation when the alert is shown. This is accomplished using the following piece of code (in the `show` method of `ui.alert`):

```
setTimeout ( function () {
  self._containerElement.style.opacity = "1"; }, 50 );
setTimeout ( function () {
  self._alertElement.style.opacity = "1";
UI.styleElement ( self._alertElement, "transform",
"scale3d(1.05, 1.05,1)" ) }, 125 );
setTimeout ( function () {
  UI.styleElement ( self._alertElement, "transform",
  "scale3d(0.95, 0.95,1)" ) }, 250 );
```

```
setTimeout ( function () {
  UI.styleElement ( self._alertElement, "transform",
  "scale3d(1.00, 1.00,1)" ) }, 375 );
```

In this snippet, the `opacity` property is set to 1 (remember, the stylesheet uses 0 as the default), which makes everything appear with a fade-in animation. Then, three `transform:scale3d()` styles are scheduled for 125 ms, 250 ms, and 375 ms after the initial appearance of the alert. The changes in scale (1.05 to 0.95 to 1.00) generate the visual bounce. Likewise, when the alert is hidden, a similar series of animations fade the alert out (YASMF doesn't provide a bounce when the alert is hidden—just a fade).

That's it, as far as YASMF's alerts are concerned. Of course, depending on your needs, you may not need all the styles or animations, but these give a reasonably native-like experience visually.

Implementing the data model

Now that we've covered the Capture API and alerts, we can build the video note data model. It's very similar to the image and audio note models:

videoNote (+baseNote)	
r/o	.video
p	_updateUnit()
p	_updateModificationDate)
o	setMediaContents (filename)
o	destroy()

. property	**r/w** read/write	**r/o** read-only		
p private	**o** override	↖ notification		

Getting on with it

Let's get coding. Let's build the model's shell at `www/js/app/models/videoNote.js` using the following code:

```
define ( ["yasmf","app/models/baseNote", "app/models/videoManager"],
function ( _y, BaseNote, VideoManager ) {
   var _className = "VideoNote";
   var VideoNote = function () {
      var self = new BaseNote();
      self.subclass ( _className );
      // the following code inserted here
```

```
        return self;
    }
    // add translations here
    return VideoNote;
});
```

First, we need to create a property that will hold our `VideoManager` class we created earlier:

```
self._video = null;
self.getVideo = function () {
    return self._video;
}
Object.defineProperty ( self, "video", {
get: self.getVideo, configurable: true});
```

Since we're a video note, we need to override the representation and unit labels appropriately:

```
self._representation = "film";
self.unitLabels = [ "app.vn.SECONDS", "app.vn.SECOND",
"app.vn.SECONDS" ];
```

We also need a method that can update our `unitValue` function to the duration of our captured video and another method to update the modification date:

```
self._updateUnit = function () {
    self.unitValue =
    Math.round(self._video.capturedDuration);
}
self._updateModificationDate = function () {
    self._modifiedDate = new Date();
}
```

We need to override the `setMediaContents` method so that we can create a new `VideoManager` instance:

```
self.overrideSuper ( self.class, "setMediaContents",
self.setMediaContents );
self.setMediaContents = function ( theMediaContents ) {
    self.super ( _className, "setMediaContents", [
    theMediaContents ]);
    if (self._video !== null) {
        self._video.destroy();
        self._video = null;
    }
```

```
self._video = new VideoManager();
self._video.init ( theMediaContents );
self.notify ( "mediaContentsChanged" );
self._video.addListenerForNotification ( "videoCaptured",
self._updateUnit );
self._video.addListenerForNotification ( "videoCaptured",
self._updateModificationDate );
}
Object.defineProperty ( self, "mediaContents", {
get: self.getMediaContents, set: self.setMediaContents,
configurable: true});
```

Finally, we need to override our `destroy` method so that we can dispose off our `VideoManager`:

```
self.overrideSuper ( self.class, "destroy", self.destroy);
self.destroy = function () {
    self._video.destroy();
    self._video = null;
    self.super ( _className, "destroy" );
}
```

One last thing. We need to add a couple of translations:

```
_y.addTranslations ( {
    "app.vn.SECOND": { "EN": "second", "ES": "segundo" },
    "app.vn.SECONDS": { "EN": "seconds", "ES": "segundos" }
});
```

What did we do?

In this section, we defined the model for a video note and implemented the corresponding code.

Implementing the user interface

Next, let's implement the user interface. We need to define the template HTML, and then define the code. Again, it's very similar to the previous project.

Before we start writing code, let's define the view's model. It should appear very familiar by now, as shown in the following diagram:

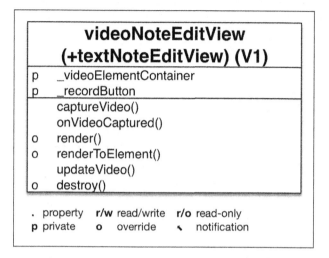

Getting on with it

First, create a new template at `www/html/videoNoteEditView.html`. It's very similar to our image note edit view's template. I've highlighted the differences in the following code:

```
<html>
  <body>
    <div class="ui-navigation-bar">
      <div class="ui-title"
      contenteditable="true">%NOTE_NAME%</div>
      <div class="ui-bar-button-group ui-align-left">
        <div class="ui-bar-button ui-tint-color ui-back-button">
        %BACK%</div>
      </div>
      <div class="ui-bar-button-group ui-align-right">
        <div class="ui-bar-button ui-destructive-color">
        %DELETE_NOTE%</div>
      </div>
    </div>
    <div class="ui-scroll-container ui-avoid-navigation-bar">
      <div class="video-container">
        <div class="video-element"></div>
        <div class="video-actions">
          <div class="ui-glyph ui-background-tint-color ui-glyph-
circle-outlined"></div>
        </div>
```

```
      </div>
      <textarea class="ui-text-box"
      onblur="this.classList.remove('editing');"
onfocus="this.classList.add('editing');">
%NOTE_CONTENTS%</textarea>
    </div>
  </body>
</html>
```

Next, we need to create the view's shell in `www/js/app/views/videoNoteEditView.js`:

```
define ( ["yasmf", "app/models/noteStorageSingleton",
          "text!html/videoNoteEditView.html!strip",
          "app/views/textNoteEditView", "hammer"],
function ( _y, noteStorageSingleton, videoNoteViewHTML,
           TextNoteEditView, Hammer ) {
    var _className = "VideoNoteEditView";
    var VideoNoteEditView = function () {
        var self = new TextNoteEditView();
        self.subclass ( _className );
        // insert the following code here
        return self;
    }
    return VideoNoteEditView;
});
```

We need two private properties to track the record button and the video container:

```
        self._recordButton = null;
        self._videoElementContainer = null;
```

We need a method that we can call to start a video capture session. We create a listener for `videoCaptured` in the following code so that we can be notified when the video session is over:

```
        self.captureVideo = function () {
            self._note.video.addListenerForNotification ( "videoCaptured",
self.onVideoCaptured );
            self._note.video.captureVideo()
                .catch ( function ( anError ) {
                        self._note.video.removeListenerForNotification
                          ( "videoCaptured", self.onVideoCaptured);
                        console.log (anError );
                    })
                .done();
        }
```

When a video recording has finished, we need a mechanism to update the view with the newly recorded video:

```
self.onVideoCaptured = function ()
{
  self._note.video.removeListenerForNotification (
  "videoCaptured", self.onVideoCaptured );
  self.updateVideo();
}
```

When a video is recorded (or loaded), we need to display the video inside of our `video-element` DIV. Unlike prior projects, we need to determine the physical location of the video on the filesystem using `getNativeURL`. This method essentially asks our filesystem for the `nativeURL` of the root directory and then appends the path of the video. This is a little simpler than using an asynchronous call to determine the physical file path, but it makes the assumption that the video is in the persistent filesystem (which, in our case, it is). Also, note that we use a cache-busting mechanism to ensure that the browser will always pick up the most recent version of the video:

```
self.updateVideo = function () {
  var html = "<video controls src='%URL%?%CACHE%'></video>";
  var fm = noteStorageSingleton.fileManager;
  var nativePath = fm.getNativeURL (
  self._note.mediaContents );
  var cacheBust = Math.floor(Math.random() * 100000);
  self._videoElementContainer.innerHTML = _y.template (
  html, {
      "URL": nativePath,
      "CACHE": cacheBust} );
}
```

Next, we override `render` so that the correct template is used:

```
self.overrideSuper ( self.class, "render", self.render );
self.render = function () {
  return _y.template ( videoNoteViewHTML, {
                      "NOTE_NAME": self._note.name,
                      "NOTE_CONTENTS":
                      self._note.textContents,
                      "BACK": _y.T("BACK"),
                      "DELETE_NOTE":
                      _y.T("app.nev.DELETE_NOTE")
                      });
}
```

In order to attach event handlers to the DOM elements we care about, we need to override `renderToElement`:

```
self.overrideSuper ( self.class, "renderToElement",
self.renderToElement );
self.renderToElement = function () {
    self.super ( _className, "renderToElement" );
    self._recordButton = self.element.querySelector (
    ".video-container .video-actions .ui-glyph");
    self._videoElementContainer = self.element.querySelector
    (".video-container .video-element" );
    Hammer ( self._recordButton ).on("tap",
    self.captureVideo);
    self.updateVideo ();
}
```

Finally, we should always write the code that cleans up when we're done:

```
self.overrideSuper ( self.class, "destroy", self.destroy );
self.destroy = function () {
    self._recordButton = null;
    self._videoElementContainer = null;
    self._note.video.removeListenerForNotification (
"videoCaptured", self.onVideoCaptured );
    self.super ( _className, "destroy" );
}
```

What did we do?

Most of the preceding actions should be fairly self-explanatory. With that said, let's look at the HTML5 `video` tag for a brief moment. It's not a complicated tag, and if you want to know more about HTML5 video, there are a lot of resources out there that cover it. Needless to say, not every platform supports it equally well. Android 4.x does a pretty good job with local content, as does any recent version of iOS. But get too far back or wander too far off the beaten path, and you may find that you need other mechanisms to play videos (such as native plugins).

All the code we're using displays a video element *with* playback controls. This is important—it is what lets the user interact with the video. There are other attributes that can be applied as well (such as `autoplay`, `loop`, and `poster`).

Once the user taps the video, it will start to play. Whether the video plays inline or fullscreen is up to the platform and the form factor, in addition to a preference you can set in `config.xml`. If you need this functionality, add (or modify, if it already exists) the `AllowInlineMediaPlayback` preference in your `config.xml` and set the value to `true`. You'll need to add the `webkit-playsinline` attribute to any video tag, as is done in the following code:

```
// in config.xml
<preference name="AllowInlineMediaPlayback" value="true">

// video tag in HTML
<video controls webkit-playsinline src='…'></video>
```

What else do I need to know?

Probably the best resource to learn more about the HTML5 `video` tag is
`http://www.html5rocks.com/en/tutorials/video/basics/`. It's
important to recognize that not all platforms support every option, and you'll
probably need to do some experimentation to find what works best for your app.

Should you need to implement video on an older version of Android that doesn't
support the HTML5 `video` tag, you can use a third-party plugin. The `VideoPlayer`
plugin was originally authored by Simon MacDonald for PhoneGap 2.x, and has been
updated by Raul Duran for Cordova 3.x. You can add it to your project using the
following command:

```
cordova plugin add https://github.com/raulduran/VideoPlayer.git
```

To play a video, you can then use the following code:

```
cordova.plugins.videoPlayer.play ( "file:///path/to/movie.file" );
```

In order to implement this in our app, we would require a view more like the audio
note edit view rather than the way we've implemented it in this chapter. This is left
as an exercise for the reader.

Putting it all together

There are a few pieces of code that we still need to create and edit in order to tie
everything together. Let's get started.

Getting on with it

First, we need to modify our factories. First, edit `www/js/app/factories/noteFactory.`
`js` as shown in the following code:

```
noteFactory.createNote = function ( noteType ) {
    switch ( noteType.toUpperCase().trim() ) {
        …
        case noteFactory.VIDEONOTE:
            return new VideoNote();
        …
    }
```

```
    }
    noteFactory.createAssociatedMediaFileName =
    function (noteType, uid) {
    …
    switch (noteType.toUpperCase().trim()) {
        …
        case noteFactory.VIDEONOTE:
        extension = { "ios": "mov", "android": "3gp" };
        newFileName = "movie";
        break;
        …
    }
```

Next, edit www/js/app/factories/noteViewFactory.js:

```
    noteViewFactory.createNoteEditView = function ( noteType ) {
        switch ( noteType.toUpperCase().trim() ) {
            …
            case noteFactory.VIDEONOTE:
                return new VideoNoteEditView();
            …
        }
    }
```

Next, we need to slightly adjust www/js/app/views/noteListView.js. First, add a method to create a new video note:

```
self.createNewVideoNote = function () {
  self._createAndEditNote(noteFactory.VIDEONOTE);
};
…
```

Then, we need to add an event handler to the video camera icon in renderToElement:

```
    self.renderToElement = function ()
    {
…
        Hammer ( self._newTextNoteButton ).on ("tap", self.
createNewTextNote );
        Hammer ( self._newAudioNoteButton ).on ("tap", self.
createNewAudioNote );
        Hammer ( self._newImageNoteButton ).on ("tap", self.
createNewImageNote );
        Hammer ( self._newVideoNoteButton ).on ("tap", self.
createNewVideoNote );
```

```
    ...
        }
    ...
    _y.addTranslations (
        {
            "APP_TITLE":  { "EN": "Filer" },
            "BACK":  { "EN": "Back", "ES": "Volver" },
            "TRASH": { "EN": "Trash", "ES": "Borrar" },
            "CANCEL": { "EN": "Cancel", "ES": "Cancelar" },
            "DELETE": { "EN": "Delete", "ES": "Eliminar" }
        });
    ...
```

In order to make the note deletion a bit safer, we need to add a confirmation when deleting notes in `www/js/app/views/textNoteEditView.js` (which will be inherited by all our other views):

```
    self.deleteNote = function () {
        var areYouSure = new _y.UI.Alert();
        areYouSure.initWithOptions ( {
            title: _y.T("app.nev.action.DELETE_NOTE"),
            text: _y.T(
            "app.nev.action.ARE_YOU_SURE_THIS_ACTION_CANT_BE_UNDONE"),
              promise: true,
              buttons: [ _y.UI.Alert.button ( _y.T("DELETE"), {
              type: "destructive" } ),
                        _y.UI.Alert.button ( _y.T("CANCEL"), {
                        type: "bold", tag: -1 } ) ]
        });
        areYouSure.show()
            .then ( function ( idx )  {
                if (idx>-1) {
                    noteStorageSingleton.removeNote (
                    self._note.uid );
                    self.navigationController.popView();
                    }
                })
            .catch ( function ( anError )  {
                return; // happens when a cancel button is
                pressed
                })
            .done();
    }
```

Because we're displaying a new message to the user, we need to add some translations near the bottom of the file:

```
_y.addTranslations ( {
    "app.nev.DELETE_NOTE": {
        "EN": "Delete",
        "ES": "Eliminar"
    },
    "app.nev.action.DELETE_NOTE": {
        "EN": "Delete Note", "ES": "Eliminar Nota"
    },
    "app.nev.action.ARE_YOU_SURE_THIS_ACTION_CANT_BE_UNDONE": {
        "EN": "Are you sure? This action can't be undone.",
        "ES": "¿Está seguro? Esta acción no se puede deshacer."
    }
});
```

Finally, we need to add some styles in `www/css/style.css`. For the sake of brevity, we'll leave out the code—it's all very familiar. Take a look at the code in the package for this book if you want to explore it.

What did we do?

First, we updated our factories so that they know how to create video notes and video note edit views. Next, we updated the note list view so that it can create a video note.

After that, we modified the text edit note view so that it confirms if the user wants to delete a note. Because all our other edit note views inherit from this view, our other views get this behavior for free.

Finally, we updated the stylesheet to accommodate our new view. There's nothing you've not seen before, so we won't go over the additions.

Game Over..... Wrapping it up

You're done! You've been introduced to capturing videos using the Capture API and to playing it back using the HTML5 `video` tag. Finally, you added a confirmation alert to delete notes.

 You won't be able to record video in this app if it is running on the iOS simulator due to the lack of camera support. Run this app on a real device instead.

Can you take the HEAT? The Hotshot Challenge

This is a pretty complicated challenge, but it revolves around the concept of video posters. The `video` tag permits the specifying of an image as a video's poster, and it makes sense to display a thumbnail from the video itself. The only problem is that there's no easy way to generate thumbnails from videos without using a third-party plugin. But if you're up for a challenge, take a crack at it.

 The plugin at the following website might help: `https://github.com/ photokandyStudios/PKVideoThumbnail`.

Project 8
Sharing Content

Social networks and mobile devices go together like bread and butter. If your app has built-in content or your user can create their own content, most of the other apps would benefit from the sharing of that content with social networks. Fortunately, there are several plugins available that make it extremely easy to add this functionality.

What do we build?

Our Filer app supports quite a few content types, but there's no way to get that content out of the app and share it with anyone else—except if the user copies and pastes their own notes. By adding sharing capabilities, the user can avoid this tedious copy and paste step and share (with a single tap) in the social networks that the mobile supports.

What does it do?

Cordova/PhoneGap doesn't support sharing by default, and so we need to add a plugin in order to support this functionality. There are a lot of great plugins that offer various features, some offer e-mail composition, some integrate only with Twitter, and so on, but the one we use will use the native support on the mobile device. If the device can send a tweet or post to Facebook, this particular plugin will use those social networks.

Why is it great?

Typically, most plugins only support text sharing, which is fine, but our app supports so much more. The plugin we will use also supports the sharing of images, which covers one additional type of note. If you want to add sound and video sharing, you'll be able to add that functionality as a challenge at the end of this chapter.

Although not as exciting, there's also something else we need to cover: various device events. These events cover the gamut: the `pause`/`resume` events for the application, the `online`/`offline` events for the network connect, battery events, and more. We won't build robust solutions for each, because how your app handles each event will vary based on the app. However, we'll provide the tips to get you started.

How are we going to do it?

Here's what we'll be covering:

- Handling device events
- Working with the sharing plugin
- Modifying the text note edit view
- Modifying the image note edit view

Handling device events

So far, we haven't handled various application and device events, but most apps need to support these before they are deployed to production. We've already dealt a little with one particular event (the back button event), but there are many more events that your app may need to know.

Getting ready

The documentation for all these events is located at `http://cordova.apache.org/docs/en/edge/cordova_events_events.md.html#Events`. We will cover most of the events in detail, but there are additional events that we won't cover and you might want to check out.

There are two plugins that need to be added if you want to respond to the `battery` and `network information` events:

```
cordova plugin add org.apache.cordova.battery-status
cordova plugin add org.apache.cordova.network-information
```

Getting on with it

Let's add support for event handling by editing `www/js/app/main.js`. First, we'll add some boilerplate code at the top of `APP.start`, which adds listeners for the events we care about, as shown in the following code:

```
var gN = _y.UI.globalNotifications;
var notifications = {
```

```
  "pause":
  { notification: "applicationPause",   handler: APP.onPause },
  "resume":
  { notification: "applicationResume",  handler: APP.onResume },
  "online":
  { notification: "applicationOnline",  handler:
    APP.onConnectionStatusChanged },
  "offline":
  { notification: "applicationOffline", handler:
    APP.onConnectionStatusChanged },
  "batterycritical":
  { notification: "batteryCritical",    handler:
    APP.onBatteryStatusChanged },
  "batterylow":
  { notification: "batteryLow",         handler:
    APP.onBatteryStatusChanged },
  "batterystatus":
  { notification: "batteryStatus",      handler:
    APP.onBatteryStatusChanged },
  "menubutton":
  { notification: "menuButtonPressed",  handler:
    APP.onMenuButtonPressed },
  "searchbutton":
  { notification: "searchButtonPressed",handler:
    APP.onSearchButtonPressed }
};
for ( var DOMEvent in notifications ) {
  if ( notifications.hasOwnProperty ( DOMEvent ) ) {
    var notification = notifications[DOMEvent];
    gN.registerNotification( notification.notification );
    gN.addListenerForNotification( notification.notification,
      notification.handler );
    (function (notification) {
      window.addEventListener( DOMEvent, function () {
        var args = Array.prototype.slice.call(arguments);
        gN.notify(notification, args);
      }, false);
    })(notification.notification);
  }
}
```

This code uses a tool provided by YASMF: the `globalNotifications` object. It does nothing special on its own—it serves as a way to pass notifications around in a global fashion. This object is guaranteed to exist in a YASMF app, and so any view can listen for the notifications that interest them. This is, in most parts, very similar to the way the `backbutton` event is currently handled, but the `backbutton` event is only sent to the most recent listener. These events are sent to anyone and everyone who is listening.

The preceding code then creates a notification object that contains an entry for each event that we care about. We'll soon go over how each of these events work. The events in this list contain every event, except `deviceready`, `backbutton`, and events specific to BlackBerry.

What your app will and won't need in order to handle the events really depends on your app. If you are working with the network, you'll need to intercept the connection status events. If your app needs to be sensitive to the user's current battery status (for example, to stop a heavy computation if the battery level is critical), then you'll want to respond to the battery events.

The bottom portion of the code iterates through each item in the notifications object and performs the following operations:

- Registers the notification using `gN.registerNotification`.
- Adds the specified handler using `gN.AddListenerForNotification`.
- Using an **immediately invoked function expression (IIFE)**, we call `window.addEventListener` with the event we care about and a handler that sends a notification using `gN.notify`. Any arguments passed to the handler are passed along with the notification.

If you're not using YASMF, you can simply use `window.addEventListener` and attach an event handler directly.

Now, let's add the event handlers above `APP.start`. First, let's create the `onPause` and `onResume` handlers using the following code:

```
APP.onPause = function () {
  console.log ( "Application paused" );
  // on iOS, this isn't processed until a resume event,
  // since calls to the native layer are delayed
}
APP.onResume = function () {
  console.log ( "Application resumed" );
}
```

These two handlers react to the `pause` and `resume` events, respectively. These two events deal with the state of the application—whether the application is being put in the background by the operating system (`pause`) or whether it is coming out of the background (`resume`). Although our implementation does very little (just logs the fact to the console), a production app should do much more.

For a `pause` event, you should perform the following operations:

▸ **Save any unsaved content**: Whether or not the content is saved to temporary or persistent storage depends upon the needs of your app.

▸ **Save the application state**: The application state is typically stored to some configuration file or temporary storage. Here, the goal is to bring your app to the same state when the app resumes.

For a `resume` event, you should perform the following operations:

▸ **Restore the application state**: This will restore the same view that was visible when the application was paused.

▸ **Restore unsaved content**: Apps should never lose data in a production state. If the content was saved to a temporary place, restore it as if the user never left off. If you saved the content to persistent storage during the `pause` event, you should be able to load the same file.

When working with iOS devices, however, you need to be very careful with both events. When a `pause` event is received, your app cannot make any calls to native plugins or execute native code. So, while you might expect to simply use the File API to save your unsaved content, this API is a native plugin, which means you can't use it during the `pause` event. Instead, any calls get queued up and executed when the application is resumed, which is a big problem if the app never gets resumed. Using `localStorage` should be safe, but even then there are issues. As of Cordova 3.4, it appears that writing to `localStorage` during a `pause` event doesn't flush the changes to storage. So, if the app never resumes, the data is lost. Hopefully, there is a workaround by the time you are reading this, because otherwise there is no sure-fire method to restore the application state on iOS.

When a `resume` event is received, if you need to use any code that is native and interactive (such as a Javascript alert), be sure to wrap it in a `setTimeout` call. Otherwise, your app may crash or become unresponsive:

```
setTimeout ( function () { alert(1); }, 0 );
```

If you would like to see an example of saving data during a `pause` event, refer to the `pause-resume-handling.md` document in the code package for this book.

The next block of code handles the `online` and `offline` events, and it needs the network information plugin to be added. Our code tries to be a little smart: it only generates an alert if the status has changed, and not if we receive the same event multiple times in a row. The code is also designed to avoid spamming the user with multiple alert boxes. If there's one that the app has already built, that alert is used instead. Consider the following code:

```
APP._lastConnectionStatus = "unknown";
APP._lastConnectionAlert = null;
APP.onConnectionStatusChanged = function (sender, notification) {
  var friendlyMessage = "";
  if (APP._lastConnectionStatus == "applicationOffline" &&
  notification == "applicationOnline") {
    friendlyMessage = _y.T("Your Internet Connection has been
      restored.");
  }
  if (APP._lastConnectionStatus !== "applicationOffline" &&
  notification == "applicationOffline") {
    friendlyMessage = _y.T("Your Internet Connection is
      offline.");
  }
  APP._lastConnectionStatus = notification;
  if (friendlyMessage !== "") {
    if (APP._lastConnectionAlert === null) {
      APP._lastConnectionAlert = new _y.UI.Alert.OK( {
        title: _y.T("Notice"),
        text: _y.T(friendlyMessage)
      });
      APP._lastConnectionAlert.show();
    }
    else {
      APP._lastConnectionAlert.text = _y.T(friendlyMessage);
      if (!APP._lastConnectionAlert.visible) {
        APP._lastConnectionAlert.show();
      }
    }
  }
}
```

Typically, the response time for these events is around 1 second from the moment the network state actually changes. You shouldn't rely on receiving an online event immediately after startup on iOS. It will take a second or two to receive the initial online event.

Depending on the platform, you may need to do more in order to prevent network access while offline. In this case, you could have additional listeners to handle view-related network activity, or store the value in a global variable in the APP object.

If you're not using YASMF

You'll need to modify the preceding code a bit. Assuming your handler takes an event as the first parameter, you can inspect the event's type using `event.type` and use that instead of the earlier notification parameter. Make sure you change `applicationOffline` to `offline` and `applicationOnline` to `online`. In addition, you'll need to handle native alerts differently, since they stack. There's no mechanism for changing a native alert after it is displayed.

We will get the following alert in our code when the device loses its network connection:

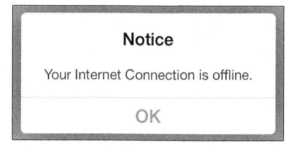

When our device regains its network connection, we will get the following alert:

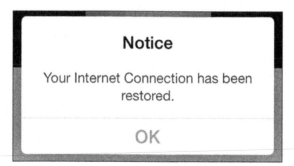

Don't forget!

Be sure to localize any notifications for your users so that they can understand what's going on.

The battery events are `batterystatus`, `batterylow`, and `batterycritical`, and they require the Battery Status plugin to be added. They all transmit the same additional information (the level and whether or not the device is plugged in), but each event is fired at various times, depending on how much charge the battery has. Most apps probably don't need to worry about responding to these events, but if you need to suspend some intensive activity when the battery is critical, it might be helpful to listen.

```
APP.onBatteryStatusChanged = function (sender, notification, data)
  {
  console.log ( "Battery status: " + data[0].level + "; is plugged
    in? " + data[0].isPlugged );
}
```

If you're not using YASMF

The battery information is reported to your handler as part of the first parameter. Assuming your event handler takes an event as the first parameter, you can access the battery information by using `event.level` and `event.isPlugged`.

The last two events are tailored for Android. The `menubutton` event is fired when the user presses the hardware menu button, and the `searchbutton` event is fired when the user presses the hardware search button, as shown in the following code:

```
APP.onMenuButtonPressed = function () {
  if (typeof APP.navigationController !== "undefined") {
    if (typeof APP.navigationController.topView.onMenuButton !==
      "undefined") {
      APP.navigationController.topView.onMenuButton();
    }
  }
}
APP.onSearchButtonPressed = function () {
  if (typeof APP.navigationController !== "undefined") {
    if (typeof APP.navigationController.topView.onSearchButton !==
      "undefined") {
      APP.navigationController.topView.onSearchButton();
    }
  }
}
```

In the preceding implementation, we look at the top-level view (`APP.navigationController.topView`) and see if it supports a method we recognize. If it does, we call it, and if not, we do nothing. This means a view could implement `onMenuButton` and display something appropriate when the button was pressed.

What did we do?

In this section, we created code to handle application-specific events, battery status events, and network status events. We also added code to handle the menu and search hardware buttons on Android.

What else do I need to know?

Every platform has various quirks when it comes to handling these events. If you're branching out to other platforms (perhaps Windows Phone 8 or BlackBerry), be certain to refer to the documentation for any quirks you might not be expecting.

Working with the sharing plugin

Now that we've dealt with the device events, let's get to the real meat of the project: let's add the sharing plugin and see how to use it.

Getting ready

Before continuing, be sure to add the plugin to your project:

```
cordova plugin add https://github.com/leecrossley/cordova-plugin-
social-message.git
```

Getting on with it

This particular plugin is one of many socialnetwork plugins. Each one has its benefits and each one has its problems, and the available plugins are changing rapidly. This particular plugin is very easy to use, and supports a reasonable amount of social networks. On iOS, Facebook, Twitter, Mail, and Flickr are supported. On Android, any installed app that registers with the intent to share is supported.

The full documentation is available at `https://github.com/leecrossley/cordova-plugin-social-message` at the time of writing this. It is easy to follow if you need to know more than what we cover here.

To show a sharing sheet (the appearance varies based on platform and operation system), all we have to do is this:

```
window.socialshare.send ( message );
```

`message` is an object that contains any of the following properties:

- `text`: This is the main content of the message.

- ▶ `subject`: This is the subject of the message. This is only applicable while sending e-mails; most other social networks will ignore this value.

- ▶ `url`: This is a link to attach to the message.

- ▶ `image`: This is an absolute path to the image in order to attach it to the message. It must begin with `file:///` and the path should be properly escaped (that is, spaces should become `%20`, and so on).

- ▶ `activityTypes` (only for iOS): This supports activities on various social networks. Valid values are: `PostToFacebook`, `PostToTwitter`, `PostToWeibo`, `Message`, `Mail`, `Print`, `CopyToPasteboard`, `AssignToContact`, and `SaveToCameraRoll`.

In order to create a simple message to share, we can use the following code:

```
var message = {
    text: "something to send"
}
window.socialshare.send ( message );
```

To add an image, we can go a step further, shown as follows:

```
var message = {
    text: "the caption",
    image: "file://var/mobile/…/image.png"
}
window.socialshare.send ( message );
```

Once this method is called, the sharing sheet will appear. On iOS 7, you'll see something like the following screenshot:

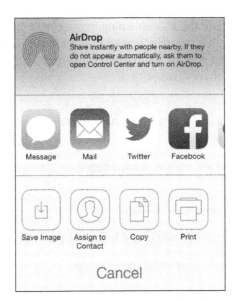

On Android, you will see something like the following screenshot:

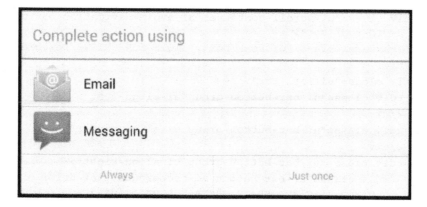

What did we do?

In this section, we installed the sharing plugin and we learned how to use it. In the next sections, we'll cover the modifications required to use this plugin.

Modifying the text note edit view

We've dispatched most of the typical sections in this project—there's not really any user interface to design, nor are there any changes to the actual note models. All we need to do is modify the HTML template a little to include a share button and add the code to use the plugin.

Getting on with it

First, let's alter the template in `www/html/textNoteEditView.html`. I've highlighted the changes:

```html
<html>
  <body>
    <div class="ui-navigation-bar">
      <div class="ui-title"
        contenteditable="true">%NOTE_NAME%</div>
      <div class="ui-bar-button-group ui-align-left">
        <div class="ui-bar-button ui-tint-color ui-back-
button">%BACK%</div>
      </div>
      <div class="ui-bar-button-group ui-align-right">
        <div class="ui-bar-button ui-destructive-
          color">%DELETE_NOTE%</div>
```

```
        </div>
      </div>
      <div class="ui-scroll-container ui-avoid-navigation-bar ui-
        avoid-tool-bar">
        <textarea class="ui-text-box" >%NOTE_CONTENTS%</textarea>
      </div>
      <div class="ui-tool-bar">
        <div class="ui-bar-button-group ui-align-left">
        </div>
        <div class="ui-bar-button-group ui-align-center">
        </div>
        <div class="ui-bar-button-group ui-align-right">
          <div class="ui-bar-button ui-background-tint-color ui-
            glyph ui-glyph-share share-button"></div>
        </div>
      </div>
    </body>
  </html>
```

Now, let's make the modifications to the view in `www/js/app/views/`
`textNoteEditView.js`. First, we need to add an internal property that references the share button:

```
self._shareButton = null;
```

Next, we need to add code to `renderToElement` so that we can add an event handler to the share button. We'll do a little bit of checking here to see if we've found the icon, because we don't support sharing of videos and sounds and we don't include that asset in those views. If we didn't have the `null` check, those views would fail to work. Consider the following code snippet:

```
self.renderToElement = function ()
{
  ...
  self._shareButton = self.element.querySelector ( ".share-button"
    );
  if (self._shareButton !== null) {
    Hammer ( self._shareButton ).on("tap", self.shareNote);
  }
  ...
}
```

Finally, we need to add the method that actually shares the note. Note that we save the note before we share it, since that's how the data in the DOM gets transmitted to the note model. Consider the following code snippet:

```
self.shareNote = function () {
  self.saveNote();
  var message = {
    subject: self._note.name,
    text: self._note.textContents
  };
  window.socialmessage.send ( message );
}
```

What did we do?

First, we added a toolbar to the view that looks like the following screenshot—note the new sharing icon:

Then, we added the code that shares the note and attaches that code to the **Share** button.

Here's an example of us sending a tweet from a note on iOS:

What else do I need to know?

Don't forget that social networks often have size limits. For example, Twitter only supports 140 characters, and so if you send a note using Twitter, it needs to be a very short note. We could, on iOS, prevent Twitter from being permitted, but there's no way to prevent this on Android. Even then, there's no real reason not to prevent Twitter from being an option. The user just needs to be familiar enough with the social network to know that they'll have to edit the content before posting it.

Also, don't forget that the subject of a message only applies to mail; most other social networks will ignore it. If something is critical, be sure to include it in the text of the message, and not the subject only.

Modifying the image note edit view

The image note edit view presents an additional difficulty: we can't put the **Share** button in a toolbar. This is because doing so will cause positioning difficulties with TEXTAREA and the toolbar when the soft keyboard is visible. Instead, we'll put it in the lower-right corner of the image. This is done by using the same technique we used to outline the camera button.

Getting on with it

Let's edit the template in www/html/imageNoteEditView.html; again, I've highlighted the changes:

```
<html>
  <body>
    <div class="ui-navigation-bar">
      <div class="ui-title"
        contenteditable="true">%NOTE_NAME%</div>
      <div class="ui-bar-button-group ui-align-left">
        <div class="ui-bar-button ui-tint-color ui-back-
          button">%BACK%</div>
      </div>
      <div class="ui-bar-button-group ui-align-right">
        <div class="ui-bar-button ui-destructive-
          color">%DELETE_NOTE%</div>
      </div>
    </div>
    <div class="ui-scroll-container ui-avoid-navigation-bar">
      <div class="image-container">
        <div class="ui-glyph ui-background-tint-color ui-glyph-
          camera outline"></div>
```

```
            <div class="ui-glyph ui-background-tint-color ui-glyph-
               camera non-outline"></div>
            <div class="ui-glyph ui-background-tint-color ui-glyph-
               share outline"></div>
            <div class="ui-glyph ui-background-tint-color ui-glyph-
               share non-outline share-button"></div>
         </div>
         <textarea class="ui-text-box"
            onblur="this.classList.remove('editing');"
            onfocus="this.classList.add('editing');
            ">%NOTE_CONTENTS%</textarea>
      </div>
   </body>
</html>
```

Because sharing an image requires a little additional code, we need to override `shareNote` (which we inherit from the prior task) in `www/js/app/views/imageNoteEditView.js`:

```
self.shareNote = function () {
  var fm = noteStorageSingleton.fileManager;
  var nativePath = fm.getNativeURL ( self._note.mediaContents );
  self.saveNote();
  var message = {
    subject: self._note.name,
    text: self._note.textContents
  };
  if (self._note.unitValue > 0) {
    message.image = nativePath;
  }
  window.socialmessage.send ( message );
}
```

Finally, we need to add the following styles to `www/css/style.css`:

```
div.ui-glyph.ui-background-tint-color.ui-glyph-share.outline,
div.ui-glyph.ui-background-tint-color.ui-glyph-share.non-outline
{
  left:inherit;
  width:50px;
  top: inherit;
  height:50px;
}
{

  -webkit-mask-position:15px 16px;
  mask-position:15px 16px;
}
```

```
div.ui-glyph.ui-background-tint-color.ui-glyph-share.non-outline
{
  -webkit-mask-position:15px 15px;
  mask-position:15px 15px;
}
```

What did we do?

Like the previous task, we first modified the template to add the share icon. Then, we added the `shareNote` code to the view (note that we don't have to add anything to find the button, because we inherit it from the Text Note Edit View). Finally, we modify the style sheet to reposition the **Share** button appropriately so that it looks like the following screenshot:

What else do I need to know?

The image needs to be a valid image, or the plugin may crash. This is why we check for the value of `unitValue` in `shareNote` to ensure that it is large enough to attach to the message. If not, we only share the text.

Game Over..... Wrapping it up

And that's it! You've learned how to respond to device events, and you've also added sharing to text and image notes by using a third-party plugin.

Can you take the HEAT? The Hotshot Challenge

There are several ways to improve the project. Why don't you try a few?

- Implement the ability to save the note when the app receives a pause event, and then restore the note when the app is resumed.

- Remember which note is visible when the app is paused, and restore it when the app is resumed. (Hint: `localStorage` may come in handy.)

- Add video or audio sharing. You'll probably have to alter the sharing plugin or find another (or an additional) plugin. You'll probably also need to upload the data to an external server so that it can be linked via the social network. For example, it's often customary to link to a video on Twitter by using a link shortener. The File Transfer plugin might come in handy for this challenge (`https://github.com/apache/cordova-plugin-file-transfer/blob/dev/doc/index.md`).

Project 9

Devices of
Different Sizes

Up until this point, we've only dealt with building apps for smaller devices such as mobile smartphones with small screens. We've also only worried about one orientation: portrait. Once we branch out from smartphones, we find that a lot of mobile devices span the spectrum with regard to screen size. Many of these are tablets—devices that have large screens, especially when compared to smartphones (although they are usually not as large as those of laptops). Devices that fit between tablets and smartphones are often referred to as phablets—a portmanteau of phones and tablets. Phablets range anywhere between five and seven inches (diagonally), while tablets start at seven inches and increase in size from there.

Screen sizes vary widely and so do aspect ratios. Most devices have adopted a 16:10 or 16:9 aspect ratio (to better display movies). However, that doesn't mean you should not worry about other ratios—case in point is the iPad, which has a 4:3 aspect ratio.

It's also important to recognize that devices often support different orientations; for example, the landscape and portrait orientations apply different resolutions and aspect ratios (although inverted). This adds an additional level of complexity to user interface design because if your app needs to support multiple orientations, it may need one layout for the landscape orientation and another for the portrait.

Thus, it is important to carefully consider your app's user interface and its appearance on these devices. For some apps, it is sufficient to scale the user interface to the screen's size—something that often works for games—whereas for other apps, the same user interface can be used with small tweaks to adapt to the different screen sizes. Finally, there are times when there simply is no choice; the user interface must be completely rethought for a different screen size.

What do we build?

This will be the first project in which we aren't actually worried about adding functionalities to our app. Instead, we'll look at how to expand the app's reach to tablets and phablets.

What does it do?

When you've been solely developing for a small screen and contemplate a larger form factor, you often ask the question, *what does one do with all that space?* When you are familiar with a 600 x 800 or 640 x 1136 portrait resolution (and often, an effective resolution such as 320 x 568), it can be difficult to imagine what else can be done to fill in all those extra pixels, especially when the pixel count is often in the millions. The iPad Air has a screen size of 2048 x 1536 (which is more than 3 million pixels in the landscape orientation) and measures about 10 inches in length (diagonally). The Kindle Fire HDX has a screen size of 2560 x 1600 (which is more than 4 million pixels in the landscape orientation) and measures at nine inches in length. The two devices sport very different aspect ratios: the iPad Air uses a 4:3 ratio (landscape) and the Kindle Fire HDX uses a 16:10 ratio (landscape).

Thankfully, we don't have to worry about each physical pixel. Most devices with these high-DPI displays (or retina displays, as Apple likes to call them) present a small collection of these physical pixels as a single logical pixel to our app. This means our app will see a Retina iPad as though it has a resolution of 1024 x 768. Sometimes, this is painful (especially if one needs physical pixel perfection), but most of the time, this works in our favor. The following diagram illustrates the difference between physical and logical pixels:

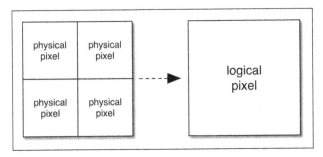

In this project, we'll rethink the user interface to better utilize the larger real estate. However, even with these changes, there's no change in functionality, just appearance.

Why is it great?

There are apps that scream for a large screen; note-taking apps aren't any exception. A bigger screen means a larger onscreen keyboard and more space for the app's content.

How are we going to do it?

First, we'll cover the responsive design and all that it entails. Then, we'll look at the three common responses to building an interface for larger screens and differing orientations:

- What is responsive design?
    - Response 1: scaling up
    - Response 2: changing layout
    - Response 3: split view

What is responsive design?

If you're familiar with web development, you're probably already familiar with the term. Responsive design is simply a method to craft websites that provide an optimal viewing experience across different devices. For a while, websites have largely targeted desktop browsers; however, since the increased popularity of mobile devices, these sites now support mobile devices as well.

For a long time, the approach was always to split the site into two: the main site, which would serve desktop browsers (that can run on computers capable of rendering complex content), and a watered-down mobile site, which would serve mobile devices. In the early days, of course, this was almost a requirement; mobile devices had very limited bandwidth and capabilities. Unfortunately, as mobile devices advanced, this particular approach persisted.

As browsers became more powerful and the capabilities and bandwidth of mobile devices increased, it became possible to build one site that could fit a desktop browser as well as a mobile device. This meant dealing with a new set of challenges—text that is readable on both devices, images that are appropriately scaled, and a drastically different layout. Desktop browsers permitted wide layouts, but the smaller mobile devices often required tall, narrow layouts.

For the longest time, this could only be accomplished using some fancy JavaScript, but once media queries were introduced into CSS, the feature really took off. Here was a feature that allowed the web designer specify the site's appearance with regard to different screen sizes, orientations, and types (such as print or other media).

Sometimes, images are better than words; this is one of those times. Here's an example of how responsive design looks on the Web. In the following screenshot (from `http://mediaqueri.es/rwd/`), the width of the screen has progressively increased, and you can see how the layout has changed according to expanded space:

Of course, the responsive design isn't limited to the width of a device; it can (and for hybrid apps, needs to) respond to the device's height as well. Alternatively, it is often useful to respond to the device's orientation or screen quality and capabilities.

There's no one way to build responsive apps. You'll need to use a wide assortment of tools to get there, and that's what we'll cover in the following sections.

Before we get started, you'll need to verify the support on your target platforms for the CSS rules we will discuss. A great resource to determine the features that are supported on various platforms is `http://caniuse.com`.

Position your containers

Containers are block elements that contain other elements, perhaps even other containers. For example, a navigation bar is a container—it comprises the title and buttons within. The same applies to views—the elements that make up the view are usually contained within another element. Up until this point, you've seen this visually demonstrated in each project when we drew the DOM layouts for our user interface designs.

Generally, you want containers to attach to the edges of the screen or of their parent element. This means your containers need to be absolutely positioned using the `position: absolute` style. The attachments are specified using the `top`, `left`, `right`, and `bottom` styles. These specify offsets in pixels or other units from the edge of the parent (assuming the parent is in the `absolute` or `relative` position). We can also specify the width and height of the element if a specific edge should not be attached to that of the parent.

Let's look at the following code snippet:

```
.ui-container {
  position: absolute;
  top: 0;    left: 0;
  right: 0; bottom: 0;
}
```

Each corner of this element will be attached to that of its parent, because we've not specified an offset from the edges. Also note that we've not specified any actual pixel position. If this were a top-level block element, it would fill any screen size. What makes this technique so useful is that if it is nested within another element and that element doesn't fill the screen, this element will be constrained to the parent's size.

The following is a visual representation of the parent element:

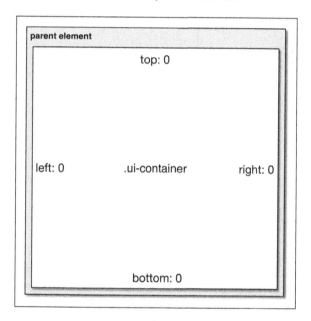

In the preceding diagram, the element classed `ui-container` fills its parent element. For clarity, there is a gap between the two elements, but in reality, the parent element is completely filled.

We can use any combination of these properties to achieve various affects. For example, for a specific width but a variable height, we can use the following code:

```
.ui-container .left-side {
  position: absolute;
  top: 0;        left: 0;
```

```
    width: 320px; bottom: 0;
  }
.ui-container .right-side {
    position: absolute;
    top: 0;    left: 320px;
    right: 0; bottom: 0;
  }
```

The preceding code results in the following layout:

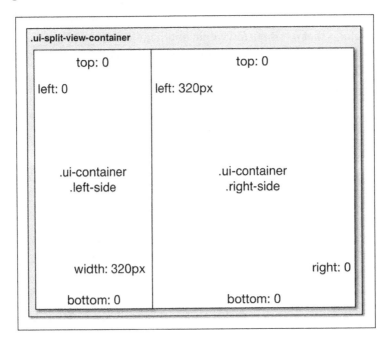

Of course, we assume that it will work on screens with at least 320 pixels across, but you get the point. Note that we changed `right` to `width` for the left container. You could do the same if you needed a container with variable width but a fixed height.

Positioning parents

When positioning elements absolutely, make sure that their parents are either absolutely or relatively positioned. This ensures that absolutely positioned children can refer to their parent to obtain the necessary frame.

If we want the container to be half the width of the parent element, we can use `width: 50%` instead, which leads us to the next section.

Using percentages instead of pixels where plausible

Based on the preceding example, it's easy to see why we should use percentages instead of pixels where plausible. Our left-most container wouldn't fit a screen that was only 240 pixels wide. If it makes sense in the context of the element, the following code is probably better:

```
.ui-container .left-side {
  position: absolute;
  top: 0;      left: 0;
  width: 30%; bottom: 0;
}
```

However, what if you want to enforce some practical limits? Perhaps the container needs to be 320 pixels wherever possible, but allow for other possibilities.

Using minimum and maximum values

Because all modern browsers work with minimum and maximum values, it's possible to write something like the following:

```
.ui-container {
  position: absolute;
  top: 0; left: 0;
  width: 100%; max-width: 320px; min-width: 240px;
  bottom: 0;
}
```

This ensures that the element has a reasonably sane width at all times; it will always be between 240 px and 320 px. This requires that the parent be at least 240 px wide, but it also ensures it will be capped at the maximum size when presented with a wider parent.

Using media queries (or similar)

Media queries allow you to specify that a set of styles applies only to specific media. Here, media has a broad definition, but you can craft a set of rules that applies to a device with a screen resolution of 2048 x 1536, and another set of rules that apply to a device with a screen resolution of 640 x 1136.

The concept is to ensure that your layout is effective when targeted at various media and sizes. For example, you might change the position, order, and size of elements on a narrow screen (say, a smartphone), but allow ample space for the content on a larger screen.

You can accomplish all this and more by using media queries. Essentially, they let you do something like the following:

```
.ui-container {
  position: absolute;
  top: 0;          left: 0;
  width: 320px; bottom: 0;
}

@media screen and (max-device-width: 319px)
             and (min-device-width: 240px) {
  .ui-container {
    width: 100%;
  }
}

@media screen and (max-device-width: 239px) {
  .ui-container {
    display: none;
  }
}
```

This essentially duplicates our previous example, but with the added bonus of the variable width taking effect only if the device's screen width falls within 240 px to 319 px. If the device's screen is wider, then we cap at 320 px, and if it is narrower, we hide the element.

Media queries are incredibly powerful, and their full use is unfortunately outside the scope of this book. For more information and excellent documentation regarding media queries, see `https://developer.mozilla.org/en-US/docs/Web/Guide/CSS/Media_queries`.

Most frameworks provide other mechanisms to achieve similar effects, and YASMF is no exception. If you inspect the `body` element in a browser, you'd see many classes attached:

- The platform classes: `ios`, `android`, `mac`, `windows`, `linux`, `unknown`, and so on
- The OS-version classes: `ios7`, `ios6`, `ios5`, and so on
- The form-factor classes: `tablet` and `phone`
- The orientation classes: `portrait` and `landscape`
- The device classes: `ipad`, `iphone`, `droid-tablet`, `droid-phone`, and so on
- The pixel-density classes: `loDPI` (non-retina) and `hiDPI` (retina)

These classes duplicate the functionalities of media queries in three ways: the form-factor, orientation, and pixel-density classes. That is, you could use a media query to determine whether the app is running on a tablet in the landscape orientation with a retina display or a phone-sized device in the portrait orientation with a non-retina display.

However, these classes are more powerful than media queries, because they allow us to write CSS that targets a specific platform (which we've been making use of in our project this far), a specific device class, and even a specific OS version. All these can be combined to make some very powerful style rules that are often more self-documenting than media queries.

For example, consider the following code:

```
.ui-container {
  position: absolute;
  top: 0;     left: 0;
  right: 0;   bottom: 0;
}

.tablet.landscape .ui-container {
  right: inherit;
  width: 320px;
}

.tablet.portrait .ui-container {
  display: none;
}

.ipad.ios7 .ui-container {
  top: 20px;
}
```

The preceding code looks fairly simple. Yet these simple rules lead to complex behavior. For example, if run on an iPad with iOS 7 in the landscape orientation, the container would be offset from the top of the parent by 20 px. If the same iPad were in a portrait orientation, the container wouldn't be visible at all. If this code were run on an Android tablet, the same would apply, except the container wouldn't be offset from the top by 20 px.

YASMF automatically applies all these classes at startup and whenever the device's orientation changes. If you want to implement something similar, refer to *Project 3, Mobile Application Design*, near the end of the *Implementing the note list view* section.

Using resolution-independent assets when possible

If you look at our apps so far, you'll note that we've never worried about the sizes of our assets. This is because we use small-sized icons (60 x 60 pixel) and have never gone above this value. If we did exceed it, we'd start to see interpolation by the browser, resulting in some blurriness.

It is also important to note that when we render to non-retina screens, we draw at a particular fraction of the icon size. This isn't necessarily ideal; a 50 percent reduction will usually generate good results, but a different screen size may result in a blurry icon.

It's best to use resolution-independent assets when possible for this very reason. These would typically be web fonts or SVG elements. The benefit is that the assets can remain very sharp at large and small sizes beyond which they would be considered "pixel-perfect". For example, a web font might have glyphs that render to a 16 x 16 pixel grid when the font size is also 16 px. Nevertheless, the font will still appear sharp at 20 px, where a bitmap icon exhibits blurriness, uneven line thickness, and other visual artifacts.

If you can't use resolution-independent assets directly (for example, some platforms might face problems in rendering SVG or web fonts, or drawing these assets might be too slow), the next best thing is to build your assets using vectors and then generate the necessary bitmap assets. For example, I always create icons using a vector drawing tool, like Adobe Illustrator or Sketch. The benefit is that the shapes are always resizable depending on various needs. Then, I save a specific size as a bitmap that the app can use.

If you want to be accurate, it's best to generate a bitmap for each scaling factor. For example, YASMF supplies icons with `@2x` in the filename. These are rendered for screens with a 2x scaling factor, where one logical pixel dimension contains exactly two physical pixels in that dimension. For a scaling factor of 1x, we could use `@1x`, though typically a filename without any scaling factor is assumed to be 1x.

Note that the scaling factors aren't integers, that is, you can end up with a scaling factor of 1.4x, 1.5x, or 1.75x—any value is possible. This means, if our icons only support a 2x scaling factor, the browser must scale them down to the actual scaling factor, which may or may not be appealing. Scaling down to a 1x factor will usually result in a reasonable-looking image, but if the factor is anything in between, the result will almost certainly be a blurry mess.

This is why many apps will use assets pre-rendered for a specific scaling factor. That is, one might have the same icon rendered at 1x, 1.4x, 1.5x, 1.6x, 2x, 2.5x, and so on.

To go a step further, many designers will also tweak the icon for each scaling factor. For example, an icon at 2x might appear blurry when scaled down to 1x simply because of too much detail that is juxtaposed. Rendering the 1x icon with less detail will keep the end result sharp, but it requires much more work on the part of the designer and developer.

As you know, we've only worried about icons for a scaling factor of 2x. We've been allowing the browser to scale according to the device, but this isn't always optimal. For the purposes of our book, it's sufficient; however, when creating your own apps, you should go to the next step and ensure the assets are sharp for all scaling factors.

Media queries can come to your rescue here because you can apply styles based on specific pixel ratios, as follows:

```
.icon {
  background-image:url('./icons/icon@1x.png');
}

@media screen and (-webkit-min-device-pixel-ratio:1.4) {
  .icon {
    background-image:url('./icons/icon@1_4x.png');
  }
}
@media screen and (-webkit-min-device-pixel-ratio:2) {
  .icon {
    background-image:url('./icons/icon@2x.png');
  }
}
```

Plan ahead

When you take all these into account from the very beginning, scaling up an iPhone app is pretty easy. On the other hand, if you've planned everything down to the pixel and built an app for a 320 x 480 screen, you will have to change all those pixels around on a larger screen. When dealing with simple productivity apps such as Filer, building a layout that can scale to a larger screen isn't terribly difficult, but once you get into more complex layouts and graphics, it starts to become a challenge.

In some ways, highly graphical games have it both the hardest and the easiest. A game is probably going to keep the same user interface when scaling to a new screen, with perhaps a few minor tweaks to the button placement or size. The graphics, however, are going to be the same visually. However, underneath the hood, those graphics may be rendered at vastly different resolutions. A certain graphic might work fine on a small screen, but get that up to a larger screen, and it will either seem too large or too small. To avoid forcing the browser to scale everything (which always slows things down and results in some blurriness), it is better to re-render the graphics for the target screen. Because we never know what kind of screens will be out in the future, it is, for this reason, preferable to always create your graphics in a vector format. This way you can create a new rendition when a new size is needed.

One of the hardest things to deal with properly is full-screen images. These might be in-game backgrounds, menu backgrounds, splashes, and so on, and you want them to look as sharp as possible. One approach is to add letterboxing around the image if the aspect ratio of the screen is substantially different (think of a wide-screen movie appearing on a TV that is not widescreen). The other would be to scale and crop the image, potentially blurring it a bit, and losing portions of this image. The only other realistic option is to create an image specifically for each supported resolution.

For the best visual appearance, you should always render your images at the device's native resolution. For a Retina iPad, this would be 2048 x 1536 for a full-screen image when in the landscape orientation. This, of course, is different for just about every Android device, and there's no terribly easy way to deal with it, as previously mentioned. The best image quality will result by rendering an image specifically for each supported resolution and scaling factor.

On the other hand, non-game apps can be terribly painful to scale up. You might be dealing with a lot of content that is, for example, formatted in a reasonably complex manner. It looks great given a specific screen size, but on another, things may break in odd places, especially when simply scaling. Sometimes, the fact that we're working in HTML and CSS will save us—it's meant to deal with a complicated layout, but just as often as not, it'll cause the look and feel to go awry in a way that you hadn't envisioned.

This is when creating code and layout specifically for tablet-sized screens may be necessary. You can do things in your JavaScript, HTML, and CSS to handle these sizes. You can put a `DIV` classed with `tablet` in your HTML, and have a CSS rule that hides it on anything but a tablet. Likewise, you could hide the phone UI elements if you're trying to create a universal app that can run on both phone- and tablet-sized screens. Or, if you're positioning certain things with JavaScript, you can always look at the type of device you're running the app on to get a good idea about what to do; in the worst case, look at the width or height of the screen. Again, using media queries can help when dealing with multiple resolutions.

Response 1 – scaling up

Many apps often respond to a larger screen size by scaling everything up to fill the space. Whether this is appropriate is a different matter. If one has written their styles and layouts correctly, the app should scale automatically.

Getting on with it

Just to show you how this looks, try running our app as it stands on a tablet device. It should work without further modification and should look like a scaled-up phone app. That is, the list of notes is wide (especially in the landscape orientation) and there's a lot of wasted space. Adjust the orientation of the device and note how the views appropriately resize when the width and height of the screen change.

The list view will look like the following when in the landscape orientation:

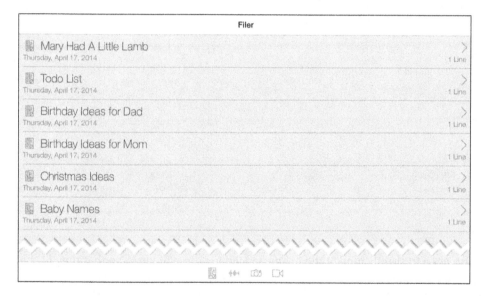

This, in my opinion, does not look great. There's a large amount of space wasted, and it really does look like the developer didn't even bother trying. For many users, this is going to leave a bad taste in their mouth.

What did we do?

In this section, we ran our app on a tablet-sized device. We changed orientations to see how the app appropriately fills the screen even when the dimensions change. We also noted that the list view doesn't look particularly great on larger devices (especially in the landscape orientation).

Response 2 – changing the layout

Another common response to a larger screen, or to a change in orientation, is simply to change the layout. This can be as simple as stacking elements vertically when in the portrait orientation and placing them together horizontally when in the landscape orientation. Or, the layout can change in very complex ways, for example, a list can turn into a carousel or grid.

Getting ready

We can adjust the layout of the list of notes when we have a larger screen. Instead of generating a very wide list, we could generate a grid of items, which is more visually appealing, and it would better fill the space. Consider the following screenshot:

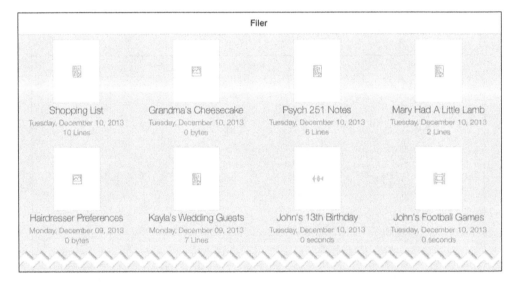

We also need to slightly modify the image and video note edit views so that they fit the large screen size better. For example, when in the landscape orientation, it makes more sense to display the image or video to the left of the note instead of above it, whereas in the portrait orientation, keeping the top and bottom layout makes more sense, especially when the soft keyboard is on the screen.

Getting on with it

In order to accomplish this, we'll need to make a few tweaks to the note list view and the note list item template. After this, we'll have to alter a few styles to better fit the larger screens.

First, let's adjust the template for the note list item at `www/html/noteListItem.html`. The changes are highlighted in the following code. All we're doing is adding a wrapping `DIV` tag around the icon representation for a note:

```html
<html>
  <body>
    <div class="ui-list-item-contents" data-uid="%UID%">
      <div class="note-page">
        <div class="ui-glyph note-representation ui-glyph-
%REPRESENTATION%"></div>
      </div>
      <div class="ui-label note-name">%NAME%</div>
      <div class="ui-label note-modified-date">%MODIFIED%</div>
      <div class="ui-label note-info">%INFO%</div>
      <div class="ui-indicator ui-arrow-direction-right"></div>
    </div>
    <div class="ui-list-action-group">
      <div class="ui-list-action ui-background-destructive-color"
data-uid="%UID%"><div>%TRASH%</div></div>
    </div>
  </body>
</html>
```

Next, we alter the note list view at `www/js/app/views/noteListView.js`. We'll focus on the changes to `renderList`, but you are free to look at the code package for this book to see all the changes we made.

At the top of the method, we check whether we are on a tablet-sized device and our DOM element is at least 320 pixels. The logic here is that we might want to render a list of notes in a narrow view rather than in a grid. This ensures that if this app is on an iPhone, it looks as it always has. Consider the following code:

```
if (_y.device.isTablet() &&
    parseInt(window.getComputedStyle ( self.element
).getPropertyValue ( "width" ),10) >= 320)
    {
```

If it turns out we are on a tablet or in a wide container, we then mark the DOM element by adding a `wide` class. Our style sheet will catch this and style the list appropriately. Consider the following code:

```
    self.element.classList.add ("wide");
}
```

The remainder of the code is nearly identical; save for the portion where we need to handle gesture support. Swipe-to-delete doesn't make much sense in a grid, so we add a long-press gesture to each element, which will pop up a list of available options. The code is self-explanatory, and so we'll leave it to you to look at the code package for the book.

The real work is done in the style sheet; we need to create all the styles that will generate a grid instead of a list. However, since we need to run on a smaller device as well, we won't change the existing styles. We'll just create new ones under the `wide` class. Add the following styles to `www/css/style.css`.

The first rule creates the grid itself—note that it is set to an inline block element. This allows the browser to wrap a series of this element as if it were a line of text. With a `width` of `25%`, the browser will always render four per row. Consider the following code:

```
.noteListView.wide .ui-list-item {
  border-bottom: 0;
  margin-left: 0; margin-right: 0;
  display: inline-block;
  width: 25%;  min-height: 200px;
  vertical-align: top;
  padding-left: 0;
}
```

The following styles render the item itself, including the white rectangle that is representative of a page as well as the icon inside:

```
.noteListView.wide .ui-list-item .note-page {
  background-color: #FFFFFF;
  margin: 0 auto;
  width: 100px;  height: 130px;
  border: 1px solid rgba(0,0,0,0.125);
}
.android .noteListView.wide .ui-list-item .note-page {
  background-color: #242424;
  border: 1px solid rgba(255,255,255,0.125);
}
.android .noteListView.wide .ui-list-item .note-representation {
  background-color: #808080;
}
.noteListView.wide .ui-list-item .note-representation {
  float: inherit;
  height: inherit;
  width: inherit;
}
```

Next, we need to specify where the text lives; in this case, below the page element:

```
.noteListView.wide .ui-list-item .note-name {
  font-size: 20px;
  margin-left: 0;
  margin-right: 0;
  text-align: center;
}
.noteListView.wide .ui-list-item .note-modified-date,
.noteListView.wide .ui-list-item .note-info {
  text-align: center;
  float: inherit;
}
```

We hide the indicator and the action group, since they don't make sense in a grid layout:

```
.noteListView.wide .ui-list-item .ui-indicator {
  display: none;
}
.noteListView.wide .ui-list-item .ui-list-action-group {
  display: none;
}
```

We also need to adjust the layout for the video and image note views:

```
.VideoNoteEditView .video-container .video-element video {
  width: 100%;
  height: 100%;
}
.tablet.portrait .ImageNoteEditView .image-container,
.tablet.portrait .VideoNoteEditView .video-container {
  height: 50%;
}
.tablet.landscape .ImageNoteEditView .image-container,
.tablet.landscape .VideoNoteEditView .video-container {
  width: 50%;
  height: 100%;
  display: inline-block;
  vertical-align: top;
}
.tablet.portrait .ImageNoteEditView .ui-text-box,
.tablet.portrait .VideoNoteEditView .ui-text-box {
  height: 50%;
}
.tablet.landscape .ImageNoteEditView .ui-text-box,
.tablet.landscape .VideoNoteEditView .ui-text-box {
```

```
    height: 100%;
    width:49%;
    width: calc(50% - 10px);
    display: inline-block;
}
```

If you recall, the text box animates over the image or video element when on a smaller screen. On a large screen, that stops making sense, so we override those settings:

```
.tablet.portrait  .ImageNoteEditView .ui-text-box.editing,
.tablet.portrait  .VideoNoteEditView .ui-text-box.editing {
  height: 50%;
  margin-top: 0;
}
.tablet.landscape  .ImageNoteEditView .ui-text-box.editing,
.tablet.landscape  .VideoNoteEditView .ui-text-box.editing {
  height: 100%;
  margin-top: 0;
}
```

What did we do?

At this point, you should be able to run the app again on a tablet device and add some notes. As you add notes, you will see them appear in a grid pattern rather than as a list. If you then run the same code on a smartphone, the list will be used instead.

Response 3 – split view

The split view layout is by far one of the most popular methods to scale your app to the tablet. It also has the benefit of flattening the application's information hierarchy, which is a way of saying that it takes fewer taps to get somewhere in the app.

Most tablet platforms implement this view in similar ways. In the landscape mode, the sidebar is always visible on the left-hand side of the screen (although sometimes on the right). In the portrait mode, it's usually hidden, ready and waiting for when the user taps a button to call it out. Other times, the view is always visible in the portrait mode, but this depends on the type of app and whether the loss of content real estate is worth having the split view always visible.

In our case, this really isn't the best view for the app. Since Filer is a document-based app, the work we've done to this point is sufficient. However, in order to demonstrate the split view element, we'll add it to the app as well. We won't hide and show the sidebar; instead we'll opt to have it always visible. We'll worry about hiding and showing the sidebar in the next project.

Getting ready

The split view is really just two views put side by side. That's the easy way to think about it—one view is on the left-hand side in a smaller sidebar, while the second is on the right. The left view is technically called the master view and the right view is called the detail view. Technically, this pattern is the **master-detail** pattern. It is most obvious when working with data records, where the record selection occurs in the master view (on the left) and the detail of the record shows in the detail view (on the right).

In our app, we're going to make the notes list the master view so that the note content itself can be the focus of the user. This means that a specific note will become the detail.

The following is our desired result:

The associated DOM layout is as follows::

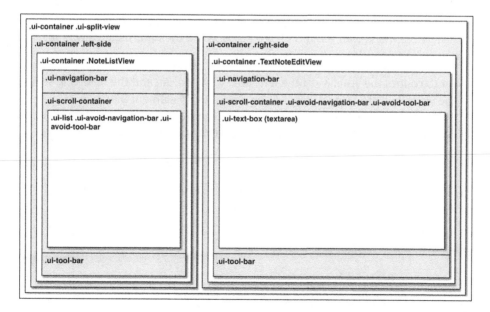

Getting on with it

Before we start writing code, let's go over how split views work. Split views aren't terribly complex; they are essentially two containers laid out side by side. Where typical top-level containers are expected to fill the screen, the left-most container must fill only a small portion of the screen, and the right-most container must fill the remainder.

Any view or element can be added as either side's child. If we need to maintain a view stack, a navigation controller is usually inserted. This would then manage all the views inside. If a view stack is not necessary, the navigation controller can be ignored, and the view can be added directly. In our code, we will always assume that the navigation controller is present.

The parent DOM element is given the classes of `ui-container` and `ui-split-view`. The left-most DOM element within is given the classes `ui-container` and `left-side`. You can imagine what the right-most DOM element is given (`ui-container` and `right-side`). Within a style sheet, we can create several styles that give us the desired layout, like the following:

```
.ui-split-view { width: 100%; }
.ui-container .left-side {
  width: 320px;
  border-right: 1px solid #808080;
  z-index: 3;
  transform: translateZ(3px); }
.ui-container .right-side {
  width: calc(100% - 320px);
  left: 320px; }
```

These styles are sufficient to generate a split view that has both sides always visible. The left-most view is always given a width of 320 pixels, while the right-most view is adjusted to fill the remaining screen space.

If we want to control the visibility of the left-most view, we can add the following styles and control the visibility by toggling a class on the parent DOM element between `ui-left-side-invisible` and `ui-left-side-visible`. Because the default styles show the left-most view, we only need to define styles to hide the view, shown as follows:

```
.ui-split-view.ui-left-side-invisible .ui-container.left-side
{ display: none; }
.ui-split-view.ui-left-side-invisible .ui-container.right-side
{ left: 0; width: 100%; }
```

There are other types of split views. The two popular types are the off-canvas view and the split overlay view. The off-canvas view places the master and detail views side by side, but provides a wider canvas than the screen width. When the left-most view is visible, the screen viewport includes the left-most view at the expense of losing a portion of the right-most view. When the left-most view is invisible, the screen viewport slides over to the right, hiding the left-most view and revealing the complete right-most view. The split-overlay view works in a similar manner, except the left-most view appears above the right-most view when visible and is hidden when invisible.

The styles for both are very similar and simple:

```
.ui-off-canvas-view {
  width: calc(100% + 320px);
  transform: translateX(-320px);
  transition: transform 0.3s ease-in-out; }
.ui-off-canvas-view.ui-left-side-invisible {
  transform: translateX(-320px);
}
.ui-off-canvas-view.ui-left-side-visible {
  transform: translateX(0);
}
.ui-split-overlay-view { width: 100%; }
.ui-split-overlay-view.ui-left-side-invisible .ui-container.left-side
{
  transform: translateX(-320px);
  transition: transform 0.3s ease-in-out }
.ui-split-overlay-view.ui-left-side-visible .ui-container .right-side
{
  transform: translateX(0);
  transition: transform 0.3s ease-in-out }
.ui-split-overlay-view .ui-container.right-side {
  left: 0; width: 100% }
```

All split views generally work in the same way, that is, they all support showing and hiding the left-most view. In all cases, if you want the user to have control over when the left-most view is shown, you'll need to add a button (or a swipe gesture handler) so that the user can toggle the state. In our app, we'll use the default split view and won't worry about hiding the left-most view—it'll always be visible. We'll look into toggling the visibility of the left-most view in the next project.

So far, you've seen how to visually represent a split view controller, but what about the code to back everything up? It's remarkably simple; you'll need a few properties to keep track of the views and which side they are on and a mechanism to toggle the sidebar. Consider the following code:

```
self._leftViewStatus = "invisible" // or visible
self.setLeftViewStatus = function ( viewStatus ) {
  self.element.classList.remove ( "ui-left-side-" + self._
leftViewStatus );
  self.element.classList.add ( "ui-left-side-" + viewStatus );
  self._leftViewStatus = viewStatus;
}

self._viewType = "split" // or off-canvas or split-overlay
self.setViewType = function ( viewType ) {
  self.element.classList.remove ( "ui-" + self._viewType + "-view" );
  self.element.classList.add ( "ui-" + viewType + "-view" );
  self._viewType = viewType;
  self.leftViewStatus = "invisible";
}

self.toggleLeftView = function () {
  if (self._leftViewStatus === "visible") {
    self.setLeftViewStatus ( "invisible" );
  } else {
    self.setLeftViewStatus ( "visible" );
  }
}

self._leftElement = null;
self._rightElement = null;
self._createElements = function () {
  self._leftElement = document.createElement ("div");
  self._rightElement = document.createElement ("div");
  self._leftElement.className = ".ui-container .left-side";
  self.rightElement.className = ".ui-container .right-side";
  self.element.appendChild ( self.leftElement );
  self.element.appendChild ( self.rightElement );
}

self._assignViewToSide = function ( whichSide, theView ) {
  if (self._leftElement == null || self._rightElement == null)
  {
    self._createElements;
```

```
    }
    // allow the child view to communicate with us
    theView.splitViewController = self;
    // make the view a child of the specified side
    theView.parentElement = whichSide;
  }

  self.getLeftView = function () { return self._leftElement; }
  self.getRightView = function () { return self._rightElement; }
  self.setLeftView = function ( theView ) {
    self._assignViewToSide ( self._leftElement, theView ); }
  self.setRightView = function ( theView ) {
    self._assignViewToSide ( self._rightElement, theView ); }

  // the following properties are also defined:
  // viewType, leftViewStatus, leftView, rightView
```

Now that we've got a split view controller, how do views on one side communicate with those on the other? One mechanism is to walk the view hierarchy to reach the appropriate view. Another mechanism is to send global notifications that the view on the other side is expected to understand. In our case, we'll walk the view hierarchy, like the following:

```
self.navigationController.splitViewController
  .rightView.pushView ( aView );
```

For our purposes, this is sufficient. However, there is a problem in this approach; it requires our code to know the view hierarchy of our app. This is a form of tight coupling—something most projects should avoid. In more complicated applications, it would be better to send notifications, which are a form of loose coupling.

Of course, it's possible to detect the view hierarchy and decide on the appropriate course of action, but it's best to avoid coupling this tight in production apps:

```
if (typeof self.navigationController !== "undefined") {
  if (typeof self.navigationController.splitViewController !==
"undefined") {
    self.navigationController.splitViewController
      .rightView.pushView (aView)
  } else {
    self.navigationController.push (aView);
  }
}
```

Visually, walking the view hierarchy looks like the following:

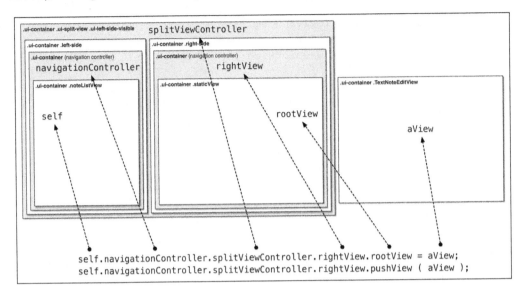

All of this is implemented in YASMF using the split view controller. If you want to look at the code in the code package (it's very similar), go to `/framework/lib/yasmf/ui/splitViewController.js` or visit `https://github.com/photokandyStudios/YASMF-Next/blob/master/lib/yasmf/ui/splitViewController.js`.

Now that we've covered how you can implement split views, let's go over the code changes for our project.

First, we need to create a new view. We'll call it a static view because its only purpose is to indicate that the user should select a note from the list or create a note. The view does this just by displaying some text to the user. If we didn't do this, the user might not know what to do initially (especially in the first run).

This view is very, very simple. So simple that we're not going to duplicate the code here. You can copy the template and view from our sample project to yours. The template is at `www/html/staticView.html` and the view is at `www/js/app/views/staticView.js`.

Next, we need to alter the note list view (`www/js/app/views/noteListView.js`) in order to enable communication between both views that are on the screen. Where we would normally just call our view's navigation controller and push a new view, we now need to determine whether the view is inside a split view controller. If the view is, it needs to put the new view in the right-hand side of the screen. To do this, we create a new private method that takes care of putting a new note edit view in the proper place:

```
self._displayEditView = function ( theView ) {
```

First, we check for the existence of `SplitViewController`:

```
if (typeof self.navigationController
  .splitViewController !== "undefined") {
```

If it is there, we ask for the `rightView` variable so that we can interact with it:

```
var rightView = self.navigationController
  .splitViewController.rightView;
```

Next, we look at the `class` of this view's `topView`. If it isn't `StaticView`, then a note is edited and we need to save it first. Note that we use `topView` here instead of `rootView` to ensure that we target the currently visible view. If we were pushing multiple views on to the right-most view's stack, `rootView` would point at the very first view pushed, and that wouldn't be visible. Consider the following code:

```
if (rightView.topView.class !== "StaticView" ) {
  rightView.topView.saveNote();
}
```

Once we've saved a note that may be visible, we then ask `rightView` to assign the new edit view as its `rootView`. This is different from pushing a view, which would add the view to the view stack with the potential for animation. Here, we're replacing the root view itself, and there will be no animation:

```
self.navigationController.splitViewController
  .rightView.rootView = theView;
} else {
```

If we're not in the split view, push the new view like we always have (in order to support the app on a phone-sized device):

```
    self.navigationController.pushView ( theView );
  }
}
```

Next, we need to alter each `createNew...` method and the `editExistingNote` method to call `_displayEditView` whenever they want to display a view. Instead of pushing the view, the code should now look similar to the following:

```
self.createNewTextNote = function () {
  ...
  self._displayEditView ( aNoteEditView );
}
```

Deleting a note is now more difficult, since it is entirely possible that the note is currently visible and would need to be removed from the screen after the deletion. Alter deleteExistingNote as follows:

```
self.deleteExistingNote = function ( e ) {
  ...
  noteStorageSingleton.removeNote ( theUID );
  if (typeof self.navigationController
    .splitViewController !== "undefined") {
      var topView =
      self.navigationController.splitViewController
      .rightView.topView;
      if (topView.class !== "StaticView") {
```

If, and only if, the note that is being edited is the same as the one being deleted (by checking UIDs), do we need to worry about removing it off the screen. We do this by creating a new static view and assigning it to the right-most view's rootView:

```
        if (topView.getNoteUID() == theUID) {
          var staticView = new StaticView();
          staticView.initWithOptions ();
          self.navigationController.splitViewController
          .rightView.rootView = staticView;
        }
      }
    }
  }
```

In the text note edit view (www/js/app/views/textNoteEditView.js), we need to add code for popping the view when the **Delete** button is tapped, and we also need to add a new method to get the UID of the currently visible note.

First, let's add the method to get the UID of the view's current note so that the note list view can check whether a note being deleted is the same note that we are editing:

```
self.getNoteUID = function () {
  return self._note.UID;
}
```

Next, we need to create a method that can pop our view off the view stack when running on a phone-sized device, but one that can replace the right-most view with a static view when running in a split view:

```
self.popView = function () {
  if (typeof self.navigationController
```

```
          .splitViewController !== "undefined") {
            var staticView = new StaticView();
            staticView.initWithOptions ();
            self.navigationController.splitViewController
            .rightView.rootView = staticView;
          } else {
            self.navigationController.popView();
          }
        }
```

Now, replace any occurrences of `self.navigationController.popView` in the remaining code with `self.popView`.

Finally, we need to alter `www/js/app/main.js` to create a split view controller when running on a tablet. In `APP.start`, note that the defined portion of the code needs to be updated to refer to the new static view (look in the code package of this book if you need to see this). The first section of code should look familiar:

```
var rootContainer = _y.get("rootContainer");
var noteListView = new NoteListView ();
APP.noteListView = noteListView;
noteListView.init ( );
```

Now, we create a variable so that we can easily toggle between the split and normal views without creating multiple projects. If the device is a phone, we proceed to override whatever was just indicated, because a split view doesn't make sense in our case on a smartphone:

```
var whichAppStyle = "split";
if ( _y.device.isPhone() ) {
  whichAppStyle = "normal";
}
switch (whichAppStyle)
{
  case "split":
    var leftNavigationController,
    rightNavigationController,
    splitViewController,
    staticView;
```

First, we need a static view created. This will be displayed on the right. We need this because split view controllers will not work if two views are not ready to go:

```
staticView = new StaticView();
staticView.initWithOptions ();
```

Next, we create the left-hand side's navigation controller and add the note list view to it:

```
leftNavigationController =
  new _y.UI.NavigationController();
leftNavigationController.initWithOptions (
  { rootView: noteListView } );
```

Now we create the right-hand side's navigation controller. The static view is attached to it:

```
rightNavigationController =
  new _y.UI.NavigationController();
rightNavigationController.initWithOptions (
  { rootView: staticView } );
```

Then, we create the split view controller. We attach the left and right navigation controllers to the left and right views. We also indicate the view type. (This can also be off-canvas, which we'll cover in the next project, or split-canvas, which you can experiment with on your own.) We also make sure the sidebar is visible (by default, it is invisible). Consider the following code:

```
splitViewController =
  new _y.UI.SplitViewController();
splitViewController.initWithOptions (
  { leftView: leftNavigationController,
  rightView: rightNavigationController,
  parent: rootContainer,
  viewType: whichAppStyle,
  leftViewStatus: "visible" } );
APP.splitViewController = splitViewController;
break;
default:
```

If we don't want a split view app, just start the app like we always have:

```
var navigationController =
  new _y.UI.NavigationController();
  navigationController.initWithOptions (
    { rootView: noteListView,
    parent: rootContainer } );
  APP.navigationController = navigationController;
}
```

What did we do?

In this section, we discussed how to create split view controllers and modified our app to support them.

What else do I need to know?

We haven't gone into detail about how to handle the physical back button when working with split views. The proper method is to build a navigation stack, akin to your browser history. Whenever the back button is pressed, you can navigate to the previous navigation state on the stack. This is easier said than done, especially for complex apps. In our case, it's not necessary because each side can only display one view at a time, and views are replaced when they are displayed, not pushed. This means the view stack is only one level deep.

Game Over..... Wrapping it up

At this point, you've got an app that can function as a scaled app with an alternate layout or as a split-view app on a tablet. The app works as it always has on a smartphone device, and so, we've essentially created a universal app—one that works on smartphones and tablets.

Can you take the HEAT? The Hotshot Challenge

Why don't you try few of the following challenges:

▸ Convert the app to use an off-canvas split view. This was popular on the iPad Facebook app and was also available on the iPhone app. The benefit is that the menu can remain offscreen until called on by the user. The method used to request the menu to appear is often a menu (or hamburger) icon (three horizontal lines stacked one on top of the other) as well as a left-to-right swipe near the left edge of the screen.

▸ Modify the existing split view app so that the user can hide the sidebar in order to gain more space to work with their note. This is often done with a toggle button in the navigation bar.

▸ Try moving the sidebar to the right-hand side of the screen instead of the left-hand side.

▸ Add a second sidebar on the right-hand side that appears when the user requests it. (This is also seen in the iPad Facebook app as the chat sidebar.)

Project 10

Maps and GPS

Although unthinkable only a few years ago, it's unlikely that you don't have a device on you that knows how to locate itself, either by inferring the location from the WiFi signal or from the GPS network. The accuracy of the calculated location depends on the method used, but GPS signals permit a high degree of accuracy. Given that this used to be the mainstay of expensive GPS gadgets not so long ago, it's amazing how quickly this feature has become ubiquitous and expected. Because of this, users expect their apps to be location-aware.

What do we build?

Our project utilizes the Google Maps API (as of writing this, Version 3.15.16). We will use this API to display an interactive map that is centered on the user's current location. Our project will also use the geolocation features that Cordova/PhoneGap provide in order to obtain the user's location over a period of time to allow the app to record the path the user takes during the same period. Instead of a voice recorder, think of the app as a path recorder.

What does it do?

In order to actually use Google Maps, we have to load the API libraries. We have to approach this a little bit differently because we are using RequireJS—we can't actually do anything related to map in the app until the libraries have loaded.

We'll also cover a little bit of the Google Maps API itself. The subject, on the whole, is worth a book on its own; consider this as a jumping-off point.

While the visual star is the Google Map, the main feature of the app is to record paths. This means that we'll have to use the geolocation features provided by Cordova/PhoneGap. It is important to note that if the system browser has a reasonable implementation of these features, Cordova/PhoneGap won't override the browser's implementation.

When the project is done, the app will be able to record the device's location and then display the recorded path when asked. There are all sorts of possibilities here: you could share the path with a friend, create an animation of the path taken, or even export the path to KML to share it with other applications.

What is KML?

Keyhole Markup Language (**KML**) is an XML file format that specifies various locations by longitude and latitude, along with various attributes such as descriptions, images, 3D renderings, and so on. Various applications can display KML files, including Google Earth. For more information, visit `http://developers.google.com/kml/documentation/`.

Why is it great?

Geolocation and interactive maps are features that users expect in modern apps. If you display an address, it is expected that you can display an interactive map to go along with it. If you offer searches by location, it is expected that you can locate where the user is and provide them with relevant results that are nearby. Geolocation and interactive maps aren't just for turn-by-turn directions or helping someone who got lost—they are invaluable features in many other applications as well.

How are we going to do it?

In order to accomplish our project, we'll be performing the following tasks:

- Developing our UI and look and feel
- Exploring geolocation
- Developing our data models
- Loading the Google Maps API
- Implementing our data models
- Implementing our path edit view
- Putting it all together

What do I need to get started?

Unlike the previous projects, we're starting this one from scratch. Therefore, you need to create a new project:

```
cordova create pathrec com.packpub.phonegaphotshot.pathrec pathrec
--copy-from path/to/template
```

```
cordova platform add ios android
```

Because the two projects are somewhat similar, it's possible to take the last Filer app, copy the www folder, and edit the resulting files (be sure to alter the `index.html` and `config.xml` files if you do). It may, however, be just as easy to create a new project.

Be sure to add the following plugins:

```
cordova plugin add org.apache.cordova.globalization
cordova plugin add org.apache.cordova.keyboard
```

Designing our app's UI and its look and feel

This will be our first new app—we won't be adding anything to Filer anymore. Even so, the look and feel will be very similar: a list of recorded paths, or the recorded paths view, and an interactive map (or the map view).

Getting on with it

Let's take a look at the mock-up for the tablet version of the app. The following image isn't quite representative of what appears onscreen. We're using an off-canvas split view in this app, which essentially means that the screen of the device is a window on this wider view. In order to show the leftmost sidebar, the rightmost view is only partially displayed. In order to show the entirety of the rightmost view, the sidebar must be offscreen. This arrangement is still a split view, but one that is wider than the screen. Consider the following image:

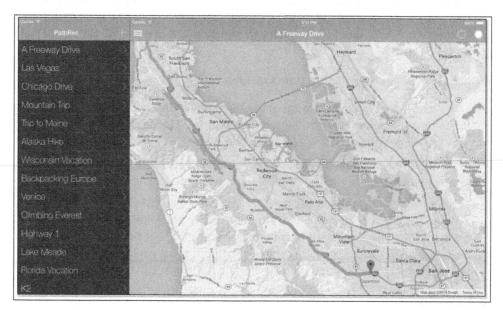

Here's the corresponding DOM structure and CSS classes:

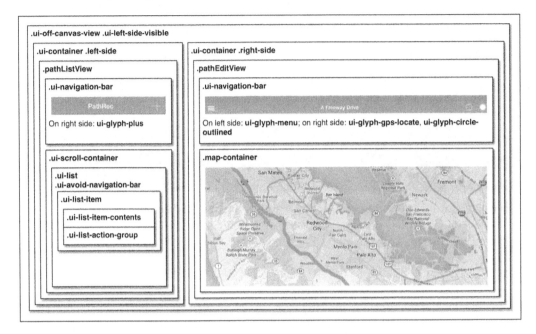

Most of this shouldn't require much explanation by now; the largest element is the Interactive Map. Since it is provided by Google, most of the interaction a user would expect is already present, without any work on our part. This includes panning the map as well as zooming in or out. Take special notice of the green line running from the red marker to top-left corner of the view—this is the representation of a recorded path. Although we have to do the work to record the path, Google provides the ability to display it with only a small amount of code necessary on our part.

There are a few other elements that you should notice:

▶ The icon in the upper-left corner of the map view (often referred to as the hamburger icon) is the menu button. This button will slide the offscreen canvas to the left or right, exposing and hiding the sidebar.

▶ The teardrop-shaped marker near the bottom-left corner of the map view is provided by Google, and it is used in our app to indicate the user's current location.

▶ The leftmost icon in the upper-right corner of the map view is the locate icon. When tapped, it centers the map around the user's location. During recording, the map usually stays centered on the user's location, but the user should also be able to explore the map on their own without being constantly returned to their current location. After some exploration, the user can tap this button to return the map to their current location.

▶ The rightmost icon in the upper-right corner of the map view is the record path icon. When tapped, the view will begin to record the user's position as often as it changes and draw a line following the user's progress. During recording, the icon changes to a pause icon, which, if tapped, will pause the recording operation.

Unlike a standard split view, an off-canvas split view can work equally well on tablet-sized and phone-sized devices. On a phone-sized device, the sidebar takes up nearly all the available real estate, but there's enough of the rightmost view visible so that the user can tap the menu icon to hide the sidebar.

 The off-canvas split view as implemented by YASMF works on iOS 6, iOS 7, and Android 4.4. On Android versions less than 4.4, use either a regular split view or a split-overlay view.

What did we do?

In this section, we designed the mock-up for the new path recording app and discussed the various interactive elements.

Exploring geolocation

Geolocation is one of those rare APIs that does what it was made for very simply and with a minimum of fuss; it's a very succinct API. There's also another benefit: as a W3C standard, many browsers have implemented it and it isn't specific to Cordova/PhoneGap.

What Cordova/PhoneGap does offer, however, is akin to a polyfill. If the browser implementation being used does not support geolocation, then Cordova/PhoneGap will provide its own implementation. As such, what works on one platform can work on many different platforms, including desktop browsers.

The API documentation can be found at `https://github.com/apache/cordova-plugin-geolocation/blob/dev/doc/index.md`.

Getting ready

Before you use the geolocation features, be sure to add the plugin to your project:

```
cordova plugin add org.apache.cordova.geolocation
```

Getting on with it

There's only one concept you have to worry about when it comes to the geolocation API: position data. The API lets you obtain the device's current position as accurately as possible. This means you can obtain the latitude, longitude, altitude, heading, and speed of the device.

In order to facilitate obtaining the position, there are two main methods: you can ask for it once or you can be notified whenever it changes (for however long you'd like to listen).

To ask for the position once, you can make use of the following code:

```
navigator.geolocation.getCurrentPosition ( successFunction,
errorFunction, { enableHighAccuracy: true});
function successFunction ( position ) {
  alert ( JSON.stringify(position) );
}
function errorFunction ( error ) {
  alert ( error.message );
}
```

If an error occurs, `errorFunction` will be called with an error message. If the position is obtained successfully, `successFunction` will be called with the position data.

Any error that occurs will be one of the `PositionError` constants. There are three possible error codes:

- `PositionError.PERMISSION_DENIED`: This indicates that the user did not allow the app access to the device's location

- `PositionError.POSITION_UNAVAILABLE`: This indicates that the position is not available (perhaps because there is no access to a WiFi or cellular network or the user is in a location where GPS is not available)

- `PositionError.TIMEOUT`: This indicates that the position took too long to determine

The `enableHighAccuracy` option is used to request a highly accurate position fix. This may use satellite positioning instead of the device's WiFi or cellular network. Keep in mind that this may also reduce battery life significantly.

Android Simulator Quirk

If you want to test in the Android Simulator, use `enableHighAccuracy:true` as in the preceding example. If you don't, it is possible you won't see any position at all. This only affects Android 2.x.

> **iOS Simulator Quirk**
>
> You may get an error like `the operation could not be completed` or the app might crash when you attempt to use geolocation services. The simulator has several recorded paths that simulate a moving device. Just open the **Debug** menu and open the **Location** submenu. You should see several paths that you can choose from, or you can enter a custom location. This will prevent the error or crash from occurring. Thankfully, this particular issue does not affect physical devices.

There are other options that can be passed as well, including `timeout` and `maximumAge` (both are specified using milliseconds).

- ▸ `timeout`: This indicates how long our app is willing to wait for a result. If the position can't be determined within the timeframe, `errorFunction` is called with a `timeout` error message instead.

- ▸ `maximumAge`: This, on the other hand, allows us to improve performance a bit by allowing cached position results. For example, if you set this to `10000` milliseconds (10 seconds), the API could return a location that was determined up to 10 seconds ago. Although this doesn't initially seem useful, it does reduce how often the API needs to calculate the position of the device (and therefore the number of requests made to the network or satellites), and as such, it can be a useful battery-saving feature.

When `successFunction` is called, the position data looks like the following:

- ▸ `position.timestamp`: This gives the date/time when the position was obtained.

- ▸ `position.coords`: This gives the coordinate information. It has the following properties:

    - ❑ `position.coords.latitude`: This gives the latitude (decimal degrees).

    - ❑ `position.coords.longitude`: This gives the longitude (decimal degrees).

    - ❑ `position.coords.altitude`: This gives the altitude in meters if available.

    - ❑ `position.coords.altitudeAccuracy`: This gives the accuracy of the altitude in meters, if available. Android devices return null.

    - ❑ `position.coords.heading`: This gives the heading (or direction of travel) in degrees (clockwise relative to true north).

    - ❑ `position.coords.speed`: This gives the speed in which the device is traveling in meters per second.

While you could technically poll for the position, it's easier to use a `watch` function that notifies your code whenever the user's location changes. Allowing the device to notify the app (instead of polling continuously) allows better resource optimization, and also saves battery life. For example, instead of continually sending position information, a phone might only send a notice when the location has changed significantly.

To use this functionality, you can use the following code:

```
var watchID = navigator.geolocation.watchPosition ( successFunction,
errorFunction, { enableHighAccuracy: true});
```

The `successFunction` will be called whenever there is a significant location change. The `errorFunction` may also be called many times over if there is a problem (especially if there's a timeout). Don't make any assumptions as to what constitutes a significant location change, as this varies by platform and device.

> **Don't assume the position will change between notifications**
> Some devices send notifications based on an internal polling interval. Therefore, it is possible that the position you receive hasn't changed at all.

The position data sent is exactly the same as the previous method, and so it is possible to use one function for both types of functionality. We'll do this in our app—the user can request a current position at any time, and they can also request that their position be watched over a period of time.

One interesting difference is the return value of this method. It can be used to cancel the watch as shown here:

```
navigator.geolocation.clearWatch (watchID);
```

You will want to be absolutely certain this is called when you no longer need to watch the position. There's nothing worse than the user thinking the device is no longer tracking their position, only to find out that their battery is exhausted in short order because the app never released the location watch.

What did we do?

In this section, we covered the geolocation API, including its installation, how to request a position once, and how to listen for changes in position.

Designing our data models

Although this is a new app, there's quite a bit of similarity between this app and the Filer app. Instead of `noteStorage` and `textNoteEditView`, we'll be using `pathStorage` and `pathEditView`. Of course, there are some changes in the data models to be aware of, including new models to handle position data.

Getting on with it

The biggest difference between this new app and Filer is the type of data it processes. A note only had a few properties, but a path can have dozens (even hundreds) of places within it. It should be apparent that we're dealing with two separate objects: `Place` and `Path`. Of course, as it was necessary in the Filer app, we'll also need a storage mechanism for these objects. Consider the following diagram:

place

r/o	.altitude
r/o	.formattedLatitudeLongitude
r/o	.googleLatitudeLongitude
r/o	.heading
r/w	.JSON
r/o	.latitude
r/o	.longitude
r/w	.position
r/o	.speed
r/o	.timestamp
p	_getGoogleMarker()
o	init (UID)
	initWithJSON (JSON)
✎	positionChanged

path

r/o	.createdDate
r/o	.JSON
r/w	.name
r/o	.modifiedDate
r/w	.places[]
r/w	.uid
	addPlace()
o	init (UID)
	initWithJSON (JSON)
o	initWithOptions (options)
✎	nameChanged
✎	pathChanged
✎	uidChanged

pathStorage

p	_paths
r/o	.collection
	createPath()
	getPathAtIndex(index)
	getPathByUID (UID)
	getPathIndexByUID (UID)
	loadCollection()
	removePathAtIndex (index)
	removePathByUID (UID)
	saveCollection()
	savePath (note)
p	_collectionChangedListener
o	init()
✎	collectionChanged
✎	collectionFailedLoading
✎	collectionFailedSaving
✎	collectionLoading
✎	collectionLoaded
✎	collectionSaving
✎	collectionSaved
✎	pathChanged
✎	pathCreated
✎	pathFailedRemoving
✎	pathFailedSaving
✎	pathRemoved
✎	pathSaved

. property **r/w** read/write **r/o** read-only
p private **o** override ✎ notification

Much of this should look pretty familiar by now. You can see that the `Place` model directly mirrors most of the position data obtained from the geolocation API. Only the extra properties have to do with formatting the latitude and longitude in a human-readable form as well as in a Google-parsable form. There's also a method to obtain a Google Marker (which appears as a red marker on the map).

A `Path` object, likewise, is very similar to `Note` in our previous projects. Instead of content, however, we store an array of `Places`. To support the addition of new places to a path, the `addPlace` method is present.

As far as storage goes, `pathStorage` is largely very similar to `noteStorage` with only a few additional methods that can be used to find paths by their unique ID.

What did we do?

In this project, we built the `Path` and `Place` data models for our app. We also built the storage model for paths.

Loading the Google Maps API

The Google Maps API is an extremely powerful mapping and visualization API. To cover the entire API would require an entire book, if not multiple volumes. As such, we're only touching on the API very briefly. Should you require further information, visit `https://developers.google.com/maps/documentation/javascript/tutorial`.

Getting ready

You may want to sign up for an API key at the preceding URL. You don't need one to use the API (and we don't use one in this app), but having a key allows you to track usage metrics. If your app becomes popular enough, access to the API may be throttled by Google. However, if you have a key, you can pay to avoid the otherwise low caps enforced on non-paying users.

Getting on with it

Google has their own code to load maps asynchronously, and if you're more comfortable using that code, you're welcome to do so. However, it would be nice to integrate the Google Maps API into RequireJS.

In order to do so, we first need to download a plugin for RequireJS. The plugin is called `async`, and you can probably infer its purpose already. This allows RequireJS to load libraries asynchronously while still using them as dependencies for our modules.

The plugin itself is part of a collection of plugins, so you can install the entire collection or just one. For our purposes, you just need the file at `https://github.com/millermedeiros/requirejs-plugins/raw/master/src/async.js` or you can install the entire repository at `https://github.com/millermedeiros/requirejs-plugins`.

When you download it, be sure to save it as `async.js` in the `www/js/lib` directory. If you're using the template you created in *Project 2*, *Localization and Globalization*, to create your projects, it would be a good idea to add this file to the template as well. If you're using the template provided by the code package for this book, the plugin is already present.

Now we can load Google Maps by using RequireJS, and this is done as follows:

```
define ( ['async!http://maps.google.com/maps/api/js?v=3&sensor=true'],
    … )
```

This works great, but it's a little verbose. It'd be nicer to have something shorter to refer to. Furthermore, Google always places its code under the `window.google.maps` namespace —who wants to type that out each time we want it?

To address both issues, create a new file named `gmaps.js` at `www/js/lib` (note that if you are using the template in the code package for this book, this file already exists):

```
/**
 * This encapsulates the long async!http://... google maps
 * API string so that it's easier to require
 *
 * Based on http://blog.millermedeiros.com/requirejs-2-0-
 * delayed-module-evaluation-and-google-maps/
 */
define ( ['async!http://maps.google.com/maps/api/js?v=3&sensor=true'],
function() {
    return window.google.maps;
});
```

This shortens the code needed to load Google Maps to the following:

```
define ( ['gmaps'], function ( gmaps) { … } );
```

It also removes the need to refer to the entire `window.google.maps` namespace; we can just refer the library as `gmaps`.

What did we do?

In this section, we downloaded the `async` plugin that allows RequireJS to load libraries asynchronously. We also created a shim around the Google Maps library so that we can refer to it more easily.

What else do I need to know?

We haven't mentioned it yet, but notice the `sensor=true` portion of the URL that loads the Google Maps API. This forces Google Maps to use the geolocation features of the device rather than solely relying upon the network location information. Essentially, this means the maps will have better position accuracy at the cost of battery life.

It's also important to recognize that the `async` plugin can do much more than simply load the Google Maps API. It can load other scripts asynchronously, but it can also be used to load **JSON with padding** (**JSONP**), which makes this plugin very useful to deal with web services that use JSONP. Essentially, any service that returns JSONP and accepts a parameter that specifies the JavaScript callback method can be utilized.

To use the `async` plugin in order to simply load another library, use it as we did earlier:

```
async!url://to/library?parameters
```

To use the `async` plugin to load JSONP, use it as follows:

```
async!url://to/web/service?parameters[!callbackParameterName]
```

Most JSONP APIs use `callback` as the parameter name that specifies the `callback` method, so you usually don't need to specify the latter portion (indicated in brackets). Some services don't follow along and use another parameter to specify the callback. In this latter case, you need to specify it. For example, Flickr uses `jsoncallback`. You would need to use this to get a photo feed (this is directly from the example code for the `async` plugin available at `https://github.com/millermedeiros/requirejs-plugins/blob/master/examples/async.html`):

```
async!http://api.flickr.com/services/feeds/photos_public.
gne?id=27041612@N06&format=json!jsoncallback
```

Implementing our data models

Now that we've loaded the Google Maps API successfully, we can implement our data models.

Getting on with it

By now, you should be familiar with most of the code that we'll be using to implement our data models, and so we won't include the full code listing. You can get the full code by downloading the code package for the book or viewing the online GitHub repository.

The `Place` object is defined in `www/js/app/models/place.js`. Most of the code is mundane, the majority of it deals with creating the various properties as seen in the model graphic. There are a couple of interesting pieces of code, however.

`setPosition` is an interesting method:

```
self.setPosition = function ( position ) {
  var tempPosition = {};
  var properties = [ "latitude", "longitude", "altitude",
    "heading", "speed" ];
  var setProperty = function ( property ) {
    if ( typeof position.coords !== "undefined" ) {
      if ( typeof position.coords[property] !== "undefined" ) {
      tempPosition.coords[property] = position.coords[property]; }
    }
    if ( typeof position[property] !== "undefined" ) {
    tempPosition[property] = position[property]; }
  }
  if ( typeof position !== "undefined" ) {
    if ( typeof position.timestamp !== "undefined" ) {
    tempPosition.timestamp = position.timestamp; }
    if ( typeof position.coords !== "undefined" ) {
      tempPosition.coords = {};
    }
    properties.forEach ( setProperty );
  }
  self._position = tempPosition;
  self.notify ( "positionChanged" );
}
```

An incoming position might be a position from the geolocation API. In that case, it will contain a `coords` component that contains the latitude, longitude, and so on. However, an incoming position could also be an existing `place` object. In this case, it won't have a `coords` component. Rather than writing two separate methods to handle each case, it is possible to handle both cases at once.

Notice that the list of properties we care about is declared at the top of the method. Below this, we define a method called `setProperty`. This will check for the existence of the property in the `coords` component, if it exists, and copy that value. It will also check for the existence of the property outside of the `coords` component and copy that value as well.

Near the bottom of the method, `forEach` is called on the list of properties. This causes `setProperty` to be called for each property that we care about.

Each `place` property is designed to handle the possibility of having a `coords` component and not having one. For example, the `latitude` property looks like the following:

```
self._getCoordinateProperty = function ( theProperty ) {
  if (self._position !== null) {
    var coords = (typeof self._position.coords !== "undefined") ?
      self._position.coords : self._position;
```

```
          return coords[theProperty];
      }
      return undefined;
  }
  self.getLatitude = function () {
      return self._getCoordinateProperty ( "latitude" );
  }
```

The next interesting method is `getGoogleLatitudeLongitude`:

```
  self.getGoogleLatitudeLongitude = function () {
      return new gmaps.LatLng( self.latitude, self.longitude );
  }
```

When sending the latitude and longitude of a place to Google, we have to use a `LatLng` object. Usually, this method comes in handy when converting a path from our app's internal representation to that required by Google.

The `path` object is defined in `www/js/app/models/path.js`. Most of this code should also be familiar, but there are two sections that are interesting.

First, unlike the notes in our prior projects, a `path` object needs to store multiple places. Here's the code for that property:

```
  self._places = [];
  self.getPlaces = function () {
      return self._places;
  }
  self.setPlaces = function (thePlaces) {
      self._places = thePlaces;
      self.notify("pathChanged");
  }
  Object.defineProperty(self, "places", {get: self.getPlaces, set:
  self.setPlaces, configurable: true});
```

This isn't particularly different from other property definitions, other than initializing the backing variable with a blank array. In order to add a place, however, we need the following code:

```
  self.addPlace = function ( aPlace ) {
      self._places.push ( aPlace );
      self.notify ( "pathChanged" );
      self._modifiedDate = new Date();
  }
```

Again, this is not too different from what we've encountered before, but this all sets up how we can serialize and deserialize a path. First, let's look at _serialize:

```
self._serialize = function () {
  var serializedPlaces = self._places.map(function (place) {
return place.JSON; });
  return JSON.stringify ({
    "uid":          self.uid,
    "createdDate":  self.createdDate,
    "modifiedDate": self.modifiedDate,
    "name":         self.name,
    "places":       serializedPlaces
  });
}
```

The very first line of the method calls the map method of our internal _places property. This calls the function inside with each place in the array, which returns the JSON of each place. This is collated into an array of JSON representations of each place. Near the end of the method, we use this array when generating the JSON for the path object.

Now, let's look at _deserialize, where we need to parse the JSON for a path and add all the places contained within it:

```
self._deserialize = function (theSerializedObject) {
  try {
    var aPath = JSON.parse(theSerializedObject);
    self.uid = aPath.uid;
    self._createdDate = new Date(aPath.createdDate);
    self.name = aPath.name;
    var serializedPlaces = aPath.places;
    self._places = serializedPlaces.map(
      function (JSON) {
        var aNewPlace = new Place();
        aNewPlace.initWithJSON(JSON);
        return aNewPlace;
      });
    self._modifiedDate = new Date(aPath.modifiedDate);
    return true;
  }
  catch (e) {
    return false;
  }
};
```

First, the method parses the entire `path` object and copies the data into the object. This works for everything but the list of places. If the data were simply copied, the places would have only data and no corresponding code. Since we call methods attached to `places`, it is important not to eliminate this code.

Instead, the code calls `map` on the array that contains the JSON for each place. This calls the internal function that creates a new place and initializes it with the JSON. When these steps are complete, we have a `path` object with fully functional `place` objects as well.

Finally, let's go over the interesting portions of the `pathStorage` object (in `www/js/app/ models/pathStorage`. Firstly, it is important to note that the internal collection of paths is an array and not a dictionary as we used in the Filer app. Both work equally well, but changing this to an array enables us to cover a few more interesting facets of array enumeration.

With that in mind, let's look at the `saveCollection` method:

```
self.saveCollection = function () {
  self.notify ( "collectionSaving" );
  try {
    localStorage.setItem ( "paths", JSON.stringify (
      self._paths.filter ( function ( thePath ) { return thePath
!== null; } )
        .map ( function ( thePath) { return thePath.UID; } )
    ) );
    self.notify ( "collectionSaving");
  }
  catch ( anError ) {
    self.notify ("collectionFailedSaving", [anError.message] );
  }
}
```

If you recall from the previous projects, a deleted item is marked with a `null` entry. We could just as easily use a `for` loop and check each entry prior to saving it, but instead we use the `filter` method of our `_paths` array. This method calls the internal function for each member of the array, passing each member as the parameter. If the method returns `true`, the member is added to a new array, while if the method returns `false`, the new array doesn't contain the member. In our case, when complete, a new array that contains all the non-null members is generated.

The method then calls the `map` method on this new array to return the UID for each `place`. By doing so, the code generates a list of UIDs, while ignoring all `null` entries.

There's one more piece of code to discuss, this time in `getPathIndexByUID`:

```
self.getPathIndexByUID = function ( theUID ) {
  var theIndex = self._paths.reduce (
    function ( previousValue, currentValue, index, array ) {
      if ( array[index] !== null) {
        return Math.max ( ( array[index].UID == theUID ? index : -
1 ), previousValue );
      }
      else {
        return previousValue;
      }
  }, -1 );
  return theIndex;
}
```

Some newer browsers have a `find` method that can search for an item in an array. This method doesn't use it, because it's not new enough to be on many modern devices. Instead, it uses the `reduce` method instead. This lets it check each path in the array, and if the path's UID matches the one we're looking for, it returns the index. Technically, we return the maximum of `-1` or the last known index. So, if an item isn't found, `-1` will be the return value.

What did we do?

In this section, we implemented the `Path`, `Place`, and `pathStorage` data models. We also discussed the `map`, `reduce`, and `filter` array methods that simplify looping over and working with array elements.

What else do I need to know?

The modern array methods are pretty amazing. There's quite a lot of material on how they all work, but the one of best references can be found at `https://developer.mozilla.org/en-US/docs/Web/JavaScript/Reference/Global_Objects/Array`.

Do pay attention to the experimental methods; they may only work on certain browsers. If you need to use the experimental methods, there are polyfills available. They can implement these features on other browsers. In fact, the preceding reference has code for many of the experimental methods. Alternatively, you might want to use a library that implements these for you, such as `Underscore.js` (which is available at `http://underscorejs.org`).

Implementing our path edit view

Because our app is so similar to the previous projects, we won't cover every view in this section. If you want to look at the code for these views, please refer to the code supplied for this book.

All that said, here's the model for each view:

pathListView	
p	_navigationBar
p	_scrollContainer
p	_pathList
p	_addPathButton
p	_menuButton
p	_displayEditView (view)
	createNewPath()
	deleteExistingPath()
	editExistingPath()
	exposeActionsForPath()
	hideActionsForPath()
	onOrientationChanged()
o	render()
o	renderToElement()
	renderList()
	quitApp()
o	init(parentElement)
o	initWithOptions(options)
o	destroy()

pathEditView	
p	_backButton
p	_currentPositionMarker
p	_isRecording
p	_keepMapCentered
p	_lastKnownPosition
p	_locateButton
p	_map
p	_mapContainer
p	_menuButton
p	_nameEditor
p	_navigationBar
p	_path
p	_polyline
p	_recordButton
p	_scrollContainer
p	_watchID
p	_geolocationError()
p	_updateLastKnownPosition (position)
	centerMapAroundLocation()
	togglePathRecording()
	getPathUID()
	goBack()
	popView()
	releaseBackButton()
o	render()
o	renderToElement()
	savePath()
o	init(parentElement)
o	initWithOptions(options)
o	destroy()

staticView	
p	_menuButton
o	render()
o	renderToElement()
o	init(parentElement)
o	initWithOptions(options)
o	destroy()

. property	**r/w** read/write	**r/o** read-only
p private	**o** override	**⬉** notification

Getting on with it

The primary view is the path edit view that contains the interactive map and the recording controls. As usual, let's build the template for our path edit view in `www/html/pathEditView.html` (interesting portions are highlighted):

```html
<html>
  <body>
    <div class="ui-navigation-bar">
      <div class="ui-title"
        contenteditable="true">%PATH_NAME%</div>
      <div class="ui-bar-button-group ui-align-left">
        <div class="ui-bar-button ui-background-tint-color
          ui-glyph ui-glyph-menu"></div>
        <div class="ui-bar-button ui-tint-color
          ui-back-button">%BACK%</div>
      </div>
      <div class="ui-bar-button-group ui-align-right">
        <div class="ui-bar-button ui-background-tint-color
          ui-glyph ui-glyph-gps-locate"></div>
        <div class="ui-bar-button ui-background-tint-color
          ui-glyph ui-glyph-circle-outlined"></div>
      </div>
    </div>
    <div class="ui-map-container"></div>
  </body>
</html>
```

The highlighted portion in the prior code is what generates the menu (or hamburger) icon in our view. This code is also present in `staticView` so that the sidebar can be displayed at any time.

The code for the view can be found in `www/js/app/views/pathEditView.js`. Most of it should be very familiar, but let's look at the more interesting portions. First, let's go over some of the properties and how they are used:

- `_mapContainer`: This is used to hold the reference to the `map-container` element. This is where the Google Map will be inserted.

- `_locateButton`, `_recordButton`, and `_menuButton`: These are store references to the icons on the navigation bar.

- `_path`: This is a reference to the specific path this view is editing.

- ▶ `_lastKnownPosition`: This does what it's name implies. It tracks the last known position of the device from the geolocation API.

- ▶ `_watchID`: This stores the identifier that is obtained when the user begins a recording operation. Later, this is used to cancel the watch when the recording session stops.

- ▶ `_currentPositionMarker`: This stores the red marker used to denote the current position on the map. It's shaped like an upside-down teardrop.

- ▶ `_keepMapCentered`: This is used to determine whether the map should stay centered continually. It is set to `false` the moment the user pans or zooms on the map, but is set back to `true` when they tap the locate button.

- ▶ `_isRecording`: This indicates whether we're actively recording the user's position.

- ▶ `_map`: This stores the reference to the actual Google Map object.

- ▶ `_polyline`: This stores the reference to the actual polyline object of Google. This depicts a recorded path on the map. This is similar in a way to our `Path` object, as a polyline is simply a collection of positions.

Next, let's look at some of the interesting methods. First, let's look at `renderToElement` This is the code that links up any DOM elements with the event handlers. However, more importantly for this app, it creates the Google Map in our view. The code is fairly long, so we'll break it up into more manageable bits as we discuss it. Consider the following code:

```
self.renderToElement = function () {
  self.super(_className, "renderToElement");
  self._navigationBar = self.element.querySelector
(".ui-navigation-bar");
  self._nameEditor = self.element.querySelector
(".ui-navigation-bar .ui-title");
  self._backButton = self.element.querySelector
(".ui-navigation-bar .ui-back-button");
  self._menuButton = self.element.querySelector
(".ui-navigation-bar .ui-glyph-menu");
  self._locateButton = self.element.querySelector
(".ui-navigation-bar .ui-glyph-gps-locate");
  self._recordButton = self.element.querySelector
(".ui-navigation-bar .ui-glyph-circle-outlined");
self._mapContainer = self.element.querySelector(".map-container");
  Hammer(self._backButton).on("tap", self.goBack);
```

So far, nothing here is worth our attention. But, the next bit of code is definitely new:

```
Hammer(self._menuButton, {prevent_default:true}).
on("tap", function () {
self.navigationController.splitViewController.toggleLeftView() });
```

This small snippet of code is how we can toggle the display of the sidebar whenever the menu button is tapped. This particular part of YASMF's `SplitViewController` only does one thing: it toggles the CSS class on the offscreen canvas between `ui-left-side-visible` and `ui -left-side-invisible`. Consider the following code:

```
Hammer(self._locateButton).on("tap",
self.centerMapAroundLocation);
Hammer(self._recordButton).on("tap", self.togglePathRecording);
_y.UI.backButton.addListenerForNotification("backButtonPressed",
self.goBack);
```

Again, the preceding isn't terribly new, but the next portion is. Now, we get into the real work of creating an interactive Google Map with our path displayed within. The first thing you should notice is that all of this code is wrapped in a `setTimeout` call that waits 100 milliseconds. This is important, because without it, it is possible that the Google Map will be created before the view has a defined size. If this happened, the map renders incorrectly. However, if we wait a few milliseconds to give the view time to figure out its size on the screen, the map will always correctly render. Consider the following code:

```
setTimeout ( function () {
  self._map = new gmaps.Map (
    self._mapContainer, {
      disableDefaultUI: true,
      center: new gmaps.LatLng(40,-90),
      zoom: 15,
      mapTypeId: gmaps.MapTypeId.ROADMAP
    }
  );
```

First, the method creates a new Google Map object. We give it an initial latitude and longitude, a zoom value, and indicate that the map type should be a roadmap (not satellite). We also remove the Google user interface (we'll only allow interaction by gestures). Consider the following code:

```
gmaps.event.addListener ( self._map, 'dragstart', function () {
  self._keepMapCentered = false;
});
```

This code ensures that when a map receives a drag gesture, the map will no longer automatically center itself based on the user's position:

```
self._currentPositionMarker = new gmaps.Marker( {
  map: self._map,
  title: "Current Position"
}
);
```

The preceding section creates the Google Marker that we use for the user's current position (interestingly enough, the text isn't actually displayed). Consider the following code:

```
// and create a polyline that we can work with
self._polyline = new gmaps.Polyline ( {
  strokeColor: '#60E020', strokeOpacity:0.85,
  strokeWeight:10 } );
self._polyline.setMap ( self._map );
```

The preceding code creates a new polyline and sets its style and colors. We've chosen a } color that matches that of our navigation bar. We've also chosen a fairly thick weight for the stroke, mainly to make it visible in screenshots for this book. You may prefer a smaller value. Consider the following code:

```
self._path.places.forEach (
  function ( place )
  {
    self._polyline.getPath().push
( place.googleLatitudeLongitude );
  }
)
}, 100);
}
```

After the polyline is created, we need to add each place in our path to it. We use this by pushing the `LatLng` object returned from our place onto the path returned by Google's `polyline` object.

Next, let's look at the code for `togglePathRecording` (called whenever the user taps the record button):

```
self.togglePathRecording = function () {
  if (self._isRecording) {
    self._isRecording = false;
    navigator.geolocation.clearWatch( self._watchID );
    self._watchID = null;
    self._recordButton.classList.remove
( "ui-glyph-pause-filled" );
    self._recordButton.classList.add
( "ui-glyph-circle-outlined" );
  }
  else {
    self._watchID = navigator.geolocation.watchPosition(
      self._updateLastKnownPosition, self._geolocationError, {
        enableHighAccuracy: true
      }
```

```
    );
    self._recordButton.classList.remove
( "ui-glyph-circle-outlined" );
    self._recordButton.classList.add ( "ui-glyph-pause-filled" );
    self._isRecording = true;
  }
}
```

The code is written in the reverse order. First, look at the bottom section within the `else` clause. As long as the app isn't recording, it calls `watchPosition` and saves the watch ID for later (so that it can be cancelled). Then, the icon of `_recordButton` is changed to a pause icon. Notice that we define `_updateLastKnownPosition` to be the handler whenever the location of the device changes.

Going to the top of the code, if the app is recording, it now needs to stop. To do this, it clears the geolocation watch by calling `clearWatch`. Then, it changes the class on `_recordButton` from a pause icon to a record icon.

Next, let's look at `centerMapAroundLocation`, which is called whenever the user taps the locate button:

```
self.centerMapAroundLocation = function () {
  self._keepMapCentered = true;
  if (!self._isRecording) {
    navigator.geolocation.getCurrentPosition(
      self._updateLastKnownPosition,
      self._geolocationError, {
        enableHighAccuracy: true
      }
    );
  }
}
```

Essentially, if the app isn't recording, this method makes a call to `getCurrentPosition` in order to obtain the user's current position. If the app is recording, there's little point—there's already a watch in place and the map will center at the next update. The interesting part of this code is the handler for location notice. It's the same as we defined earlier for the watch: `_updateLastKnownPosition`.

`_updateLastKnownPosition` is where the hard work happens. Let's look at the code:

```
self._updateLastKnownPosition = function ( position ) {
  if (self._lastKnownPosition === null ) {
    self._lastKnownPosition = new Place();
    self._lastKnownPosition.init ( position );
```

```
    }

    else {
      self._lastKnownPosition.position = position;
    }
```

This first bit of code simply updates our internal property to the incoming position. Note that the code creates the `Place` object on-the-fly, and only if necessary. Consider the following code:

```
    var googleLatLong =
    self._lastKnownPosition.googleLatitudeLongitude;
```

Next, we ask `_lastKnownPosition` for a Google `LatLng` object (which is how Google represents latitude and longitude). We'll need it for the following code:

```
    if ( self._keepMapCentered ) {
      self._map.panTo ( googleLatLong );
    }
```

This should be obvious: if the map is supposed to keep the user's location centered. The method will pan to the latitude and longitude of the incoming position. Consider the following code:

```
    self._currentPositionMarker.setPosition ( googleLatLong );
```

This code updates the position of the current position marker so that the user has a visual indication of their current position. Consider the following code:

```
    if ( self._isRecording ) {
      self._polyline.getPath().push ( googleLatLong );
      var newPlace = new Place();
      newPlace.init ( position );
      self._path.addPlace ( newPlace );
    }
    };
```

Finally, if the app is recording, we push the new position onto the polyline and on our `path` object's list of places. This forces the polyline to update itself so that the user will be able to watch the path draw on the map as recording progresses.

There's one last bit of code we need to point out: `popView`. This is called whenever the view is about to go away and we need to ensure that we stop recording. It simply checks whether we are recording, and if so, it calls `togglePathRecording`.

What did we do?

In this task, we created the path edit view, which holds the interactive map. We implemented a path recording feature and touched very lightly on some of the features of the Google Maps API.

Putting it all together

There are a lot of little tweaks and changes that need to be made before you can actually test the app. Because the code is so familiar (and there's not a lot of it), we'll just indicate the files you need to look at.

Getting on with it

You'll need to look at the code that comes with the book in order to complete the following files:

- ▶ www/css/style.css
- ▶ www/html/pathListItem.html
- ▶ www/html/pathListView.html
- ▶ www/html/staticView.html
- ▶ www/js/app/views/pathListView.html
- ▶ www/js/app/views/staticView.html
- ▶ www/js/app/models/pathStorageSingleton.js
- ▶ www/js/app/main.js

All of the changes in each file are minor (mostly of the search-and-replace variety). If you prefer, you can simply copy the files from our code without making all the required modifications.

There are a few styles that we need to touch on very briefly. In www/css/style.css, we added the following:

```
.pathEditView .map-container
{
  width: 100%;
  height: 100%;
}
```

All this does is ensures that the map fills the entire view. Without it, there'd be no visible map. Consider the following code:

```
.ui-split-view .ui-navigation-bar .ui-glyph-menu,
.ui-container .ui-navigation-bar .ui-glyph-menu {
  display: none;
}
.ui-split-overlay-view .ui-navigation-bar .ui-glyph-menu,
.ui-off-canvas-view .ui-navigation-bar .ui-glyph-menu {
  display: inline-block;
}

.ui-off-canvas-view .ui-container.left-side .ui-navigation-bar .
ui-glyph-menu {
  display: none;
}
```

As in the prior project, you can actually run the app with different split view types. The styles described earlier display the menu button as appropriate. First, if the split view is a normal split view (where the leftmost view is always present), the menu button isn't shown. Likewise, the menu button is hidden if the app isn't running in a split view at all.

If the split view is an off-canvas view (as is the default for this project), the menu button needs to be visible only on the rightmost view. This is done by hiding it from the leftmost side when the app is using an off-canvas view.

On the other hand, if the split view is an overlay view (where the leftmost view can appear over the rightmost view), the menu button needs to appear in both views as the leftmost view would be displayed over the rightmost view. You'll notice that there is code in `pathListView` that handles the menu button.

In addition, we've modified `main.js` a little to reflect the fact that the app can be run using many different split-view configurations. We won't duplicate the code here, it's very similar to Filer's `main.js`.

There's one last thing we need to go over, and it has to do with the status bar of iOS 7. Typically, the status bar consists of dark text, which works great when it is displayed above light backgrounds. In this case, even though the background is light, white text works better. In order to control the status bar, we need to add a plugin to the project:

cordova plugin add org.apache.cordova.statusbar

Next, we need to add a few lines of code to `APP.start` in `main.js`:

```
if (_y.device.platform() == "ios") {
  StatusBar.styleLightContent();
}
```

You can do lots more with the status bar. To learn more, check out the documentation at `http://plugins.cordova.io/#/package/org.apache.cordova.statusbar`.

What did we do?

In this section, you finished the app by making the various adjustments necessary based on our provided code for the book. Most of the changes were of the search-and-replace variety.

Game Over..... Wrapping it up

Now that the app is complete, you should be able to build and deploy it to your device. You should be able to create a new path document, change the title, record a path, and save it. You should be able to interact with the map by swiping and pinching to zoom.

Can you take the HEAT? The Hotshot Challenge

There are a lot of ways this project could be improved. Why don't you try a few?

- ▶ When loading a path, hardcoded coordinates are used. This means it might not be obvious whether there is even a recorded path on the map. Add code to pan the map to the first recorded place in the path. You might also try to use some math to determine the size of a path and select an appropriate zoom level that displays the entire path.

- ▶ Additionally, center the map on the user's position automatically if there are no places in the path.

- ▶ Add a sharing mechanism so that other users can see the path you took.

- ▶ Add the path-recording feature to the Filer app.

- ▶ Allow the user to add annotations at specific places. Also, allow the user to edit the path, including clearing the path, removing and adding points, and so on.

- ▶ Create an audio tour by recording audio at certain positions, and then trigger when the user is near those locations.

Project 11

Canvas Games and the Accelerometer

Smartphones are no strangers to little fun games that help pass the time. From the seemingly eternally existing Solitaire to Snake, Tetris, or Pop-the-Bubble variants, we've found ways to pass the time with our mobile devices. Even if you nearly always write productive applications, sooner or later, the "bug" to write a game is likely to bite.

What do we build?

In this project, we're going to put together a game called **Cave Runner**. Okay, it won't win any prizes based on the originality of the game (or the title), nor will it win "the best game of the year" prize. But it's amusing and has a lot of potential to expand in various ways, so it serves as a good base, especially for the *quick and diverting* category many games try to fit into.

What does it do?

To accomplish this, we're going to heavily rely upon the HTML5 Canvas, which is the only way we're going to achieve anything even approaching 60 frames per second (the target for most games). Even so, only recent and powerful devices are going to meet this target, so we will also need to use some mathematics in order to create a game that isn't reliant on hitting 60 fps. If the game's timing relied solely on hitting 60 fps, 30 fps would feel as if we're playing the game in slow motion. Instead, we have to act like we're running at 60 fps—even if we can't display that many frames—so that we avoid this effect. (It won't keep the game from feeling jumpy, especially if the frame rate varies inconsistently, but it will keep the speed of the game at an appropriate level.)

While controlling a game character on a console, portable game machine, or PC is pretty obvious (keyboard, mouse, D-pad, joystick, and so on), how does one control a game character on a mobile device that usually has none of those features? There are two answers: use the multi-touch screen, which can be used to simulate a joystick or D-pad, or use the device's built-in accelerometer. We'll talk about using both in this task.

Why is it great?

Hopefully you'll have a bit of fun with the game as it stands now, but even as a simple game, it introduces you to the concepts you'll need to create complex games further down the road. We'll work on keeping the game going at the same speed regardless of frame rate. We'll also work out how to control the game using the touch screen and the accelerometer. All of these things combine to create a good game, and you should have a good base from which to build on for any future endeavor.

How are we going to do it?

We're going to approach this project much like we have the prior projects:

- ▸ Designing the game
- ▸ Implementing the Start view
- ▸ Implementing the Options view
- ▸ Implementing the Game view
- ▸ Generating levels
- ▸ Drawing to the canvas
- ▸ Performing updates
- ▸ Handling touch-based input
- ▸ Handling the accelerometer

What do I need to get started?

Unlike prior projects where we've suggested creating the project from scratch by following along, we're suggesting in this project that you download the project from the code package for this book, compile it for your device, and play with it so that you get a good feel for how the game works. Then, you can either work from that project as you proceed through the various steps, or you can start over from scratch with a much better idea of what we're aiming for than when approaching the project blindly.

If you want to play the game without compiling the project just yet, an iOS demo is available at https://app.io/kAxEF4. (Everything works, except the accelerometer, since the demo is running on a simulated device.)

Designing the game

Although in prior projects we developed the user interface and the interactions between the various widgets and views, we'll be designing how our game looks and acts instead in this project. While similar, there's often a lot more that has to go into designing games (graphic assets, level design, character design, animation, and so on). Unfortunately, we can't go over everything given the breadth of the subject material, but we can give you a good start.

Getting on with it

The primary theme of the game may already be evident from the title, Cave Runner. These kinds of games have been around since the first computers, even if the graphical quality was somewhat coarse and blocky.

In short, we're going to develop a game that has a series of levels through which the player (who controls a ship) has to navigate safely in order to advance. Each level will be more difficult than the previous, and in our particular version, as long as the player can keep up, there's no end to the levels. In all practicality, there will be a point where the player can't navigate safely through a given level, so the game always ends with a crash. Think of it as an endurance run where we already know the outcome—it's the journey that matters. (This is often the point in so-called *twitch* or *impossible* games.)

The level consists of a cave-like structure with walls on both sides of the screen. These walls are irregular and random and together form a safe path for the ship. If the ship touches the edges, the game is over.

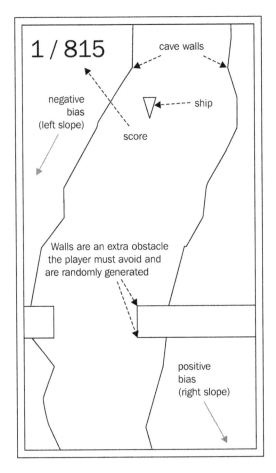

To make things a little more difficult, there are obstacles (called **walls**) that get in the ship's way. In the first few levels, they don't appear very often, but as the levels get harder, the obstacles appear more often. The obstacle looks like a wall with an opening cut out, and the ship must pass within the opening in order to be safe.

Our levels will be randomly generated according to certain parameters in order to create an ever-changing landscape. Even though our levels are random, you could easily create static levels and load them in as necessary—something we suggest you do at the end of the project.

Our ship will be very simple: a triangle. Yes, one can get a lot more complicated with animation, but for the simple visual style of our game, it works well for our needs.

In order to move the ship, the player has three options: use the left and right onscreen buttons, swipe the screen, or tilt the device. The ship will move according to the direction of the button tapped, the swipe, or the tilt, that is, tapping the left button, tilting left, or swiping right-to-left will move the ship left and vice versa.

Since we're calling our character a ship, we're intentionally introducing some fuzzy mechanics to the movement. In other words, the ship doesn't respond instantly, nor does it stop instantly. Think of the ship as if it has thrusters on it and is operating in a low-gravity environment. Of course, we could have decided that the position of the ship was directly related to the position of the finger on the screen or the degree of the tilt—for some games, this would be appropriate. It is always important to recognize that you should tailor your control mechanism to your game and use what makes sense.

Our game itself will be contained within one view—the Game view. Outside of the game, the Start view and an Options view will live. The Start view contains two buttons: **Play** and **Options**. Tapping on **Play** will switch to the Game view, while the **Options** button will switch to the Options view.

The Options view gives three options for the control scheme: one for tilting the device, one for sliding a finger across the screen, and one for tapping left and right buttons. Tapping any of these elements will select that method as the control scheme. An additional **Back** button lets the user get back to the Start view.

Inside the Game view, we have several items that need to be displayed—of course the level and the ship are required, but games often display other information as well. In our case, we'll display the current level and the player's score (which is a combination of distance travelled minus the horizontal movements of the ship). Should we need to display a message (such as ***Crash!*** or **Level Up!**) we'll show it in the middle of the screen along with two buttons: one to restart or continue, depending on the situation and one to go back to the Game view.

That's it, really! It's not a complicated game, yet it can provide a base for more complicated endeavors in the future.

What did we do?

In this task, we designed our game and the control mechanics. We figured out the views we need as well.

What else do I need to know?

By no means is game design this simple. We can proceed this quickly through this particular game partly because it is simple and the mechanism is well known. Even slightly more complex games will require much more time to design, and it is best to do so before writing even a single line of code. Figure out your visual style, your sound style, and the mechanics of the game, control mechanisms, levels, and animations. All of this will take time and lots of paper.

Implementing the Start view

The Start view is very simple. Think of it as a menu screen that allows the player to start the game or to make changes to how the game works. There's also one component that's not terribly obvious if you haven't played the game yet: the title is animated.

When done, we'll have a view that looks like the following screenshot:

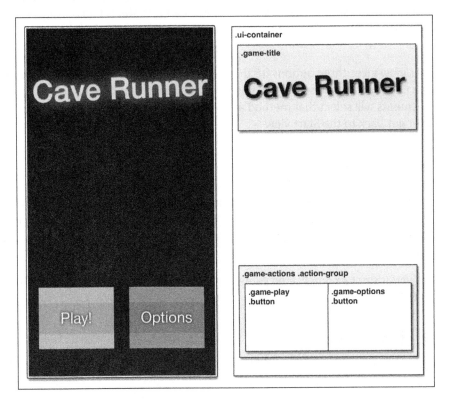

Getting on with it

As always, let's first start with the template in `www/html/startView.html`. Use the following code:

```
<html>
<body>
<div class="ui-container">
<div class="game-title">%APP_TITLE%</div>
<div class="game-actions action-group">
<div class="game-play button">%PLAY%</div>
<div class="game-options button">%OPTIONS%</div>
</div>
</div>
</body>
</html>
```

As templates go, this is nothing new by any stretch of the imagination. There's one thing you should take note of: we've previously used a navigation bar—that's totally absent here and it's on purpose. We want the game to be immersive, so from the very beginning, the experience should feel unique.

Note that there are no graphical elements—everything is accomplished via CSS. Let's go over that portion of code now (from `www/css/style.css`).

It's probably difficult to see from the screenshot, but there is a gradient (black to dark-blue) for the background of each view. The following is the CSS:

```
.startView, .optionsView, .gameView{
  background-color: #081020;
  background-image: -webkit-linear-gradient(top,
                  rgb(0, 0, 0) 0%, rgb(16, 32, 64) 100%);
}
```

As you can see in the preceding screenshot and in the preceding template, buttons are grouped together into action groups. The following code provides some basic styling so that they are all consistent:

```
.action-group {
  position: absolute;
  left: 0; right: 0;
  height: 100px;
  line-height: 100px;
  text-align: center;
  color: #FFFFFF;
  font-size: 25px;
}
```

The buttons within the action groups also receive styles with a default appearance (in our case, the blue buttons are considered the default style):

```
.button {
  display: inline-block;
  box-sizing: border-box;
  margin-left: 10px; margin-right: 10px;
  width: 40%;
  border: 25px solid rgba(128,192,255, 0.5);
  border-left: 0; border-right: 0;
  background-color: rgba(128,192,255,0.75);
  line-height: 50px;
  text-shadow: 0 0 5px black;
}
```

The following CSS specifies where the buttons should live on the Start view:

```
.startView .action-group {
  bottom: 65px;
}
```

We also want the **Play** button to use a different color, so use the following code:

```
.startView .game-play {
  border: 25px solid rgba(192,255,128, 0.5);
  background-color: rgba(192,255,128,0.75);
}
```

Animation of the app's title is accomplished by first defining keyframes. These define the various styles at specific intervals, and the browser will interpolate between them during animation to create a smooth result. In the following case, the title rotates from -5 to +5 degrees, and the title has a glowing element that slowly pulsates:

```
@-webkit-keyframes animateTitle
{
from {
    -webkit-transform: rotate(-5deg);
    text-shadow: 0 0 15px white;
  }
  25% {
    -webkit-transform: rotate(0deg);
    text-shadow: 0 0 35px white;
  }
  50% {
    -webkit-transform: rotate(5deg);
```

```
    text-shadow: 0 0 15px white;
  }
  75% {
    -webkit-transform: rotate(0deg);
    text-shadow: 0 0 35px white;
  }
  to {
    -webkit-transform: rotate(-5deg);
    text-shadow: 0 0 15px white;
  }
}
```

Next, we define the basic style of the title. Note that we didn't actually specify the keyframe name in the preceding code—this is to prevent the title from animating when we don't want it to (such as during game play). We have specified that the animation cycle should take 10 seconds, should last forever, and that the interpolation should be linear. Let's define the basic style using the following code:

```
.startView .game-title{
  line-height: 200px;
  font-size: 50px;
  font-weight: bold;
  color: yellow;
  text-align: center;
  -webkit-transform: rotate(-5deg);
  text-shadow: 0 0 25px white;
  -webkit-animation-duration: 10s;
  -webkit-animation-iteration-count: infinite;
  -webkit-animation-timing-function: linear;
}
```

Now, let's go over the interesting portions of code in www/js/app/views/startView.js. For the code we omit, please refer to the code package for this book.

The first method of interest is init, wherein we add listeners for the appearance and disappearance of the view so that we can trigger/stop the animation as appropriate. Let's use the init method in the following code:

```
self.overrideSuper ( self.class, "init", self.init );
self.init = function ( theParentElement ) {
  self.super ( _className, "init",
    [undefined, "div", "startView ui-container",
     theParentElement] );
  self.addListenerForNotification(
    "viewWillAppear", self.startAnimation);
```

```
    self.addListenerForNotification(
      "viewWillDisappear", self.stopAnimation);
}
```

In `startAnimation`, we assign the name of the keyframe we defined earlier—this starts the title animation. Let's assign it in the following code:

```
self.startAnimation = function () {
  var e = self.element.querySelector(".game-title");
  e.style.webkitAnimationName = "animateTitle";
}
```

Likewise, `stopAnimation` stops the animation so that it can't slow down game play. Let's define `stopAnimation` in the following manner:

```
self.stopAnimation = function () {
  var e = self.element.querySelector(".game-title");
  e.style.webkitAnimationName = "inherit";
}
```

What did we do?

In this task, we created the Start view's code, the template, and its associated styles. We've seen how to trigger an animation from code, and how to stop it so that it doesn't impact the rest of the app while the view is not visible.

What else do I need to know?

CSS3 Animation is a topic all its own—there are limitless possibilities. In order to learn more about animating in this way, you can visit the following sites:

▶ https://developer.mozilla.org/en-US/docs/Web/Guide/CSS/Using_CSS_animations

▶ http://coding.smashingmagazine.com/2011/09/14/the-guide-to-css-animation-principles-and-examples/

 It's important to point out that Android devices using version 4.3.x or lower sometimes exhibit problems with this kind of animation. The fix is to change any `overflow` style of all the parent elements to `visible`.

Implementing the Options view

In this task we'll focus on the Options view located in `www/js/app/views/optionsView.js`. It's only moderately more complex than the Start view, so much of the code is very similar.

When you're done, you'll have something that looks like the following screenshot:

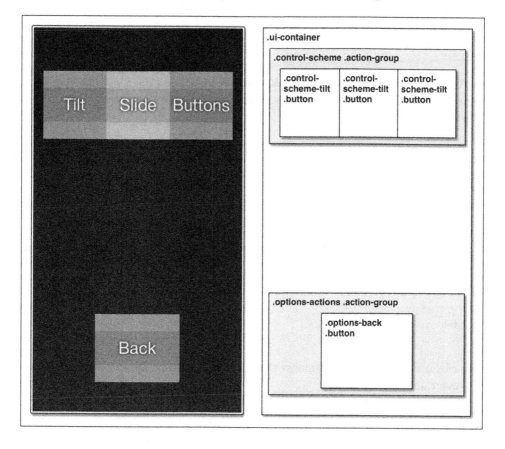

Note that in this view, the selected control scheme is the one marked in green.

Getting on with it

First, the following is the template for the view (in `www/html/optionsView.html`):

```
<html>
<body>
<div class="ui-container">
<div class="control-scheme action-group">
```

```
<div class="control-scheme-tilt button">%TILT%</div>
<div class="control-scheme-slide button">%SLIDE%</div>
<div class="control-scheme-buttons button">%BUTTONS%</div>
</div>
<div class="options-actions action-group">
<div class="options-back button">%BACK%</div>
</div>
</div>
</body>
</html>
```

There's nothing terribly difficult here! Notice that we've defined three possible control schemes that the user can select from as well as provided a **Back** button at the bottom of the view.

A few styles are necessary to make this work visually (again, in `www/css/style.css`). The first one declares where the **Back** button lives on the screen, as shown in the following code:

```
.optionsView .options-actions.action-group {
  bottom: 65px;
}
```

Next, we declare where the control scheme group lives. The `font-size` attribute collapses any possible gaps between the buttons:

```
.optionsView .control-scheme.action-group {
  top: 65px;
  font-size: 0;
}
```

The size of these buttons is much smaller than the other buttons we've worked with, so we need to override that as follows:

```
.optionsView .control-scheme.action-group .button {
  width: 30%;
  margin: 0;
  font-size: 25px;
}
```

We also want the selected control scheme to have a different color, so use the following code:

```
.optionsView .control-scheme.action-group .button.selected {
  border: 25px solid rgba(192,255,128, 0.5);
  background-color: rgba(192,255,128,0.75);
}
```

Next, let's look at the interesting code in `www/js/app/views/optionsView.js`.

The first interesting method is `updateControlScheme`. When the view appears or the user selects a control scheme, we need to update the visible elements so that only the selected control-scheme is visibly selected. Note that the `slide` control scheme is the default:

```
self.updateControlScheme = function () {
  var controlSchemes = { "tilt" : self._tiltButton,
                         "slide" : self._slideButton,
                         "buttons": self._buttonsButton };
  for ( var scheme in controlSchemes ) {
    if (controlSchemes.hasOwnProperty (scheme)) {
      controlSchemes[scheme].classList.remove ("selected");
    }
  }

  var controlScheme = "slide";
  if ( typeof localStorage.controlScheme !== "undefined" ) {
    controlScheme = localStorage.controlScheme;
  }
  controlSchemes[controlScheme].classList.add ("selected");
}
```

The preceding method is also called in the event handlers for each control scheme (note that we use `localStorage` to store the settings). The following is one of them:

```
self.controlSchemeTiltSelected = function () {
  localStorage.controlScheme = "tilt";
  self.updateControlScheme ();
}
```

What did we do?

In this task, we created the Options view, the associated styles, and the associated template.

What else do I need to know?

What if the user sees this screen and decides that `swipe` is the control method they want? This means we never set a property within `localStorage`, which in turn leads us to question that when the game starts, how will it know which control method to use?

Simple—we'll do a check there too—if there's nothing in `localStorage`, we'll assume the user wants to use the `swipe` method. The key here is to be consistent. If the game decided to use the `tilt` method instead, but displayed the `swipe` as the default in our Options view, the player would obviously be confused as to which option means what.

Implementing the Game view

Next, let's write the code for the Game view. We won't cover all the code—there's a good amount of it that should be familiar, and there are some portions that we'll break out into additional sections. When we're done with the project, we'll have a view that looks like the following screenshot:

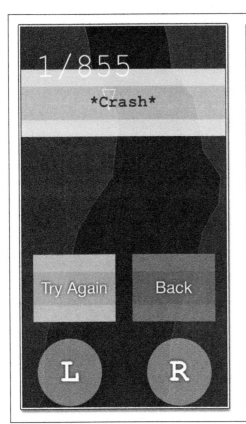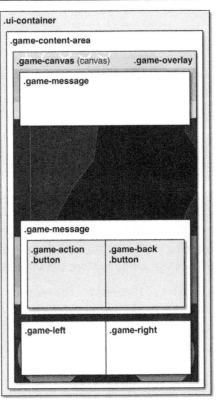

Getting on with it

First, let's get the template out of the way (in `www/html/gameView.html`):

```
<html>
<body>
<div class="ui-container">
<div class="game-content-area">
<div class="game-overlay">
<div class="game-left">L</div>
<div class="game-right">R</div>
```

```
<div class="game-message">%TAPTOSTART%</div>
<div class="action-group">
<div class="game-action button">%START%</div>
<div class="game-back button">%BACK%</div>
</div>
</div>
<canvas class="game-canvas"></canvas>
</div>
</div>
</body>
</html>
```

Again, there's nothing terribly difficult here, but it's important to pay attention to the various elements here. The `game-overlay` class contains all the interactive elements and will also be the swipe detector (for some reason, the `CANVAS` element doesn't like event handlers to be attached to it). The `game-left` and `game-right` items are the left/right buttons that the user can tap to control the ship if they've selected the buttons control scheme. These will be hidden if the control scheme is anything else.

There are some styles that need to be added to `www/css/style.css`. First, game messages appear near the top of the screen in the Courier font, as follows:

```
.gameView .game-message {
  position: absolute;
  top: 65px;
  height: 100px;
  left: 0; right: 0;
  background-color: rgba(255,255,255,0.75);
  font-family: "Courier New", "Arial", sans-serif;
  font-size: 25px;
  font-weight: bold;
  text-align: center;
  line-height: 50px;
  border: 25px solid rgba(255, 255, 255, 0.5);
  border-left: 0; border-right: 0;
  color: #242424;
}
```

The action group is near the bottom of the screen but elevated in order to avoid the left/right buttons, as shown in the following code:

```
.gameView .action-group {
  bottom: 150px;
  color: #FFFFFF;
  font-size: 25px;
}
```

The action button (which is used for starting and continuing the game) gets a green color, while the **Back** button gets a red color as shown in the following code:

```
.gameView .game-action {
  border: 25px solid rgba(192,255,128, 0.5);
  background-color: rgba(192,255,128,0.75);
}
.gameView .game-back {
  border: 25px solid rgba(255, 64,128, 0.5);
  background-color: rgba(255, 64,128,0.75);
}
```

The left/right buttons are circular buttons that appear to float above the game canvas. Let's define them in the following code:

```
.gameView .game-left, .gameView .game-right {
  position: absolute;
  bottom: 25px;
  width: 100px; height: 100px;
  border-radius: 50px;
  line-height: 100px;
  text-align: center;
  margin: 0; padding: 0;
  background-color: rgba(255,255,255, 0.5);
  color: white;
  font-size: 50px;
  font-family: "Courier New", "Arial", sans-serif;
  font-weight: bold;
  text-shadow: 0 0 5px black;
}
.gameView .game-left {
  left: 25px;
  box-shadow: 5px 5px 25px 0 rgba(0,0,0,.5);
}
.gameView .game-right {
  right: 25px;
  box-shadow: -5px 5px 25px 0 rgba(0,0,0,.5);
}
```

When pressed, they appear to move closer to the game canvas. Let's complete the implementation of the Game view using the following code:

```
.gameView .game-left.pressed, .gameView .game-right.pressed {
  bottom: 20px;
  box-shadow: 0 0 20px 0 rgba(0,0,0,.5);
  background-color: rgba(255, 255, 255, 0.75);
}
```

```
.gameView .game-left.pressed {
  left: 30px;
}
.gameView .game-right.pressed {
  right: 30px;
}
```

Now let's look at the interesting non-game code in `www/js/app/views/gameView.js`. First, let's go over the variables we define near the top of the module. The first set has to do with the various DOM elements in the view:

- ▸ `_overlay`: This refers to the `game-overlay` button
- ▸ `_backButton`: This refers to the `game-back` button
- ▸ `_message`: This refers to the `game-message` overlay
- ▸ `_leftButton` and `_rightButton`: These refer to the `game-left` and `game-right` buttons, respectively
- ▸ `_actionButton`: This refers to the `game-action` button (this displays messages such as **Start**, **Continue**, or **Try Again**
- ▸ `_actionGroup`: This refers to the group that holds the `_actionButton` and the `_backButton` elements

The following variables deal with the width and height of the game canvas:

- ▸ `_canvasWidth` and `_canvasHeight`: These store the width and height of the CANVAS element obtained from computing the styles for the BODY element (`window.getComputedStyle(document.body)`)
- ▸ `_canvasMiddle`: This stores the value of half the width of the CANVAS element
- ▸ `_pixelRatio`: This stores the pixel ratio of the device (`window.devicePixelRatio`)

Level generation requires a fair amount of the following variables:

- ▸ `_generateWidth`: This indicates the width we should use when generating the level.
- ▸ `_scale`: This is used to scale the generated level up or down in order to fit on the canvas. It's calculated by dividing `_canvasWidth` by `_generateWidth`.
- ▸ `_segmentLength`: This determines the length of each cave segment—this is hardcoded to 20 for a rough-edged cave.

- ▶ `_segments`: This stores the various *x* coordinates for each side of the cavern in addition to the coordinates for any wall obstacles. The *y* coordinates can be obtained from the segment index. Technically this is a multidimensional array: `_segments[0]` lists the *x* coordinates for the left-hand side of the cave wall, `_segments[1]` lists the *x* coordinates for the right-hand side of the cave wall, and `_segments[2]` and `_segments[3]` list the *x* coordinates for each side of any wall obstacle.

The game state is managed by the following variables:

- ▶ `_currentTop`: This indicates how far into the level the player has reached; we use this to calculate what portion of the cave to display on screen.

- ▶ `_currentLevel`: This indicates the current level number.

- ▶ `_score`: This indicates the player's score.

- ▶ `_timer`: This stores the ID for `setTimeout` or `requestAnimationFrame` (which is used to maintain the frame rate).

- ▶ `_startTime`: This is used to calculate the time difference between one frame and the next.

- ▶ `_ship`: This is an object that stores the *x* and *y* positions of the ship (the *y* position is hardcoded at 30 px) as well as the acceleration of the ship.

- ▶ `_canvas` and `_context`: These are utilized to perform drawing actions; they are cached to prevent continuous lookups.

- ▶ `_collidingLines`: This is a multidimensional array that is recalculated every time the cavern is drawn onscreen. This is utilized when determining whether the ship has crashed.

The control scheme and input from the user are controlled by the following variables:

- ▶ `_controlSchemes`: This relates the name of the various control methods with the associated index. `_controlScheme` represents the specific control scheme chosen by the user.

- ▶ `_desiredDirection`: This indicates the direction the user wants the ship to travel. If the value is less than zero, the ship should travel left. If the value is greater than zero, the ship should travel right. If the value is zero, the ship should decelerate.

- ▶ `_lastTouch`: This stores the *x* and *y* coordinates of the user's last touch.

- ▶ `_amTouching`: This indicates if the user is currently touching the screen.

- ▶ `_touchTimer`: This lets us decelerate the ship if the user keeps his/her finger in the same place on the screen for a long(-ish) period of time.

- ► `_tiltWatch`: This stores the ID obtained when watching the accelerometer for changes.

- ► `_previousAccelerometer`: This stores the most recent *x*, *y*, and *z* values obtained from the accelerometer.

Let's look at `init`; this is where we load the user's desired control scheme. Note that we also add an event listener so that the game is stopped when the view is popped, as shown in the following code:

```
self.overrideSuper(self.class, "init", self.init);
self.init = function (theParentElement) {
  self._controlScheme = self._controlSchemes["slide"];
  if (typeof localStorage.controlScheme !== "undefined" ) {
    self._controlScheme =
      self._controlSchemes[localStorage.controlScheme];
  }
  self.super(_className, "init", [undefined, "div",
    self.class + " gameView ui-container", theParentElement]);
  self.addListenerForNotification(
    "viewWasPopped", self.stopGame);
  self.addListenerForNotification(
    "viewWasPopped", self.releaseBackButton);
  self.addListenerForNotification(
    "viewWasPopped",  self.destroy);
}
```

When the player has finished the level or has crashed their ship, we need to tell them about it (or, if there is no message, we hide the message-related elements):

```
self._showMessage = function ( m ) {
  var newStyle = "block";
  if (m==="") { newStyle = "none"; }
  self._message.style.display = newStyle;
  self._actionGroup.style.display = newStyle;
  self._message.innerHTML = m;
}
```

Of course, we need to actually set up the game canvas so that we can draw on it. We do that in `renderToElement`. Setting the canvas up isn't as simple as one would expect, especially when dealing with retina or high-DPI displays. The actual `width` and `height` properties are set to the desired width multiplied by the device's pixel ratio, while the equivalent CSS styles are set to the desired width (and not multiplied by the pixel ratio). It's a convoluted method but it keeps the canvas looking sharp on all screens:

```
self._canvas = self.element.querySelector(".game-canvas");
self._context = self._canvas.getContext("2d");
```

```
self._canvas.setAttribute ( "width",
  self._canvasWidth * self._pixelRatio );
self._canvas.setAttribute ( "height",
  self._canvasHeight * self._pixelRatio );
self._canvas.style.width = "" + self._canvasWidth + "px";
self._canvas.style.height = "" + self._canvasHeight + "px";
```

What did we do?

In this section, we defined the template for the Game view, the visual styles, and some of the code for the view. In the next few tasks, we'll cover the actual game logic.

Generating levels

It's hard to imagine a game without at least one level, and that level needs to have some sort of content in it. In this task, we'll examine how to generate content for the levels in our game.

Getting on with it

There are a few ways one can generate a level. You can use random content, procedurally-generated content, or static content. The first is pretty easy—just use random numbers for everything. Unfortunately, this doesn't usually result in terribly nice levels, and there's little guarantee of winnability or difficulty.

The third method is also pretty easy—use static content. This means that you've determined the entire level ahead of time and stored it in a file. When the game requests the level, it can be read back. This means it is the same every time, which can be good (or bad), depending on the game, but it also means that you have a clear way to ensure both winnability and difficulty. For puzzle games, this is nearly always the method used.

Our method will be to procedurally generate the level. We'll be using plenty of random numbers—we don't want perfectly straight cave walls or easily guessed paths. However, we also want to build in some level of increase in difficulty over time as well as restrict the levels to a few parameters to help ensure (though not guarantee) winnability. It is possible to guarantee that a level can be winnable with enough code, but we won't go quite that far in this game.

Let's go through the code used to generate a level in `www/js/app/views/gameView.js`. As we progress through the code, the following diagram might be helpful:

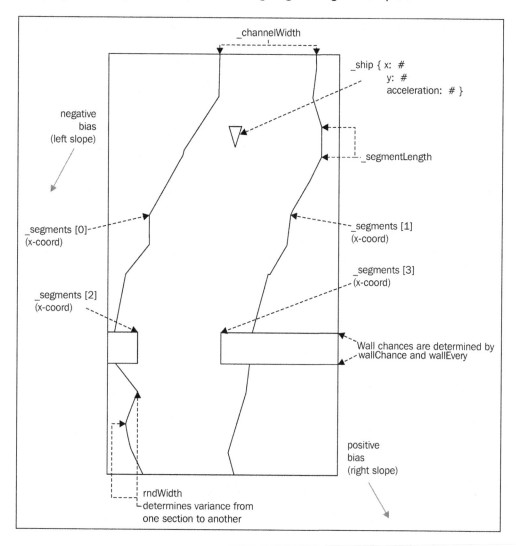

The level generation is contained in the `generateLevel` method. Let's first initialize the arrays using the following code:

```
self._segments = [[], [], [], []];
```

First we initialize our `segments[]` array with four arrays within it. The first two arrays contain the left and right *x* coordinates that make up the cave wall. The last two contain the edges (*x* coordinates, again) of any obstacle opening, or -1 if there is no obstacle in place. The *y* coordinate is inferred from the segment index in the array, as follows:

```
var generateWidth = self._generateWidth;
```

A word on `_generateWidth`: technically, this can be any number. In the previous edition of this book, it was the width of the screen. The issue is that different sized devices have radically different game play—large screens ended up with easier levels. To fix that, this number is set to a fixed value (defined earlier as `320`), and it is then scaled up. It's not a perfect solution, but it's better than a game that's too easy on a tablet. Next, let's set the following two variables:

```
var lastLeft= (generateWidth/5);
var lastRight=(generateWidth/5);
```

Here, we have two variables that store the last calculated positions for the sides of our cavern. Here we define their starting values, which simply creates a nice wide opening at the start of the level. We need this to avoid starting the level with an immediate obstacle the user can't avoid.

```
var bias = 0;
```

The `bias` method controls the direction our cave walls will tend towards. They'll still be randomly generated, but we introduce a bias whenever the walls hit the edge of the screen so that there is always some movement. Initially, the bias is zero, which means the cavern will meander until it reaches one edge of the screen.

```
var rndWidth = Math.floor(generateWidth/ 10) + (lvl*10);
if (rndWidth > 150) { rndWidth = 150; }
```

The `rndWidth` variable controls how much our cave wall can vary over a particular distance. In this case, it is controlled by `generateWidth` and our current level. This means the cave gets harder to navigate as we progress through our levels.

```
var channelWidth = Math.floor(generateWidth / 1.85)
                   - (lvl*16);
if (channelWidth < 30) { channelWidth = 30; }
```

The `channelWidth` variable, on the other hand, limits just how close the cave walls can get.

```
var wallChance = 0.5 - (lvl/12);
if (wallChance < 0.15) { wallChance = 0.15; }
```

A wall obstacle is only generated very often—we don't want an obstacle to appear at every segment. So we generate some sort of chance that is also based on the level. Easier levels will have fewer obstacles, while harder levels will have several.

```
var wallEvery = Math.floor(30 - (lvl/2));
if (wallEvery < 5) { wallEvery = 5; }
```

The `wallEvery` variable also factors in to how often obstacles appear, but in a different way. It controls how many segments must be between an obstacle before it can have a chance to be generated. In this case, we'll start off at 29 segments, but will steadily lower it as the levels increase. This means obstacles will not only appear more often, but more closely together. The following code will serve this purpose:

```
var i;
for (i=0; i<30; i++) {
  // left of corridor
  self._segments[0].push (lastLeft * self._scale);
  // right of corridor
  self._segments[1].push (lastRight * self._scale);
  // no wall
  self._segments[2].push (-1);
  self._segments[3].push (-1);
}
```

At the start of every level, we define a straight portion of the cavern. This is crucial to avoid surprising the player with an immediate obstacle.

```
for (i=0; i< Math.floor(300 + ( 125 * (lvl/2) ) ); i++) {
```

We need to create a cave several hundred segments long. The first level will start out with 725 segments and will only increase from there. Let's use the following code to determine the sides of the cave:

```
var newLeft = lastLeft + ( bias ) + ( (rndWidth/2) - Math.floor(
Math.random()* (rndWidth+1) ) );
var newRight = lastRight + ( bias )  + ( (rndWidth/2) -
Math.floor( Math.random()* (rndWidth+1) ) );
```

For each segment, we determine the left-hand side and right-hand side of the cave. We base this on the previous segment, add in the `bias` method and then add a random number within our allowed width. This gives us a cavern wall that will vary by a random amount, but not by so much (at least in the first few levels) that the level will be impossible:

```
if ( newLeft < 10 ) {
  newLeft = 10;
  bias = Math.floor( Math.random()* (self._segmentLength/2));
```

```
    }
    if ( newLeft > (generateWidth-channelWidth-10) ) {
      newLeft = generateWidth-channelWidth-10;
      bias = -Math.floor( Math.random()* (self._segmentLength/2)); }
    if (generateWidth-newRight < newLeft+(channelWidth/1.25)) {
      newRight = generateWidth-(newLeft+(channelWidth/1.25));
    }
    if (generateWidth-newRight>newLeft+(channelWidth*1.25)) {
      newRight = generateWidth-(newLeft +(channelWidth*1.25));
    }
    if ( newRight < 10 ) {
      newRight = 10;
      bias = -Math.floor( Math.random()* (self._segmentLength/2)); }
    if ( newRight > (generateWidth-10)) {
      newRight = generateWidth-10;
      bias = Math.floor( Math.random()* (self._segmentLength/2));
    }
```

Of course, without a few restrictions on the sides, it would be possible for the cave to wander off the screen, which does the player no good if they can't see it. So we keep the cave on the screen. When the cave is about to go offscreen, we also affect the `bias` method—this will tend to give the cave a zig-zag pattern overall. The `bias` method is a random value, which means the cave may quickly (or slowly) move in a particular direction. Let's use the following code to add the cave segments to the array:

```
    self._segments[0].push ( newLeft * self._scale);
    self._segments[1].push ( newRight * self._scale);
    lastLeft = newLeft;
    lastRight = newRight;
```

Finally, we added the points to the array and stored them for future reference (the next iteration in the loop). Note that we multiply these points by the ratio of `generateWidth` and the actual screen size—better here than later (when we have to be as fast as possible with drawing a frame). Next, we determine if it is time to put an obstacle in the way using the following code:

```
    if ( (i % wallEvery) === 0 && ( i > 30 ) ) {
```

First, we only check every so often (`wallEvery`), and we also restrict any obstacle from appearing within the first 30 segments of the cave. Next, we decide if a wall will appear at this point using the following code:

```
    if (Math.random()>wallChance) {
```

This makes obstacles pretty rare early on, but they add up in later levels. Now, for the obstacle, we create an opening that is a smaller opening than the width of the cave, as shown in the following code—this means the wall juts out from the cave by some amount:

```
if (Math.random()>wallChance) {
  var openingWidth = channelWidth/1.35;
  var caveWidth = ((generateWidth-newRight) - newLeft)
                  - openingWidth;
  var wallOpening = Math.floor (Math.random() * caveWidth);
  self._segments[2].push ( (newLeft + wallOpening) *
                            self._scale );
  self._segments[3].push ( (newLeft + wallOpening +
                              openingWidth) * self._scale );
}
else {    // no wall
  self._segments[2].push ( -1 );
  self._segments[3].push ( -1 );
}
}
else {    // no wall
  self._segments[2].push ( -1 );
  self._segments[3].push ( -1 );
}
```

We then determine some random value within the range of the cave's opening, and that's where the opening will go. If we aren't in a place where there should be an obstacle, we push -1. This is the flag that indicates that there is no wall on this segment.

What did we do?

In this task, we generated the levels for our game based on pseudorandom generation, with some specific rules in place to create levels that increase in difficulty over the course of the game.

What else do I need to know?

This isn't the only way to generate a procedurally generated level, of course. There are all sorts of methods that are beyond the scope of this book, and there are steps you can take to ensure that a level always stays winnable. Level generation is a subject of its own (with many, many smart people working in the field), so it won't take long to get your mind blown with some of the level generation techniques out there. Visit http://en.wikipedia. org/wiki/Procedural_generation to look for examples of games that generate their levels procedurally as well as some links to articles describing various ways to generate levels procedurally. Keep in mind this is highly specific to the kind of game you're developing.

Drawing on the canvas

Of course, it does no good to generate a level if we don't display it to the player. That's what we'll be doing in this task.

Getting on with it

We've already set our canvas up in a prior section. Now, however, we need to define the code that actually draws a frame. We need this code to be quick; however, we have to do it in 16 milliseconds if we hope to approach 60 fps. The drawing code is in the _doAnim method in `www/js/app/views/gameView.js`. Let's start with the following code:

```
if (typeof timestamp == "undefined") {
  timestamp = (new Date()).getTime(); }
var diff = timestamp - self._startTime;
```

The very first step is to determine the difference between the current time (or the time passed in to the function) and the time the last frame was rendered. This is critical in order to keep the game speed from lagging when frames are dropped.

```
var ctx = self._context;
```

Next, we copy the context to a shorter, local variable, because we're going to be using it a lot to draw lines and shapes to the canvas.

```
ctx.save();
ctx.scale (window.devicePixelRatio, window.devicePixelRatio);
ctx.clearRect ( 0, 0, self._canvasWidth, self._canvasHeight);
```

Before we do any rendering, we set up a few properties and then clear the canvas. It is critical to clear the canvas for every frame; otherwise, you'll end up leaving ghosts of the previous frame behind.

```
self._collidingLines = [[],[]];
```

We also clear out the array that will hold all the lines we draw on the screen—we'll use this later to handle collision checking. Then we draw both sides of the cave by looping over each cave segment for each side of the cave, as follows:

```
for (var i=0; i<2; i++) {
  var seg, x, y, j;
```

Based on which part of the cave we're drawing, we assign either the 0 or 1 index of segments[] to another variable, seg, as follows:

```
var offX = -10;
if (i===0) { seg = self._segments[0]; }
if (i===1) {
  seg = self._segments[1];
  offX = self._canvasWidth+10; }
```

This lets us avoid having to double-index the points array such as segments[i][j] and use seg[j] instead. We also define the left-hand side or the right-hand side of the wall that is offscreen. This comes in handy for drawing the cave, since we need to fill the cave walls to make them solid. This means we are essentially drawing a big rectangle with one portion of it very rough—the rough side being the cave wall. Let's start the process of drawing one side of the cave as follows:

```
ctx.fillStyle = "#402010";
ctx.strokeStyle = "#804020";
ctx.beginPath();
ctx.moveTo ( offX, -self._segmentLength );
self._collidingLines.push ( { x: offX,
                              y: -self._segmentLength } );
```

At this point, we actually started the process of drawing one side of the cave. First, the fill and stroke colors are defined, and then the path is started. We move to the very first part of the shape: the top-left corner of the screen (slightly offscreen, actually) for the left-hand side of the cave (and vice-versa for the right-hand side). Let's loop through the visible segments as follows:

```
for (j = Math.floor ( self._currentTop /
                      self._segmentLength )-1;
    j < Math.floor ( self._currentTop /
                     self._segmentLength ) +
   ((self._canvasHeight+(2*self._segmentLength)) /
                     self._segmentLength );
    j++) {
```

At this point, we loop through segments in the array, but only the ones necessary. If the player is halfway through the level, there's no point in drawing the previous segments, nor is there any point in drawing parts of the cave that are beyond the screen's height. In order to keep the motion of the cave smooth, we multiply the current index (j) by the segment length and subtract our current position in the level, as follows:

```
x = seg[j];
y = (j * self._segmentLength) - self._currentTop;
```

Technically, this would result in a jumpy view at the first and last drawn index, but we're drawing a couple of segments beyond both edges, so any jumpiness is kept offscreen. Next, we draw a line to the position indicated by the current segment, as follows:

```
if (i==1) { x = self._canvasWidth - x; }
ctx.lineTo ( x, y );
self._collidingLines[i].push ( { x: x, y: y } );
```

If we're working on the right-hand side, the position is to the left of the screen's right edge, which is the right-hand side of the cave. Now, If we have an obstacle to display, we also draw a line to the point and then a vertical line of one segmentLength high, as follows:

```
if ( self._segments[2][j] > -1 ) {
  ctx.lineTo ( self._segments[i+2][j], y );
  self._collidingLines[i].push (
    { x: self._segments[i+2][j], y: y } );
  ctx.lineTo ( self._segments[i+2][j],
    y+self._segmentLength );
  self._collidingLines[i].push (
    { x: self._segments[i+2][j],
      y: y+self._segmentLength } );
}
```

This will cause the obstacle to appear like a wall with an opening in it. Later, we'll redraw this wall in a different color to make it stand out. Finally, we draw a line offscreen again, and then proceed to fill and strike the path, as follows:

```
ctx.lineTo ( offX,
  ((self._canvasWidth+2)*self._segmentLength) );
self._collidingLines[i].push ( {x: offX,
  y: ((self._canvasWidth+2)*self._segmentLength) } );
ctx.closePath();
ctx.fill();
ctx.stroke();
```

The player will only see the rough edges of the cave wall. Once, the edge of the cave is drawn, we draw the wall obstacles in another color, as follows:

```
for (j = Math.floor ( self._currentTop /
                      self._segmentLength )-1;
     j < Math.floor ( self._currentTop /
                      self._segmentLength ) +
     ((self._canvasHeight+(2*self._segmentLength)) /
                      self._segmentLength );
     j++) {
  y = (j * self._segmentLength) - self._currentTop;
```

```
        if ( self._segments[2][j] > -1 ) {
          x = self._segments[i+2][j];
          ctx.fillStyle = "#804020";
          ctx.strokeStyle = "#C06030";
          ctx.beginPath();
          ctx.moveTo ( offX, y );
          ctx.lineTo ( x, y );
          ctx.lineTo ( x, y+self._segmentLength );
          ctx.lineTo ( offX, y+self._segmentLength );
          ctx.closePath();
          ctx.fill();
          ctx.stroke();
        }
      }
```

Drawing the wall obstacles in another color helps them stand out better to the player, and makes it more clear that they aren't just a natural cave formation. After we draw the cave walls, we need to draw the ship. In this case, we draw a simple triangle, as follows:

```
ctx.strokeStyle = "#FFFFFF";
ctx.beginPath();
ctx.moveTo ( (self._ship.x-10) * self._scale, self._ship.y-(
5 * self._scale) );
ctx.lineTo ( (self._ship.x+10) * self._scale, self._ship.y-(
5 * self._scale) );
ctx.lineTo ( (self._ship.x) * self._scale   , self._ship.y+(
25 * self._scale) );
ctx.lineTo ( (self._ship.x-10) * self._scale, self._ship.y-(
5 * self._scale) );
ctx.closePath();
ctx.stroke();
```

Most games need to display some text. In the following code, we display the level and the score:

```
ctx.fillStyle = "#FFFFFF";
ctx.font = "50px 'Courier New',Arial,sans-serif";
var aString = "" + self._currentLevel + "/" +
  Math.floor(Math.max(0,self._score));
 ctx.fillText ( aString, 25, 75 );
```

Finally, if the user's control method is swiping, we display a translucent circle where the user is touching (assuming it is at the bottom of the screen) so that the user knows that the touch has been registered. Let's use the following code for this purpose:

```
if (self._amTouching) {
  ctx.fillStyle = "rgba(255,255,255,0.25)";
```

```
    ctx.beginPath();
    ctx.arc ( self._lastTouch.x, self._lastTouch.y, 50, 0,
      2*Math.PI, false );
    ctx.closePath();
    ctx.fill();
  }
  ctx.restore();
```

Keep in mind that when drawing a frame, we need to be quick—and thankfully the following operations are. Depending on the hardware, we can draw a frame in only a few milliseconds.

```
    self._doUpdate ( 60/(1000/diff) );
    self._startTime = timestamp;
```

If we stay under 17 milliseconds, we can achieve nearly 60 fps, though on older hardware, this is more like 20-30 milliseconds, so we need to do something else: drop frames so that the game doesn't feel too sluggish. The factor calculated in the preceding code allows us to adjust our calculations of the ship and the scroll speed of the cavern to keep things nice and fast, even if we can't hit 60 fps.

What did we do?

In this task, we drew the level on the canvas, displayed the ship, and put various kinds of text on the canvas as well. We also kept it quick—something we could only do by using the `Canvas` tag.

What else do I need to know?

Of course, the preceding code only draws one frame. We need to call it multiple times in order to achieve fluid scrolling. There are two ways to do this: we can use `setTimeout` or use `requestAnimationFrame`. The latter is preferred as it has better resolution than `setTimeout`, but it isn't yet supported in all mobile browsers. For our purposes, we use `setTimeout` only if using `requestAnimationFrame` isn't available. It's called in `doUpdate`, which we'll go over later rather than in `doAnim`. If you want to know which browsers support `requestAnimationFrame`, visit `http://caniuse.com/requestanimationframe`.

In addition, we've only used a few of the methods available to draw on a canvas. In order to learn about all the possibilities, visit the following sites:

▶ `http://diveintohtml5.info/canvas.html`
▶ `https://developer.mozilla.org/en-US/docs/Web/Guide/HTML/Canvas_tutorial`

Performing updates

Of course, drawing the same frame over and over won't do any good. We need to update the game too. This includes responding to user input, checking for collisions, and moving us along the cave.

Getting on with it

We'll be doing all our updating in... guess what—doUpdate in www/js/app/views/ gameView.js.

If you recall from the last task, the only incoming parameter is the incoming frame multiplier. We want this to be 1, but it might be 2 if we're getting 30 fps, or 4 if we're getting 15 fps. We'll use the frame multiplier at various points to multiply any updates so that everything moves as if we were getting 60 fps, even when we aren't. Let's use the following code for this purpose:

```
self._doUpdate = function ( f ) {
var gameOver = false;
var levelOver = false;
var oldShip = {x: self._ship.x,
               y: self._ship.y };
```

The first step of our update process is to record the current value of the ship. We need this to properly detect collisions later as the position of our ship will change.

```
if (f > 0 && f != Infinity) {
```

Sometimes f comes in as 0 or Infinity. This is most often at the start of a game, when we have to pass in a time difference, but there's not really been any. In this case, the division in doAnim will return Infinity. We don't want to do anything in either case, so we make sure that we only perform an update if f is a reasonable value.

```
if (self._controlScheme != self._controlSchemes["tilt"]) {
  if (self._desiredDirection !== 0) {
    if (Math.abs(self._ship.acceleration)<1)
      { self._ship.acceleration = self._desiredDirection ; }
    self._ship.acceleration = self._ship.acceleration +
      ( self._desiredDirection * self._deviceFactor);
    if (self._ship.acceleration < -10) {
      self._ship.acceleration = -10; }
    if (self._ship.acceleration > 10) {
      self._ship.acceleration = 10; }
  } else {
    self._ship.acceleration = self._ship.acceleration / 1.5;
    if (Math.abs(self._ship.acceleration)<0.25) {
```

```
        self._ship.acceleration = 0; }
    }
    self._ship.x += (self._ship.acceleration*f);
```

The `_desiredDirection` variable reflects the user's input if they are using touch or button controls. If they are swiping to the left-hand side, the value will be negative. If they are going to the right-hand side, the value will be positive. If they aren't doing anything, it will be zero. If they are using tilt controls, we'll calculate this value differently, but we'll show that in the next task.

If the value is non-zero, we build up some acceleration, as if a thruster was on the ship. Since thrusters can't react instantly, the ship takes a little bit of time to react. This has the effect of making the game a little harder—you have to take into account the reaction time of the ship.

If the value is zero, we reduce the acceleration, as if the ship was coasting to a stop. Once we reach a certain threshold, we stop the ship entirely, but until that point, there is some movement. Again, this adds difficulty as it must be considered when moving the ship.

One important variable in the preceding code is `deviceFactor`. This is subjective—while the ship's movement felt right on an Android device, it felt too slow on an iOS device, and so this variable compensates a bit for that difference. Never be afraid to tweak the movement mechanics on different devices so that it feels the same, even if it isn't technically the same.

Note that we multiply the acceleration by `f`. This keeps the ship's movement working as if it were happening in a game with 60 fps.

```
        self._score -= Math.floor(self._ship.acceleration*f);
    } else {
        // calculate the position based on the accelerometer data
    }
```

The scoring mechanism in this game penalizes players for movement. Therefore, we subtract points based on the acceleration. This means the best scores are only possible with frugal maneuvering. Next, we calculate the vertical distance through the cave, which is done by adding a number to `currentTop`, as follows:

```
    var speed = ((4+self._currentLevel) * (f));
    self._currentTop+= speed;
    oldShip.y -= speed;
```

We adjust it slowly based on the current level as well, so higher levels will get faster and faster. Again, we multiply by `f` to keep things feeling smooth. We also adjust the *y* coordinate for the previous ship data. This is so we can later use the line segment formed by the old position of the ship and the current version to determine collisions. We also update the score (and if the game is running slowly, we don't want to penalize the user, so we also multiply it by `f`), as follows:

```
if (!gameOver && !levelOver) {
  self._score += (self._currentLevel * f);
}
```

If the player has managed to navigate the entire level, we need to stop the game and tell the user that they made it. When they continue, they'll pick up at the next higher level, as follows:

```
if ( Math.floor (self._currentTop/self._segmentLength) > self._
segments[0].length ) {
  self._actionButton.innerHTML = _y.T("CONTINUE");
  self._showMessage (_y.T('NEXT_LEVEL'));
  levelOver = true;
}
```

There are various methods of doing collision detection: we can use pixel-based detection or mathematics-based detection. Pixel detection is simple (although complicated by the fact that one needs to exclude pixels that shouldn't count as a collision) but comes at a price: doing so requires examining the data on the canvas, and this is slow. Mathematical collision detection is harder but faster and more accurate. Furthermore, we can vary our response based on what the player has collided with. We could do this with pixel-based detection as well, but the objects would need to be in different colors.

Essentially, what we want to do is represented by the following diagram:

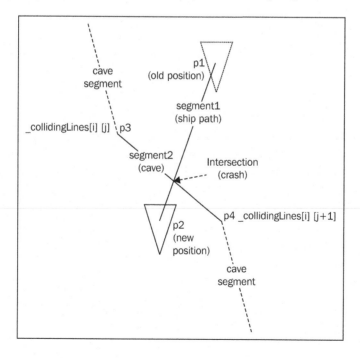

To do this, we need to know how to determine whether two line segments intersect. We can do this with the following code:

```
function doSegmentsIntersect ( segment1, segment2 ) {
  // from: http://stackoverflow.com/a/16725715
  function CCW (p1, p2, p3) {
    var a = p1.x, b = p1.y,
        c = p2.x, d = p2.y,
        e = p3.x, f = p3.y;
    return (f - b) * (c - a) > (d - b) * (e - a);
  }
  var p1 = {x: segment1.x1, y: segment1.y1 },
      p2 = {x: segment1.x2, y: segment1.y2 },
      p3 = {x: segment2.x1, y: segment2.y1 },
      p4 = {x: segment2.x2, y: segment2.y2 };
  return (CCW(p1, p3, p4) != CCW(p2, p3, p4)) &&
         (CCW(p1, p2, p3) != CCW(p1, p2, p4));
}
```

If you want to know why the preceding code works, it's simple enough to graph everything out. If you're not a math whiz, you'll have to assume that it does.

```
var gameOver = false;
var levelOver = false;
var shipCollided = false;
var segment1 = { x1: oldShip.x * self._scale,
                 y1: oldShip.y,
                 x2: self._ship.x * self._scale,
                 y2: self._ship.y },
    segment2;
```

Now that we have the mechanism to determine whether two line segments intersect, we need to determine whether our ship has collided with any of the lines we've drawn on the screen. This isn't terribly difficult! In doAnim, we stored each line segment we drew, so all we need to do is iterate over each segment. But first we need another line, and that's obtainable by using the position of the ship now and what it was at the beginning of the method. If that line intersects any line drawn to the screen, we know we have a collision. Let's use the following code for this purpose:

```
for (var i=0; i<2; i++) {
  for ( var j=0; j< self._collidingLines[i].length-1; j++ ) {
    segment2 = { x1: self._collidingLines[i][j].x,
                 y1: self._collidingLines[i][j].y,
                 x2: self._collidingLines[i][j+1].x,
                 y2: self._collidingLines[i][j+1].y };
```

```
    if (doSegmentsIntersect( segment1, segment2)) {
      shipCollided = true;
      break;
    }
  }
}
  if (shipCollided) { break; }
}
```

Why a line and not a point?

If the ship is travelling too fast, it would be possible for a point to skip over a large portion of the screen, potentially skipping over any obstacles. A line, however, drawn from the old and current positions allows us to test for a collision over the entire path of the ship.

The preceding code searches through each line we've drawn on the screen to see whether the ship's path crosses any of those lines. If it has, then we mark the ship as having collided with something. This is a very naive approach—you could optimize this in many different ways (for example, you could search only those lines within the vicinity of the ship's path).

```
if (shipCollided) {
  self._actionButton.innerHTML = _y.T("TRY_AGAIN");
  self._showMessage (_y.T('CRASHED'));
  gameOver = true;
  self._currentLevel = 0;
}
```

In the preceding code, if the ship has collided, we mark the game as over and tell the user about it.

```
if (!gameOver && !levelOver) {
  var requestAnimationFrame = window.requestAnimationFrame ||
                      window.webkitRequestAnimationFrame;
  if (typeof requestAnimationFrame !== "undefined") {
    self._timer = requestAnimationFrame ( self._doAnim)
  } else {
    self._timer = setTimeout ( self._doAnim,17);
  }
}
```

Finally, our code keeps everything going by either requesting the next animation frame or using a setTimeout property with a delay of 17 values. We do this unless the game is over or the level is over. If you wanted to add a pause feature, you would also avoid setting a timer at this point.

The 17 here is intended to get us as close to 60 fps as possible. It doesn't work out to that in reality—browsers don't have good timer resolution, so the next frame could arrive in 12 milliseconds or in 30 milliseconds. WebKit, thankfully, has something of the order of 4 milliseconds resolution, so it isn't likely to be far off from 17, and so we can get up to 56 fps, assuming a modern device.

For devices that support `requestAnimationFrame`, however, the results are better. We truly can get 60 fps (assuming we've drawn and calculated everything in 16 milliseconds) because the timer resolution is much more accurate.

Now that we have a full game loop, we need mechanisms to stop (`stopLevel`) and start it (`startLevel`). Let's start with `startLevel` first:

```
self.startLevel = function () {
self._showMessage("");
self._currentLevel++; // increment the level number
if (self._currentLevel == 1) {
  self._score = 0; // reset score at first level
}
// reset ship positions and top of the level
self._currentTop = 0;
self._ship = {x: (self._generateWidth / 2) - 10,
              y: 100,
              acceleration: 0 }
// zero out any other game state
self._desiredDirection = 0;
self._touchTimer = -1;
self._lastTouch.x = -1;
self._lastTouch.y = -1;
self._amTouching = false;
self._previousAccelerometer = { x:0, y:0, z:0 };
// generate a new level
self._generateLevel(self._currentLevel);
// set the start time:
self._startTime = (new Date()).getTime();
// draw our first frame:
self._doAnim(self._startTime+0);
}

self.stopGame = function () {
  if (typeof self._timer !== "undefined") {
    var cancelAnimationFrame = window.cancelAnimationFrame ||
                        window.webkitCancelAnimationFrame;
    if (typeof cancelAnimationFrame !== "undefined") {
      cancelAnimationFrame ( self._timer)
```

```
    } else {
      clearTimeout ( self._timer );
    }
  }
  self._timer = undefined;
}
```

What did we do?

In this task, we handled the updating of the ship's position, the position in the cave, and whether or not we crashed or completed the level. We also added code to start a new level and to stop the game entirely.

Touched-based input

As we don't have a physical keyboard or joystick or D-pad, we have to emulate one on the screen. One control scheme does this with two buttons on the screen for our game—one to go left, and one to go right. Another way is to allow for the differences in how a swipe might occur—a slow movement when our ship is not in danger, or a sudden movement when we need to avoid an obstacle in a hurry. Another method would be to simply link up the touch position on the screen to the ship—essentially our finger would have to trace the path through the cave. For smaller devices this might be fine, but for larger devices, it is better to go with some other method.

Getting ready

In our game, if the user has selected the slide control scheme, our touch input can handle swipes (where the finger isn't always on the screen) to move the ship in short bursts, and can handle long drags where the finger is always on the screen and slight movements provide the steering.

Put simply, if we move to the left-hand side, the ship should move left, and vice versa. However, if we need to get out of an obstacle's way in a hurry, we shouldn't have to move a long distance. We should be able to move a short distance in a quick burst, and so we also measure the distance between movements so that we can tune the ship's movement to how fast our finger is moving. If the finger is moving slowly, the ship moves slowly. If the finger moves quickly, the ship moves quickly.

If the user has selected the button control scheme, our touch input is somewhat simpler. Here, however, we encounter a new problem: there's no way for the user to indicate urgency. This means that we need to increase the acceleration of the ship for as long as a button is held so that a long hold gets a ship out of danger, while a short hold moves it only a short distance.

None of this is hard. In fact, the hardest part isn't making it work, it's making it work well. It's hard to make a control method feel entirely natural, and I won't claim to have mastered it here. It takes lots of testing to get a control mechanism just right.

The code to handle the left/right button control scheme is straightforward. If the left button is pressed, _desiredDirection is set to -1, and if the right button is pressed, _desiredDirection is set to 1. doUpdate will then move the ship appropriately. As this is reasonably straightforward, I'll leave it to you to look up the code.

For the slide control scheme, we attach event listeners to the game overlay. Remember, this isn't the canvas but a separate DIV element that takes up the entire screen. In my testing, canvases don't always like touch events on them. These are attached in renderToElement as follows:

```
if (self._controlScheme == self._controlSchemes["slide"])
{
  self._overlay.addEventListener ( "touchstart",
    self._canvasTouchStarted );
  self._overlay.addEventListener ( "touchmove",
    self._canvasTouchMoved );
  self._overlay.addEventListener ( "touchend",
    self._canvasTouchEnded );
}
```

Next, we define the handlers for the slide control scheme, which requires us to keep track of where the user has touched the screen. The first handler is _canvasTouchStarted, and it is called when the user first touches the screen. In it, we record the initial touch and tell the game that a finger is touching the screen. If you remember doUpdate, this last part tells the game to draw a translucent circle at the *x* position of the touch to give the user feedback, as follows:

```
self._canvasTouchStarted = function (evt) {
  if (typeof evt.touches !== "undefined") {
    self._lastTouch.x = evt.touches[0].pageX;
    self._lastTouch.y = evt.touches[0].pageY;
  } else {
    self._lastTouch.x = evt.pageX;
    self._lastTouch.y = evt.pageY;
  }
  self._amTouching = true;
}
```

When the player's finger moves, `_canvasTouchMoved` is called. At this point, we need to calculate the distance between the last *x* position and the new *x* position. We then give `_desiredDirection` a negative or positive value based on the direction of the movement. We also divide it if the movement was slow. If it was a fast movement (over five pixels), we'd have values of -1 for left and +1 for right, but a slow movement might return -0.2 and +0.2, as follows:

```
self._canvasTouchMoved = function (evt) {
  if (!self._amTouching) { return; }
  if (typeof self._touchTimer !== "undefined") {
    clearTimeout(self._touchTimer);
    self._touchTimer = undefined;
  }
  var curTouchX = evt.touches[0].pageX;
  var deltaX = curTouchX-self._lastTouch.x;
  if (Math.abs(deltaX) > 1) {
    self._desiredDirection = ((deltaX) / Math.abs(deltaX) ) /
                             (8/Math.min(Math.abs(deltaX),8)));
    self._lastTouch.x = curTouchX;
  } else {
    self._desiredDirection = 0;
  }
```

If the finger hasn't moved by much (it needs to have moved by more than one pixel to register movement to the ship), and then we set `_desiredDirection` to 0 so that the ship will coast to a stop. We also set up a timer to fire in a few short milliseconds to turn `_desiredDirection` to zero as well. This is because we won't receive a `touchMove` event if the finger stays absolutely still—so we need a way to catch this. If a movement is received before the timer expires, we cancel the timer (defined in the preceding code) so that the value never becomes zero as long as there is adequate movement, as follows:

```
  self._touchTimer = setTimeout ( function() {
    self._desiredDirection = 0;
  }, 25 );
}
```

When the finger is lifted, we will instantly allow the ship to coast to a stop, and stop displaying the translucent circle:

```
self._canvasTouchEnded = function (evt) {
  self._pressedButton = 0;
  self._amTouching = false;
}
```

This isn't the only way to create movement, and I urge you to experiment with different ways of processing touch-based input.

What did we do?

In this task, we dealt with touch-based input in order to allow the user to move our game's ship.

Accelerometer-based input

In order to respond to the tilt of the device, we need to use the device's accelerometer. These aren't the easiest things to deal with, and our implementation is... a bit naive. Unfortunately it doesn't take long until you start getting into math that's more than a bit complicated and so lies outside the scope of this project.

Getting ready

First, we need to add a plugin to the project to support the accelerometer, as follows:

```
cordova plugin add org.apache.cordova.device-motion
```

Getting on with it

Accelerometer-based input is hard, really hard, to get. It is so hard, in fact, that the game doesn't have a particularly good implementation of it. You are encouraged to experiment with a lot of devices and algorithms to come up with a good control scheme.

To turn on the accelerometer check, we first have to set up a watch for it in `renderElement`, as follows:

```
self._tiltWatch = navigator.accelerometer.watchAcceleration
                ( self._updateAccelerometer,
                  self._accelerometerError,
                  { frequency: 40 } );
```

This sets up a 40 millisecond watch—not really quite as fast as I'd like, but workable. Every 40 milliseconds, the `_updateAccelerometer` method will be called. If an error occurs, then `_accelerometerError` will be called.

So what do we get with the accelerometer? We get an object that contains four values: a timestamp, an *x* value, a *y* value, and a *z* value. These values indicate the acceleration in a given direction. If the device is lying flat on a table, the *x* and *y* values will be zero, while the *z* value will be equal to the force of gravity. Generally, we can assume that the *x* value corresponds to left/right tilt (assuming the device is upright), which is all we need for our game. Let's use the following code for this purpose:

```
self._updateAccelerometer = function ( a ) {
  var p = self._previousAccelerometer;
  var avgX = (p.x * 0.7) + (a.x * 0.3);
  self._previousAccelerometer = a;
  self._previousAccelerometer.x = avgX;
}
```

When we receive an update, we apply a weighted average of the new input and the previous input, only if we have a calibrated value, giving more weight to the previous input. It turns out that accelerometer-based input is really, really noisy, and so we only give the new input small importance. This has the side effect, unfortunately, of making movement feel a little sluggish. The fractional values make a big difference in how well the ship responds, but at the trade-off of a ship that feels jittery. Feel free to experiment with these numbers, but they need to add up to one.

Next, in `_doUpdate`, we add the following:

```
if (self._controlScheme != self._controlSchemes["tilt"]) {
  ...
} else {
  var previousX = self._ship.x;
  self._ship.x = (self._canvasMiddle -
    (self._previousAccelerometer.x * 32)) / self._scale;
  var deltaX = Math.abs(previousX - self._ship.x);
  if (deltaX<3) {
    self._ship.x = previousX;
    deltaX = 0;
  }
  if ( self._ship.x < 0 ) {
    self._ship.x = 0;
  }
  if ( self._ship.x > self._generateWidth) {
    self._ship.x = self._generateWidth;
  }
  self._score -= Math.floor(deltaX);
}
```

Here we make the assumption that with no tilt, the ship should be in the middle of the screen (which is `self._canvasMiddle/2`). We then subtract the value of the *x* value from the last accelerometer sample and multiply it by 32. This number is really quite arbitrary—feel free to experiment here. Personally, 32 felt about right, not requiring the device to tilt all the way over, but also requiring sufficient tilt to make movement feel substantial.

The remainder of the code ensures that the ship can't go off the edges of the screen.

We also need to stop watching the accelerometer when the view disappears:

```
self.destroy = function () {
  ...
  if (typeof self._tiltWatch !== "undefined") {
    navigator.accelerometer.clearWatch ( self._tiltWatch );
    self._tiltWatch = undefined;
  }
  ...
}
```

What did we do?

In this task, we dealt with handling accelerometer-based input.

What else do I need to know?

Working with the accelerometer is no simple task. While our code is pretty simple, there are a lot of complicated algorithms out there to reduce the noise but at the same time keep the movement from feeling sluggish—something I can't say we've really accomplished here.

Another alternative is to use the device's gyroscope. These values aren't based on acceleration, but on the position of the device itself and though noisy, they aren't as noisy as the accelerometer values. As such, they can be easier to work with. The problem is that only iOS exposes these to a browser; on Android, one would need to write a plugin to work with this type of sensor. Furthermore, not every device has a gyroscope, so you would need to provide a fallback to the accelerometer just in case.

 The accelerometer is only available on physical devices; in order to use it, please run this app on a real device.

Game Over..... Wrapping it up

Whew! That was a lot of work, but the result is pretty fun. See how far you can get before it gets too hard. Let me tell you, it doesn't take me very long to crash and burn.

There's one last thing we ought to mention: on iOS 7, the status bar overlays the game canvas, which would be fine, except we want the experience to be immersive. To get rid of the status bar, we can add the Status Bar plugin to the project, as follows:

```
cordova plugin add org.apache.cordova.statusbar
```

Then, add the following in `www/js/app/main.js` at the top of `APP.start`:

```
if (_y.device.platform() == "ios") {
  StatusBar.hide();
}
```

Can you take the HEAT? The Hotshot Challenge

There are a lot of ways this game could be enhanced—why don't you try a few that are given:

- ▸ The game currently lacks a pause option—why don't you add one?
- ▸ Our game is naive with regard to multitasking. Once resumed, it will happily extrapolate where we should be in the cave after what might be a very long time. A better method would be to pause the game when it is backgrounded.
- ▸ Try various control schemes until you find some you like, or change the existing schemes until you find something you prefer.
- ▸ Use the gyroscope if available.
- ▸ Add power-ups or other objects in the map that could affect the player for good or bad.
- ▸ Make static levels for the game that could be loaded on demand.
- ▸ Add logic to make sure any level is winnable.
- ▸ Add sound and music to the game. You may want to investigate a plugin for low latency audio (`http://plugreg.com/plugin/floatinghotpot/cordova-plugin-lowlatencyaudio`).

Project 12

Building a Backend – Working with Parse

Many apps will eventually need to store some data on an external server; something that isn't local to the device. For example, if an app provided the ability to sync data from one device to another, this will require some sort of backend. If a game wanted to have an achievements system where players could see how they were rated against each other, it would need some sort of backend as well. In fact, even apps that seem to need no backend often do need something of the sort, even if it is very simple. You can consider, for example, an app that simply needs to update its content from an external server on a regular basis; this server will be the app's backend.

Backends have historically required users to set up their own servers. This is often a costly endeavor, and many small developers may not have the funds needed to support the server and the incoming or outgoing bandwidth. Further, these often introduce security issues that small shops don't typically understand well.

Thankfully, there are services that can act as our backend without having to set up our own server. These are technically considered **Backends as a Service (BaaS)**. Many offer free tiers of service, and these services require payment only if the app goes viral. We'll work with Parse (`http://www.parse.com`) in this project, but there are some others that you may want to use instead. Be sure to look at the pricing structure and the features they offer when making a choice:

- Parse (`http://www.parse.com`)
- Kinvey (`http://www.kinvey.com`)

What do we build?

In this project, we'll modify our game from the previous project so that it can submit scores to a global leader-board and display the top scores from that leader-board within the app.

What does it do?

We could have written lots of code in a server-side language and provided all sorts of instructions for creating a server from scratch to serve our app, but there is an inherent difficulty here—it is far too easy to introduce security holes unawares, and one needs to have a deep understanding of how the operating system, database, and server-side code interact to perform as a backend. As such, it involves a lot of code, a lot of security discussions, and those are, frankly, out of the scope of this book. Parse, on the other hand, takes care of many of the security issues, doesn't require an additional server to maintain, and supports a simple database model where we can store records and execute queries to retrieve them again. It also offers a lot of other features, including push notifications, code-in-the-cloud, and more, but we don't need those here.

For our app, we'll just build a simple database on Parse that will store the score of every user who plays the game. We can then query this information in our app to display a leader-board listing the very best players.

Until our app becomes incredibly popular, Parse is free. A new arrangement is required only when our app crosses a certain threshold (which is quite high; at the time this book was written, 30 API requests per second). Until then, it is free, free, and free. (Other features may have other limits.)

Why is it great?

It's rare to encounter an app today that doesn't have some need for a backend, and now that BaaSs are so simple to use and have such a low barrier to entry, there's really no reason at all not to work with them. While our needs for this project are very simple, you can use the skills presented in this project as a stepping-stone to bigger and better projects that require even more backend functionality.

How are we going to do it?

We'll approach this project much as we have in the previous chapters:

- ▸ Configuring Parse
- ▸ Modifying the Options view
- ▸ Submitting scores

- ▸ Displaying scores
- ▸ Modifying the Start view

Configuring Parse

There are a few steps that one needs to do in order to have the app communicate with Parse's servers. This enables real-time analytics for us, but also allows Parse to know how their products are being used (and whether or not we need to be billed for our use).

Getting on with it

First, let's navigate to `www.parse.com`:

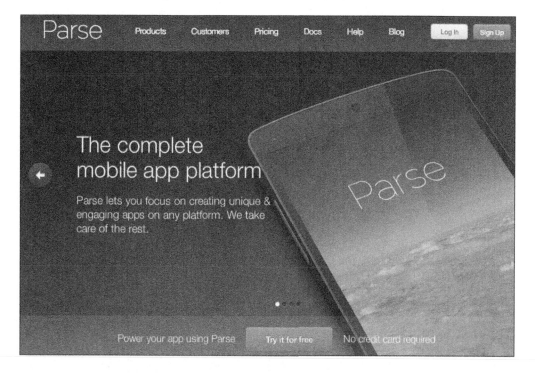

If you've already got an account, simply log in as usual. Otherwise, click on **Sign Up** to create an account. You will see the following screen:

Follow the signing up process, and when done, you will be asked to create your very first app. If you've just logged on, however, you can create a new app by clicking on the **+ Create New App** button in the upper-right of the window, as shown in the following screenshot:

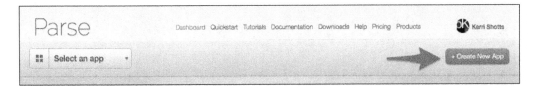

At this point, you should have the following screen:

Type in an app name (in our case, we used `CaveRunner`), and then click on **Create app**. The following screen will appear:

At this point, you need to copy the **Application ID** and **Javascript Key** values (pointed to by arrows in the prior screenshot). You'll need them later in this chapter. If you don't want to copy them now, you can always access them later from within Parse.

Now, click on the **Data Browser** button, and you should be presented with the following screen:

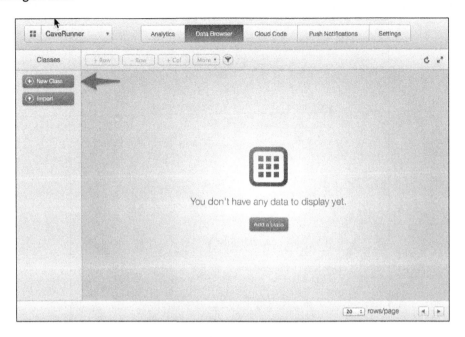

Now, let's create a new table, or class, as Parse calls it. Technically, we don't have to do this; Parse's API will lazily create this for us when our code runs. However, I find that it helps to define this up-front so that any errors will be caught immediately, rather than detecting after the data has already been stored in the table.

Click on **New Class** (indicated by the arrow in the prior screenshot). You should be presented with something like what is shown in the following screenshot (we've already filled in the fields):

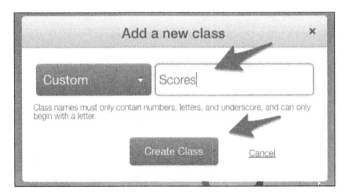

Enter a name for the table (we used `Scores`). Make sure the dropdown next to this field is set to **Custom**. Then click on **Create Class**. You should then see that the `Scores` table has been added in the left-hand list (indicated by a circle in the following screenshot):

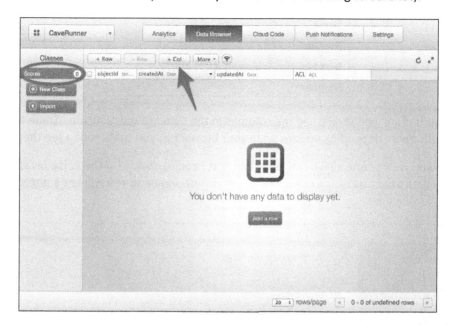

Now, we need to add columns. Click on **+ Col** (indicated by an arrow in the prior screenshot) and you will see the following screenshot:

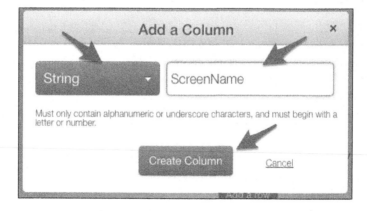

Change the dropdown to **String** and give the column a name of `ScreenName`. Then, click on **Create Column**.

Repeat the same procedure for the following columns:

Type	Name
String	ControlType
Number	HighestLevel
Number	TotalDistance
Number	Score

When this is done, you should see the columns in the data browser's header. Some fields may be offscreen; depending on how wide your browser is, you can scroll to see them all.

At this point, we've done all we can here. We next need to download the Parse Javascript SDK. Navigate to `https://parse.com/docs/downloads` and you will see a page similar to the following one:

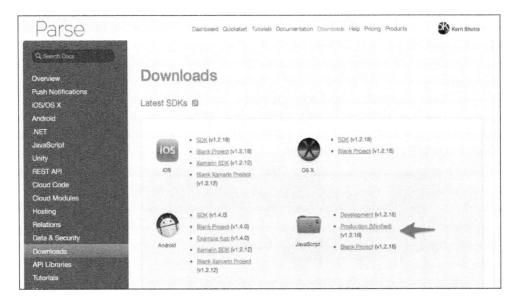

Right-click on the **Production (Minified)** link and save it to your project's `www/js/lib` `directory as parse.min.js` file. Alternatively, you can use the version in the template in the code package of this book.

Next, we need to indicate to the app that it should load this library. Open up `www/index.` `html` and add the following line just prior to the `script` tag that loads `RequireJS`:

```
<script type="text/javascript" src="js/lib/parse.min.js"></script>
```

Although this will load the library, it doesn't actually do anything yet; we need to initialize the library with our **Application ID** and **JavaScript Key**. Open `www/js/app.js` and add the following line just before `document.addEventListener( "deviceready", …)`:

```
Parse.initialize("YourApplicationID","YourJavascriptKey");
```

Now, our app is ready to work with Parse.

What did we do?

In this section, we created an account with Parse (if you didn't already have one). We created an app and retrieved its **Application ID** and **JavaScript Key** values, which are required in order for our app to interface with Parse's servers. Finally, we downloaded the SDK, loaded the script, and initialized the library.

What else do I need to know?

Communication with Parse assumes the ability to contact Parse's servers. This does mean that the Internet needs to be accessible. Thankfully, Parse does a good job not failing loudly in this particular context, but it does mean that any data sent to Parse while offline is not saved. (In our particular instance, it really isn't important if we submit a score or not. In a different app, you might need to notify the user that they needed to be online, or you might instead want to cache the data until the next time the user is online.)

What's also important is the concept of domain whitelists in Cordova. By default, apps come with the whitelist set to allow access to every domain; however, in a production-level app, you should restrict these domains to only those required to run the app. For more information, visit `http://cordova.apache.org/docs/en/edge/guide_appdev_whitelist_index.md.html#Whitelist%20Guide`.

Modifying the Options view

At this point, we're nearly ready to start using Parse. However, before we can, we need a mechanism to identify players; simply submitting a score does no good if there isn't a name attached to it. Furthermore, we should be certain that users want to participate in this global leader-board. As such, we need to modify the Options view so that it can allow the user to choose a screen name and opt-in to the submission of scores online.

When done, we'll have a view that looks like what is shown in the following screenshot:

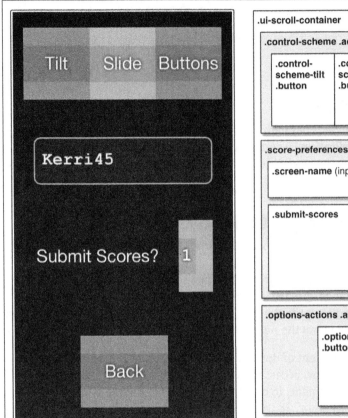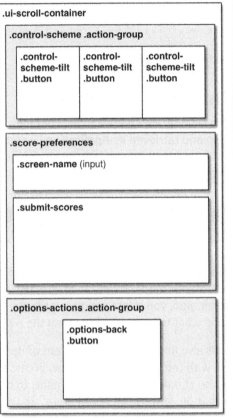

Getting on with it

This requires work in every file related to the Options view. Let's start in the template at `www/html/optionsView.html`. I've highlighted the changes:

```html
<html>
  <body>
    <div class="ui-scroll-container">
      <div class="control-scheme action-group">
        <div class="control-scheme-tilt button">%TILT%</div>
        <div class="control-scheme-slide button">%SLIDE%</div>
        <div class="control-scheme-buttons button">%BUTTONS%</div>
      </div>
      <div class="score-preferences">
```

```
        <input class="screen-name" type="text" size=10
placeholder="%SCREEN_NAME%" />
        <div class="submit-scores">%SUBMIT_SCORES%</div>
      </div>
      <div class="options-actions action-group">
        <div class="options-back button">%BACK%</div>
      </div>
    </div>
  </body>
</html>
```

So far, nothing difficult. We do change the container to use a scroll container, because we're asking for text later on. We need to be scrollable should the soft keyboard shorten our view significantly. Otherwise, everything's pretty self-explanatory.

What may not be obvious is how the **Submit Scores** item works. Essentially, it's a toggle switch. Two states are shown as follows:

Off; don't submit   On; submit

Next, let's work on the styling in www/css/style.css—there have been some changes, but most of it is self-explanatory. You can see all the changes by looking at the code package of the book, but in the following section, we'll only focus on the interesting changes.

The first interesting styles are those that create the appearance of the Screen Name text box. Notice the appearance:none rule; this prevents the browser from supplying its own styling for an input box (which usually adds some styling and borders). If we didn't do this, our styles will clash with the default appearance of an input field. Also, notice that we enable text selection using user-select:none; without it, the text inside the input field is unselectable. This is not something that a user expects.

```
.optionsView .score-preferences .screen-name {
  -webkit-appearance: none;
  appearance: none;
```

```
    background-color: rgba(48, 48, 48, 0.5);
    border: 2px solid rgba(192,255,128, 0.75);
    border-radius: 10px;
    color: white;
    font-size: 25px;
    font-family: "Courier New", Arial, sans-serif;
    padding-left: 10px; padding-right: 10px;
    line-height: 50px;
    width: 100%;
    margin-bottom: 50px;
    box-sizing: border-box;
    font-weight: bold;
    display: inline-block;
    width: 40%;
    min-width: 260px;
    -webkit-user-select: text;
    user-select: text;
}
```

To simulate an on-off switch, we add a pseudo-element to `submit-scores` DIV that is colored red and has `0` (the universal "off" symbol) inside:

```
.optionsView .score-preferences .submit-scores:before {
    position: absolute;
    right: 0;
    top: 0;
    border: 25px solid rgba(255, 64,128, 0.5);
    background-color: rgba(255, 64,128,0.75);
    border-right: 0;
    font-family: "Courier New", Arial, sans-serif;
    width: 25px;
    text-align: center;
    text-shadow: 0 0 5px black;
    font-weight: bold;
    content: '0';
}
```

However, if the element is on, we need to change the color and use `1` as the `content`, as shown in the following code snippet:

```
.optionsView .score-preferences .submit-scores.selected:before
{
border: 25px solid rgba(192,255,128, 0.5);
background-color: rgba(192,255,128,0.75);
```

```
border-left: 0;
content: '1';
}
```

Now, let's work on the code in www/js/app/views/optionsView.js. There's not a lot that's new (and most of it is fairly obvious), so we'll only cover the interesting portions.

The first interesting method is updateScorePreferences, where we update the visual elements with the stored preferences in localStorage. This handles the **Submit Scores?** on-off switch by adding a selected class if the value is YES, as shown in the following code snippet:

```
self.updateScorePreferences = function () {
  if (typeoflocalStorage.screenName !== "undefined") {
    self._screenName.value = localStorage.screenName;
  }
  self._submitScores.classList.remove ("selected");
  if (typeoflocalStorage.submitScores !== "undefined") {
    if (localStorage.submitScores == "YES") {
      self._submitScores.classList.add ("selected");
    }
  }
}
```

When the user taps on the **Submit Scores?** on-off switch, it needs to toggle the state, as shown in the following code snippet:

```
self.toggleSubmitScores = function () {
  var selected = self._submitScores.classList.contains
    ("selected");
  selected = !selected;
  localStorage.submitScores = selected ? "YES" : "NO";
  self.updateScorePreferences();
}
```

When the user edits their screen name, it should be saved immediately.

```
self.saveScreenName = function () {
  localStorage.screenName = self._screenName.value;
}
```

To handle the screen name update, we attach a listener to the screen name text box so that when the focus leaves, the value is saved inside (in renderToElement) as shown in the following code snippet:

```
self._screenName = self.element.querySelector (".screen-name");
self._screenName.addEventListener ( "blur", self.saveScreenName );
```

We also need to add the event handler to toggle the submission of scores, shown as follows:

```
self._submitScores = self.element.querySelector
  (".submit-scores");
Hammer (self._submitScores).on("tap",
  self.toggleSubmitScores);
```

At the end of `renderToElement`, we force our first update so that the values are there when the view appears, shown as follows:

```
self.updateScorePreferences();
```

What did we do?

In this task, we modified the Options view by adding a field that indicates the user's screen name. Initially, this field is blank, but the user can put any value they want in it. We also added an on-off switch for the submission of scores. By default this is off, but the user can opt-in by tapping it. We also converted the view into a scrollable view in case the soft keyboard overlaps a portion of our view.

What else do I need to know?

You might be asking why we simply don't assume that the player wants to participate in the leader-board. The reason is privacy. Perhaps they are terrible at the game and don't want to be embarrassed, or perhaps they're just wary of online services in general. Either way, always respect the privacy of your users when it comes to sending information online and allow them to either opt in or out of the service.

To fully respect privacy, we should probably add a second option that will disable Parse completely by not even executing `Parse.initialize` in the first place.

Furthermore, in a production app that is distributed to others, always create a privacy policy and post it on your website or in the app store. Some stores will require a privacy policy just to list your app.

Submitting scores

When the game is over, we need to submit a score to Parse. For all the complicated work going on underneath the surface, this is deceptively simple.

Getting on with it

In order to submit scores, we need to add a method to our Game view (www/js/app/views/gameView.js) named _reportScore, shown as follows:

```
self._reportScore = function () {
  // verify submitScores is set in localStorage
  if (typeof localStorage.submitScores !== "undefined") {
    // if it is, check if it is set to YES
    if (localStorage.submitScores == "YES") {
      // if we're supposed to submit scores, check
      // if the user has set their screen name
      if (typeof localStorage.screenName !== "undefined") {
        if (localStorage.screenName !== null) {
          // Set the screen name (trim it just in case)
          var screenName = localStorage.screenName.trim();
          // get the player's score
          var score = Math.floor(self._score);
          // and the highest level obtained
          var highestLevel = self._currentLevel;
          // and calculate the total distance (including the
          // distance the user must have travelled in prior
          // levels.
          var totalDistance = Math.floor(
            self._currentTop/self._segmentLength);
          for (var i=0; i< (highestLevel-1); i++) {
            totalDistance += Math.floor(600+(125*(i+1)) );
          }
          totalDistance = Math.floor(totalDistance *
          self._segmentLength) + 30;
          // get the name of the control type
          var controlType = self._controlSchemesArray[
            self._controlScheme];
          // report the data, if the screen name isn't empty
          if ( screenName !== "" ) {
            // create a new class based on the Scores table
            var GameScore = Parse.Object.extend("Scores");
            // create a new object based on that class
            var gameScore = new GameScore();
            // and set the data (these are the same fields
            // we created earlier
            gameScore.set ( "ScreenName", screenName );
            gameScore.set ( "Score", score );
            gameScore.set ( "HighestLevel", highestLevel );
```

```
                    gameScore.set ( "TotalDistance", totalDistance ) ;
                    gameScore.set ( "ControlType", controlType ) ;
                    // and save to Parse
                    gameScore.save( null,
                      { success: function ( gameScore ) {
                          console.log ( "Saved Score!") ;
                        },
                        error: function ( gameScore, error ) {
                          console.log ( error ) ; }
                      } ) ;
                  }
                }
              }
            }
          }
        }
```

We also need to add one line near the top of the Game view class, under `self._` `controlSchemes={…}`, as shown in the following code:

```
    self._controlSchemesArray =[ "slide", "tilt", "buttons" ] ;
```

This lets us get from the numeric `_controlScheme` (which is 0, 1, or 2) back to a human-readable value for the database. (We could have stored this number instead, but it's easier to read the data without having to interpret this number each time.)

Next, we need to actually call `_reportScore`. There are two places we should do this. In `self.goBack()` (but only if we've actually been playing), use the following code:

```
    self.goBack = function () {
      if (self._currentLevel> 0) {
        self._reportScore() ;
      }
      self.navigationController.popView() ;
    }
```

In `self._doUpdate()`, when we crash, use the following code:

```
    if (shipCollided) {
      self._actionButton.innerHTML = _y.T("TRY_AGAIN") ;
      self._showMessage (_y.T('CRASHED')) ;
      gameOver = true;
      self._reportScore() ;
      self._currentLevel = 0;
    }
```

That's it! You should be able to run the app on your device, enter your screen name, opt-in to submitting your score, and then play a few times. Each time you finish the game, your score will be sent to Parse.

You can verify this by refreshing the Parse Data Browser. Your scores should be recorded there.

What did we do?

In this section, we modified the Game view so that it will submit a score when a game is finished.

What else do I need to know?

The Parse SDK documentation is quite good, and it covers a lot more than what we'll be going over in this chapter. Learn more about working with Parse by visiting `https://parse.com/docs/js_guide`.

Displaying scores

Submitting scores is great, but the whole point is to be able to compare ourselves against the rest of the world. To do that, we need to create a new view: the High Scores view. When done, it will look like what is shown in the following screenshot:

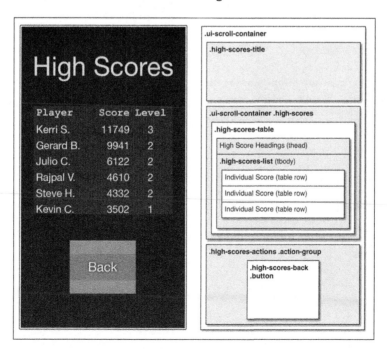

Just for full disclosure, all these scores are mine and not of the people mentioned in the preceding screenshot. This is just a nice shout-out to some of those who have been involved with the book.

Getting on with it

First, let's create a couple of templates. The main template will be for the view, while each particular score will have a simpler template.

In `www/html/highScoresView.html`, let's create a template for view:

```html
<html>
  <body>
    <div class="ui-scroll-container">
      <div class="high-scores-title">%HIGH_SCORES%</div>
        <div class="ui-scroll-container high-scores">
          <table class="high-scores-table">
            <thead>
              <tr><th width="25%" align="left">%PLAYER%</th>
                <th width="25%" align="right">%SCORE%</th>
                <th width="25%" align="center">%LEVEL%</th>
                <th width="25%" align="right">%DISTANCE%</th>
              </tr>
            </thead>
            <tbody class="high-scores-list">
            </tbody>
          </table>
        </div>
      <div class="high-scores-actions action-group">
        <div class="high-scores-back button">%BACK%</div>
      </div>
    </div>
  </body>
</html>
```

This view defines a title at the top of the view and a table underneath. This table is initially blank, but we'll fill it with scores later. At the bottom of the view, there is a **Back** button.

Next, let's define the template for a single score in `www/html/highScoreItem.html`, shown as follows:

```html
<html>
  <body>
    <tr>
```

```
      <td>%SCREEN_NAME%</td>
      <td align="right">%SCORE%</td>
      <td align="center">%LEVEL%</td>
      <td align="right">%DISTANCE%</td>
    </tr>
  </body>
</html>
```

All this requires some styling, so let's modify our style sheet in www/css/style.css shown as follows:

```
.startView, .optionsView, .gameView, .highScoresView {
  background-color: #081020;
  background-image: -webkit-linear-gradient(top, rgb(0, 0, 0) 0%,
rgb(16, 32, 64) 100%);
}
...
.highScoresView .high-scores-title {
  font-size: 50px;
  text-align: center;
  color: yellow;
  margin-top: 50px;  margin-bottom: 50px;
  line-height: 50px;
}
.highScoresView .high-scores-actions.action-group {
  bottom: 65px;
}
.highScoresView .ui-scroll-container.high-scores {
  background-color: rgba(255, 255, 255, 0.125);
  left: 25px; right: 25px;
  top: 150px; bottom: 215px;
}
.highScoresView .high-scores-table {
  color: white;
  width: 100%;
}
.highScoresView .high-scores-table td,
.highScoresView .high-scores-table th {
  padding: 5px;
}
.highScoresView .high-scores-table th {
  font-family: "Courier New", Arial, Sans-serif;
  font-weight: bold;
  color: yellow;
}
```

Next, we need to write the code in www/js/app/views/highScoresView.js. Most of this is old hat by now, so we'll only focus on the interesting portions of code. The rest are available in the code package of this book.

When the view appears, getHighScores will be called to get the high scores from Parse, shown as follows:

```
self.getHighScores = function () {
  // Create a class from the Scores table
  var GameScore = Parse.Object.extend("Scores");
  // create a query from this class
  var query = new Parse.Query( GameScore );
  // determine which control method the player is using
  var controlType = "slide";
  if (typeof localStorage.controlScheme !== "undefined") {
    controlType = localStorage.controlScheme;
  }
  // get all the scores with the same control type
  query.equalTo ( "ControlType", controlType );
  // and sort by the score (in descending order)
  query.descending ( "Score" );
  // but only get the top 20 results:
  query.limit ( 20 );
  // run the search...
  query.find()
  .then( function (results) {
    // and fill the high scores table with the
    // results
    self._highScoresList.innerHTML =
    results.reduce (
      function ( previousValue, currentValue,
      index, array ) {
        return previousValue +=
        _y.template(highScoreItemHTML,
        {"SCREEN_NAME":
          currentValue.get("ScreenName"),
          "CONTROL":
          currentValue.get("ControlType"),
```

```
        "LEVEL":
        currentValue.get("HighestLevel"),
        "DISTANCE":
        currentValue.get("TotalDistance"),
        "SCORE":
        Math.max(0,currentValue.get("Score"))
      });
    }, "" );
  });
}
```

In `init`, we add a listener for `viewWillAppear` so that we can request the high scores when the view appears. Consider the following code snippet:

```
self.addListenerForNotification("viewWillAppear", self.getHighScores);
```

What did we do?

In this task, we created a new view that requests a list of the highest scores from Parse and then displays that to the user.

What else do I need to know?

Without Internet access, of course, the list remains blank. In a production app, you should probably indicate an error of some sort rather than the user wondering if the leader-board is simply broken.

Also, note that the results returned by Parse may be estimates in some cases (especially regarding counts of rows), depending on how much data Parse has to process. The Parse documentation fully details when this might occur.

Modifying the Start view

At this point, you could run the app on your device and play the game, but you wouldn't be able to see the high scores. In order for that to work, we need to modify the Start view a little. When done, it'll look like what is shown in the following screenshot:

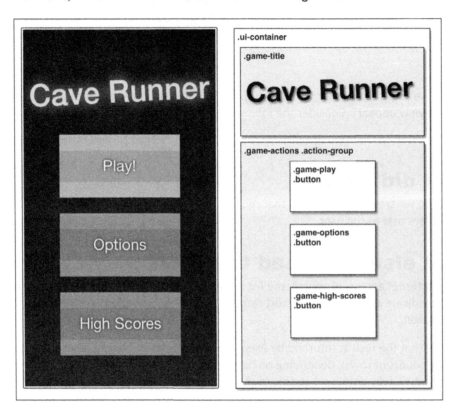

Getting on with it

First, we need to modify the template a little bit (in `www/html/startView.html`), shown as follows:

```
<html>
  <body>
    <div class="ui-container">
      <div class="game-title">%APP_TITLE%</div>
      <div class="game-actions action-group">
        <div class="game-play button">%PLAY%</div>
```

```
        <div class="game-options button">%OPTIONS%</div>
        <div class="game-high-scores button">%HIGH_SCORES%</div>
      </div>
    </div>
  </body>
</html>
```

Next, we need to adjust the styling a little bit in www/css/style.css, since we now need to display the three buttons differently on small screens. Consider the following code snippet:

```css
.startView .action-group {
  bottom: 25px;
  height: auto;
}

.startView .game-play {
  border: 25px solid rgba(192,255,128, 0.5);
  background-color: rgba(192,255,128,0.75);
  border-left: 0; border-right: 0;
}

.startView .action-group .button {
  width: 90%;
  max-width: 200px;
  margin-bottom: 25px;
}
```

Of course, we need to modify the code in www/js/app/views/startView.js to display the high scores when asked; it's all very straightforward. As such, you can take a look at the code package of the book for the changes we made.

What did we do?

In this section, we modified the Start view so that we can display the high scores whenever the user wants to view it.

Game Over..... Wrapping it up

Compared to the effort we would have had to have put forth in the past in order to create a backend capable of supporting our app, what we just did was essentially a piece of cake—thanks to Parse and a well-designed SDK. We've just scratched the surface of what Parse can do for our app; the possibilities are limitless!

Can you take the HEAT? The Hotshot Challenge

There are several ways this project could be improved; why don't you try one or more of them?

- ▸ Add an achievements system like Game Center or Open Feint
- ▸ Add a way to match up against other players
- ▸ If you want a real challenge, create a multiplayer mode where both players receive the same level and can see each other's ship on the screen
- ▸ Add a local high score chart as well so that the player can see their own score history
- ▸ Use some analytics to rate the player based on the global scores, for example, "You rank 152 out of 893 players"

User Interface Resources

While it is important for your app to be unique and stand out from the crowd, it is also important to realize that some things are already pretty standardized, and that there is no need to reinvent the wheel. For example, when building a sign-in screen, you know you need to ask for a username or an e-mail ID and a password—that's because this has become a pretty standard design pattern, and users are familiar with it from their various experiences with websites and other apps. There are many sites that provide examples of these patterns, and they can often be a source of inspiration as well.

Of course, as a hybrid app, your user interface is not actually native. That means you have to rely on a framework to provide the basic look and feel (or build your own look and feel from scratch). This appendix provides links to various frameworks and UI libraries that you might find useful, as well as links to sites that describe the implementation of various controls from scratch.

Finally, it's also critical to respect the guidelines for your target platform's human interface (especially when targeting iOS).

Flat versus skeuomorphic

If there's one thing all the current platforms have in common, it's their relative flatness. Whereas iPhones were initially full of realistic textures, knobs, push buttons, and so on, the modern platforms are much flatter.

During the transition to visually flat platforms, the prior platforms were often described as overly skeuomorphic. Apple's Game Center and Calendar apps were often paraded as excellent examples of this due to their felt and leather textures, respectively. While it served as a rallying cry, it is important to recognize that the modern platforms have not actually abandoned skeuomorphism—only the often over-baked textures that accompanied it.

A skeuomorph is simply a representation of a real, physical object; this helps users feel more at home when using the app. When presented with a knob, button, or switch, users know that it can be turned, pushed, or toggled, respectively. None of the modern platforms have abandoned these concepts. Furthermore, many app designs still feature skeuomorphs as well—calculator and calendar apps being prime examples.

Therefore, when designing your app, don't completely eschew skeuomorphism. When used properly, it can give your users instant insight into how your app works. Use it with care, however, an improper skeuomorph is perhaps worse than none at all.

Human Interface/Design Guidelines

It is vital to follow the **Human Interface Guidelines (HIG)** for your platform. On some platforms (such as Apple's iOS), failure to follow the HIG is grounds for rejection of your app. No matter what you feel about it, the HIG is designed to ensure that all apps have some degree of consistency and user friendliness. The HIG isn't there to pound you into submission, rather for legitimately good (and well-thought-out) reasons.

See these guides for more information:

- Apple's iOS HIG:

  ```
  http://developer.apple.com/library/ios/#documentation/
  UserExperience/Conceptual/MobileHIG/Introduction/Introduction.
  html
  ```

- Android's UI Guidelines:

  ```
  http://developer.android.com/guide/practices/ui_guidelines/
  index.html
  ```

Should you target another platform not covered in this book, you'll want to search for the corresponding HIG. It may not always be named quite the same, but every platform has something similar, even if it isn't enforced to the same degree as Apple's.

Mobile pattern references

Patterns are incredibly useful. They allow us to standardize common practices and appearances and can relieve the developer of having to reinvent the wheel continuously. Of course, there are situations where you'll need to develop your own patterns for your app (depending on what it does), but you might be surprised how often a pattern that meets your specific needs has already been developed.

Don't copy a pattern's visual design pixel for pixel; you'll almost certainly need to tweak the design elements to fit in with your app's design language. If you don't, your app may end up feeling like a hodgepodge of various screens with no unifying thread.

The following websites are great resources for pattern discovery and inspiration:

Websites	Platforms	Form factors	Notes
http://www.mobile-patterns. com/	iOS, Android	iPhone, Phone	No commentary, searchable, actual screenshots
http://inspired-ui.com/	iOS, Android	iPhone, iPad, Phone	No commentary, searchable, actual screenshots
http://pttrns.com/	iOS	iPhone, iPad	iOS 7 section, no commentary, searchable, actual screenshots, zoom loupe
http://www.mobiletuxedo. com/category/ui-patterns/	iOS, Android	iPhone, Phone	No commentary, not searchable, actual screenshots, other resources
http://www.androidpatterns. com	Android	Phone	Searchable, commentary, mockups
http://androidux.com	Android	Phone	Not searchable, actual screenshots, fail section
http:// mobiledesignpatterngallery. com/mobile-patterns.php	iOS, Android, Windows, Web	Varies	Not searchable, actual screenshots, anti-patterns
http://www.game-patterns. com	Varies	Varies	Game-related, searchable

User interface frameworks/libraries

When crafting hybrid apps, we are responsible for the entire look and feel of the app, often needing to combine CSS, HTML, and JavaScript in complicated ways. Use of YASMF in this book has simplified a lot of the typical boilerplate code, but YASMF does not implement every possible user interface widget, and it is still rather new. If you'd prefer another user interface framework, these are some that I found interesting and promising. Most of the following are more than simply user-interface frameworks. Many are app frameworks as well, which implies learning how each framework manages views and the application state:

- **Framework 7** (`http://www.idangero.us/framework7/`): This is an iOS 7-specific framework with awesome transitions and good performance.

- **Chocolate Chip UI** (`http://chocolatechip-ui.com`): This is a cross-platform framework with updated visuals for iOS 7, Android Jelly Bean, and WP8.

- **Fries** (`http://getfri.es`): This is an Android-specific framework.

- **Kendo UI** (`http://www.telerik.com/kendo-ui`): This is a cross-platform framework with open source and professional versions.

- **Sencha Touch** (`http://www.sencha.com/products/touch/`): This is a cross-platform framework with built-in support for Cordova.

- **Intel App Framework** (`http://app-framework-software.intel.com`): This is a cross-platform framework, and was previously known as jqMobi.

- **jQuery Mobile** (`http://jquerymobile.com`): This is a cross-platform framework based on jQuery. Be careful with this one—it can be nice, but it does tend not to perform as well as the other frameworks.

- **Zepto JS** (`http://zeptojs.com`): This is not a UI framework, but useful as a lightweight jQuery replacement in order to gain some performance.

User interface tips

Often, the details are what matter. Here are some tips to help make sure you have not only a great-looking app but also a great-feeling one. Consider the following points:

- Avoid novel or undiscoverable interactions. Or, if you do want to use such interactions, try to provide a second discoverable method to achieve the same thing. We could argue that the slide menu in Facebook is novel, but the gesture should be discoverable: the button that triggers the menu is highly visible and likely to be tapped.

▸ Respect your users' expectations of what UI elements and gestures do. At first, this seems obvious; you wouldn't send an e-mail by clicking on a trash can. That said, there are plenty of ways you can do things, even in a subtle manner, that your users didn't expect. Your users' expectations are highly specific to the platform, so following your platform's HIG will help out significantly in this area.

▸ Do blend in. By this I mean that your app should look like it belongs on your user's device. That is, your app should respect the HIG for the platform. It also means your app needs to have the appearance of a native app. Failing to do so may cause your users to feel like your app is a second-class citizen. Even with a native appearance, your app should also do its best to *feel* native; that is, it should have the speed and response time close to that of a native app. (It may not always be easy, or even possible, on some platforms using Cordova. In this case, you should try to get as close as you can, without impacting your project and its timeline.)

▸ Be a perfectionist. By this I mean that you should make sure that all your objects align well, your textures blend seamlessly, images are scaled correctly (especially according to the aspect ratio), and so on. This requires painstaking attention to detail; however, eventually, your app will look and feel better.

▸ Be responsive. Whenever possible, avoid freezing the user interface. If you must freeze the UI, then put up an indicator to the user so they know their inputs will be ignored. When it comes to being responsive, this isn't simply about being responsive to a tap on a button, it also includes scrolling performance. If an app scrolls in a herky-jerky fashion, the app will feel slow.

▸ Sip your data. While your app may often be used on a Wi-Fi connection, don't forget about users who may have to deal with a cellular connection instead. Their connections may not just be slower, but they are usually under pretty onerous data caps. Cache extensively. Avoid downloading what you've already downloaded. If it can be compressed, by all means, compress it. Alternatively, give your user an "out," if your app is going to use a lot of data no matter what. You might want to let them disable the portions of your app that use a lot of data when on a cellular connection.

▸ Properly handle "no data" situations. Unless your app ships with all the data it ever needs, there may be times when there isn't any data to display. In a social network app, for example, the network may be down. In a content-generation app, the user may not have generated any content yet. In each case, your app should handle the situation as best as it can. For example, if the user needs to do something first, indicate that in place of an empty view.

B

Tips, Tricks, and Quirks

Even though we've been building apps specifically for Cordova/PhoneGap, there are still numerous differences between platforms and between operating systems within the platforms. Especially with Android, it's common for quirks to be present only on a particular brand, for example, an app might render oddly on an HTC smartphone but work perfectly on a Samsung device. It's impossible to test every configuration in cases like these, but it's worth documenting issues when you find them.

Tips

These tips are things I've encountered while working on this book and while writing other Cordova/PhoneGap apps. There's no real common theme here, but it might help save you a few minutes should you encounter the same problem in the future.

Prevent highlighting and outlines when tapping

Mobile browsers are not like desktop browsers. This may sound obvious at first glance, but mobile browsers have to deal with large, squishy fingers, whereas most desktops still use mice or trackpads which have much greater accuracy. This means that it is easier to tap on the wrong item when using a mobile browser. It can also be more difficult to know when a tap has been registered.

To accommodate this profound difference between mobile and desktop browsers, mobile browsers offer affordances to users so that they know that, yes, their tap was registered, and that this is what they tapped. This is usually done by highlighting the element with a specific color or outlining the element in a color, or both.

While it is important for native apps to have affordances, the browser doesn't typically render the affordance in the way the user would like. Some of this can be changed (the color can be modified, for example), but more often than not, the affordance rendered by the browser does not match the designer's vision.

There is a fix, however, to disable these browser-driven affordances. Remember, though, that you should provide your own affordances when applicable if you turn these browser affordances off globally.

These rules can disable both the highlight and outline affordances. Remember to add the browser prefixes in your code as follows:

```
tap-highlight-color: rgba(0,0,0,0);
tap-highlight-color: transparent;
outline: none;
```

To apply these rules globally, you can attach them to the `body` element in your CSS. For most native apps, this is what you'll generally want.

 The transparent rule is for some Android devices. See `http://phonegap-tips.com/articles/essential-phonegap-css-webkit-tap-highlight-color.html`.

Include affordances

Now that we've essentially removed all the affordances provided by the browser, we need to add some back for the sake of user experience. Generally, these include changing the text or background color of buttons and list items.

As long as the item in question has an event handler registered that uses a `touchstart` event, you can create CSS rules using the `active` pseudo-element as follows:

```
.ui-list-item:active {
  background-color: blue;
}
```

Prevent unwanted text selection

Native interfaces generally don't allow users to include user-interface widgets inside selections. By default, however, the mobile browser used by Cordova/PhoneGap will permit this, resulting in a decidedly odd experience.

To turn it off globally, attach the following to the `body` element:

```
user-select: none;
```

For elements that need to support selection (such as actual content or text inputs), replace `none` with `text`.

Improve text rendering

By default, the mobile browser renders text fairly poorly; it doesn't support ligatures, kerning, or the like. However, you can enable this feature to use better typography in the app (for fonts that support it). Again, attach to the body element as follows:

```
text-rendering: optimizeLegibility;
```

That said, this shouldn't be used on Android devices, since some versions don't calculate the text boundaries correctly. For Android, turn it back off as follows:

```
body.android {
  text-rendering: auto !important;
}
```

Use native scrolling

On a desktop, one would typically use `overflow: scroll` or `overflow: auto` to make certain elements scrollable. This works to a degree on most mobile devices, but the experience is decidedly non-native on iOS. For example, there may not be inertial scrolling or rubber-banding effects.

To enable this on iOS 5 and above, add the following to any scrollable container:

```
-webkit-overflow-scrolling: touch;
```

Keep in mind that native scrolling of this form works only on iOS 5 and higher. It doesn't hurt to use the property on Android devices (or any WebKit browser) since if the browser doesn't know what to do with it, it will ignore the property.

If Android is not using native scrolling, try this:

For Android platforms, adding a z-index to the scrollable area may trigger native-feeling scrolling if Android wasn't applying it before. It's possible anything that creates a new stacking context may also force the issue (so `position:absolute` may also work).

Use a scrolling library

If you can't use native scrolling or need to support a platform where you need to offer a fallback, use a scrolling library.

There are several available, but I can't recommend iScroll enough, it's not perfect (no scrolling library ever is), but it's the closest I've seen and supports a wide variety of platforms. You can get it at `https://github.com/cubiq/iscroll`.

Use 3D transforms to use the GPU

When you add a 3D transform to an element, it will use the GPU to composite the element instead of the software renderer. This can improve performance during animations and scrolling, but it does come at a cost: memory. This works best on items that aren't more than four times (or so) the size of the screen—more than this may cause visual artifacts (as the GPU must use tiling to draw the element).

There are a couple of methods you can use. The first one is as follows:

```
transform: translateZ(0);
```

Alternatively, you can use:

```
transform: translate3d(0,0,0);
```

When using 3D transforms, hide the backface

You may notice that elements flicker when using the GPU. If this is the case, hide the back face:

```
backface-visibility: hidden;
```

Remember perspective while using the GPU

Even though 3D transforms don't automatically default to rendering elements with perspective like in a 3D game, perspective itself is still used. This means that when animating elements over each other, it's possible that you may see elements being rendered in the wrong order. Your first instinct will be to add `z-index`, which is fine for non-GPU elements, but it won't do anything when using the GPU. Instead, use a specific z-value to ensure that the element renders closer to the user than those behind it. For example, consider the following code snippet:

```
z-index:9;
transform: translateZ(9px);
```

The `z-index` here has no specific save function to make it clear that this element is intended to render above other elements. The actual work, however, is accomplished by the `translateZ(9px)` portion—this renders the element `9px` closer to the user's view than other elements. Since there's no perspective, there's no apparent change in size as elements move along the *z*( )axis, so the user doesn't notice, but the browser rendering engine surely does.

Use click prevention or prevent default actions

It's possible that you may encounter what seem to be spurious events occurring immediately after a tap (or other gesture) that invokes a navigation animation. There are a couple ways around this:

▸ **Use a "click prevention" DIV**: This `DIV` is put up prior to the animation once the gesture is detected and is removed from the `DIV` after the navigation is complete. This `DIV` is told to fill the entire screen and is transparent, so the user never sees it, but the DOM won't pass events below it. If you inspect YASMF's Navigation Controller, you'll notice that it throws up a click prevention `DIV` during a view navigation animation for this very reason.

▸ **Prevent the default browser action**: This works as well, if not better, than the prior, since it doesn't involve manipulating the DOM. `Hammer.js` makes this really easy to do—one can enable it by passing `prevent_default:true` as an option, as shown in the following code:

```
Hammer(contentsElement, { prevent_default:true }).on("tap",
function (e) {} _;
```

Complex effects hinder performance

Although most modern devices come with powerful GPUs, this hasn't always been the case. Even with GPUs, it's still pretty easy to bog down the compositor so that performance lags and stalls.

There's no one-size-fits-all fix to handle this, though. Here are some general pointers, however:

- **Avoid using gradients**: The gradients take time to compute.
- **Avoid scaling images**: The interpolation of an image is painfully slow.
- **Avoid shadows**: These require underlying elements to be composited first, and then the shadow to be composited on top. This takes time. Additionally, any blur in the shadow has to be calculated.
- **Avoid partial transparency**: Like shadows, this requires composition. It's a little faster, since the shadow blur doesn't have to be calculated.
- **Avoid rounded corners**: Creating rounded corners requires computations.
- **Avoid a lot of elements in the DOM**: The more the elements in the DOM that have events or need to be positioned by the browser, the slower things run due to the required calculations. This means that you shouldn't ever attach an event handler to a DOM element that doesn't need it (even if it does something cool), and you should limit the amount of positioning calculations the browser has to go through.

Audio/video file extensions matter

Although one would hope that things have progressed to the point where the file type could be inferred from the file itself, we're still sadly stuck with the fact that file extensions matter. Therefore, don't create a video file with a `.video` extension, or an audio file with a `.audio` extension. This will fail, simply because the extension is important in determining how to parse the file.

Instead, use the proper file extensions. The extensions we used in this book are as follows:

Platform	Audio	Video
Android	`.3gp`	`.3gp`
iOS	`.wav`	`.mov`

Careful with XHR/AJAX status values

When working with XHR status values, especially when dealing with content on the local filesystem, be sure to handle both `0` and `200` return values. Different platforms return different values for a successful operation.

Android quirks

There are simply some things that go wrong when you least expect it on Android, and it can feel like you're always down on your luck since you never know when an Android device is going to come along that totally messes with your app. We can't cover every device, obviously, nor every quirk, but here are some of the ones I've run into.

SVG renderings for masks (<4.4)

For Android Versions lower than 4.4, you can't use SVG for masking. Attempting to do so results in a solid block of color.

For Android 4.4 and higher, the problem is solved, due to the new system browser.

Poor rendering for rounded corners (2.x)

Although it doesn't affect us greatly since we target Android 4.x in this book, it's still worth noting that Android 2.x doesn't apply anti-aliasing to rounded corners. This means they look horrible when compared to other platforms and operating system versions. Thankfully the problem was resolved in later versions, but 2.x still consumes a large portion of the market. If you're targeting those devices, it's worth recognizing.

Canvas artifacts (4.1x — 4.3.x)

It just so happens that if you run our game in *Project 11, Canvas Games and the Accelerometer*, and *Project 12, Building a Backend – Working with Parse*, on these particular versions of Android, you'll encounter the situation where the very first frame of the game is persisted underneath the actual game, even though we execute a `clearRect` on the canvas. We were unable to eliminate this artifact on our device (2012 Nexus 7), but you might have more luck with some of these potential fixes:

- https://medium.com/p/ffcb939af758
- https://code.google.com/p/android/issues/detail?id=35474
- http://stackoverflow.com/questions/13071528/html5-canvas-issues-on-android-4-1-1
- http://stackoverflow.com/questions/12804710/android-4-html5-canvas-not-redrawing
- http://stackoverflow.com/questions/13280195/phone-android-html5-hardware-acceleration-canvas

CSS animation artifacts (4.x; fixed for 4.4+)

If you run our game in *Project 11, Canvas Games and the Accelerometer*, and *Project 12, Building a Backend – Working with Parse*, on these particular versions of Android, you'll also encounter this issue. The title of the game animates correctly, but the non-animated version is also visible. Some of the fixes in the previous section work—the fix that worked immediately for us was to ensure `overflow: visible` on all parent elements. (Of course, this may result in other issues, such as scrolling of views that wasn't intended.)

Horrid canvas performance (4.4.x)

When Android 4.4 (KitKat) was released, great rejoicing occurred because the system web view was finally backed by Chromium. The hope was that this would alleviate a lot of the quirks of the old system web view (which was horribly out of date and broken in many places). Unfortunately, Google broke the Canvas element. Essentially it is not accelerated at all, and as such, it is next to useless for games that require anything more than about 4 or 5 frames per second.

There is, unfortunately, no fix. Google is aware of the issue, and hopefully, the problem will be fixed in a future Android release. You might have luck with Project Crosswalk (`https://crosswalk-project.org`). It can supply a hardware accelerated canvas to your Cordova app that should have much improved performance.

Blob support (<4.4)

Android Versions prior to 4.4 don't natively support easy creation of Blobs. You can use a polyfill that will provide this support without having to make changes to the rest of your code as shown in the following code snippet:

```
// Copyright (c) 2013 The Chromium Authors. All rights reserved.
// Use of this source code is governed by a BSD-style license that can be
// found in the LICENSE file.

// modification by KS for PhoneGap Hotshot
try {
  new Blob([]);
} catch (e) {
  var nativeBlob = window.Blob;
  var newBlob = function(parts, options) {
    if (window.WebKitBlobBuilder) {
      var bb = new WebKitBlobBuilder();
      if (parts && parts.length) {
        for (var i=0; i < parts.length; i++) {
          bb.append(parts[i]);
        }
```

```
    }
    if (options && options.type) {
      return bb.getBlob(options.type);
    }
    return bb.getBlob();
  }

  newBlob.prototype = nativeBlob.prototype;
  window.Blob = newBlob; // clobber the global
}
```

Floating input boxes

Some companies have decided to theme their flavor of Android, and this can occasionally cause problems. Older HTC devices tend to be a big problem: HTC re-themed the input boxes that the web view generates and then preceded to ignore any CSS applied. This often results in horrible renderings on these devices.

And there's no fix if you encounter a device with this problem. The only fix is to flash a new ROM that does away with HTC's theming, and most users simply aren't going to do that.

The Android Emulator is slow

If you've tested any of our apps on your development machine using the emulator, you already know just how slow this can be. Startup times lasting several minutes aren't uncommon, and then once the emulator is going, performance is absolutely horrible.

There is some hope, in the form of GenyMotion (`http://www.genymotion.com`). It provides a faster emulation environment, and makes testing much, much easier.

Even so, don't assume that GenyMotion or the Android Emulator always reflect how your app will look and feel on a real device. Even GenyMotion's emulator is rarely as smooth as a physical device. Furthermore, graphical glitches when using Host GPU acceleration aren't uncommon—but thankfully they do not appear on a real device. All of this is why it is so important to test on real devices.

Finally, do not assume that the emulator can provide every feature that a real device can. Both Android and GenyMotion can simulate various features, but not every feature is available. For more information, see `http://developer.android.com/tools/devices/emulator.html` and `http://www.genymotion.com/features/`.

iOS quirks

iOS isn't without its own set of quirks that get in the way of things. The only upside here is that there are fewer device permutations available to cause problems. The downside is that any problem you do discover likely impacts a larger percentage of users.

Don't use private file paths

Although you'd never use it on purpose, some plugins return a `private` file path, as in a path that is of the form `file:///private/var/...` or `/private/var/....` Even if this path ultimately points into the app's sandbox, it will still fail.

On iOS 6, `localhost` may be returned instead of `private`. You'll need to remove the `localhost` portion before the file path will work. For an example of how this is done, refer to `_resolveLocalFileSystemURL` in YASMF's `FileManager` (`/framework/lib/yasmf/util/fileManager.js`).

Watch the status bar

When iOS 7 was released, the status bar became transparent. This means that the underlying content could show through. Because of this, the metrics for content at the top of the screen are different when targeting iOS 7 compared to previous versions.

For example, when creating a navigation bar at the top of the screen, make it 64 pixels high instead of 44 pixels to account for the 20-pixel-high status bar. (The status bar isn't always 20 pixels high—think of the in-call status bar—but it appears that a 20-pixel offset or a 64-pixel-high navigation bar still works in this case.)

System fonts

The system fonts for iOS 7 are different from iOS 6 and before. This is a subtle difference perhaps, but it is something to pay attention to.

To use the new iOS 7 system font, use a font stack like this:

```
font: 18px/44px -apple-system-font, "Helvetica Neue", Helvetica,
Arial, sans-serif;
```

Note the `-apple-system-font` portion; this will apply the new font on iOS 7. For any other version, the fallback fonts will be used instead.

Rotation and viewport changes can disable scroll views

Frustrating, yes. Thankfully, there's an easy fix (see `http://stackoverflow.com/a/3485654`). Whenever the orientation changes, execute something like this:

```
if ( _y.device.platform() == "ios" )
{
  self._scrollContainer.style.display = "none";
  setTimeout (function () { self._scrollContainer.style.display = "";
} );
}
```

Unfortunately, the same issue can also occur in views that have text input when the soft keyboard is raised. If the view prior to the raising of the keyboard did not scroll, the view will often fail to scroll after the keyboard is raised. If the view scrolls prior to the raising of the keyboard, it will work after the keyboard appears. One might be able to attach event handlers for the `blur` and `focus` events to fix the issue, or simply ensure the view is always large enough to scroll, even by a few pixels.

Never use IFRAME with native scrolling

Bad things happen. What actually happens seems somewhat random and a bit spurious. That is to say that sometimes you'll get by with using that IFRAME with no problem. Other times, depending upon the configuration of the DOM or the specific device, you'll run into problems with scrolling. This can be as simple as some areas not responding to scrolling gestures and as serious as some areas actually scrolling in the wrong direction. Sometimes one even has to swipe horizontally in order to scroll vertically.

So don't do it. It's not worth your sanity.

The iOS simulator has quirks

The iOS simulator is just a simulator. It inherits all the resources of your development machine, including lots of memory and a fast CPU. Generally, this means your app will run more slowly on a real device, since a real device has a slower CPU and less memory. (About the only exception is GPU acceleration: the physical device usually has smoother animation than the simulator.)

Furthermore, the simulator isn't emulating a real device at all—your app is recompiled to target an Intel x86 processor (instead of the ARM chip in iPhones and iPads), which means there is always the chance your app won't behave exactly the same when run on a desktop and when run on a physical device. More than once, I've encountered strange bugs that occur only on the simulator and not on the physical device (and vice versa). This is one reason why it is so very important to test on real hardware.

Also, don't forget that the simulator doesn't provide all the features of a real device. For example, our Filer app can't record audio, take a picture, or capture video in the simulator, because these features aren't available. For information about what is available and what is not available in the simulator, see `https://developer.apple.com/library/ios/documentation/IDEs/Conceptual/iOS_Simulator_Guide/TestingontheiOSSimulator/TestingontheiOSSimulator.html`.

Index

Symbols

_actionButton element 355
_actionGroup element 355
_amTouching variable 356
_backButton element 355
_canvasHeight variable 355
_canvasMiddle variable 355
_canvas variable 356
_canvasWidth variable 355
_collidingLines variable 356
_context variable 356
_controlSchemes variable 356
_currentLevel variable 356
_currentTop variable 356
_desiredDirection variable 356
_generateWidth variable 355
_lastTouch variable 356
_leftButton element 355
_message element 355
_overlay element 355
_pixelRatio variable 355
_previousAccelerometer variable 357
_rightButton element 355
_scale variable 355
_score variable 356
_segmentLength variable 355
_segments variable 356
_ship variable 356
_startTime variable 356
_tiltWatch variable 357
_timer variable 356
_touchTimer variable 356
_updateModificationDate property 206
_updateUnit property 206

A

accelerometer-based input, Cave Runner game
    378-380
Ackuna
    URL 71
Adobe PhoneGap 3.x 13
allowEdit property 208
alsoSaveToPhotoAlbum property 215
Android developer downloads
    URL 81
Android quirks
    about 419
    Blob support 420
    canvas artifacts 419
    CSS animation artifacts 420
    Horrid canvas performance 420
    input boxes, floating 421
    poor rendering, for rounded corners 419
    SVG renderings, for masks 419
Android Simulator Quirk 316
Android's UI Guidelines
    URL 408
animating
    URLs 348
Apple's iOS HIG
    URL 408
AppLingua
    URL 71
asynchronous callback, File API 131
async plugin 320
audio note edit view 204

B

BaaS 383
Babble-on
   URL 71
backbutton event 266
backend 383
backend, for Cave Runner game
   about 384
   features 384
   Options view, modifying 391-396
   Parse, configuring 385-391
   scores, displaying 399-403
   scores, submitting to Parse 396-399
   Start view, modifying 404, 405
   steps 385
   working 384
Backends as a Service. *See* BaaS
BackgroundColor property 51
base note model
   about 83
   createdDate property 84
   deserialize method 84
   implementing 87-95
   initialization method 84
   JSON property 84
   mediaContents property 84
   modifiedDate property 84
   name property 84
   representation property 84
   serialize method 84
   textContents property 84
   UID property 84
   unitLabels property 84
   unitValue property 84
batterycritical event 270
batterylow event 270
batterystatus event 270
Battery Status plugin 270
bias method 360

C

Camera API
   overview 207-216
cameraDirection property 208, 215

camera manager
   creating 209, 210
camera property 206
cameraSource property 215
Capture API
   about 234
   overview 234, 235
   URL, for documentation 234
   video manager, creating 236-240
Cave Runner game
   about 339
   accelerometer-based input 378-380
   code, for drawing to canvas 364-368
   designing 341-343
   features 340
   Game view, implementing 352-358
   levels, generating 358-363
   Options view, implementing 349-351
   prerequisites 341
   Start view, implementing 344-348
   steps 340
   touched-based input 375-377
   updates, performing 369-375
CDVFile/filesystem scheme format 224
centerMapAroundLocation 333
channelWidth method 360
Chocolate Chip UI
   about 410
   URL 410
command-line interface (CLI) 25
configuration items, RequireJS
   baseUrl 127
   paths 127
   shim 127
   urlArgs 127
configuration, Parse 385-391
configuration, SDK
   about 16
   Android development 23
   for Mac/Linux 20, 21
   for Windows 8 21
   iOS development (Xcode) 22
containers
   about 284
   positioning 284-286
Cordova 3.x
   installing 26, 27

Cordova CLI
about 47
plugin, installing 33, 34
plugin, listing 34
plugin, removing 34, 35
used, for building Hello World app 39
used, for creating Hello World app 29
used, for deploying Hello World app 42
Cordova/PhoneGap 3.x
about 14
installing 25
Cordova plugin
URL 74
correctOrientation property 208
CSS
implementing, for mobile application design
115-123
CSS3 Animation 348

D

data model
creating, for CameraManager object 209, 210
designing, for image note 205, 206
implementing, for image note 218-220
data model, Media API
designing 175, 176
implementing 176-178
data model, mobile application design
base note model 83
designing 82- 86
Note Storage model 83
data models, geolocation and interactive maps
designing 319, 320
implementing 322-327
dates
formatting 57-64
destinationType property 207
destroy property 206
device
Hello World app, deploying 41
device events
handling 264-271
devices of different sizes project
about 282
features 282
steps 283

directory entries, File API 135
DirectoryEntry
entries, obtaining in 140, 141
methods 135, 136
properties 135
DisallowOverscroll property 51
document object model (DOM) 52

E

editingAllowed property 215
encodingType property 208, 215
entries
obtaining, in DirectoryEntry 140, 141
Essence icons
URL 80
events, FileReader object
onabort 138
onerror 138
onload 138
onloadend 138
onloadstart 138
events, FileWriter object
onabort 139
onerror 139
onwrite 139
onwriteend 139
onwritestart 139

F

File API
about 129
asynchronous callback 131
contents, reading of file 137, 138
data, writing to file 139, 140
directories, removing 142
directory entries 135
entries, obtaining in DirectoryEntry 140, 141
file entries 136
files, copying 141
files, moving 141
files, removing 142
filesystems 132
filesystems, requesting 133, 134
overview 131
properties, reading of file 137, 138

quota, requesting 133
URLs, for information 131
wrapping 143-145
File API project
features 130
prerequisites 130
steps 130
working 130
file entries, File API 136
FileEntry
methods 137
properties 137
FileManager
properties 146
FileManager file
overview 145, 146
FileManager, proxies to File API
changeDirectory (path) 147
copyDirectory (sourceDirectory,
    targetDirectory, newName) 147
copyFile (pathToFile, pathToDirectory,
    newName) 147
createDirectory (path) 147
deleteFile (pathToFile) 147
getFileEntry (path) / getDirectoryEntry
    (path) 146
getFileURL (path) / getDirectoryURL
    (path) 146, 147
moveDirectory (sourceDirectory,
    targetDirectory, newName) 147
moveFile (pathToFile, pathToDirectory,
    newName) 147
readDirectoryContents (path, options) 147
readFileContents (path, options, kind) 147
removeDirectory (pathToDirectory,
    recursively) 147
resolveFileSystemURL (theURL) 146
writeFileContents (path, options, data) 147
Filer app 203, 263
FileReader object
events 138
methods 139
properties 139
filesystems, File API
about 132
persistent 132

requesting 133, 134
temporary 132
FileWriter object
events 139
methods 140
properties 140
flat platforms
versus skeuomorphic 408
forEach method 323
Framework 7
about 410
URL 410
Fries
about 410
URL 410
fullscreen property 51

G

Game view, Cave Runner game
DOM elements, in view 355
implementing 352-358
variables 355, 356
generateLevel method 359
generic factory 86
geolocation
exploring 315-318
geolocation and interactive maps
building 311, 335, 336
data models, designing 319, 320
data models, implementing 322-327
features 312
functioning 311, 312
geolocation, exploring 315-318
Google Maps API, loading 320-322
path edit view, implementing 328-334
prerequisites 312, 313
steps 312
UI, designing 313, 314
getFormattedUnitValue property 206
getGoogleLatitudeLongitude method 324
getPathIndexByUID 327
globalization 45
globalNotifications object 266
Glyphish Complete
URL 80
Google Chrome 131

Google Maps API
  loading 320-322
Google's App Translation Service 71
Google Translate 65

H

Hammer.js
  about 179
  swipe-to-delete 180-182
  tap detection, speeding up 179
  URL, for downloading 179
Hello World app
  building 14, 38
  building, Cordova CLI used 39
  building, PhoneGap CLI used 39, 40
  building, steps 14
  creating 28
  creating, with Cordova CLI 29
  creating, with PhoneGap CLI 29, 30
  deploying, Cordova CLI used 42
  deploying, PhoneGap CLI used 43, 44
  deploying, to device 41
  deploying, to simulator 41
  features 14
  hotshot challenge 44
  platform, managing 30
  plugin, managing 32
  prerequisites 15
  wrapping up 44
HideKeyboardFormAccessory 51
HIG (Human Interface Guidelines) 408
HTML5 Canvas 339

I

ICanLocalize
  URL 71
IcoMoon
  URL 81
Icons 8
  URL 80
image capture project
  user interface, designing for 204, 205
image note
  data model, designing for 205, 206
  data model, implementing for 218-220
image note edit view

about 204, 205
  modifying 277-279
immediately invoked function
    expression (IIFE) 266
installation, Cordova 3.x 26, 27
installation, Cordova/PhoneGap 3.x 25
installation, node.js 16-20
installation, PhoneGap 3.x 27
Intel App Framework
  about 410
  URL 410
iOS quirks
  about 422
  IFRAME, avoiding with native scrolling 423
  private file paths, avoiding 422
  rotation and viewport changes can
      disable scroll views 423
  status bar, viewing 422
  system fonts 422
iOS Simulator Quirk 317

J

jQuery Mobile
  about 410
  URL 410
JSON with padding (JSONP) 322

K

Kendo UI
  about 410
  URL 410
Keyhole Markup Language (KML) 312
key-value observing (KVO) 85
Kinvey
  URL 383

L

layout
  modifying 294-298
levels, Cave Runner game
  generating 358-363
locale
  about 53
  determining, of user 53-56
localization 45

M

master-detail pattern 299
Media API
  building, steps 159-161
  data model, designing 175, 176
  data model, implementing 176-178
  features 160
  file path, for Android 163
  file path, for iOS 162
  hotshot challenge 201
  MediaError 166
  media manager, creating 166-174
  overview 161-165
  prerequisites 161
  styles, modifying 198-200
  URL, for documentation 161
  user interface, designing 174
  user interface, implementing 187-197
  working 160
  wrapping up 200
MediaError 166
mediaFilter property 215
media manager, Media API
  creating 166-174
Media object
  duration property 163
  getCurrentPosition() method 163
  getDuration() method 163
  pause() method 163
  play() method 163
  position property 163
  release() method 164
  seekTo() method 163
  setVolume() method 164
  startRecord() method 163
  stop() method 164
  stopRecord() method 164
media queries
  URL, for information 288
  using 287-289
mediaType property 208
menubutton event 270
methods, DirectoryEntry
  copyTo(targetDirectoryEntry, [newName],
    success, failure) 136
  createReader() 136

getDirectory(path, options, success,
    failure) 136
getFile(path, options, success, failure) 136
getMetadata(success, failure) 136
getParent(success, failure) 136
moveTo(targetDirectoryEntry, [newName],
    success, failure) 136
removeRecursively(success, failure) 136
remove(success, failure) 136
setMetadata(success, failure, metadata) 136
toURL() 136
methods, FileEntry
  copyTo(targetDirectoryEntry, [newName],
    success, failure) 137
  createWriter() 137
  file(success, failure) 137
  getMetadata(success, failure) 137
  getParent(success, failure) 137
  moveTo(targetDirectoryEntry, [newName],
    success, failure) 137
  remove(success, failure) 137
  setMetadata(success, failure, metadata) 137
  toURL() 137
methods, FileReader object
  abort() 139
  readAsArrayBuffer(file) 139
  readAsBinaryString(file) 139
  readAsDataURL(file) 139
  readAsText(file) 139
methods, FileWriter object
  abort() 140
  seek(toPosition) 140
  truncate(bytes) 140
  write(data) 140
Misnamed API 160
mobile application design
  about 73
  base note model, implementing 87-95
  building 73
  CSS, implementing 115-123
  data model, designing 82-86
  deploying 123-127
  features 74
  hotshot challenge 128
  index.html file, defining 125, 126
  note list view, implementing 101-109
  Note Storage model, implementing 95-101

plugin, adding 127
prerequisites 74
short files, defining 123, 124
steps 74
text note edit view, implementing 110-115
user interface, designing 75-82
working 73, 74
mobile pattern
references 409

N

native alerts
overview 240-250
native-like alerts
overview 240-250
node.js
installing 16-20
URL 16
non-native alerts
overview 240-250
note list view
about 204
implementing 101-109
Note Storage model
about 83
implementing 95-101
modifying 148-155
numbers
formatting 57-64

O

onPause event handler 266
onResume event handler 266
Options view, Cave Runner game
implementing 349-351
Orientation property 51

P

Parse
configuring 385-391
URL 383
path edit view, geolocation and interactive maps
implementing 328, 329
properties 329, 330
pause event

operations 267
PhoneGap 1.x 14
PhoneGap 2.x 14
PhoneGap 3.x
about 14
installing 27
PhoneGap Build
about 47
URL 25, 38, 40
PhoneGap CLI
plugin, installing 35, 36
plugin, listing 36
plugin, removing 37
used, for building Hello World app 39, 40
used, for creating Hello World app 29, 30
used, for deploying Hello World app 43, 44
Place object 322
platform, Hello World app
adding 31
listing 31
managing 30
removing 32
updating 32
plugin
about 32
URL 32
plugin, Hello World app
managing 32
managing, with Cordova CLI 33
managing, with PhoneGap CLI 35
popoverOptions property 208
portable media player
history 159
reference link 159
project
creating, based on existing template 49-52
Promises
overview 143
properties, controlling image source
allowEdit 208
cameraDirection 208
correctOrientation 208
destinationType 207
encodingType 208
mediaType 208
popoverOptions 208
quality 207

saveToPhotoAlbum 208
sourceType 208
targetHeight 208
targetWidth 208
properties, DirectoryEntry
fullPath 136
isDirectory 135
isFile 135
name 136
properties, FileEntry
fullPath 137
isDirectory 137
isFile 137
name 137
properties, FileManager
actualQuota 146
currentWorkingDirectory 146
cwd 146
fileSystemType 146
FILETYPE 146
PERSISTENT 146
requestedQuota 146
TEMPORARY 146
properties, FileReader object
error 139
readyState 139
result 139
properties, FileWriter object
fileName 140
length 140
position 140
readyState 140

Q

Q.js
overview 143
quality property 207, 215
quota, File API
requesting 133

R

renderToElement 330
RequireJS
configuration items 127
URL 48

RequreJS text plugin
URL 48
resolution-independent assets
using 290
responsive design
about 283, 284
containers, positioning 284-286
further planning 292
maximum values, using 287
media queries, using 287-289
minimum values, using 287
percentage, using instead of pixels 287
resolution-independent assets, using 290, 291
resume event
operations 267
rndWidth method 360

S

saveCollection method 326
saveToPhotoAlbum property 208
scaling up 293
SDK
configuring 16
configuring, for Mac/Linux 20, 21
configuring, for Windows 8 21
searchbutton event 270
Sencha Touch
about 410
URL 410
setMediaContents property 206
setPosition method 323
setProperty method 323
sharing plugin
about 263
features 263
steps 264
working 263
working with 271-273
simulator
Hello World app, deploying 41
singleton 100
skeuomorph 408
skeuomorphic
versus flat platforms 408
sourceType property 208

split view controllers
  creating 300-304
split view layout 298-309
src property 215
Start view, Cave Runner game
  implementing 344-348
still images
  working with 203

T

Tabs icons
  URL 80
targetHeight property 208
targetSize property 215
targetWidth property 208
template
  creating 48, 49
text
  translating 65-70
text note edit view
  about 204
  implementing 110-115
  modifying 273-277
tips
  3D transforms, using for GPU usage 416
  affordances, including 414
  audio/video file extensions matter 418
  backface, hiding while 3D transforms usage 416
  cautious, with XHR status values 418
  complex effects hinder performance 418
  highlighting, preventing when tapping 413, 414
  native scrolling, using 415
  outlines, preventing when tapping 413, 414
  perspective, while GPU usage 417
  scrolling library, using 416
  text rendering, improving 415
  unwanted text selection, preventing 415
tips, for user interface 410, 411
touched-based input, Cave Runner
          game 375-377
translatable text
  adding, to app 65-70
translators
  Ackuna 71
  AppLingua 71

Babble-on 71
Google's App Translation Service 71
ICanLocalize 71

U

updates, Cave Runner game
  performing 369-375
useCorrectOrientation property 215
user
  locale, determining 53-56
user interface
  designing, for image capture project 204, 205
  designing, for video note edit view 232, 233
  implementing, for image capture project 221-225
  implementing, for video capturing project 253-257
  resources 407
  tips 410, 411
user-interface frameworks
  Chocolate Chip UI 410
  Framework 7 410
  Fries 410
  Intel App Framework 410
  jQuery Mobile 410
  Kendo UI 410
  Sencha Touch 410
  Zepto JS 410
user interface, geolocation and interactive maps
  designing 313, 314
  elements 314
user interface, Media API
  designing 174
  implementing 187-197
user interface, mobile application design
  designing 75-82

V

video capture project
  about 231
  features 232
  implementing 257-260
  steps 232
  user interface, implementing for 253-257
  working 231

video manager
  creating 236-240
video note data model
  building 250
  implementing 251, 252
video note edit view
  user interface, designing for 232, 233
video recording session
  duration property 234
  limit property 235
video tag
  URL, for information 257
view stack
  overview 182-186

W

wallChance method 360
wallEvery method 361
webviewbounce property 51

X

XHR (XMLHttpRequest) 71

Y

**YASMF (Yet Another Simple
    Mobile Framework) 243, 266, 289**
YASMF v0.4 (YASMF-Next) 52

Z

Zepto JS
  about 410
  URL 410

Thank you for buying
PhoneGap 3.x Mobile Application Development HOTSH⊕T

About Packt Publishing

Packt, pronounced 'packed', published its first book "*Mastering phpMyAdmin for Effective MySQL Management*" in April 2004 and subsequently continued to specialize in publishing highly focused books on specific technologies and solutions.

Our books and publications share the experiences of your fellow IT professionals in adapting and customizing today's systems, applications, and frameworks. Our solution based books give you the knowledge and power to customize the software and technologies you're using to get the job done. Packt books are more specific and less general than the IT books you have seen in the past. Our unique business model allows us to bring you more focused information, giving you more of what you need to know, and less of what you don't.

Packt is a modern, yet unique publishing company, which focuses on producing quality, cutting-edge books for communities of developers, administrators, and newbies alike. For more information, please visit our website: www.packtpub.com.

About Packt Open Source

In 2010, Packt launched two new brands, Packt Open Source and Packt Enterprise, in order to continue its focus on specialization. This book is part of the Packt Open Source brand, home to books published on software built around Open Source licenses, and offering information to anybody from advanced developers to budding web designers. The Open Source brand also runs Packt's Open Source Royalty Scheme, by which Packt gives a royalty to each Open Source project about whose software a book is sold.

Writing for Packt

We welcome all inquiries from people who are interested in authoring. Book proposals should be sent to author@packtpub.com. If your book idea is still at an early stage and you would like to discuss it first before writing a formal book proposal, contact us; one of our commissioning editors will get in touch with you.

We're not just looking for published authors; if you have strong technical skills but no writing experience, our experienced editors can help you develop a writing career, or simply get some additional reward for your expertise.

PhoneGap 3 Beginner's Guide

ISBN: 978-1-78216-098-4   Paperback: 308 pages

A guide to building cross-platform apps using the W3C standards-based Cordova/PhoneGap framework

1. Understand the fundamentals of cross-platform mobile application development from build to distribution.

2. Learn to implement the most common features of modern mobile applications.

3. Take advantage of native mobile device capabilities—including the camera, geolocation, and local storage—using HTML, CSS, and JavaScript.

PhoneGap Mobile Application Development Cookbook

ISBN: 978-1-84951-858-1   Paperback: 320 pages

Over 40 recipes to create mobile applications using the PhoneGap API with examples and clear instrucions

1. Use the PhoneGap API to create native mobile applications that work on a wide range of mobile devices.

2. Discover the native device features and functions you can access and include within your applications.

3. Packed with clear and concise examples to show you how to easily build native mobile applications.

Please check **www.PacktPub.com** for information on our titles

PhoneGap Social App Development

Consume social network feeds and share social network content using native plugins and PhoneGap

Kerri Shotts   [PACKT]

Instant PhoneGap Social App Development

ISBN: 978-1-84969-628-9   Paperback: 78 pages

Consume social network feeds and share social network content using native plugins and PhoneGap

1. Learn something new in an Instant! A short, fast, focused guide delivering immediate results.

2. This book will guide you through using the Twitter JSON API and PhoneGap as a simple way to consume social media content. You'll also be able to share content to Twitter using the Twitter Web Intents.

3. Learn how to consume content using Twitter's JSON API.

WordPress Mobile Applications with PhoneGap

A straightforward, example-based guide to leveraging your web development skills to build mobile applications using WordPress, jQuery, jQuery Mobile, and PhoneGap

Yuxian Eugene Liang   [PACKT]

WordPress Mobile Applications with PhoneGap

ISBN: 978-1-84951-986-1   Paperback: 96 pages

A straightforward, example-based guide to leveraging your web development skills to build mobile applications using WordPress, jQuery, jQuery Mobile, and PhoneGap

1. Discover how we can leverage on WordPress as a content management system and serve content to mobile apps by exposing its API.

2. Learn how to build geolocation mobile applications using WordPress and PhoneGap.

3. Step-by-step instructions on how you can make use of jQuery and jQuery Mobile to provide an interface between WordPress and your PhoneGap app.

Please check **www.PacktPub.com** for information on our titles

CPSIA information can be obtained at www.ICGtesting.com
Printed in the USA
BVOW08s0559041214

377644BV00004B/13/P